FROM FREUD TO JUNG

A C.G. JUNG FOUNDATION BOOK
PUBLISHED IN ASSOCIATION WITH DAIMON VERLAG,
EINSIEDELN, SWITZERLAND

The C.G. Jung Foundation for Analytical Psychology is
dedicated to helping men and women grow in conscious
awareness of the psychological realities in themselves
and society, find healing and meaning in their lives and
greater depth in their relationships, and live in response
to their discovered sense of purpose. It welcomes the
public to attend its lectures, seminars, films, symposia,
and workshops and offers a wide selection of books for
sale through its bookstore. The Foundation also pub-
lishes *Quadrant*, a semiannual journal, and books on
Analytical Psychology and related subjects. For information about Foundation programs or membership,
please write to the C.G. Jung Foundation, 28 East 39th
Street, New York, NY 10016.

LILIANE FREY-ROHN

FROM FREUD TO JUNG

A Comparative Study of the Psychology
of the Unconscious

Translated by Fred E. Engreen and Evelyn K. Engreen

Foreword by Robert Hinshaw

SHAMBHALA
Boston & Shaftesbury
1990

SHAMBHALA PUBLICATIONS, INC.
Horticultural Hall
300 Massachusetts Avenue
Boston, Massachusetts 02115

SHAMBHALA PUBLICATIONS, INC.
The Old School House
The Courtyard, Bell Street
Shaftesbury, Dorset SP7 8BP

9 8 7 6 5 4 3 2 1

First Shambhala Edition

Printed in the United States of America on acid-free paper
Distributed in the United States by Random House
and in Canada by Random House of Canada Ltd.
Distributed in the United Kingdom by Element Books Ltd.

LIBRARY OF CONGRESS CATALOGING-IN-PUBLICATION DATA

Frey-Rohn, Liliane.
    [Von Freud zu Jung. English.]
    From Freud to Jung: a comparative study of the psychology of the
unconscious / Liliane Frey-Rohn; translated by Fred E. Engreen and
Evelyn K. Engreen.
        p. cm.
    Translation of: Von Freud zu Jung.
    Reprint, with new foreword. Originally published: New York:
Putnam for the C.G. Jung Foundation, 1974.
    "Published in association with Daimon Verlag Einsiedeln."
    "A C.G. Jung Foundation book."
    Includes bibliographical references.
    ISBN 0–87773–572–7 (alk. paper)
    1. Subconsciousness. 2. Jung, C. G. (Carl Gustav), 1875–1961.
3. Freud, Sigmund, 1857–1939. I. Title.
BF315.F74 1990   89-48068
150.19'54—dc20   CIP

TABLE OF CONTENTS

CONTENTS

CONTENTS

CONTENTS

FOREWORD

Originally written twenty years ago, *From Freud to Jung* is a timeless classic, one that goes straight to the essence in comparing the basic influences, ideas, and contributions of the two great pioneers of depth psychology in their context, without frills. This is not a biography but a deep and scholarly investigation of the *opus* by a lifelong student of Jung who knows his ideas literally inside and out: she has lived a long and rich "Jungian life." Fortunately, she has shared some of what she has learned with us.

In today's "fast-food" world with its emphasis on techniques and technologies leading to quick results, it is more important than ever to try and regain a sense of our origins, to help us be aware of where we are and where we might be going. This book is not modern in the current sense of the word, but it can be nourishing, providing us with some urgently needed orientation and ground for understanding, for growing our own food for thought.

In the course of many years of close association with Carl Gustav Jung, Liliane Frey-Rohn became ever more curious about and fascinated with the influence of the person and the teachings of Sigmund Freud, particularly upon Jung's early work. Although Jung seldom spoke of his relationship with Freud, whenever the subject did arise, either publicly or privately, she was very aware of Jung's feeling of indebtedness to Freud, both emotionally and intellectually.

After meeting Jung in 1929 and beginning an analysis, first with an assistant and later with Jung himself, she endeavored to verse herself more thoroughly in the history of the development of depth psychology. With a Ph.D. in philosophy from the University of Zurich, Liliane Frey was already familiar with many of the works used as sources by both Freud and Jung, and she continued to pursue this interest for several decades, publishing some of her conclusions and ideas along the way in articles such as "Die Anfänge der Tiefenpsychologie" (The Beginnings of Depth Psychology), which was published in 1955 in a *Festschrift*[1] (celebratory volume) honoring Jung's eightieth birthday.

Upon Jung's death in 1961, she intensified her efforts, completing the manuscript for the original German edition of this book, and it was published in 1969 as *Von Freud zu Jung: Eine vergleichende Studie zur Psychologie des Unbewussten* (Zurich: Rascher Verlag). The book was very well received and became a standard work for the German-language Jungian training institutes, a status that holds true today more than ever.

1. *Studien zur analytischen Psychologie C.G. Jungs*, vol. 1 (Zurich: Rascher, 1955).

When the Rascher Verlag ceased activity not long thereafter, the book went out of print for a time, but the newly founded Daimon Verlag issued a revised edition of *Von Freud zu Jung* in 1979 as one of the very first titles on its list of Jungian classics.

Work on the English-language edition consisted of an unusually intense collaboration between the author, who speaks and writes English fluently, and the highly competent professional translators Fred and Evelyn Engreen. Under the auspices of the C. G. Jung Foundation of New York, it finally made its appearance in English in 1974 (published by Putnam) and quickly extended its excellent reputation to English-language training institutions and lay readers alike.

What makes this book particularly unique is the fact that Liliane Frey-Rohn was *there* through many of Jung's most productive years, from the late 1920s until his death in 1961. She has thorough knowledge of his work as he thought, practiced, and lived it, and she had the privilege of training with him, reading and discussing his papers as he was writing them, and actively participating in his many courses, including the famous Zarathustra Seminars,[2] which extended over a period of many years. She was there during his Eranos lectures in Ascona, the seminars at the Eidgenössische Technische Hochschule and at the Psychological Club in Zürich, to name just a few. In addition, she has thorough knowledge of the history of European thought and of philosophy, and is thus able to provide us with a scholarly presentation of the historical and philosophical *context* from which both Freud and Jung were emerging.

The author establishes her theme with a brief sketch of some events in Jung's life, and then a summary of young Freud's first works leads to Jung's encounter with *Studies on Hysteria* and *The Interpretation of Dreams*, followed by the seven years of intense relationship between the two men. After the final tragic split in 1913, Jung sank into a depression and, according to his own account, spent the next several years trying to understand what had happened, while at the same time encountering the depths of the unconscious face to face, as it were, as his thoughts, interests, and energies became ever more independent of Freud's influence. While it is regrettable that more of the personal aspects of the relationship are not addressed in the book, it must be remembered that this work was designated a treatment of both men's thought and not a biography, a premise to which the author has held fast and which also has its advantages. Rather, the book focuses on *basic Freud and Jung*, a goal that it admirably achieves. In so doing, it deals in great detail with the period of the seven years of their personal relationship and the six

2. Recently published as *Nietzsche's Zarathustra: Notes of the Seminar Given in 1934–1939 by C.G. Jung*, ed. James L. Jarrett, Bollingen Series (Princeton: Princeton University Press, 1988).

ensuing years. Jung's work from the time after Freud's death in 1939 until his own death in 1961 are treated in an appendix.

Liliane Frey-Rohn, now eighty-eight years of age, continues to live in her beloved Zurich, where she maintains a small analytic practice. In her several decades as a close associate of Jung she was, to name just a few of her many activities, instrumental in the founding of the C. G. Jung Institute of Zurich in 1948, where she was one of the original five Curatorium members (i.e., members of the board of directors) designated by Jung. From the beginning, she has been an official training analyst and frequent lecturer at the Institute, the Psychological Club in Zurich, and elsewhere, and has taught seminars and been an examiner for trainees, best known for her expertise in the very subject of this book, the history and development of depth psychology, particularly in relation to Freud and Jung. Her main fields of collaborative study with Jung himself concerned the phenomena of synchronicity and astrology.

It was also Jung who ignited her passion for the writings of the German philosopher Friedrich Nietzsche, whose ideas had considerable influence on his own. Although she had lectured and earlier published an article on Nietzsche's work,[3] it was not until she was over eighty years old that she became intensely involved with Nietzsche's thought during a period that was to last a good four years and during which she feverishly wrote her second full-length book, as thorough and well-researched as the first: *Friedrich Nietzsche: A Psychological Approach to His Life and Work* (1984; English edition published by Daimon in 1988). Also concerned with psychologically approaching the phenomenon of death, she recently co-authored, together with Marie-Louise von Franz and Aniela Jaffé, a book on this subject, scheduled to appear soon in English.[4]

For historians and scholars, for students and trainees, for all who are interested in the historical development of depth psychology from its roots in philosophy to recent times, *From Freud to Jung* is indispensable reading. I am pleased that it is one of the first titles in the important new series of Jungian works to be published jointly by Shambhala Publications, the C. G. Jung Foundation, and Daimon Verlag. May the readership be widespread and inquisitive and may this book help prepare the ground for the next generation of psychological thought.

Robert Hinshaw, Publisher
Daimon Verlag
Einsiedeln, Switzerland

3. "The Shadow Revealed in the Works of Friedrich Nietzsche" in *The Well-Tended Tree* (New York: Putnam, 1971).
4. *Im Umkreis des Todes* (*On Death*) (Zurich: Daimon Verlag, 1980, 1984).

PREFACE

This book is an outgrowth of my interest in the historical point of view. It represents a continuation of my paper on "The Beginnings of Depth Psychology" (1955). Since this earlier study was limited to the field of medical psychology in the period from Mesmer to Freud, later developments were sketched only briefly. It is thus understandable that I wished to continue the historical perspective. The present work, however, is not intended as a broad compendium of the later developments in depth psychology. It is focused rather on outlining the basic concepts of Freud and Jung and by this comparison to gain a more comprehensive understanding of the work of Jung. In other words, I have attempted to bring out more clearly the specific aspects of Jung's views of man and the cosmos. To this end I have found it essential to trace the development of Jung from his initial fascination with Freud's ideas to his gradual liberation from these powerful concepts, leading to the final breakthrough into his own unique being.

Accordingly, this goal required comparatively more attention to the first thirteen years of Jung's work, during which his basic ideas were shaped in constant debate with Freud. Such an approach seems to be justified since Jung not only came into an extensive and profound inheritance but developed and tested his own insights by consistent confrontation with this inheritance.

In this study I have tried to combine an historical-developmental and a systematic approach, but I have had to forego the biographic background as well as the personal psychology reflected in each basic concept. Because of space limitations it was also impossible to give examples illustrating the basic concepts or to include a critical evaluation of the pertinent literature.

In presenting the psychological theories of Freud and Jung, I deliberately restricted myself to the psychology of the unconscious. Such a limitation seemed warranted because Freud's investigations up to the 1920's were concentrated on the unconscious, and this area also remained the predominant focus of Jung's interest. Nevertheless, its relationship to psychology as a whole made some excursions into ego psychology and the psychology of consciousness unavoidable. Still, I had to refrain from discussing Jung's theory of types to any great extent—although this is an important part of his psychology—because there is nothing in Freud's work which could be considered analogous. Finally, I have touched only occasionally on the problem of how the basic theoretical assumptions affect the practice of psychotherapy, because such an attempt would call for a much broader study.

Certain other difficulties were encountered in presenting the fundamental psychological concepts. It would have been tempting to select certain periods and to compare the statements of both investigators during that time. Regretfully, this plan was not feasible because, generally speaking, Jung referred to corresponding theories of Freud only much later, often many years after their formulation. To give just two examples: It was mainly in 1906–1907 (*Studies in Word-Association* and *The Psychology of Dementia Praecox*) and again in 1913 (*The Theory of Psychoanalysis*) that Jung discussed Freud's theory of hysteria, developed between 1892 and 1900. Similarly, Jung appraised Freud's *Three Essays on the Theory of Sexuality* (1905), particularly the hypothesis of sexual trauma during infancy or early childhood, only when he was beginning to break away from Freud, that is, in the years 1911–1913 (*Transformations and Symbols of the Libido*[1] and *The Theory of Psychoanalysis*). Furthermore, after parting from his former friend, Jung referred to him only sporadically as new concepts developed, and even then such references were almost exclusively to Freud's discoveries during the years 1893–1910.

Equally unproductive was my attempt to contrast the two ideologies in a predominantly systematic manner, not the least because complete disregard of chronology would have impeded the understanding of Jung's ideas, in a state of constant growth. These considerations influenced my decision to combine the chronological and the systematic approaches. More precisely, starting with the discoveries of Jung, I attempted to compare his ideas with those of Freud and then to trace the structural transformations that came about in the course of time. Even this approach had its disadvantages, owing to the unavoidable differences of phase in the intellectual interests of the two innovators.

In my presentation I have largely confined myself to concepts published up to the year of Freud's death (1939). In order to do justice to the extraordinarily important discoveries in the last writings of Jung, which rounded off his entire work, it seemed best to treat them briefly in an appendix. They are principally the "archetype-as-such" and the archetype of the self.

[1] This is a literal translation of Jung's title *Wandlungen und Symbole der Libido* (1911–12), used in preference to that of the Hinkle translation, *Psychology of the Unconscious*, or of the Hull translation of Jung's 1952 revision, *Symbole der Wandlungen = Symbols of Transformation*, the text of which is greatly altered.

Quotations of the 1911–12 work are given in either the Hinkle or Hull translations, as indicated.

This volume is the result of many years devoted to studying the ideas of both investigators. The manuscript was started in the last year of Jung's life, and he never saw the draft. But in previous years we had discussed the subject on many occasions, and I would like to express appreciation here for his constant intellectual support. In the final stages of preparation, Dr. Jolande Jacobi was of great help by offering positive criticism and making valuable suggestions, for which I would again like to express deeply felt thanks. The perceptive interpretation of the translators, Dr. Fred E. Engreen and Evelyn K. Engreen, has enabled me to clarify many points for this edition, and I am deeply appreciative. The greatest gratitude, however, I feel toward my dear husband, who contributed essentially to the completion of this book by steady encouragement and intellectual clarification.

L. F.-R.

NOTE OF ACKNOWLEDGMENT

For permission to quote from the *Collected Works of C. G. Jung*, acknowledgment is made to Princeton University Press, publishers of Bollingen Series, which includes the *Collected Works*. For permission to quote from the *Standard Edition of the Complete Psychological Works of Sigmund Freud*, translated from the German under the general editorship of James Strachey, acknowledgment is made to Sigmund Freud Copyrights Ltd., the Institute of Psycho-Analysis, and the Hogarth Press, Ltd. London. Acknowledgment is also made to Basic Books, Inc., New York, for quotations from *The Interpretation of Dreams* and *From the History of an Infantile Neurosis (Collected Papers of Sigmund Freud*, Volume III, edited by Ernest Jones, M.D.); W. W. Norton & Co., New York, for quotations from *The Ego and the Id;* and Allen & Unwin, Ltd., in Canada, for quotations from *The Interpretation of Dreams.*

TRANSLATORS' NOTE

In spite of its many Germanic roots, the English language often defies translation from the German idiom. Throughout this work the translators have endeavored to convey the author's intention and to interpret the feeling behind her words. But wherever necessary we have adhered strictly to her terminology—certainly in so far as technical terms are concerned and also in order to simplify indexing. Often we felt that a more concise, more readable English text might have resulted if less consideration had been given to these requirements.

The translators have been working as a writing team for many years, producing many documented papers on medical and psychiatric subjects. This experience contributed to the exacting research that went into compiling over 200 English references which replace those cited by Dr. Frey in original German sources.

If the present version of this work makes a worthy contribution, it is because of the close collaboration between the translators and the author. Although separated by more than a third of the globe, Dr. Frey and the translators painstakingly checked every page of the draft and brought each chapter into a compatible English version. We are immensely grateful for Dr. Frey's patient and diligent cooperation. Thanks are also due to Dr. Hilde Kirsch; to Ruth Cron, administrative secretary, The C. G. Jung Institute, Los Angeles; to John Connor, head librarian, and other personnel of the Los Angeles County Medical Association Library; and to the various library facilities of the University of California at Los Angeles.

Los Angeles, California
May 1973

Fred E. Engreen, Ph.D.
Evelyn K. Engreen

FROM FREUD TO JUNG

INTRODUCTION

1. The Origin of Jung's Point of View

The complexity and uniqueness of Jung's personality were already revealed in his early occupation with psychology. The range of his interest included philosophy as well as psychopathology; Schopenhauer and Kant captivated him as much as the enigmas of mesmerism and spiritualism. Whether the question was one of knowledge or abnormal psychic phenomena, it was always the mystery of the human personality that fascinated Jung and challenged his thinking. Even in medical school a trait of his personality which was to endure until his last years became manifest: the passion for understanding extraordinary phenomena. Expanding his knowledge of factual data also meant broadening his psychological experience. As C. A. Meier[1] has correctly stressed, Jung had an "unerring scientific instinct" which led him to make discoveries in the realm of the human psyche. What applied to his doctoral dissertation dealing with occult phenomena was equally true of his last works, for example, the essay in which he explored the phenomenon of the "modern myth" of flying saucers.

Jung's interest in the human personality awakened very early, as documented in his *Memories, Dreams, Reflections.*[2] He soon became thoroughly convinced that the human personality comprised everything that was the living expression of the soul—the vital manifestation as well as intuitive understanding, feeling as well as action. The contemporary notion of the human personality, limiting it to acts of volition and cognition, seemed to Jung to convey a most incomplete picture. It lacked the emotional elements which alone can account for paradoxical behavior and make the tendency to unconscious lies and self-deception understandable.

The environment in which Jung spent his early years only too frequently gave rise to disappointing human experiences. The petit-bourgeois surroundings of a parsonage, the milieu of his native town, Basel, deeply imbued as it was by the spirit of humanism, and last but not least the threatening proximity of the two big powers, France and Germany—all these influences were merged into the perception that the light in a personality cannot exist without the shadow (a concept which one could say was the *leitmotiv* of Jung's later works). With such

---

[1] *Jung and Analytical Psychology* (1957), p. 8. (For full references to works cited, see the bibliography.)

[2] (1963), pp. 44ff. (Cited hereafter as *Memories*.)

a background, we can understand Jung's early admiration for Nietzsche, whose intuitive sense of the tragic ambiguity of the human condition and biting criticism of morality and truth left an indelible imprint on Jung.[3] Out of all these impressions his own direction of investigation became more and more clearly crystallized. The goal that he set himself in 1914 was already characteristic of his thinking at the turn of the century: "I wanted to understand what really goes on in people's minds."[4]

Jung's peculiar bent first became apparent in his choice of the subject of his dissertation,[5] which dealt with the occult phenomena that science had rejected as abstruse and undeserving of serious study. The stimulus to this investigation was his encounter with the abnormal states of an hysterical 15-year-old girl who, while in trance during spiritualistic sessions, reported strange dreams and visions. In writing his thesis, Jung was guided by his wish to deepen and expand the understanding of hysterical and somnambulistic states of semiconsciousness and to detect their relationship to normal psychological problems.[6] His investigation of automatisms and somnambulistic personalities as well as states of dissociation and "double consciousness" brought Jung into contact with the contemporary spiritualistic literature (Myers, Mitchell, Kerner, and others) and also with the French psychopathologists (Binet, Azam, Ribot, Richer, etc.), but above all with Charcot and Janet. Jung found Janet's point of departure particularly valuable, that is, the concept of the unity of the personality, but he could not accept Janet's rationalistic definition of the personality as successive gradations of consciousness. In his studies of neurosis, Janet exhibited an intellectual attitude of taking no account of emotional values and neglecting the vital strata of the individual personality. For Jung, Janet's approach made it impossible to have an adequate understanding of the emotional states of the patient, of his violent passions or mania, and certainly not of disintegration of the personality.

While Jung did not explicitly spell out his reservations about Janet in his dissertation—sometimes he even followed in his footsteps—he expressed his dissent indirectly but clearly. Even at that time, he suggested the possibility of a teleological significance in somnambulism and hallucinations[7] and also referred to the "heightened unconscious performance"[8] which is characteristic of many automatic

---

[3] Frey-Rohn, "The Shadow Revealed in the Works of Friedrich Nietzsche" (1971).
[4] "Some Crucial Points in Psychoanalysis: A Correspondence Between Dr. Jung and Dr. Loÿ" (1914), p. 258.
[5] "On the Psychology and Pathology of So-Called Occult Phenomena" (1902).
[6] Ibid., p. 4.   [7] Ibid., p. 79.   [8] Ibid., p. 80.

processes. He went so far as to suspect "that the phenomena of double consciousness are simply new character formations, or attempts of the future personality to break through."[9] This last remark we may regard as a first hint of developmental processes within the psyche. And finally he professed—in blunt opposition to Janet—that there are cases of somnambulistic heightened performance "which postulate a highly developed intellectual activity of the unconscious."[10]

Jung found a fertile field for the investigation of emotional and vital events at the Burghölzli Mental Hospital, whose staff he joined in the year 1900. Initially, he confined himself to observing patients only symptomatically and evaluating them clinically. As he said in his *Memories*, his teachers "were not interested in what the patient had to say, but rather in how to make a diagnosis or how to describe symptoms and to compile statistics."[11] On the side, he engaged in physiological investigations and practiced hypnosis. Neither of these activities, however, satisfied Jung, because his principal interest was the understanding of the human personality—the deranged personality—and the psychiatry of those days gave him little stimulation in that direction.

During this period of searching for an objective approach to the irrational phenomena of the psyche, two of Freud's works struck Jung like bolts of lightning. *Studies on Hysteria* and *The Interpretation of Dreams*[12] "pointed the way to a closer investigation and understanding of individual cases."[13] What impressed Jung most deeply was that Freud was the first to "introduce psychology into psychiatry."[14]

The Interpretation of Dreams was of incisive significance to Jung. It seemed to him to be a most important scientific achievement that somebody dared to unlock a dark area such as the world of dreams, to make it accessible to systematic investigation, and even to describe it as a "highly important source of information about the unconscious processes."[15] Jung was particularly impressed that—in an era when the ideal of science was to be free of emotions and value judgments— Freud not only had the courage to include affects but even to use them as guides through the thicket of the unconscious depths of the psyche.

As Jung once told me, he had never doubted the reality of the unconscious, but during those early years he was lacking an effective tool with which to investigate in an objective way the unconscious

---

[9] Ibid., p. 79.   [10] Ibid., p. 87.   [11] *Memories*, p. 114.

[12] Even though at the time he found much of this book unclear, it seemed to him important in blazing the trail toward future developments. See *Memories*, pp. 146–47.

[13] Ibid., p. 114.   [14] Ibid.

[15] "In Memory of Sigmund Freud" (1939), p. 44.

5

utterances of the individual's personality, his feelings and emotions, his conflicts and defeats, and particularly his suffering.

> To me, the unconscious was at all times self-understood. It seemed natural to me that psychic events occurred in myself and in others which one really could not know but could only divine. From my earliest days I was highly intrigued by the fact that people could say and do things for which they could give no reason, for which they did not feel answerable nor responsible, which immediately after they could not remember and therefore could deny in good conscience. But there was no objective approach for understanding the nature of the human personality.[16]

Jung found it difficult to accept the idea that the theoretical bases of psychoanalysis grew mainly out of "practical empiricism" and lacked experimental verification. Even though he never doubted that "all human ideas are determined, in a most wonderful way, by psychological laws,"[17] he sought the "secure framework" from which the unconscious data would become evident. In his own words, "the association experiment has helped us to overcome these first and most important difficulties."[18]

With unsurpassed feeling, Alphonse Maeder in 1956 described the atmosphere at the Burghölzli during the first years of the twentieth century:

> Upon my return to Zurich (1906) I found Eugen Bleuler an outstanding clinical teacher and a scientifically productive scholar; from C. G. Jung, at that time first assistant physician, I received an enthusiastic introduction to psychoanalysis. For the first time I heard the name of Freud. . . . Soon I had the privilege of becoming a collaborator of these two outstanding men, a truly fortunate relationship lasting for several years. . . . In addition to all he taught me and stimulated in me, as well as the example he set of a man who devoted his life to inquiry, I owe Jung something else: he was the first truly remarkable man whom I met personally and became close . . . and who took me seriously. His profound and universal knowledge, the secure instinct with which he tracked down problems of depth psychology, made a deep impression on me. . . . As far as I was concerned, behind Bleuler and Jung there was in the distance the fascinating figure of the master, S. Freud, with whom I was in

---

16 Personal communication, 1958.
17 "Psychoanalysis and Association Experiments" (1906), p. 289.
18 Ibid., p. 290.

contact through letters and the exchange of publications and whom I later met personally at the International Congress for Psychoanalysis at Nürnberg. All of those who were the vanguard of the movement congregated at that time, among them Adler, Stekel, Ferenczi, Sadger, Federn, Jones, Abraham, Eitingon, and from Switzerland, in addition to Jung, L. Binswanger and O. Pfister. This was the era of the most vehement rejection and unimaginably passionate attacks on psychoanalysis. Those few dozen men from the four corners of the globe clustered almost like brothers around the venerated founder of the movement, who clearly exhibited the traits of a patriarch.[19]

2. Freud's Contributions Before the Turn of the Century

In order to understand Jung's work correctly and to keep his discoveries distinct from the insights of Freud, we must review the range of the ideas with which he came in contact. At the outset, Jung found himself confronted not only with a wealth of original observations regarding the origin of neuroses, but also with Freud's revolutionary method of inquiry, which attempted systematically to understand human behavior as stemming from *unconscious motivations*. Freud's essential contribution was to grant to emotions and affects the principal emphasis in treating neuroses; he drew attention to the dangers of one-sided glorification of the intellect while neglecting the vital aspects of the psyche. Already at the time of his collaboration with Breuer, Freud emphasized—partly through Charcot's influence—the causative role of psychic trauma in the development of neuroses. His investigations were focused on the relationship between trauma and symptom, and in this context he understood trauma as a psychic shock which the subject was unable to handle because of its incompatibility with his conscious concepts. From the very beginning, Freud's main theme was the stressful power play between opposing tendencies, in which the overwhelming tendency brought about the defense against the affect-laden experience or else forced it into the unconscious. This acceptance of Herbart's remarkable concept of repression, when viewed in the dynamic perspective, culminated in assuming a mechanism of dissociation or, in other words, severing the total irritation from the related event; in regard to content, it resulted in the formation of an unconscious focus of disease. The finding that "derailed affects" persist in the unconscious and retain their total energy was—as Bleuler cor-

19 Maeder, "Mein Weg von der Psychoanalyse zur Synthese" (1956), p. 94. (Here tr. F.E.E. and E.K.E.)

rectly pointed out—one of Freud's discoveries which cannot be disregarded by psychology.[20]

Of equal importance was Freud's recognition that, instead of a more or less conscious conflict between ego and trauma, an unconscious antagonism developed which led to symptom formation. Accordingly, Freud's concept of the symptom was that it expressed the tension created by the unconscious antagonism: It was substitute-formation, but the form it took—conversion, transposition, or projection—depended on the type of conflict situation. Freud's discovery that neurosis results from the ego's miscarried attempt at defense[21] made him the pioneer of modern psychotherapy. He was also in the vanguard in assuming an axiomatic determination of neurotic symptoms; that is, symptoms are not only appropriately determined but, like psychic events in general, are always related to specific causes.

Freud's invention of the technique of "free association," that is, the use of spontaneous thoughts as they arise, became immeasurably important in the further development of psychology. The laws of association, it is true, had been investigated by Locke and Hume, but in Freud's work they assumed an entirely new significance and application. With the cooperation of the subject of the therapeutic process,[22] Freud unexpectedly gained entrance to the patient's personal life history; he believed that through such uncovering the puzzling nature of the disease could be disclosed. In addition, Freud discovered the extraordinarily significant factor of the patient's resistance[23] to the therapeutic process, explaining the frequent failures of therapy, particularly therapy using hypnotic suggestion. He also recognized in the patient's resistance to associations the cause of memory disturbance, which in psychotherapy takes the shape of "cutting off ideas" or "disrupting continuity," known technically as blocking and obstruction. The experiences with the association technique were very revealing in the theoretical perspective. They enabled Freud to observe not only the "enchaînement," the uninterrupted linking of psychic events, but also the concentric arrangement of repressed memories around so-called "nuclei or centres of crystallization."[24] These experiences made Freud the first in the field of medical psychology to achieve an empirical demonstration of the unconscious, that is, the demonstration of a coherent unity and a dynamic structure in the material of unconscious memories.

20 E. Bleuler, "Die Psychoanalyse Freuds" (1910).
21 Freud, "Further Remarks on the Neuro-Psychoses of Defence" (1896), p. 169.
22 Breuer and Freud, *Studies on Hysteria* (1893–95), p. 292.
23 Ibid., p. 268.   24 Ibid., p. 123.

Those discoveries of Freud which we have briefly sketched were the psychological tools with which Jung became adept after familiarizing himself with the *Studies on Hysteria.* The other papers which Freud published before the turn of the century, however, probably became accessible to Jung only when they were brought together in the *Collection of Shorter Writings on the Theory of the Neuroses from the Years 1893–1906.*[25]

In his early publications Freud developed primarily the theories of the "sexual trauma in childhood" and the symptom as a compromise formation. Originally he had assumed a simple causal connection between neurotic symptom, actual trauma, and defense, but he soon became convinced that this concept was insufficient: The history of every neurosis seemed in the end to go back to sexual experiences during early childhood.[26] However, this hypothesis, too, did not completely correspond with the true situation and was superseded by the assumption that symptom formation depended on a further condition, that is, the breakthrough of revived material, the return of repressed memories[27] in later years. The insight that hysterical symptoms are derivatives of memories which are operating unconsciously[28] was subsequently confirmed. Nevertheless, Freud was disappointed to find that such revived traces of memory were highly questionable as to factual content. The "reality" of fantasized sexual traumata in childhood[29] could not be maintained because the reports of hysterical patients were usually based on fiction, biased distortion of memories,[30] and even "displacement maneuvers." This new evidence meant a collapse of Freud's former values and caused him the greatest embarrassment. Still, the failure led to an extremely important result—the discovery of the pervasive significance of sexuality in the etiology of neuroses. On this finding he based the theory of sexuality;[31] he did not find it necessary to sacrifice earlier conclusions but was able to utilize them, though with some modification, and to incorporate them in the new hypotheses. As Freud himself stated, the theory of infantile sexuality arose from the previous assumption of a "sexual trauma in childhood."

[25] Jung's letter to Freud of 5 Oct. 1906 acknowledges Freud's gift of the *Collection of Shorter Writings.* See *The Freud/Jung Letters* (1974), J 1.

[26] "My Views on the Part Played by Sexuality in the Aetiology of the Neuroses" (1906), p. 273.

[27] "Further Remarks on the Neuro-Psychoses," p. 169.

[28] "The Aetiology of Hysteria" (1896), p. 212.

[29] *The Origins of Psycho-Analysis* (1887–1902), p. 216.

[30] "Screen Memories" (1899), p. 322.

[31] "Three Essays on the Theory of Sexuality" (1905).

Freud observed that censuring agents are at work in the psyche, which not only fend off incipient memories but also distort and falsify them; this discovery formed one of the basic concepts of his system. The recognition of this mechanism became important 1) in tracing neuroses from their origin in miscarried attempts at repression and 2) in trying to explain neurotic symptoms either as surrogate gratification or as compromise formations[32] resulting from the conflict between the "return of the repressed" and the censor's further efforts to repress. Both concepts were destined to become pillars of psychoanalytic theory.

Freud's research on parapraxes and dreams must be counted among his outstanding contributions to psychology and psychopathology. This work again furnished proof that not only "unconscious thoughts" and "unconscious wishes" exist, but that meaning and purpose can be recognized throughout psychic processes.[33] Those seemingly "unintentional performances," for example slips of the tongue, misreadings, forgetting, mislaying and losing objects, "are well-motivated and determined by impulses which are totally unknown to consciousness." These observations rounded out his concept of the bridge linking psychic disturbances and normal behavior. This view applied in large measure to dreams; initially, Freud had surmised that dreams were pathological phenomena, but increasingly he recognized in them the "normal prototypes of all psychopathologic structures"[34]—a finding which allowed a much more profound understanding of the neuroses. Freud was the first to recognize that the dream is a genuine psychic performance, not only ingenious but psychologically significant. Freud's dream interpretation was a classic contribution; he showed that the dream presents a structural unity of meaningfully connected parts, serving a decided function in the whole structure of the psyche, particularly its tendencies toward wish-fulfillment. The dream is intrinsically embedded in the total "enchaînement" of the psychic sphere. Moreover, his dream studies opened a path to the study of symbolism in dreams and thence to an understanding of symbols in general. Jung was deeply convinced that Freud's dream interpretation was "the boldest attempt ever made to master the enigma of the unconscious psyche on the apparently firm ground of empiricism."[35]

Freud's position regarding dreams and dream symbolism will be discussed in greater detail in a later chapter.

32 Ibid., p. 208.
33 "Introductory Lectures on Psycho-Analysis" (1916–17), p. 40.
34 "The Claims of Psycho-Analysis to Scientific Interest" (1913), p. 172.
35 Jung, "In Memory of Sigmund Freud" (1939), p. 44.

A. FROM TRAUMA
TO THE FEELING-TONED
COMPLEX

I. ASSOCIATION EXPERIMENT AND
FEELING-TONED COMPLEX

The scope and significance of Freud's discoveries are sufficient to explain the great impression they made upon Jung. He was similarly stirred by the sufferings of the mentally disturbed and found a wealth of stimulation in Freud's work. In fact, the fascination was so strong that for a time he put aside the pregnant inception of his own psychological theories in order to evaluate the teachings of Freud. His scientific attitude is epitomized by the following words:

> I told myself Freud could be refuted only by one who has made repeated use of the psychoanalytic method and who really investigates as Freud does—that is, by one who has made a long and patient study of everyday life, hysteria, and dreams from Freud's point of view.[1]

Jung saw in Freud more than the mere achievement of an individual. He regarded Freud as the embodiment of the intellectual dynamism which was characteristic of the closing nineteenth century. In part, Freud appeared to him as an offshoot of scientific materialism, intent on transferring the causal determinism and the basic mechanistic assumptions of the nineteenth century to psychic phenomena; but mainly, he recognized Freud as an exponent of the twentieth century, a forerunner who, like Nietzsche, anticipated the impact of the affects in understanding the psyche.

Still, the prevailing uncertainty regarding diagnosis and management of the psychoses, as well as the high degree of subjectivity underlying the scientific interpretation of cases, led Jung to develop a more exact method. Under the guidance of his chief, Eugen Bleuler, and in collaboration with his colleague, Franz Riklin, he worked on the association experiment, from which he expected success in the field of psychiatric diagnosis. At the same time it promised to be a test of the hypotheses on which Freud's work was based. The study of association processes was not a new venture at the Burghölzli Hospital. Some time earlier Bleuler and his collaborators[2] had begun to give

---

[1] "The Psychology of Dementia Praecox" (1907), p. 3.

[2] Before the preparation of Jung and Riklin, "The Associations of Normal Subjects" (1905), CW 2; cf. par. 1.

attention to this technique, which had been introduced into psychiatry by Kraepelin[3] and Aschaffenburg.[4]

From the beginning of his professional career, Jung, too, had included the study of the associative activity of emotionally disturbed patients in his exploration of mental disorders. With this approach he gained much illuminating insight of the patient's state of mind. The importance which Bleuler had earlier attributed to the study of associations becomes evident from his comment:

> Thus in the activity of association there is mirrored the whole psychical essence of the past and of the present, with all their experiences and desires. It thus becomes an index of all the psychical processes which we have but to decipher in order to understand the complete man.[5]

According to Bleuler, Jung's investigations were of particular value because they afforded unexpected insight into the "unconscious mechanisms" of the psyche and into the "unconscious working of the mind."[6] As Freud had already established, associations were anything but accidental; they were rather a part of the total "enchaînement" of psychic life.

In setting up the design of the association experiment,[7] Jung and his collaborators started initially from the method of Wundt and Aschaffenburg and adopted the latter's classification of associations. However, in contrast to existing methods of research, mainly designed to investigate the connection between association and disturbance of attention, Jung used his method to observe emotional disturbances. From his work on associations Jung discovered that "seemingly" accessory findings—which Wundt and his school interpreted as "mistakes" (that is, responses clashing with the meaning of the stimulus word)—were of specific value for understanding the psychic situation of the patient. The hitherto neglected disturbances in the association process—for example, "perseveration," "prolonged reaction time," "absence of reaction," and particularly mistakes in "reproduction of the stimulus words"—were those precisely destined to become of extraordinary significance as indicators of often powerful affective influences and emotions. Such evidence demonstrated to Jung the

[3] "Der psychologische Versuch in der Psychiatrie," in Kraepelin, ed., *Psychologische Arbeiten*, Vol. I (1896).

[4] "Experimentelle Studien über Assoziationen," in ibid.

[5] Bleuler, "Upon the Significance of Association Experiments" (1906), in Jung, ed., *Studies in Word-Association*, pp. 4–5.

[6] Ibid., p. 6.

[7] C. A. Meier, *Die Empirie des Unbewussten* (1968), Ch. IV.

importance of the affective aspect of associations for the "experimental investigation of pathological feeling changes and their consequences."[8]

The "faulty reactions," which formerly had been approached only from the outside and were understood as disturbances of attention, could now be studied from the inside, from the point of view of affectivity. What is more, they seemed to indicate the operation of a still unknown psychic factor, lying outside of consciousness. In other words, they could be easily interpreted as effects of concealed, feeling-toned experiences. From these observations Jung drew the conclusion —extraordinarily significant for his psychological investigations—that there are affect- and feeling-toned complexes in the unconscious psyche. In this context, then, disturbances of association were nothing less than signs of complexes, *complex indicators*.

Under "characteristics of an unconsciously constellating complex," Jung included the following: "long reaction-time, unusual reaction, failures, perseveration, stereotyped repetition of the stimulus-word . . . translation into foreign language, strong language, quotations, slips of the tongue, assimilation of the stimulus-word."[9] Later, Jung also took into consideration the reproduction experiment, which gave information mainly about gaps in memory and memory falsifications.[10]

In his investigation of somnambulistic phenomena in 1902, Jung had demonstrated the significance of feeling-toned ideas as the essential cause of dreams.[11] Only while working on the association experiments did he realize that these ideas were also factors in causing disturbances of the association process. This seemed to him to be an impressive finding in still another direction: it put ego consciousness into a position of relative significance, since in the association process ego consciousness has a much smaller role in autonomous action but rather is acted upon.

> To our ego-consciousness the association-process seems to be its own work, subject to its judgment, free will, and concentration; in reality, however, as our experiment beautifully shows, ego-consciousness is merely the marionette that dances on the stage, moved by a concealed mechanism.[12]

How did Jung's concept of the complex develop? In his earliest description of it, he defined the affect-toned complex as "the sum of

[8] Jung and Riklin, p. 191.
[9] "The Reaction-Time Ratio in the Association Experiment" (1906), p. 263.
[10] "Psychoanalysis and Association Experiments" (1906), p. 290.
[11] "On the Psychology and Pathology of So-Called Occult Phenomena" (1902), CW 1, p. 68.
[12] "The Reaction-Time Ratio," p. 245.

ideas referring to a particular feeling-toned event."[13] In a sense, he extended this definition in 1928 by referring to a "nuclear element" of the complex.[14] And finally, in 1934 he completed the definition by distinguishing between emotional and purposeful aspects.[15]

From the very beginning, Jung recognized, as a characteristic of the affect-toned complex, the feeling tone[16] and emotional dynamism that could range from a state of low affectivity to extreme irritability and frenzy. The frequency of its occurrence and the degree of intensity as well as the quality of feeling showed the affect-toned complex to be an extraordinarily significant measurement of the degree of affectivity and also a nodal point of emotional events in the psyche.

The findings in the association experiment and their evaluation—principally the discovery of the indicators of the complex—were among the earliest scientific achievements of Jung. In his mind, the great value of the experiment was that it produced objectively valid evidence of the manifestations of the unconscious psyche. In Jung's hands the association experiment was invaluable for grasping the unconscious emotional determinants of psychic disturbances and for investigating the phenomena of psychopathology. It also confirmed the applicability of Freud's association technique in establishing the etiology of neuroses—an incidental gain which should not be underestimated. It was a great satisfaction to Jung that his "method of discovering complexes" could be successfully applied to the investigation of a delinquent.[17] From then on, the association experiment served him as an indispensable tool.

Jung's method of associations opened up a new avenue not only for the understanding of neurotic and psychotic symptoms but also for clarifying affective disturbances in the "normal psyche." Investigation of the associations of normal subjects enabled him to point out that the existence of complexes was a common phenomenon, characteristic of psychic life in general. In the complexes Jung also found the key to understanding the parapraxes—slips of the tongue, forgetting, slips of the pen, and so on—which Freud had examined in *The Psychopathology of Everyday Life*.[18] Jung, however, could not agree with Freud's explanation that these phenomena can be traced back to an internal conflict between conscious and unconscious "intentions," an interpretation that appeared to him to have too much of a rationalistic tinge.

[13] Jung and Riklin, p. 72, n. 18.   [14] "On Psychic Energy" (1928), p. 11.
[15] "A Review of the Complex Theory" (1934).
[16] "The Associations of Normal Subjects" (1904), p. 72, n. 18.
[17] "On the Psychological Diagnosis of Facts" (1905), p. 220.
[18] 1901; SE VI.

I. ASSOCIATION EXPERIMENT AND FEELING-TONED COMPLEX

The insights which Jung gained from the association experiment were not confined to that study alone. They found application far beyond the experimental situation and could be confirmed wherever a dialogue between human beings took place. This concept, used as a guide from the beginning, was expressed in 1934:

> What happens in the association test also happens in every discussion between two people. In both cases there is an experimental situation which constellates complexes that assimilate the topic discussed or the situation as a whole, including the parties concerned.[19]

Jung's observations in the association experiment largely coincided with Freud's experiences in psychotherapeutic contact with his patients. All the phenomena which Jung encountered in disturbed subjects in the course of the experiment—curtailment of associative activity, disturbances of recollection, blocking the recall capacity, deficiency or falsification of memory—were also characteristic of Freud's psychotherapeutic experience (see A.II.1). Similarly, his finding of "systematic amnesias"[20] (deficiencies of attention, limited to certain coherent series of memories) tallied with the phenomenon which Freud labelled as "hysterical amnesia."

Altogether, the results of the association experiment revealed important analogies between Jung and Freud: Both investigators established an intrinsic connection between disturbances of associative processes and psychopathological phenomena. For both, the cause was an unconscious, affect-toned factor which exerted a more or less intensive effect on the conscious psyche, on the action and thought of the individual. Likewise, both men recognized as precipitating factors of neurotic disturbances the aftereffects of events which had remained unconscious—interpreted by Freud as unresolved fixation to trauma,[21] and by Jung as affect- and emotion-toned complexes. These remarkable parallels led Jung, in 1906, to make the statement that "the association experiment devised by me gives the same results in principle [as the psychoanalytic method], and psychoanalysis is really no different from an association experiment,"[22] implying that the association experiment allowed an objective test of psychoanalysis—a conclusion, however, which subsequently lost validity.

In short, Jung's association experiment created a tool which allowed an objective approach to irrational phenomena and, in general, to the

19 "A Review of the Complex Theory," p. 95.
20 "Analytical Psychology and Education" (1926), p. 109.
21 Breuer and Freud, *Studies on Hysteria* (1893–95), p. 10.
22 "Freud's Theory of Hysteria" (1906), p. 7.

unconscious psyche. What Freud had initiated, Jung continued. Freud had demonstrated empirically the role of affect-toned disturbances in the unconscious, and Jung *experimentally* confirmed these factors. Both investigators contributed to making the unconscious (formerly only a philosophical concept) accessible to empirical exploration.

Much earlier, Leibniz had recognized the necessity of supplementing conscious ideas with unconscious perceptions. Likewise, Schelling had expanded human consciousness through the concept of the eternally-unconscious. Carus and Schopenhauer, on the other hand, thought that consciousness is derived from the unconscious, and von Hartmann built his system on the assumption of an unconscious spirit, which he considered the foundation of the absolute. In contrast to these more or less speculative arguments, the empirical demonstration of the unconscious was a scientific achievement of extraordinary impact. Moreover, with the association experiment Jung created the experimental basis on which it became possible to make objective statements, independent of personal opinions, about the presence of affect-toned complexes in the background of the psyche.

II. COMPLEX AND TRAUMA

1. Acute and Chronic Complexes

Jung and Freud agreed that the approach to the unconscious should be made by investigating the circumstances which disturb habitual behavior. But while Freud conceived of the traumatic affects as the primary, precipitating causes of unconscious phenomena, for Jung the emotion-toned complexes were the central factors in the background of the psyche. A discussion of the relationship between trauma and complex, therefore, seems unavoidable. Did the two concepts coincide? Was the complex, like the trauma, characterized by intense affect discharges? How did the investigators conceive the function of trauma or complex within the total personality?

In Jung's association studies, which he used partly to test Freud's discoveries, he established a far-reaching kinship between complex and trauma. Like Freud, who had seen in trauma the initial affect leading to the development of neuroses, Jung perceived the complex as the true *causa morbi*; accordingly, "every psychogenic neurosis contains a complex."[1] As an example of the etiological function of the complex, Jung cited a case of hysteria in which the association experiment showed the very same complex as that revealed in symptoms and dreams.[2] In his investigations on dementia praecox he was able to establish that in many cases "dementia praecox has an abnormally strong affective content which becomes stabilized with the onset of the disease."[3]

Could the affect-toned complex therefore be equated with trauma? According to Jung's statements, these terms were analogous only in the case of complexes with "abnormally strong affective content"; they had a marked constellating effect on psychic life and were also major factors in the development of psychopathologic formations. Only complexes with a high degree of intensity, which Jung later liked to describe as a "complete invasion of the individual,"[4] could be compared to trauma. Concerning the chaotic, passionate affective life, Jung wrote: "It lacks the true human note, it is out of proportion, irrational, a phenomenon of nature that breaks through the human order."[5]

1 Jung, "Psychoanalysis and Association Experiments" (1906), p. 291.
2 "Association, Dream, and Hysterical Symptom" (1906).
3 "The Psychology of Dementia Praecox" (1907), p. 110.
4 "The Therapeutic Value of Abreaction" (1921), pp. 133–34.
5 *Psychological Types* (1921), p. 155.

Wherever intense complexes were involved, unexpected and incalculable effects developed. This was particularly true in states of possession which encompassed the entire thinking and feeling of the person. The changes in personality were often serious and became manifest in a restriction of psychic faculties as well as in a decline of interests. The complex could become so overpowering that it increasingly assimilated more associations and not infrequently brought even the ego under its domination.

> Anything that does not suit the complex simply glances off, all other interests sink to nothing, there is a standstill and temporary atrophy of the personality. Only what suits the complex arouses affects and is assimilated by the psyche.[6]

Intense affect could sometimes be brought about by acute events, for example, fright or threat of danger, or in cases of an unexpected death. In such instances it was easily possible to demonstrate the agreement between Freud's findings in psychotherapy and the responses of Jung's neurotic subjects during the association experiments. With both methods memory gaps and memory deficits were encountered as well as faulty reproduction of personal experiences.

The feeling-toned complex, however, was never limited to acute states. Through fantasies and religious experiences Jung discovered the significance of *chronic* complexes. Among their striking features were long-lasting effects as well as affective stability, often continuing over a number of years; in other words, a "continually active feeling-tone."[7] These were essential observations for Jung since they prompted him to expand the prevailing concepts of affectivity of Freud and other contemporaries. Freud had considered the decisive aspect of affectivity to be the "sum of excitation"[8] of sexual drives (later called the degree of excitation). But Jung came out for the qualities of "mood and content of experience" and for the feeling quality of the complex.[9] This step cannot be overestimated since it brought about a changed point of view in the empirical investigation of unconscious phenomena. From then on, the inner content of experiences was considered as important as the dynamic aspects of the symptom.

> Feeling is primarily a process . . . that imparts to the content a definite *value* in the sense of acceptance or rejection ("like" or

6 "Dementia Praecox," pp. 47–48.   7 Ibid., p. 43.
8 Freud, "The Neuro-Psychoses of Defence" (1894), p. 60.
9 Jung, "Dementia Praecox," p. 42.

"dislike"). The process can also appear isolated, as it were, in the form of a "mood."[10]

Jung, however, went a step further in his critical examination of the concept of trauma, particularly of the sexual trauma of childhood which Freud formulated in 1896. He not only opposed Freud's limitation of trauma to sexual experiences reaching as far back as early childhood, but he became more and more convinced that Freud's emphasis on trauma in the etiology of neurosis was one-sided. At the time of his separation from Freud, Jung did not yet completely deny the etiological significance of trauma in the development of neuroses; however, it seemed to him that the total emotional situation of the subject, his frame of mind and his peculiar psychology were incomparably more responsible for the specific pathologic consequence. In contrast to the mechanistic approach of Freud—based as it was on the causal nexus of trauma, frustration, and regressive return of childhood memories—Jung emphasized the psychic predisposition of the subject; it was this factor alone that determined the effect of the trauma.

The individual must meet the trauma with a quite definite inner predisposition in order to make it really effective. This inner predisposition is . . . to be understood . . . as a psychological development which reaches its climax, and becomes manifest, at the traumatic moment.[11]

It may be somewhat surprising that Jung quarreled with the "sexual trauma in childhood" as late as 1913, fifteen years after Freud recognized the weakness of his earlier theory. That, in spite of being aware of this fact,[12] Jung discussed the theory of trauma at such length seems to have been due to his effort to invalidate the meaning of the infantile fixations[13] (Oedipus complex) as well as to pave the way for understanding the significance of the "actual present."[14] A further stimulus may be the fact that Freud, even after replacing the trauma theory with that of infantile sexuality, still clung covertly, in his conversations with Jung, to the etiological significance of childhood trauma; this was clear also in his 1918 work "From the History of an Infantile Neurosis."

[10] Jung, *Psychological Types*, p. 434.
[11] Jung, "The Theory of Psychoanalysis" (1912), p. 96.
[12] "Psychoanalysis and Neurosis" (1913), pp. 243–44.
[13] Ibid., p. 244.
[14] "The Theory of Psychoanalysis," p. 166.

2. *The Inner Unity of the Complex*

A noteworthy difference may be detected between the concepts of trauma and complex when one examines their inner cohesiveness and stability. From the first, Jung's psychology was oriented toward totality of the psychic structure. Even in his doctoral thesis, while under the influence of French psychopathology, he had discovered tendencies to a personality structure in somnambulistic subjects. He regarded the connection between content and emotion as decisive for understanding the inner life of a person. This point of view continued to guide him in the investigation of the complex. In it he saw a higher psychical unity,[15] which showed a stability and a structure brought about principally by the perfect coupling of feeling-tone and idea.

In order to compare these views with Freud's concept of trauma it is best to start with the inception of his theory. Freud's studies proceeded from psychopathologic phenomena—hysteria and obsessional neurosis —until he became preoccupied with the effect of fright, the psychic trauma. It was his basic assumption that "every event, every psychic impression is provided with a certain quota of affect of which the ego (normally) divests itself by means of a motor reaction,"[16] but he considered this mechanism to be quite labile. Freud was always impressed by the *dissociative tendency of psychic connections* where intense affects were concerned, particularly by the eruption of affects. In psychic trauma he recognized a sum of excitation, which in principle could be dissociated and, under the influence of moral resistance, lead to a separation of the affect from the related idea.[17] This assumption—to which I will return when discussing the theory of repression—determined the direction of Freud's further psychological investigations. Once the dissociation of psychic trauma was accepted, it was only a step to hypothesize mechanisms of displacement and substitute-formation in the psyche. To Freud the entire level of the unconscious was flexible. He became convinced of the fundamental motility of unconscious connections[18] primarily through investigating the mechanisms of the libido. Accordingly, in the normal psyche, too, the connections between the aim of the drive and object representation were by no means stable but could easily be substituted by others, exchanged for others, or in other words, could be *split*. These loose psychic connections led Freud to some interesting explanations of, for example,

15 "Psychoanalysis and Association Experiments," p. 291.

16 Freud, "Some Points for a Comparative Study of Organic and Hysterical Motor Paralyses" (1893), p. 171.

17 "The Neuro-Psychoses of Defence," p. 52.

18 "Introductory Lectures on Psycho-Analysis" (1917), p. 359.

homosexuality and the possibility of sublimating instinctual drives. As late as 1925,[19] the motility of the libido appeared to Freud to be the essential spur to cultural achievements of both individuals and the community. Not only psychic trauma but psychic experience in general presented a very loose connection between psychic components.

In contrast to Freud, Jung was at all times cognizant of a firm connection between feeling-tone and idea. To him, the complex in the first place was complete and whole, as had been demonstrated by the association experiment. Even though the dissociative tendency of the complex was confirmed with intense affect levels, in contrast to Freud he found that this phenomenon was restricted to certain cases of schizophrenia, as will be brought out later (see G.I.2.c).

After his first reference to the complex as a "higher unit," Jung stated in 1907 (*Psychology of Dementia Praecox*) that, irrespective of content, every minute part of the complex reproduced the feeling-tone of the whole and, in addition, each affect radiated throughout the entire mass of the idea.

> This behaviour may be compared directly to Wagnerian music. The leitmotiv, as a sort of feeling-tone, denotes a complex of ideas which is essential to the dramatic structure. Each time one or the other complex is stimulated by something someone does or says, the relevant leitmotiv is sounded in one of its variants. It is exactly the same in ordinary psychic life: The leitmotivs are the feeling-tones of our complexes, our actions and moods are modulations of the leitmotivs.[20]

Jung's concept of the complex as a psychic unit was destined to be extraordinarily productive in his psychological investigations. He recognized in it the basis of structural units of the psyche as a whole. This was a twofold concept: It revealed the intimate connection between the "higher units" themselves and their relation to the totality of the psyche. A series of phenomena confirmed Jung's early assumption. In *Transformations and Symbols of the Libido* (1912) he described the archaic "primordial thoughts," the "primordial images,"[21] which showed a totality of feeling and thinking (see C.IV). Similarly, the archetypal image indicated a link between image and instinct[22] (see E.III.4). In the "pattern of behavior," Jung later attempted to give adequate expression to the inner connection between "image and

---

[19] "An Autobiographical Study" (1925), p. 56.
[20] Jung, "Dementia Praecox," p. 39, n. 4.
[21] Cf. *Symbols of Transformation* (1952), p. 293. (Regarding the use of the above English title, see Preface, n. 1.)
[22] Jung, "Instinct and the Unconscious" (1919), p. 138.

instinct," going so far as to describe the image as "the meaning of instinct."[23] This seemed to him to be extremely important for psychotherapy in connection with the problem of releasing dammed-up drives.

> . . . as biology shows, instincts are by no means blind, spontaneous, isolated impulses; they are on the contrary associated with typical situational patterns and cannot be released unless existing conditions correspond to the *a priori* pattern.[24]

In his last years, Jung still emphasized that image and instinct have a "primary connection" (1955),[25] and this seemed to him to throw light on the *numinosum*, the overwhelming power of religious ideas.

3. The Nuclear Element as the Center of the Complex

Jung expanded the theory of the complex in still another direction. He discovered a central point of reference, the so-called nuclear element,[26] which is the specific focus not only of the quality of energy—the feeling-tone—but also the quality of content, the quality of value and meaning. While Jung initially had defined the complex as the sign of an extraneous event, he later found evidence in the nuclear element which seemed to indicate an intrapsychic reality. As he came to recognize more and more clearly, the nuclear element of the complex arose from the clash between the outer and the inner reality of the individual, the germ of the nuclear element originating as much from earlier experiences and the psychic disposition as from forceful environmental influences.

> The nuclear element consists of two components: first, a factor determined by experience and causally related to the environment; second, a factor innate in the individual's character and determined by his disposition.[27]

Jung's meaning can be illustrated, for example, in the mother-complex. This is conditioned, on the one hand, by outside influences, sometimes very subtle, coming from the mother or from a foster-parent or nurse, or quite generally from the protective family circle; on the other hand; this complex arises equally from intrinsic ways of thinking and acting, which are immanent in the individual. Consequently, in

23 "On the Nature of Psyche" (1946), p. 201.
24 Jung, "Medicine and Psychotherapy" (1945), p. 92.
25 *Mysterium Coniunctionis* (1955), p. 418.
26 "On Psychic Energy" (1928), p. 11.   27 Ibid.

the concept of the complex intrinsic influences were closely connected with those from outside sources.

This concept was to be confirmed—in a way which still seems unfathomable—by the discovery of primordial images (1912)[28] and archetypal motifs (1917)[29] in the dark hinterland of the psyche. From his investigation of the instinct, Jung recognized that the unconscious contents and processes allow archaic images, deeply rooted in instinctual life, and archetypal qualities (1919)[30] to shine through. This applied essentially to the complex and particularly to the "archetype" which Jung discerned in the nuclear element. Thus, not only did his conjecture of a constitutional pattern become plausible, but the concept of the nuclear element as the carrier of archaic meaning and instinctual disposition was confirmed. These insights carried Jung one step beyond Freud's theories. He was then enabled to enlarge upon and supplement the one-sided emphasis on causation through outside impressions (traumata). While Freud had considered affect and libido merely from a dynamic point of view, Jung gave due consideration to the constitutional disposition of the individual and to the intrapsychic structure of the unconscious psyche.

In attempting to evolve methods of quantifying the effects of complexes, Jung initially adopted the same aims as Freud. Both investigators were searching for a reliable standard which would allow them to grasp the laws governing psychic events. Freud hit upon such a yardstick in the concept of libido,[31] while Jung introduced the concept of "value intensity"[32]—the energy potential of the nuclear element. On this depended the constellating power of the complex, that is, its capacity to assimilate contents which have an inner relation to the nuclear element.

The constellating power of the nuclear element corresponds to its value intensity, i.e., to its energy.[33]

Thus, an objective evaluation of the energy potential of the complex seemed to be possible and might even claim some degree of probability,

---

[28] *Transformations and Symbols of the Libido.*

[29] "The Psychology of Unconscious Processes" (1917).

[30] "Instinct and the Unconscious" (1919), p. 133.

[31] "Three Essays on the Theory of Sexuality" (1905).

[32] "On Psychic Energy" (1928), p. 12.

[33] Ibid. In the course of time, Jung modified the term "constellation." In the beginning he had in mind the effect of the complex on associations, but in later years he emphasized the point that "the outward situation releases a psychic process in which certain contents gather together and prepare for action . . . a position from which he [the individual] can be expected to react in a quite definite way" ("A Review of the Complex Theory," 1934, p. 94).

although psychic phenomena can never be estimated with the accuracy permitted by the measuring techniques of natural science. Jung considered the means of such an evaluation to be the relative number of constellated contents as well as the frequency of reactions indicating a disturbance of the complex.

The intensity of affective phenomena—that is, the physiological effects of the complex, such as changes in respiration, pulse, and skin resistance to an electrical current[34]—revealed the emotional state of the individual. Even though objective techniques for measuring elapsed time, pulse and respiration curves, etc., had been available in experimental psychology before the time of Jung, his studies on the nature of the complex laid the foundation for the investigation of psychosomatic interrelationships.[35]

In summary, Jung's interest was always concentrated on the feeling-toned complex and not on trauma. At all times, he subordinated the concept of trauma to that of the complex, which to him appeared to be of paramount significance. In the complex (more precisely, in its nuclear element) he recognized the most essential source of information concerning the inner aspects of the personality, concerning the individual's unconscious motives, hopes, and fears, as well as his hidden tendencies for development. For Jung the complex—rather than the dream, as Freud had assumed—was the "via regia" to the realm of the unconscious.

> The *via regia* to the unconscious, however, is not the dream, as he [Freud] thought, but the complex, which is the architect of dreams and of symptoms.[36]

4. Unconscious and Conscious Complexes

That complexes can be conscious was less of a problem to Jung than that they can also be unconscious. The affective intensity of complexes, which found expression in the peculiarities brought out in the association process and in the stream of consciousness generally, would have been sufficient to direct the attention of the ego to this phenomenon. In any case, Jung established again and again that the subjacent complex was usually unknown and veiled—a circumstance clearly demonstrated in the association experiment. We cannot overlook the fact that in many cases the essential psychological significance remained unconscious.[37]

34 "On Psychic Energy," pp. 13–14.   35 Meier, *Die Empirie des Unbewussten.*
36 Jung, "A Review of the Complex Theory," p. 101.
37 Ibid., p. 11.

This finding, first observed by Freud, had motivated him to develop the theory of repression (see B.III.1). According to this hypothesis, traumatic experiences which had barely approached consciousness became unconscious because of their incompatibility with the ego.[38] In other words, the affective content of trauma activated the mechanism of displacement so that the related idea was banished from consciousness as unacceptable. For Freud, psychic traumata were therefore always unconscious—a concept which did not change even in later years when he investigated the libido fixation, particularly the Oedipus complex.[39] One could raise the question whether the release of the repressed material in the course of psychoanalytic therapy would not transform the unconscious trauma into a conscious complex, but this possibility did not satisfy Freud's hypotheses. In his view, the attempt to make causative traumata conscious, that is, to become aware of them and to work through them, led to resolution and removal of the whole complex. Accordingly, Freud considered traumata and complexes as either unconscious or, after working-through and sublimation, as "terminated."

For Jung, the circumstances were more intricate. Indeed, he had the same concept as Freud, that the majority of feeling-toned complexes were unconscious. But unconsciousness was not necessarily the result of repressing formerly conscious content. As we will see later on, recent contents constellated in the background may remain unconscious because they are new and therefore strange to consciousness.[40] There are degrees of unconsciousness—in fact, an entire gamut of unconscious complexes, varying from relative unconsciousness (as in parapraxes) to states of relative independence and autonomy (see A.III) and on to those of definite possession, that is, total unconsciousness. The greater the degree of unconsciousness, the less corrigible and controllable the complex—a conclusion reached by both Jung and Freud.

In contrast to Freud, Jung maintained that there were also conscious complexes which were accessible to correction and control because of their conscious behavior. What was a conscious complex? Jung certainly did not conceive it only as the subject's "mere" knowledge that a feeling-toned complex existed. Awareness of a blind spot in

---

38 Breuer and Freud, "Preliminary Communication" (1893), in *Studies on Hysteria*, p. 10 and n. 1.

39 As early as 1906 Freud adopted the term "complex" from the Zurich School and used it from then on ("Psycho-Analysis and the Establishment of the Facts in Legal Proceedings," p. 104). His use of the term "nuclear complex of a neurosis" goes back to 1908 ("On the Sexual Theories of Children," p. 214).

40 Jung, "On Psychic Energy," p. 11, n. 19.

the psyche did not preclude the development of unconscious effects, just as it did not guarantee the possibility of the ego's control of the complex. For Jung, more important than awareness was the endeavor, whether more or less successful, to let the complex come into consciousness. By this endeavor he meant a mutual penetration of the "conscious" and the "unconscious" (see G.II.4.b), while the subject remained conscious of the opposite affects as well as of the psychological significance of the complex (see App. II.2.d). Even though such an attitude was associated with an increase in energy and improved adjustment to the outer world, it by no means implied that the complex was thus dissolved, as Freud had assumed. Jung recognized with increasing clarity that in complexes essential to life an undetermined portion of the affective nucleus always remained unconscious, since there is no conscious content which is not in some respect unconscious.[41] This is not necessarily a disadvantage, because it could be salutary for the individual to live consciously with his complex.

[41] "On the Nature of the Psyche," p. 188.

III. THE AUTONOMY
OF THE UNCONSCIOUS COMPLEX

---

1. The Ego-Complex and the Autonomous Complex

To understand Jung's psychology one must recognize that the psyche always forms a whole, with interrelated parts. This concept by no means excludes the relative independence of the parts.

> Although the separate parts are connected with one another, they are relatively independent, so much so that certain parts of the psyche never become associated with the ego at all, or only very rarely.[1]

These independent components of the psyche, which show a relative spontaneity, Jung called autonomous complexes. It is true, such unconscious contents had previously been discovered and investigated by Janet ("existences secondes") and by Freud (compulsive and obsessive phenomena). However, in Jung's psychology the aspect of autonomy assumed surprising proportions by incorporating the impersonal contents of archaic layers (collective unconscious). Anticipating a later discussion (see A.III.3), we might mention here that the impersonal complexes of psychic life showed a degree of autonomy and spontaneity which the individual experienced as utterly strange, even endowed with an odd magical power. A characteristic of these impersonal complexes was that they were always derived from the dark sphere of the unconscious and presented an undeniable superiority over conscious reality.

At first, Jung stayed on more or less known territory; among the complexes, he conceived the ego-complex as the "firmly knit union of the psyche," connected with the "powerful and ever-present feeling-tone of our own body." He considered the ego-complex as the "centre characteristic of our psyche,"[2] on which—when properly coordinated into the whole—the health of the person largely depended. Even so, the ego-complex for Jung was only one among many other complexes. As long as the ego-complex was in harmony with the unconscious background, it retained its central characteristic. However, if it arbitrarily separated itself from its base—which, according to Jung, happened when feeling-tone and connected ideas were exaggerated or

[1] Jung, "The Psychological Foundations of Belief in Spirits" (1920), p. 307.
[2] Ibid.

overemphasized—the ego-complex then fostered the development of one or more split-off complexes (in Freud: traumata due to ego defense).

> The ego-complex is, so to say, no longer the whole of the personality; side by side with it there exists another being, living its own life and hindering and disturbing the development of the ego-complex.[3]

Cases of complexes splitting-off from the ego seemed to give rise to a "secondary authority in addition to the ego-complex" which, pursuing its own purposes, thwarted the aims and objects of the ego, and "successfully competes with the intentions of the ego-complex."[4] The remarkable feature of such a "secondary authority" was—as Freud had already pointed out—that the unconscious complex with its entire tension remained operative in the unconscious. This occurred despite the great intensity which ordinarily would have required transition into consciousness. Unknown, unrecognized by the ego, wrapped in complete darkness, these effects were completely out of the reach of the ego. Janet had emphasized the persevering effect of the split-off contents, and Freud had laid great stress upon the compulsive repetition of dissociated contents; but Jung pointed out that, in addition, every dynamically laden complex was characterized by a tendency to "have a separate existence."[5] He saw this quality of autonomy in the striving of the complex to achieve its aim in opposition to the conscious psyche—a quality which Freud had traced back primarily to repression.

We have already pointed out that such autonomously functioning units are not merely split off from the ego, but that they are also due to the unconscious withdrawal of energy—or, to put it differently, what has involuntarily slipped away is the thought-complex.[6] Jung's observations in 1907 were significantly expanded with the passing of years. He recognized that the fascinating aspect of the autonomous complex was connected with the presence of an ego-alien quality—an "unconscious something"—which functioned independently from consciousness (see App. I) and was "unassailable to criticism." This strange "something" produced the most disparate effects; it could form the basis of creative processes—mainly in the case of impersonal complexes—or could lead to negative, even dangerous disturbances.

[3] Jung, "The Psychology of Dementia Praecox" (1907), p. 47.
[4] Jung, "The Reaction-Time Ratio in the Association Experiment" (1906), p. 245.
[5] "Psychoanalysis and Association Experiments" (1906), pp. 314f.
[6] "Dementia Praecox," p. 45.

III. THE AUTONOMY OF THE UNCONSCIOUS COMPLEX

Peculiar to it was often a surprising quality of authority; not infrequently it acted as an "evil spirit" which contrived all kinds of mischief and tricks. In 1936 Jung described these observations in retrospect:

> As the association experiments prove, complexes interfere with the intentions of the will and disturb the conscious performance; they produce disturbances of memory and blockages in the flow of associations; they appear and disappear according to their own laws; they can temporarily obsess consciousness, or influence speech and action in an unconscious way. In a word, complexes behave like independent beings, a fact especially evident in abnormal states of mind. In the voices heard by the insane they even take on a personal ego-character like that of the spirits who manifest themselves through automatic writing and similar techniques. An intensification of complexes leads to morbid states, which are extensive multiple dissociations endowed with an indomitable life of their own.[7]

Hallucinations and delusions were included among such invasions by unconscious complexes as well as the phenomenon of "voices" which repeat the patient's thoughts aloud.[8] Most impressive were primitive people's experiences with "ghosts," which clearly revealed the earmarks of projection of unconscious contents.

> Spirits, therefore, viewed from the psychological angle, are unconscious autonomous complexes which appear as projections because they have no direct association with the ego.[9]

Contents are thus manifested as

> spirits . . . when the individual loses his adaptation to reality, or (those) which seek to replace the inadequate attitude of a whole people by a new one. They are therefore either pathological fantasies or new but as yet unknown ideas.[10]

By recognizing the autonomy of unconscious complexes, independent of the ego, Jung may be said to have delivered a counterstroke to the most sensitive point of the then prevailing psychology of consciousness. At the same time he provided an ingenious foundation for the phenomena of obsession and compulsion which Freud had observed.

---

[7] "Psychological Factors Determining Human Behaviour" (1936), p. 121.
[8] "Belief in Spirits," p. 307, n. 3.   [9] Ibid., p. 309.
[10] Ibid., p. 315.

2. *The Unconscious Complex as Part of the Personality*

Jung observed a quality in the autonomous complexes which he had already described in his thesis as characteristic of the somnambulist's psyche. At that time his interpretation of the findings had been stimulated by the phenomena of "double consciousness" and "second existences" discovered by the French psychopathologists (Azam, Richer, Binet, Janet, etc.). Later on, these assumptions were completely confirmed in the investigation of complexes. Jung became convinced that the unconscious complex was an unconscious part of the personality, displaying a definite personality character. This insight, which fitted aptly into his concept of the inner unity of the complex, was in sharp contrast to Freud's assumption that traumatic experiences are in principle ready to split into the elemental components of emotion and idea.

With regard to the tendency to autonomy and the inclination to personification shown by the unconscious complexes, Jung was able, to a large extent, to draw on Janet's investigations. As early as 1889, Janet had observed that unconscious partial formations in hysterical patients, especially the "second existences," presented personality character. As Jung, too, was able to establish, both qualities exhibited a tendency to systematization of ideas around a stable nucleus as well as formation of a personality center. He observed this in the nuclear element (1928) and noted the presence of particular affects, particular ideas, and even a particular memory. Still, Janet's assertion of a separate ego always remained an open question to Jung. But it seemed to him that the unconscious complexes had "all the essential features" in common with the fragments of personality observed by Janet "until we come to the delicate question of fragmented consciousness."[11] It became clear to Jung that the split-off, unconscious complex formed "a miniature self-contained psyche,"[12] even a "dissociated personality."[13]

The tendency of unconscious complexes to personify and lead an independent life was by no means only a pathological phenomenon, even though it could always be detected in hallucinations, delusional systems, or possession. In this respect, the investigations by Morton Prince and Janet had been of great value to Jung. These investigators had demonstrated that increased unconsciousness may cause the unconscious psyche to split into as many as four or five partial fragments

---

11 Jung, "A Review of the Complex Theory" (1934), p. 97.
12 "Problems of Modern Psychotherapy" (1929), p. 56.
13 *Psychology of the Unconscious* (1916; tr. of *Transformations and Symbols of the Libido*, 1912), p. 37.

of personality, each with its own specific memory. Jung had uncovered similar findings in certain psychic phenomena of primitive people. For instance, the belief in demons or in the return of the souls of the deceased pointed unmistakably to the concept of a multitude of psyches. But Jung found the psychic formations of legend, dream, and myth to be the most cogent proof of tendencies to personification in the psyche of "normal" people. These productions portrayed essential aspects of the human personality (for example, typical attributes, characteristic behavior, or recurrent modes of reaction) in the guise of personifications and autonomous motives.

From such findings Jung concluded that the psyche of the individual does not constitute an indivisible unit but may be split into fragments of personality. He especially emphasized the splitting tendency of the psyche in 1936, but he by no means envisaged the destruction of the continuity of experience.

> The tendency to split means that parts of the psyche detach them-selves from consciousness to such an extent that they not only appear foreign but lead an autonomous life of their own. It need not be a question of hysterical multiple personality, or schizophrenic altera-tions of personality, but merely of so-called "complexes" that come entirely within the scope of the normal.[14]

On the other hand, it should be made clear that the split-off parts ordinarily constitute whole complex-units, or fragmentary personalities complete in themselves. Contrary to Freud's assumption that dissocia-tion of affect and idea was connected with the mechanism of repression, Jung understood personality disintegration as occurring exclusively in certain psychotic phenomena.[15] He had already emphasized in his association studies that neurosis was not associated with the destruc-tion of complexes but was based on the dissociation of two mutually exclusive complex-units (or separate personalities), each completely preserved within itself.

In 1946 Jung finally came to the opinion that the tendency to split is a general quality of the psyche which occurs in healthy as well as in sick people. He attempted to express this idea in the concept of the dis-sociability of the psyche.[16] This explanation was very important be-cause, on the one hand, it called into question the prejudice for the unity and superiority of the ego-complex and, on the other hand, the belief in an *a priori* unity of the person. Even though an image of this unity (archetype of the self) lay dormant in the psyche of man, the

14 "Human Behaviour," p. 121.   15 "Schizophrenia" (1957), pp. 269–70.
16 "On the Nature of the Psyche" (1946), p. 173.

unity did not by any means exist from the beginning of life but was rather the conception of a goal toward which the development of the individual was oriented. This conclusion proved productive in regard to the possibility of gradually integrating those still unconscious contents capable of being admitted to consciousness. It clarified the idea that the beginning of consciousness depended on integrating the still unconnected islands of consciousness and also explained the extension of consciousness through creative production.[17]

3. Personal and Impersonal Complexes

Although a more detailed discussion of impersonal complexes appears in a later chapter (see B.III.2), in order to preserve the relationship between various aspects of the theory of the complexes, I must mention here the discovery of the impersonal complexes. Jung described "personal" contents as those ideas which either belonged to the ego-complex or were split off from the ego and ignored. All personal contents, thus, were reminiscences of events which had occurred during life. "Impersonal" contents, on the other hand, originated essentially from the timeless and primary cause of the psyche; they are, therefore, completely independent from the ego and from personal memories.

The discovery of contents having a meaning common to all men and, more than that, the recognition of a timeless basis for the unconscious formations of the psyche was destined to advance the psychology of the complexes in an unanticipated manner. Jung was thus enabled to discern the essential double-layer character of the unconscious complexes. The complex pointed, on the one hand, to contents which were split off from consciousness but, on the other hand, to some which, because of their unfamiliar character, immutability, fascination, and usurping action, seemed to belong to a deep layer that far surpassed the personal sphere.

In contrast to reminiscences which could be attributed to personal experiences, such captivating ideas were derived from something

timeless; they arise from that realm of creative psychic life out of which the ephemeral mind of the single human being grows like a plant that blossoms, bears fruit and seed, and then withers and dies. Ideas spring from something greater than the personal human being. Man does not make his ideas; we could say that man's ideas make him.[18]

17 "On Psychic Energy" (1928), p. 11, n. 19.
18 Jung, "Freud and Jung: Contrasts" (1929), p. 333.

There is no parallel in psychoanalysis to Jung's assumption of double-layered unconscious complexes. Freud's psychology up to the end of the second decade of the twentieth century was based on the presupposition that contents must be understood as fundamentally personal; even in his later writings, in which he supplemented the ontogenetic motives with phylogenetic tendencies, particularly the archaic heritage, Freud rejected in principle the hypothesis of a timeless and collective unconscious (see D.III.3). Despite certain concessions regarding the presence of historical memories of bygone times, Freud's psychology, and particularly psychoanalytic psychotherapy, retained on the whole its personalistic orientation.

The hypothesis stating that the unconscious complexes belonged to the primordial foundation common to all mankind had important consequences for Jung's psychology, especially for his psychotherapy. So far as complexes shared in the superpersonal nature of the psyche, they involved not only problems which concern humankind *per se,* but also the fertile ground of creative processes. In psychotherapy, therefore, the complexes made it possible to approach the psychic suffering of man from the depths of his personality. Contrary to the reductive method of tracing back burdensome problems to personal and sexual childhood conflicts, as proposed by Freud, the perspective of an impersonal basis for the psyche opened *new* prospects which transcended personal confines and reached beyond the limits of psychopathology. Because of its genesis in the collective psyche, this new approach pointed out contents which are beyond "healthy or sick," even beyond "good and evil." We agree with Jolande Jacobi that

> Material deriving from the collective unconscious is never "pathological"; it can be pathological only if it comes from the personal unconscious, where it undergoes a specific transformation and coloration by being drawn into an area of individual conflict.[19]

[19] *Complex, Archetype, Symbol in the Psychology of C. G. Jung,* pp. 25–26.

IV. PSYCHIC CONFLICT AND COMPLEX

A discussion of the psychology of the complex would be incomplete without mentioning *psychic conflicts*. In fact, both Freud and Jung recognized that conflict, particularly moral conflict, was one of the principal causes in creating complexes (traumata). They both realized that, conversely, the traumatic complex, when intensity increases, may become the starting point of tensions and conflicts.

In keeping with his interest in the development of neuroses, Freud initially fixed his attention on the neurotic conflict. One of his earliest important scientific contributions dealt with the discovery of the stressful power-play between opposite affects. This insight brought him to the breaking point with Breuer on the theory of hypnoid hysteria.[1] Breuer had conceived of an hysterical disposition in certain traumatic conditions.[2] To him, psychic conflict seemed to be less a diminution of psychic function than an increased performance of the psyche. Freud at times traced such a conflict situation to the antagonism between conscious will and an unconscious "counter-will,"[3] or to the opposition between ego and trauma;[4] later, he ascribed it to the friction between self-preservation and sexual instincts,[5] or to the dichotomy of incest-wish and barrier against incest,[6] and finally he conceived it as the tension between the ego and the id.[7] In a word, psychic conflict essentially grew out of the tension between antagonistic affects.

Additional aspects, however, were required before pathogenic conflicts could be understood. For pathogenesis to occur, a latent infantile conflict had to be present as well as a tendency to escape from it and to revive early fixations through regression. In a normal case the conflict could be worked through and its tendency toward repetition controlled, but in the neurotic the tension of antagonistic affects remained unconscious and therefore could not be worked through, resulting in symptoms which gave the impression of an ongoing battle. Freud explicitly stressed in his "General Theory of the Neuroses"

---

1 Freud, "The Neuro-Psychoses of Defence" (1894), p. 47.
2 Breuer and Freud, *Studies on Hysteria* (1893–95), p. 285.
3 Freud, "On the Psychical Mechanism of Hysterical Phenomena" (1893), p. 32.
4 Introduction to "Psycho-Analysis and the War Neuroses" (1919), p. 210.
5 "Psycho-Analysis" (1926), p. 265.
6 "Three Essays on the Theory of Sexuality" (1905), p. 225.
7 "The Ego and the Id" (1923).

that the pathogenic conflict in neurotics is not to be confused with a normal struggle between mental impulses both of which are on the same psychological footing. In the former case, the dissension is between two powers, one of which has made its way to the stage of what is preconscious or conscious while the other has been held back at the stage of the unconscious.[8]

The manifest results of such conflict were neurotic symptoms, at times expressing the opposition of emotion-laden complexes which had not been worked through.

For Jung, too, psychic conflict arose from the tension between opposites—an "affective antithesis"—whether between ethics and sexuality, between individual desires and collective mores, or between nature and mind. Jung recognized that conflict was the precondition for every neurosis,[9] but—in contradistinction from Freud—he viewed it as an event which must be understood mainly in its relation to the normal psyche. He always approached neurosis from the point of view of the total personality. Conflict was, according to Jung, an inevitable aspect of life and developmental processes, which did not necessarily have to be interpreted as something negative. On the contrary, as early as 1912 Jung pointed out that the tension between "won't" and "will,"[10] between growth and death-wish, is in the end basic to personality structure. In this tension the polarity of the psyche appeared not only in the guise of the opposition between inside and outside, of extraneous demand and self-determination, but also as the dynamism of counter-moving phases of the life cycle (see G.I.2.a). Conflict was a phenomenon deeply rooted in the human condition, just as characteristic of the normal as of the unhealthy psyche; whether regarded as positive or as negative, this expressed "the apparent impossibility of affirming the whole of one's nature."[11]

On the whole, the degree of dissociation was a criterion of the development of neurotic conflict. As long as the opposites were joined, the conflict could be regarded as normal. The more the opposites became disunited and tended to be "at odds with themselves," the more likely was the eruption of a neurosis. Dissociation of the psyche[12] followed, a state in which the opposite poles were "kept apart by strong emotional barriers."[13] In contrast to Freud, to whom neurosis

---

[8] *Introductory Lectures on Psycho-Analysis* (1915–1917), Vol. 16, p. 433.
[9] *Symbols of Transformation* (1952), p. 173.
[10] Ibid.
[11] Jung, "A Review of the Complex Theory" (1934), p. 97.
[12] Jung, "On Psychic Energy" (1928), p. 33.
[13] Jung, "Psychoanalysis and Association Experiments" (1906), p. 315.

always indicated repressed unconscious components, Jung recognized in the neurotic conflict a tension of opposite positions in which the opposites were represented by two personality fragments, each retaining all its characteristics, but the unity of the total personality was always maintained. Dissociation of the psyche in psychosis showed essentially different characteristics. Not infrequently it took a form in which only fragments of personality formations, that is, vestiges of meaning,[14] could be recognized.

Jung differed from Freud also in other respects. While Freud traced every neurotic conflict of adults back to an antagonism with its roots in childhood, Jung put emphasis on the present and the actual attitude of the person. Therefore, the working-through of the current conflict was the guide to successful psychotherapy.

Lastly, the two psychologists were dissimilar in the evaluation of the moral conflict. Freud saw this conflict as a clash between cultural standard and instinctual desire. Until the 1930's he coordinated the unconscious pole with the immoral side. Jung, on the other hand, denied such a consistent relationship. In his view, the focus of the unconscious might have a moral or an immoral nature. Freud preferred to think of the ego as the seat of moral evaluation, resulting in the equation: unconscious = instinct-ridden = immoral. (This position was essentially changed, or at least differentiated, with the introduction of the concept of the superego.) Jung established the reverse relationship. Not infrequently it was precisely the moral tendencies which were unconscious and had remained unknown to the subject—whether because he studiously overlooked them and preferred to "forget" them, or because these tendencies could become conscious only when released from the grip of unconscious experiences. Above all, Jung's appraisal of creative products[15] led to an interpretation of psychic conflict which differed from that of Freud. In such conflicts, one pole was determined by contents, largely unknown to the subject, which had only begun to take shape out of the depths of the unconscious; the opposition encompassed a wide arc, reaching down into the archaic level of the unconscious and thereby raising great difficulties against assimilation into consciousness. Because there was no place in Freud's system for such creative products, there was no point of reference here between Jung and Freud.

14 Jung, "Psychological Factors Determining Human Behaviour" (1936), p. 122.
15 "On Psychic Energy," p. 11, n.

V. THE MEANING OF THE COMPLEX

Even though the unconscious complex as a rule pointed to personal sensibilities and inferiorities, Jung still recognized the possibility of transforming these offensive and undesirable traits by viewing them from the "greater" aspect, the superior and superpersonal elements of the psyche, thus using the personal difficulty as an instrument for expanding the constricted concepts. In clear distinction from Freud, who looked upon neurotic conflict as something rather negative, Jung detected a positive meaning even in incompatible complexes; he arrived at this by realizing that dynamism is inherent in the tension of the opposites and that whatever made the person ill usually contained the seed of cure as well. As we will see later on, the drawing power of the complex, with its tendency toward regression, can be checked and the latitude for a symbolic approach created, provided the person's attitude is favorable (see E.III.5).

Alfred Adler had already recognized the importance of directing the point of view toward a finale, although he connected it with a psychological system based on the drive for power. It was to his merit that he conceived the "guide line," "the guiding fiction,"[1] which the individual unconsciously constructed to compensate for feelings of inferiority and insecurity and as a means of "maximation of ego consciousness"[2] as well as a "preparatory action" for a "re-evaluation of all values."

Jung went farther by emphasizing very clearly the point of view that there is no emotion-laden experience, no psychic trauma, and in general no complex-related attitude to life which could not be used to good advantage as an occasion for deepening one's insight, for becoming more conscious, and for expanding the personality. The unconscious complex would lose its meaning if considered as nothing else but the outcome of adverse and painful situations. The dignity of man demands that he be viewed as the starting point of mental progress leading to a conscious confrontation with his hidden opposites, that is, with the "Yea" and "Nay" contained therein. From such speculations Jung arrived at the conviction that the complexes more than anything else represented the focal and nodal points of psychic life.

[1] *The Neurotic Constitution* (1912), p. 54.
[2] Ibid., p. 34.

A. FROM TRAUMA TO THE FEELING-TONED COMPLEX

Complexes obviously represent a kind of inferiority in the broadest sense—a statement I must at once qualify by saying that to have complexes does not necessarily indicate inferiority. It only means that something discordant, unassimilated, and antagonistic exists, perhaps as an obstacle, but also as an incentive to greater effort, and so, perhaps, to new possibilities of achievement. In this sense, therefore, complexes are focal or nodal points of psychic life which we would not wish to do without; indeed, they should not be missing, for otherwise psychic activity would come to a fatal standstill.[3]

From this we may conclude that the unconscious complex represented something negative but could also prove to be a productive factor. It may have been the weak point of psychic life, the focus of defeat, but it also was the area of potential victory!

In summary, the various aspects of the complexes resulting from Jung's investigations were emotionality and an archetypal foundation, on the one hand, with a tendency toward independence and fragmentary personality on the other; furthermore, they encompassed the unity and wholeness of the psyche and, finally, the autonomy of the complex and its incompatibility with the ego. Jung described the feeling-toned complex as

> the *image* of a certain psychic situation which is strongly accentuated emotionally and is, moreover, incompatible with the habitual attitude of consciousness. This image has a powerful inner coherence, it has its own wholeness and, in addition, a relatively high degree of autonomy, so that it is subject to the control of the conscious mind to only a limited extent, and therefore behaves like an animated foreign body in the sphere of consciousness.[4]

3 Jung, "A Psychological Theory of Types" (1928), pp. 528-29.
4 "A Review of the Complex Theory" (1934), p. 96.

B. FROM PSYCHIC "MECHANISMS"
TO THE TOTAL PERSONALITY

I. PSYCHIC MECHANISMS IN GENERAL

In all his investigations—whether on the association experiment, the complex, a neurotic symptom, the autonomy of the psyche, or the phenomena of dissociation—Jung more or less explicitly followed the same guiding principle: the concept of the "totality of the psyche."[1] This idea developed with greater and greater clarity from the time he separated from Freud.

The concept of a more comprehensive whole was always the focal point of Jung's interest. Even while studying philosophy in college, he had been captivated by the idea of the "homo maximus, of whom every person was only a reflection." Jung only later introduced into psychology the term "self" or "center of personality," but the idea was always operative as a dark-unconscious guide.

It was not by chance that Krafft-Ebing's description of the psychoses as "diseases of personality" struck Jung with such force and revived in him the concept of a wider personality. He was equally impressed by Janet's remark that neurosis is a "maladie de la personnalité" and his explanation of hysteria as a dissociation of the personality.[2]

To be sure, the acquaintance with Freud's work early in the century initially led to a slight interruption in the natural development of Jung's own budding psychology. He was fascinated not only by the methods of natural science but also by the newness of Freud's investigative procedure, which made the subject and his life-story the center of psychotherapy. Under the strong influence of Freud's theory of neurosis, Jung at first tested Freud's psychological findings by applying the psychoanalytic method. During this period he put aside his own aims, which were directed toward the perspective of combining man's surface personality with that which was "greater in him."

Consequently, in his earlier writings Jung often referred to the psychic mechanism which played such a role in Freud's psychology. According to Freud, psychic mechanisms were psychological laws determining the play or dynamism of forces in man. He distinguished the dynamism of ideas (culminating in the automatisms of condensation, displacement, and compromise-formation) from the laws of repression, that is, the process of banishing contents from consciousness. Prominent in Freud's thinking was the concept of causal determination, taking the form of an automatic interplay of forces. And what was Jung's attitude to this?

[1] Jung, "The Therapeutic Value of Abreaction" (1921), p. 138.
[2] Personal communication from Jung.

II. SUBSTITUTION AND SYMBOLIZATION

In 1929 Jung still was gratified to recall that the association experiments tended to confirm Freud's mechanisms of repression, substitution, and symbolization.[1] Indeed, even in 1936, he recognized that Freud "took as his point of departure the wholeness and indivisibility of the human personality, though, in keeping with the spirit of the age, he restricted himself to the investigation of instinctive mechanisms and individual processes." However, he considered it deplorably one-sided that Freud "narrowed the picture of man to the wholeness of an essentially 'bourgeois' collective person."[2]

It may be of historical interest to sketch the gradual transformation of Jung's views—from his initial adoption of Freud's concept of psychic mechanisms to a wider approach, which allowed for the ideas of a creative aspect in the life of the psyche, of a facet of meaning and values, and a teleological viewpoint.

In his early writings, *Studies in Word-Association* and *Psychology of Dementia Praecox*,[3] Jung interpreted under the term "substitution" a series of mechanisms which Freud had described as "screen memories"[4] and which he had also discovered were operative in parapraxes and symptomatic actions.[5] Freud traced such parapraxes to "shortcomings in our psychical functioning,"[6] caused by distortion and substitution. He stressed the point that "the appearance of an incorrect function is explained by the peculiar mutual interference between two or several correct functions."[7] The unconscious intention takes over in the conscious expression, thus substituting for and concealing the conscious function.

Jung, too, had noted that the modes of reaction in the association experiment were not infrequently "veiled" or "disguised," that is, the obvious association was masked by another intention. Like Freud, Jung at that time (1907) rejected an arbitrary psychical reaction in such cases and searched for the determinant. Thus, he attempted to trace psychotic depression to "screen causes" which in turn are the product of repression.[8]

1 Jung, "Some Aspects of Modern Psychotherapy," p. 29.
2 "Psychological Typology," p. 547.
3 Published 1904–1907 and 1907, respectively.
4 "Screen Memories" (1899). Cf. Jung, "The Reaction-Time Ratio" (1906), p. 251.
5 *The Psychopathology of Everyday Life* (1901).
6 Ibid., p. 239.　　　　　　　　　7 Ibid., p. 278.
8 "The Psychology of Dementia Praecox" (1907), p. 72.

II. SUBSTITUTION AND SYMBOLIZATION

Before we say that the patient is depressed for some "inadequate" reason, we must bear in mind the mechanisms existing in every normal person, which always strive to repress anything unpleasant and bury it as deeply as possible.[9]

Nearly forty years later Jung took a significantly different position. He then conceived of the depressive process as connected with a total change of personality: "This lowering of energy can be seen most clearly before the onset of certain psychoses."[10] This state Jung described as due to "a certain predisposition on the part of the conscious mind, namely a deficit in the form of loss of energy,"[11] or to "a sudden change of personality (a so-called mutation of character)," and finally to "the empty stillness which precedes creative work."[12]

A similar development occurred in Jung's concept of fantasy-formation and symbolization. In 1912 he had written that man in his fantasy-thinking has kept a condensation of his psychic history as it developed from the oldest layers of the human mind.[13] In the second edition (1924) of *Wandlungen und Symbole der Libido* (the original version of *Symbols of Transformation*), Jung stated more clearly "the real purpose" of the book: ". . . creative fantasy also draws upon the forgotten and long buried primitive mind with its host of images, which are to be found in the mythologies of all ages and all peoples."[14] Likewise, in 1912 he saw "the religious hymn arising from the unconscious [as] the compensating amends for the erotic . . . infantile reminiscences . . . re-awakened into life by the introversion of the libido."[15] This position was very much changed by 1952:

The [erotic] impression goes on working in the unconscious and throws up symbolical fantasies.[16]

Not last in importance, Jung dropped the initial assumption of distortion in fantasy processes (subjective thinking) and put in its place the activity of *objective* motives, independent of personal opinions. In 1952 he wrote:

But there is no real ground for assuming that it [subjective thinking] is nothing more than a distortion of the objective world-picture, for it remains to be asked whether the mainly unconscious inner motive which guides these fantasy-processes is not itself an *objective*

9 Ibid., pp. 72–73.
10 "The Psychology of the Transference" (1946), p. 181.
11 Ibid., p. 180.   12 Ibid., p. 181.
13 *Psychology of the Unconscious (Transformations and Symbols of the Libido,* 1912), p. 36.
14 *Symbols of Transformation*, p. xxix.   15 *Psychology of the Unconscious*, p. 72.
16 *Symbols of Transformation*, p. 53.

fact. Freud himself has pointed out on more than one occasion how much unconscious motives are grounded on instinct, which is certainly an objective fact.[17]

Quite generally, in the course of time Jung abandoned the concept of a mechanism of displacement, that is "repressing the conflict into the unconscious,"[18] and explained this event as "an entirely natural and automatic process of transformation."[19]

Symptomatic actions deserve particular attention. Freud investigated symptomatic acts in 1901[20] and considered them to be similar to "bungled actions."[21] He recognized these acts—which included certain kinds of gestures, expressive motions, or other motor behavior—as simply a balance or level between opposing intentions. He pointed out that symptomatic acts "give expression to something which the agent himself does not suspect in them, and which he does not as a rule intend to impart to other people but to keep to himself."[22] In particular, these acts were compromise-formations, which "satisfied two impulses"—on the one hand, the suppression of a wish, on the other, the fulfillment of an unconscious wish.[23]

Following Freud, Jung interpreted automatic action as due to a mechanism of displacement of repressed thoughts.[24] Yet as early as 1913 he substituted for the expression "symptomatic actions"— which in his view placed too much emphasis on unconscious intentions—the term "symbolic actions,"[25] intended to underline the presence of unconscious constellations. Jung found increasing satisfaction in this term because it brought out the unintentional aspect—the "purely accidental"—which pointed less to an intention than to an unconscious meaning. However, it took a long time until Jung freed himself from the concept of substitute-formations and concentrated completely on symbolic relationships. Under the influence of Freud's personality, Jung oscillated for a time between a negative and a positive evaluation of these symbolic relationships. At one time he conceived of them as expressions of vague and indefinite thinking, at another as exhibiting "the characteristics of mythological thinking."[26]

Only in 1921 did Jung's discussion of symptomatic actions come to a tentative halt. It culminated in his opposing those actions, which

17 Ibid., p. 28. 18 *Psychology of the Unconscious*, p. 73.
19 *Symbols of Transformation*, p. 59.
20 *The Psychopathology of Everyday Life*, pp. 191–216.
21 Ibid., pp. 162–90. 22 Ibid., p. 191.
23 Ibid., p. 197. 24 Jung, "Dementia Praecox," p. 49.
25 "The Theory of Psychoanalysis" (1913), p. 150.
26 "Dementia Praecox," pp. 62–63.

Freud had equated with symptoms, against the symbolic actions which seemed to be important *because* of their still hidden meaning:

> The fact that there are two distinct and mutually contradictory views eagerly advocated on either side concerning the meaning or meaninglessness of things shows that processes obviously exist which express no particular meaning, being in fact mere consequences, or symptoms; and that there are other processes which bear within them a hidden meaning, processes which are not merely derived from something but which seek to become something, and are therefore symbols.[27]

From these different clues it should become quite clear that Jung gradually came to understand symbolic actions and experiences in the context of their inherent symbolic value, while initially he had seen them as particular cases of substitution to be judged according to their symptomatic significance.

Jung's research on neurotic symptoms formed a bridge to the exploration of symbols. Because of their symbolic character, neurotic symptoms assumed importance to Jung—an insight which subsequently was extended to include the final significance.[28] Even though Freud had occasionally considered symbolic relationships—or more correctly, symbolizing relations between symptom and trauma—the causal approach remained of primary importance to him (see App. II.2.d). Essentially, the symptom was relevant as a mnemic symbol of repressed traumata.[29]

In contrast, Jung already had explained the symptom in *Studies in Word-Association* as the "symbolic manifestation"[30] of the unconscious complexes. Even though at that time he largely interpreted the symbol as an expression of inferior thought, nevertheless the hint at the symbolic character of the symptom was already a first step toward a new psychological perspective. In fact, from that time on "thinking in symbols" remained a major concern with him. When we consider that in the year 1906 he still criticized himself for lacking an adequate understanding of symbols, we cannot help but feel amazement and admiration for the progress he made from those first tentative beginnings to the fully matured understanding of the symbol as "the best possible description or formulation of a relatively unknown fact."[31]

[27] *Psychological Types* (1921), p. 478.
[28] "On the Psychology of the Unconscious" (1917/1943), p. 46.
[29] Breuer and Freud, *Studies on Hysteria* (1893–95), p. 297; Freud, "The Neuro-Psychoses of Defence" (1894), p. 49.
[30] "Psychoanalysis and Association Experiments" (1906), p. 321.
[31] *Psychological Types* (1921), p. 474.

1. The Theory of Repression in Freud's Psychology

Since the theory of repression was the central point in Freud's approach to neurosis, Jung's position in this regard is of particular interest. The subject must, therefore, be dealt with in some detail.

How did Freud arrive at this theory? What was his concept of the mechanism of repression? The idea of a defense mechanism was by no means an original discovery of Freud's; he was influenced by a number of predecessors. Still, it was a great achievement that he connected the concept of defense with the theory of affects—a feat which put his personal mark on this concept.

Herbart was among the first to propose the idea of repression.[1] While Freud was still in secondary school,[2] a book by Lindner[3] drew his attention to the psychology of Fechner[4] and to Herbart's idea of repression. This book was particularly illuminating since it was one of the first introductions to the scientific psychology of the nineteenth century.

In Herbart, Freud found hints of the concept of dynamic play between opposite ideas that impede each other and result in repression. Also, Herbart considered that unconscious ideas were indestructible and that they could not be lost, so that they could pass over the threshold of consciousness whenever the specific obstacle had been removed. As surprising as it may be to find agreement between certain of these early findings with the later concepts of Freud, the differences were so obvious that it is out of the question to consider that Freud merely developed Herbart's suggestions.

Freud also received effective stimulus from his contemporaries. Primarily there was J. M. Charcot, who made a lasting impression on Freud with his causal nexus between psychic trauma (*obnubilation du moi*) and fixation of ideas and symptoms produced by auto-suggestion.[5] Janet was also an important influence—first, with his investigations of psychic automatisms (which he traced to dissociation of insufficiently perceived ideas) and, second, for his concept of "second existences." Janet's theory of the perceptive weakness of the ego with its related

[1] J. F. Herbart, *A Text-Book in Psychology* (1816; tr. 1895).
[2] Jones, *The Life and Work of Sigmund Freud*, Vol. I (1953), p. 374.
[3] G. A. Lindner, *Manual of Empirical Psychology* (1858; tr. 1889).
[4] G. T. Fechner, *Elements of Psychophysics* (1860; tr. 1966).
[5] Frey-Rohn, "Die Anfänge der Tiefenpsychologie," in *Studien zur analytischen Psychologie C. G. Jungs*, Vol. I, p. 41.

restraint of attention originated only a few years after Breuer's theory of hypnoid states. Breuer had proposed that dreamlike (or hypnoid) states favor the development of traumatic experiences.

After a short period of enthusiastic collaboration, Freud separated from Breuer and asserted the so-called theory of defense: that it was not the hypnoid state that caused hysteria, but the psychic trauma and the resulting defense mechanism.[6] It was Freud's essential discovery that the incompatibility of trauma and ego initiates the defense against incompatible excitations. This always comes about from an exaggeration of opposites which makes impossible the working-through of the unacceptable affect. Under normal conditions the defense produces a more or less appropriate adjustment to the environment, but in the neurotic this attempt seems to fail. The psychic conflict is forced into the unconscious, where it perseveres, together with its entire tension— "perseveration" (Janet)—and where it persists, constantly ready to break through. The conflict is, so to speak, an "unredeemed spirit" which repeatedly harasses the consciousness. Two basic assumptions in psychoanalysis were derived from this concept: first, that neurosis is due to failure in attempting a defense,[7] and, second, that defense is connected with an elementary mechanism of dissociation of affect and idea.

Freud conceived this mechanism as weakening the result of trauma by severing the quantum of affect connected with it, simultaneously displacing the affect to an idea which was not in itself incompatible;[8] at the same time, the original idea, being "inadmissible to consciousness" (Breuer),[9] was forced into the unconscious.

This mechanism of displacement was entirely new; its aim was to make incompatible ideas unrecognizable, ineffective, and innocuous.[10] Later, Freud could see that displacement underlay the formal structure of a number of very important phenomena which could clarify the mechanisms of defense and screen memories[11] as well as those of distortion and falsification[12] and which, finally, would explain the mechanism of compromise formations[13] between antagonistic tendencies of the psyche. He observed that, whenever the conscious solution of a psychic conflict miscarried, an unconscious attempt at a solution,

[6] Freud, "The Neuro-Psychoses of Defence" (1894), pp. 49–50.
[7] "Further Remarks on the Neuro-Psychoses of Defence" (1896), p. 169.
[8] "The Neuro-Psychoses of Defence," p. 51–52.
[9] Breuer and Freud, Studies on Hysteria (1893–95), p. 229.
[10] "The Neuro-Psychoses of Defence," p. 49.
[11] "Screen Memories" (1899), pp. 307–308.
[12] Ibid., p. 322.
[13] "Further Remarks on the Neuro-Psychoses of Defence," pp. 170–72.

initiated by defense, appeared as an equivalent; this assumed the shape of a compromise formation. In other words, a symptom developed as a sign of the unconscious antagonism between the affect-laden forces, trauma and defense. In brief, the symptom was a mnemic symbol[14] related to traumatic events.

Freud assumed that the separation of affect and idea might lead to any one of three mechanisms: 1) conversion of the "sum of excitation" into an inadequate motor innervation (conversion hysteria);[15] 2) displacement of the affects to another idea, with a "false connection" between idea and affect (obsessional neurosis);[16] or 3) the ideas against which the ego defends itself may manifest themselves in the guise of projections to extraneous objects (paranoia).[17]

This was still a relatively simple concept of defense and symptom formation in neurosis and was to be greatly expanded. The first extension was Freud's hypothesis of the sexual trauma in early childhood (1896).[18] The new aspect was the assumption of a traumatic significance, not only of violent sexual experiences but of such experiences in earliest childhood, particularly seduction and rape. Both generated a process of primary defense. Freud also corrected his concept of the origin of neurotic symptoms; the primary defense was no longer a sufficient explanation but had to be augmented by the return of the material which had been repressed by actual rejection of instinctual drives.

Freud found an important basis for the explanation of the mechanism of repression in the distinction between primary and secondary processes (1895).[19] He discovered a fundamental dualism in the laws governing the dynamics of psychic events, a dualism which was parallel to the distinction between "unconscious" and "preconscious"—while the primary events (= unconscious events) exhibited a tendency to unimpeded discharge of energies, the secondary events (= preconscious events) were characterized by a mechanism of repression and control.[20] By this opposition Freud was the first to propose a scientifically satisfactory foundation of the mechanism of repression. What he formerly had understood as the result of a counter-force within the ego could now be traced to a process of restraint proceeding from an endopsychic censorship. Fifteen years later, even this theory was more

14 "The Neuro-Psychoses of Defence," p. 49.

15 Ibid.

16 "On the Grounds for Detaching a Particular Syndrome from Neurasthenia under the Description 'Anxiety Neurosis' " (1895), p. 96.

17 "Further Remarks," pp. 174–75.   18 Ibid., p. 163.

19 The Origins of Psycho-Analysis (1887–1902), p. 129.

20 The Interpretation of Dreams (1900), p. 599.

III. REPRESSION AND DISSOCIATION

precisely formulated. At that time Freud established a fact which was of extraordinary importance for his doctrine of neuroses: repression (= defense) also resulted in an "alteration in cathexis" to the rejected ideas[21] (cathexis = concentration of energy upon a given object). That energy, which had been fixed to the preconscious ideas, was transformed in the process of repression into unconscious free-floating energy. In other words, everything that was repressed followed the laws of the unconscious, that is, the primary processes.

Still more incisive were the modifications which Freud introduced in his theory of sexuality. In *Studies on Hysteria* the defense mechanism had been understood as a purely psychogenic reaction of the ego against trauma, but after 1905 it was founded on the biological hypothesis of the libido, that is, on an instinctual factor.[22] Freud assumed that the traumatic experiences as well as the related defensive tendencies of the ego were in essence determined by the person's constitution—an alteration which was already linguistically indicated by the change from the term "defense," with its psychological connotation, to "sexual repression," which implied somatic processes.[23] Freud saw the relationship of the ego to the individual's basic constitution as mediated by the "latency period,"[24] which is also based on constitutional factors. At the same time, he arrived at a more precise terminology by giving up the earlier vague reference to the ego as the censor and, instead, recognizing the ego as the center of the preconscious. Once the concept of the latency period had been introduced, the ego identified with the "paternal no" in curbing the instinctual drives, that is, with the incest taboo and the cultural standards based on it (see E.II.2). The decisive aspect of this period of Freud's investigations was to establish a biological basis for the theory of neuroses. There was also another change in terminology: Instead of defense, trauma, energy, and reanimation of repressed memories, as formerly used, Freud now preferred the expressions repression, sexual fixation, libido, and regression (see E.II.2). However, the biological basis of the theory of repression left unchanged the former characteristics of repression (detaching trauma from the ego, banishing the objectionable idea from consciousness, and displacing the affect); neither did it alter its basic importance in the etiology of neurosis.

Freud put great emphasis on the repression hypothesis because, for a number of years, he continued to regard repression as correlated with

[21] "The Unconscious" (1915), pp. 180–82.

[22] Freud, "Three Essays on the Theory of Sexuality" (1905), pp. 135ff.

[23] Freud, "My Views on the Part Played by Sexuality in the Aetiology of the Neuroses" (1906), p. 276.

[24] *Introductory Lectures on Psycho-Analysis* (1915–17), p. 326.

whatever is unconscious.[25] This concept became untenable only with the discovery of the superego. In the chapter on the unconscious we will return to this subject in greater detail.

Years later, while working out the basis of ego-psychology, Freud introduced radical modifications. During these investigations, the emphasis was shifted from exploring repressed drives to the study of the repressing agency, the ego.[26] He recognized that the ultimate source of repression rested in the ego ideal and in a "special psychical agency" —the forerunner of the superego. From that time on, Freud gave primary attention to changes and disturbances in the ego as an agent. Changes in the ego during the developmental years appeared to him at least as important as changes in sexual functions. Even though the mechanism of repression continued to be extremely important in explaining neurosis, it lost its central position for coordinating other mechanisms. He reintroduced the old concept of defense[27] as the overriding influence on such automatic forms of behavior. (Among the mechanisms of defense Freud included repression, regression, isolation, reaction formation, undoing, denial, introjection, projection, and sublimation, with only the last leading to positive working-through.) At the same time, he expanded the role of the superego, which was destined to become the predominant agency from which all types of defense originated.

The discovery of the superego brought about a fundamental modification of Freud's ideas in still another direction. Up to that time, he had equated the unconscious with repressed contents and had therefore assumed that whatever was unconscious was, by the same token, repressed. But now he felt he must give up this assumption, since it was evident that the superego did not fit into this rule. While it was, on the one hand, of unconscious nature, representing an unconscious part of the ego, on the other hand, it was not at all repressed but was, on the contrary, the origin of the process of repression itself. The conclusion was inevitable: The equation of "unconscious" and "repressed" could no longer be maintained. Freud confessed, therefore, in 1923:

> We recognize that the *Ucs.* does not coincide with the repressed; it is still true that all that is repressed is *Ucs.*, but not all that is *Ucs.* is repressed.[28]

25 "Repression" (1915), p. 148.
26 "On Narcissism: An Introduction" (1914), p. 94.
27 "Inhibitions, Symptoms, and Anxiety" (1926), p. 164.
28 "The Ego and the Id" (1923), p. 18.

As we will discuss in the chapter dealing with the unconscious, this insight was also the reason why Freud replaced the concept of the unconscious by that of the id (see D.I), which did not necessarily need to include repressed ideas.

One of the most debatable conclusions which Freud drew from the premises of repression and superego was his theory of the origin of the products of civilization. The whole of civilization appeared to him as nothing other than repression of instincts. According to Freud, the anxiety resulting from insecurity, as well as feelings of impotence and helplessness, induced individuals to join together and form communities. It became necessary to renounce the most pressing desires as well as urgent aggression. Or to put it otherwise: Each individual was forced to repress his instinctual desires! But more than that: Because humanity could not exist in the long run by negating everything that made life worth living, it created equivalents for what had been lost. The imposed renunciation of wish-fulfillment was internalized. A collective superego came into being which led to setting up ideals and creating works of art. One of the most doubtful consequences of the theory of repression was that Freud finally understood even religious ideas not only as an escape from the rigors of drive renunciation but also as "illusions, fulfillments of oldest, strongest, and most urgent wishes of mankind."[29] In this respect, Freud went so far as to equate the religious development of mankind as a whole with that of the child. Just as the child learned to "subdue" instinctual demands through repression and constructed a father ideal, so the human race behaved: Through its gods it attempted to make life again livable. Freud did not hesitate to say:

> Religion would thus be the universal obsessional neurosis of humanity; like the obsessional neurosis of children, it arose out of the Oedipus complex, out of the relation to the father.[30]

It is unlikely that one could formulate more harshly the idea that civilization and its products, particularly religious ideas, can be traced to nothing but repression.

2. Repression in the Light of Jung's Psychology

From the time of his association studies, Jung came back again and again to the theory of repression. Even in his latest works, Jung em-

29 "The Future of an Illusion" (1927), p. 30.
30 Ibid., p. 43.

phasized Freud's great merit of having laid the foundations of a psychology of the neuroses[31] and had pinpointed its central factor, the theory of repression. This acknowledgement, however, must not be overestimated, because Jung's statements referred mainly to Freud's early concept of repression (that is, up to about 1912). Jung took into consideration neither the theory of primary and secondary processes and the conclusions derived therefrom, nor ego psychology and the related mechanisms of defense.

Jung was first impressed with the scientific importance of repression while working on his association experiments. He was able to authenticate a series of phenomena which coincided with what Freud described as "repressed" contents. As Jung stressed in retrospect (1929), observations in the association experiments "undoubtedly tended to confirm the facts indicated by Freud, namely the facts of repression, substitution, and 'symbolization.' "[32] This applied primarily to association experiments with neurotic patients, in the course of which he was able to demonstrate certain disproportionate reactions. Marked defects of memory as well as distortions of memory suggested to him the activity of acute complexes. Like Freud, Jung recognized that this was caused by the splitting of contents which were incompatible with the ego and inadmissible to consciousness. As early as 1905, Jung made the statement that "the main part of the emotionally charged complex becomes split off and repressed [from consciousness]."[33]

This far-reaching confirmation of repression by no means meant that Jung accepted Freud's concept completely even at the time of his greatest fascination with Freud's ideas. On the contrary, from the very beginning he made certain exceptions, primarily related to Freud's tendency to a mechanistic approach and to his generalization of repression. Jung also could accept only partially the anthropological basis of a struggle between conscious beliefs and emotional experiences. For one should never overlook that, even when writing his thesis, Jung regarded the human personality as a *totality*, with an interaction of the individual parts. In this he agreed with Janet, whose concept of neurosis as a "disease of the personality" largely corresponded with Jung's experiences with so-called somnambulistic symptoms. Likewise, from his study of Eastern wisdom, Jung perceived the guiding image of "something greater" in man, which succeeded in piercing the hitherto impenetrable darkness of psychic processes. Such experiences explain the slight uneasiness which Jung had felt almost immediately toward the

31 Jung, "On the Psychology of the Unconscious" (1917/1943), pp. 9-10.
32 "Some Aspects of Modern Psychotherapy" (1929), p. 29.
33 Jung and Riklin, "The Associations of Normal Subjects," p. 119.

concept of repression; only gradually was he able to express this in a satisfactory manner.

As to the mechanistic aspect of the process of repression, the principal point with which Jung could not agree was Freud's tracing repression back to elemental forces and the laws governing them. Only during the years in which he was most strongly affected by Freud's ideas, Jung partially accepted his theories of the splitting of psychic trauma into affect and idea. Other than that, Jung maintained that a comprehensive approach to psychic phenomena was better suited to the essence of the psyche than an analytical dissection of the total experience into its elements. He went farther and farther away from his partial acceptance of the mechanisms of dissociation, although he had initially assumed it to be present in hysteria[34] and in obsessional neurosis.[35] Finally he restricted it to dementia praecox.[36] In this disease, Jung observed—as Freud did—an "incongruity between ideational content and affect,"[37] as well as a degree of inadequacy of affectivity which could progress to "atrophy of the complex"[38] (see G.I.2.c) and lead to complete disintegration of the personality. This stance Jung maintained until his last psychiatric writings.

Freud always equated the repressed with an idea which had been forced into the unconscious and was separated from all other experiences. This concept, however, in no way applied to Jung. When demarcating the concepts of the two investigators, it seems to me of decisive importance that Jung—except for the years 1907–1908—always saw a complex-connected content in the repressed, made up of feeling-tone and idea. These divergences came about partly because Freud based his theories largely on psychopathologic experiences; he built his theory of repression primarily on observations of sick people and attempted to apply these findings to the psychic make-up of normal persons. Jung's concept of repression, in contrast, was derived from a point of view that was as much concerned with normal as with sick people. This was already manifested in the early investigation of the associations of healthy subjects.

Jung's critical attitude towards Freud's theories arose also from his significant observation that the complexes which have split off from the ego by no means comprised only repressed contents, which previously had been conscious. In many cases something entirely different seemed to be present—an enigmatic "withdrawal" or "slipping away of ideas of the complex." What Freud had described as "repressed"

34 "The Psychology of Dementia Praecox" (1907), pp. 71–72.
35 Ibid., p. 72.   36 Ibid., p. 73.
37 Ibid., p. 71.   38 Ibid., p. 97.

Jung understood as an effect of the autonomous activity in the background of the psyche. As early as 1905 we encounter his conjecture that contents inadmissible to consciousness (that is, repressed) might not infrequently be the effect of impersonal complexes or may represent the activity and autonomy of the unconscious. A few years later, his investigations of the fantasies of psychotics convinced Jung that a large number of phenomena could be traced to the operation of strange contents which could not as yet be perceived and arose spontaneously from the deep level of the psyche (see D.II.3.a). From such observations Jung arrived at the remarkable conclusion that unconscious phenomena exist which are far less a product of repression than a spontaneous effect of the background of the psyche. From such statements it might clearly follow that, for Jung, Freud's equating of "repressed" with "unconscious" was in no way conclusive.

In spite of far-reaching differences in the concept of repression, Jung never went so far as to discard this term. However, he limited its meaning to "relatively inadmissible to consciousness" or "dissociated from the ego." Thus, he did not accept Freud's concept of the mechanism of displacement nor that of "alteration of cathexis." Most important, Jung differed from Freud in the question of the motives which compelled repression.

In the first place, Freud's motive of resistance—invalidation and hostility[39] against affectivity—was repugnant to Jung. In pathological cases he considered more pertinent Janet's idea that a weakness of attention (*état de distraction*) and a restraint of the sense of reality (*fonction du réel*) are found in hysteria and obsessional neurosis, respectively. Jung, however, did not wholly agree with Janet's concept, because he could not see the psyche either as a place of conflict and hostility, nor as a playing-field for the ego and automatism, but rather, on the whole, as an area of collaboration and cooperation between "conscious" and "unconscious."

In the process of repression, Jung considered the motives of "forgetting" and "devaluating" to be of primary importance. In the association studies we already find the attempt to regard hysteria as characteristically motivated by "intentional forgetting" of painful experiences, or "not wanting to understand," which covered up a "kind of playing hide-and-seek with oneself." What Jung had in mind was less a normal forgetting than an "artificial loss of memory,"[40] which seemed to be indicated by the concurrence of such phenomena with

39 Freud, "Remembering, Repeating and Working-Through" (Further Recommendations on the Technique of Psycho-Analysis, II; 1914).
40 Jung, "Analytical Psychology and Education" (1924), p. 109.

an increase in energy-tension.[41] Jung interpreted the characteristic of "habitual unconsciousness,"[42] that is, forgetting which has become a habit, as an essential aspect. In the same way, tracing back "repression" to the motive of "devaluating the reality aspect" (first attempted in 1913)[43] arose from a need to clarify motives. Jung had established that the unconscious complex in certain cases of obsessional neurosis went hand in hand with a devaluation of reality, the patient retreating to his world of complexes. It is interesting to note that Jung arrived at this hypothesis in connection with his discovery of opposite attitudes in individuals, that is, extraversion and introversion—an understanding which he gained from examining the differences between the basic psychological assumptions of Freud and Adler. He recognized that Freud referred mainly to the object, Adler to the subject.

The typical modes of behavior as well as the motives in the two forms of neurosis (hysteria and obsessional neurosis) seemed to depend on just such an opposition of attitudes. While Jung found that in hysterical extraversion "habitual forgetting" was accentuated, in compulsive neurosis the motive of devaluating reality was prominent.

Freud has taught us that in the mechanism of hysterical extraversion the personality seeks to get rid of disagreeable memories and impressions, and to free itself from its complexes, by a process of *repression*. The individual clings to the object in order to forget these painful contents and leave them behind him. Conversely, in the mechanism of introversion, the libido concentrates itself wholly on the complexes, and seeks to detach and isolate the personality from external reality. This psychological process is associated with a phenomenon which is not properly speaking "repression," but would be better rendered by the term "devaluation" of the objective world.[44]

A. DEVELOPMENT OF CONSCIOUSNESS AND REPRESSION

The discovery of the opposite types of attitude (later, the discovery also of opposite types of function) was destined to become a landmark in Jung's psychology by leading him to a new understanding of the development of consciousness and the motivations of repression. It is noteworthy that in this connection he was able to make a partial concession to Freud's motive of defense, even though based on essentially different reasoning. Whenever Jung refers to "defense" or "repression,"

41 Ibid., p. 110.   42 Jung and Riklin, p. 138.
43 Jung, "A Contribution to the Study of Psychological Types" (1913).
44 Ibid., p. 501.

he never understood these terms in the framework of a mere tension of drives but rather in the framework of *development of consciousness*. From this point of view, the motive of repression of ego-incompatible contents was never "accidental" but was basically combined with the process of the differentiation of consciousness. Jung was even of the opinion that no differentiation of consciousness could take place without "repression," or more precisely "suppression," of primitive contents which hinder adjustment. From this we can understand how Jung could regard repression as a phenomenon that also is typical of events in the "normal" psyche. In this position he differed from Freud, who on principle started out from the pathology of the neuroses.

Jung made a decisive step as early as 1912 by describing the structural opposition of "won't" and "will"[45] as a phenomenon inherent in the life-process. It was this principle that Jung enlarged upon, evolving the psychology of the development of consciousness.[46] He could do this all the more successfully as the differentiation of consciousness was based on the unfolding of the opposites. Consciousness fundamentally included directedness, culminating in the discrimination of ego and non-ego, good and evil, beautiful and ugly, true and false. Therefore, the process of the unfolding of consciousness was accompanied by the creation of the tension between the opposites of conscious and unconscious contents. The contents integrated by the conscious ego were pitted against others which remained in the unconscious due to negligence and undervaluation. The ability to be self-directed and discriminating, however, was not only a beneficence but a Danaän gift of civilization.[47] As Jung wrote in 1916:

> One-sidedness is an unavoidable and necessary characteristic of the directed process, for direction implies one-sidedness. It is an advantage and a drawback at the same time.[48]

Everything that is in opposition to the directed process and incompatible with it was either pushed back into the unconscious or existed from the very beginning in the unconscious psyche. The result was the formation of an inferior part of the personality, which encompassed the unadapted, the primitive and archaic, as well as the painful and unacceptable and, finally, also the "repressed." Jung expressed this thought in 1921 as follows:

The greater the dissociation, that is, the more the conscious attitude

45 *Psychology of the Unconscious*, p. 195. 46 *Psychological Types* (1921).
47 "The Stages of Life" (1930), p. 388.
48 "The Transcendent Function" (1916), p. 71.

becomes alienated from the individual and collective contents of the unconscious, the more harmfully the unconscious inhibits or intensifies the conscious contents.[49]

Jung still more clearly formulated this thought twenty years later:

The differentiated and differentiable functions are much easier to cope with, and, for understandable reasons, we prefer to leave the "inferior" function round the corner, or to repress it altogether, because it is such an awkward customer. And it is a fact that it has the strongest tendency to be infantile, banal, primitive, and archaic.[50]

Jung considered the "invention of consciousness as the most precious fruit of the tree of knowledge,"[51] but he recognized that, without any doubt, the process of consciousness provided a seed for splitting the personality as a whole, of dissociating the superior and inferior parts of the personality. In order to avoid misunderstandings I want to point out explicitly that such inferior parts of the personality presented all the characteristics that Jung had already ascribed to complexes; in contrast to what Freud understood as the "repressed," these inferior fragments exhibited not only a degree of centralization but also a certain organization.

Likewise, Jung's opposition of inferior and superior parts of the personality does not coincide with Freud's distinction between primary and secondary processes. The unconscious part of the personality was, in Jung's psychology, neither "free floating" nor subject to the pleasure principle, but was subordinated to the organization of the total personality, just the same as the conscious processes.

In Jung's psychology the problem of the inferior personality fragment, which is split off from the ego, manifested itself primarily in the shadow.[52]

By shadow I mean the "negative" side of the personality, the sum of all those unpleasant qualities we like to hide, together with the insufficiently developed functions and the content of the personal unconscious.[53]

The unconscious complex of the shadow most closely approached what Freud understood as the "repressed." Jung interpreted the per-

49 *Psychological Types*, p. 126.
50 "A Psychological Approach to the Dogma of the Trinity" (1940/1948), p. 165.
51 "The Meaning of Psychology for Modern Man" (1933), p. 140.
52 Frey-Rohn, "Evil from the Psychological Point of View" (1967), p. 167.
53 Jung, "On the Psychology of the Unconscious" (1917/1943), p. 66, n. 5.

sonal shadow, in the first place, as an inferior part of the personality, that is, a portion which included the traits of inferior and undifferentiated qualities of the personality, often also negative and deficient traits. As early as 1912, while still under the influence of Freud's theories, Jung used the term "shadow side of the psyche"[54] to characterize "not-recognized desires" and "repressed portions of the personality." Five years later he described this aspect of the human personality in a very graphic manner:

> We discover that the "other" in us is indeed "another," a real man, who actually thinks, does, feels, and desires all the things that are despicable and odious. . . . A whole man, however, knows that his bitterest foe, or indeed a host of enemies, does not equal that one worst adversary, the "other self" who dwells in his bosom. Nietzsche had Wagner in *himself*, and that is why he envied him *Parsifal*; but, what was worse, he, Saul, also had Paul in him. Therefore Nietzsche became one stigmatized by the spirit; like Saul he had to experience Christification, when the "other" whispered the "Ecce Homo" in his ear. Which of them "broke down before the cross"—Wagner or Nietzsche?[55]

Jung essentially identified the shadow as that unconscious personality of the same sex, that "reprehensible," inferior other which, during the development of consciousness, the individual had forgotten or had failed to recognize, had suppressed and, on account of its incompatibility, had relegated to the unconscious.

The "shadow" was, however, "negative" only when viewed from consciousness. It was essential to Jung's psychology that the inferior complex was not immoral alone, that is, comprising contents incompatible with social values (as Freud had assumed), but that potentially it also contained values of the highest morality which, to be sure, were for the time being still unknown to the ego or had not been recognized by it. Jung, therefore, did not automatically assess the shadow as negative, but saw in it also the prospect of constructive seeds for future development. This was particularly the case when there was a side hidden in the shadow personality which society valued as positive, yet which was regarded by the individual as inferior.

In discussing the "finality" of psychic life, we will see to what degree Jung was able to recognize a seed of transformation—the maternal soil which would produce something positive in the future—even in the underestimated, inferior content of the unconscious psyche so long

[54] "New Paths in Psychology" (1912), p. 266.
[55] "On the Psychology of the Unconscious," p. 35.

as the conscious attitude was suitable. From a formal point of view this was possible because the archaic-primitive aspect of the shadow personality retained its connection with the "ancient paths" in the psyche —a connection which could be revived by the contamination of the shadow with the remainder of the unconscious. In both cases the shadow personality hinted at those personality seeds which connected the individual with the whole and, therefore, could make the individual a whole. As I have emphasized in regard to the unconscious complex in general, the shadow complex could become the trigger for a meaningful, even "good" experience. To this end, however, it was necessary that the individual give credit to hitherto unknown positive potentialities, to what had been considered worthless and incompatible to the ego; furthermore, he must be open to the possibility that the rejected personality fragment might contain hidden salutary potentials. In such a case, the "shadow complex" represented the true moral problem of the individual.

The development of a shadow personality, however, could also lead to the opposite result. If the individual, owing to the acute tension between the opposites, could not withstand this conflict or was unable to recognize the rejected components as belonging to himself, there was the danger of a splitting of the personality into the opposites of "light-dark," "good-evil," or "positive-negative." In such cases, the connection between the two systems—conscious and unconscious— seemed to be restricted or even disrupted. This would produce phenomena of blockage, with consequent symptomatic actions or even neurotic symptoms.

From these few leads it might be concluded that the shadow comprised ideas which somewhat corresponded to Freud's concept of the repressed. The shadow was not only excluded from consciousness, in fact, inadmissible and incompatible with its values, but was also subjected to inhibition (resistance) from consciousness and, in general, less differentiated, if not of an inferior nature. Like complexes in general, it encompassed both feeling-tone and idea. As an integral part of the normal personality development, the shadow personality—in contrast to Freud's view—was subject neither to the mechanisms of severance and shifting nor to a "change in cathexis." Aside from its unconscious character, the inferior personality presented the same contents as the superior, that is, ideas, thought, images, and value judgments (see D.II.3.a).

Thus it again became evident that the shadow personality was by no means always pathological but might assume the characteristics of mental disease under the influence of aggravating attitudes, for example, phenomena of blockage due to regression. Although Freud, in his sexual theory, conceived the repressed complex as "normal," as a biological phenomenon connected with the latency period, he was mainly interested in the neurotic damage resulting from failure of an attempt at repression.

Up to now we have discussed the unconscious psyche chiefly from its personal aspect. But what about the impersonal contents of the unconscious, which are the "greater" in psychic life? Do they present something corresponding to the "repressed"?

B. HEIGHTENED UNCONSCIOUS PERFORMANCE AND REPRESSION

The examination of contents superior to consciousness began far back in Jung's studies. As early as 1902 he recognized, from his investigations of a somnambulistic medium, the superiority of the values of the unconscious, that is, its capacity to achieve "heightened unconscious performances,"[56] "a receptivity of the unconscious far exceeding that of the conscious mind,"[57] and "attempts of the future personality to break through."[58] Indeed, at that time he had been astonished not only by heightened performances in hypermnesia,[59] in hallucinating, and in visions, but also by heightened intellectual performances, in such form as fantastic tales and dreams.[60]

> Finally, there are cases of somnambulistic heightened performance which cannot be explained solely by the hyperaesthetic unconscious activity of the senses or by the concord of associations, but which postulate a highly developed intellectual activity of the unconscious.[61]

It also occurred to Jung that the unconscious had at its disposal a richer store of memories than Freud's repressed, as well as a greater autonomy in the combination of memories. The unconscious, as it were, premeditated the new ideas and the combinations of ideas.[62]

> The unconscious can perceive, and can associate autonomously; and the trouble is that only those associations which have once passed through our conscious minds have the quality of being known, and many of them can fall into oblivion so completely that they lose any such quality. Our unconscious must therefore harbour

[56] "On the Psychology and Pathology of So-Called Occult Phenomena" (1902), p. 80.
[57] Ibid.
[58] Ibid., p. 79.
[59] Ibid., p. 86.
[60] Ibid., pp. 66–67.
[61] Ibid., p. 87.
[62] "Cryptomnesia" (1905), p. 99.

an immense number of psychic complexes which would astonish us by their strangeness.[63]

The steadily renewed experience that certain "contents disappear from consciousness without the slightest trace of repression"[64]—which seemed to indicate a power of attraction on the part of the unconscious—again pointed in the same direction of a heightened value of the unconscious. Not less impressive was the phenomenon of cryptomnesia, that is, the emergence of ideas which only indirectly could be recognized as memory images.

The understanding of heightened psychic performances was unexpectedly expanded by the investigation of archaic images in the depth of the psyche (see C.II). Jung gained a deep insight into the hidden reaches of the unconscious, mainly through observations of the fantasies and delusional systems of mentally disturbed patients. In them he experienced the spontaneous quality, the purposive character, and also the archaic aspects of certain unconscious formations. By means of this material he also recognized a connection with the strange and incorrigible aspects of the "repressed" complex which had impressed him. In such cases, it was usually the emergence of hitherto unknown fantasy contents which brought something completely new to the individual. Particularly impressive was the fact that these fantasies, in spite of their high affective value, had only sparse bridges to consciousness, so that access to the conscious psyche had still to be established. Jung discovered this phenomenon principally in "creative products,"[65] which he understood as contents which seemed strange and which spontaneously—often without demonstrable relationship to consciousness—emerged from the dark reaches of the psyche.

From such experiences Jung learned that certain fantasies, however absurd they may seem, could never be explained exclusively through repressed (that is, personal) motives, but that in every such case one could profitably search for deeper, impersonal factors. Most of all, it became increasingly more evident to him that the strange quality and the fascinating effect on consciousness, characteristic of such formations, as well as the complete lack of any personal experience, could be explained only by the existence of something greater and impersonal, something capable of accounting for such extraordinary effects. With clear reference to Freud, Jung postulated that unconscious contents existed which could not be classified under the heading of repressed

63 Ibid., p. 98.
64 "Analytical Society and Education" (1924), pp. 109–10.
65 "On Psychic Energy" (1928), p. 11, n. 19.

contents (as defined by Freud) and which could not possibly have been repressed because they never had been conscious.

Actually, the repression theory takes account only of those cases in which a content, in itself capable of becoming conscious, is either quite consciously repressed and made unconscious, or has right from the beginning never reached consciousness. It does not take into account those other cases in which a content of high energic intensity is formed out of unconscious material that is not in itself capable of becoming conscious, and so cannot be made conscious at all, or only with the greatest difficulty. In these cases the conscious attitude, far from being hostile to the unconscious content, would be most favorably disposed towards it, as in the case of creative products, which, as we know, almost always have their first beginnings in the unconscious.[66]

From this point of view, Freud's concept of the unconscious seemed to Jung too narrow and could not do justice to the impersonal contents, particularly the creative contents of the psyche. Even though Freud increasingly drew away from equating the unconscious with the repressed, nevertheless, he failed to recognize that the realm of the originally repressed (which he considered to transcend the unconscious) might be creative, nor did he discover the archaic depth of the unconscious. There have been certain interpretations seeking to equate original repression with collective unconscious, but such attempts miscarried because we are faced with affect-toned impulses which are "blind" and totally inaccessible to cathexis or to becoming a part of the psyche. Similarly, Freud's later assumption of an archaic heritage,[67] which he understood as phylogenetic motives manifest in "preserved memories of what was experienced by their ancestors,"[68] can hardly be regarded as a parallel to Jung's hypothesis of impersonal contents of the unconscious. Freud was never prepared to acknowledge a creative activity in the unconscious psyche. Whenever such an admission seemed to be an obvious conclusion, he always relegated it to the realm of historical reminiscences of the experiences of ancestors (see D.III).

The recognition of impersonal contents in the background of the psyche had important consequences. Jung reinstituted in its entirety the concept of dissociation which he had used from the very beginning but now saw as the overall idea encompassing all complexes which were relatively inadmissible to consciousness. This pointed, on the one hand,

[66] Ibid.
[67] Freud, "Analysis Terminable and Interminable" (1937), p. 240.
[68] "Moses and Monotheism: Three Essays" (1939), p. 100.

to experiences which once had been conscious but now had become ego-incompatible (the repressed); on the other hand, it comprised events which had not yet penetrated consciousness, or else were not capable of being apperceived. In 1946 Jung aptly formulated the distinction which he had made many years earlier:

> Such a dissociation has two distinct aspects: in the one case, there is an originally conscious content that became subliminal because it was repressed on account of its incompatible nature: in the other case, the secondary subject consists essentially in a process that never entered into consciousness at all because no possibilities exist there of apperceiving it. That is to say, ego-consciousness cannot accept it for lack of understanding, and in consequence it remains for the most part subliminal, although, from the energy point of view, it is quite capable of becoming conscious. It owes its existence not to repression, but to subliminal processes that were never themselves conscious.[69]

The consequences for the understanding of neurosis and psychosis which Jung drew from this concept of dissociation will be discussed in a later chapter.

In spite of all hesitation, objections, and qualifications, Jung always attempted to do justice to the meaning hidden in the concept of repression. Again and again he emphasized that Freud's theory of repression was an important attempt to bring to light the reality of unconscious motives and to expose the individual to the mendacity underlying many of his ideals. But Jung became alienated by the reductive-negative character of Freud's theory, which explained everything that is meaningful, every emotion, every creativity as coming from nothing else than repressed drives. This position becomes understandable when one considers Jung's approach, which attributed a value, if not the highest value, to the numinous and autonomous aspects of the psyche. These qualifications notwithstanding, Jung saw the theory of repression as a magnificent achievement of moral liberation from the grip of the Victorian era, but he also recognized that Freud had become mired down in the search for immoral motivations and infantile-sexual causes of collective ideals.

> Freud's historical contribution . . . [consists] in the fact . . . that, like an Old Testament prophet, he overthrew false idols and pitilessly exposed to the light of day the rottenness of the contemporary psyche.[70]

[69] Jung, "On the Nature of the Psyche" (1946), pp. 174–75.
[70] "Sigmund Freud in His Historical Setting" (1932), p. 36.

B. FROM PSYCHIC "MECHANISMS" TO THE TOTAL PERSONALITY

Freud was "a great destroyer who [broke] the fetters of the past"[71] and thus prepared the way for a future free of illusions and for a rediscovery of true psychic values. Attaining this goal, however, required a step from the merely sexual interpretation of the unconscious to the major aspects of the psyche—from the merely subjective view of the psyche to a concept which included its objective and collective constituents (see C.II).

[71] Ibid.

IV. THE UNITY AND TOTALITY OF
THE PERSONALITY

While Freud's investigations of psychic dynamisms were determined by his overwhelming interest in neurosis, Jung's point of departure was increasingly the exploration of individuality and its characteristics. In contrast to the mechanistic-materialistic attitude that can be discerned in Freud's entire work, Jung always occupied a position in which the psychic phenomena were considered as parts of an all-encompassing whole. Whereas Freud, persisting in a view of the world which was based on universal determinism and a measurability of events, hoped that the intricate structure of the psyche could be explained by the elementary mechanisms of repression, projection, and condensation, Jung's interest was concentrated on recognizing the relationships between the partial and the total personality. While Freud considered it feasible to dissect the psyche into its elemental components and explain the entire individual on the basis of isolated drive-mechanisms and processes, Jung envisaged the totality of the human personality so as to gauge and understand the particular phenomena from the standpoint of the whole. This process of understanding the psychic individuality may be said to have reached its first culmination about 1921.[1]

The concept of the totality of the personality was—as noted above— always a guidepost for Jung. In his thesis, when he referred to somnambulist partial personalities, multiple personalities, or split personalities, in the background the concept of the unified personality was constantly alive. This attitude was the source for his remark in *The Psychology of Dementia Praecox* that "the essential basis of our personality is affectivity."[2]

Still, what Jung really meant by personality remained unclear for quite some time. At first, this term denoted a personal center of smaller or larger dimension. Even then, difficulties arose, since Jung was not always clear whether he envisaged the conscious or the unconscious part of the personality, the ego-personality, or a partial personality. The opposition of an "inferior" and a "superior" personality could be equally perplexing. Furthermore, references to splitting phenomena and multiple personalities did not always help express his opinions clearly. On the contrary, Jung occasionally used the term "personality"

[1] Jung, *Psychological Types* (1921), p. 448.
[2] "The Psychology of Dementia Praecox" (1907), p. 38.

according to its general meaning in referring to a mature, well-balanced individual. Again, he spoke of "expansion of the personality" when thinking of the incorporation of unconscious content into the ego-personality. As time went on the meaning of the term "personality" became narrower, at least in a formal sense, when Jung gave it the meaning of a firmly structured complex of attributes with a central nucleus. As early as 1902, Jung had conceived the idea of a "future personality"[3] in order to indicate something like a personality superior to the ego. Several years had to pass until his earlier conjectures of the totality of the personality could be demonstrated as clearly as he thought necessary. This did not happen until 1913, after Jung separated from Freud. He threw overboard all formalism and everything which was "confining and automatic," and dared to expose himself to what was alive in his own psyche. In confronting his own darkness, by coming to terms with the images, tendencies, and ideas of his own hidden psyche, Jung gained the conviction so essential to his psychology—that an organizing center is active in the psyche, which is generally unknown to the ego. This insight became more and more shaped to the idea of a central nucleus, inherent in each individual, which was oriented toward the totality of the psyche.

In 1916 Jung was already delineating the concepts of "individuality" and "individuation." However, at that time his concepts differed somewhat from the meaning he gave them later. He then defined "individuality" as "that which is peculiar and unique in a given combination of collective psychological elements."[4] He described individuation as "a process of development that seems to us irrational . . . particular and universal at once."[5]

Over the years, empirical evidence increased Jung's certainty of the unity and uniqueness of individuality and its antecedent existence. In 1921 he wrote:

> The psychological individual, or his *individuality*, has an *a priori* unconscious existence, but exists consciously only so far as a consciousness of his peculiar nature is present.[6]

At first glance, it might appear as if Jung's hypotheses of a multiplicity of independent fragments, complexes, and images of the psyche would indicate a primal chaos rather than a uniting principle. This, however, would be a wrong impression. Since the idea of a multiplicity

---

[3] "On the Psychology and Pathology of So-Called Occult Phenomena" (1902), p. 79.

[4] "The Structure of the Unconscious" (1916), p. 301.

[5] Ibid., p. 297.   [6] *Psychological Types*, p. 447.

logically calls for unity as its opposite, an empirically demonstrated multitude of unconscious tendencies would have as its counterpart a tendency to integrate many parts into a comprehensive unity. Jung, therefore, recognized that the tension between the tendency to dissociate and the inclination towards unity was a phenomenon intrinsically characteristic of the life process. This tension constituted the foundation of psychic dynamics. Because of it, the opposites could not only separate again, but showed the same tendency to unify. Jung's words, in 1928, are illuminating:

> Over against the polymorphism of the primitive's instinctual nature there stands the regulating principle of individuation. Multiplicity and inner division are opposed by an integrative unity whose power is as great as that of the instincts.[7]

Primarily, Jung's investigations of the fantasies arising from the unconscious helped him to demonstrate empirically that the sequence of images not only exhibited a disorderly variety of dissociated fragments but at the same time showed a tendency toward gradual centralization: "They pursue definite, unconscious lines of direction which converge upon a definite goal."[8]

> Individuation means becoming an "in-dividual," and insofar as "individuality" embraces our innermost, last, and incomparable uniqueness, it also implies becoming one's own self. We could therefore translate individuation as "coming to selfhood" or "self-realization."[9]

This developmental process was never without a goal but always led to "the unfolding of the original, potential wholeness,"[10] to "the realization, in all its aspects, of the personality originally hidden away in the embryonic germ-plasm."[11] The demonstration of a process of gradual centralization in the psyche, which was based in the self, also assumed the existence of a personality core, a "mid-point of the personality."[12] With this assumption Jung fundamentally passed beyond the confines of the area of investigation marked out by Freud. Freud's point of view, based as it was on the methods of natural science, had never permitted the hypothesis of an organizing personality core. Freud had one fundamental approach: the dynamic interplay between

---

[7] "On Psychic Energy" (1928), p. 51.
[8] "The Relations Between the Ego and the Unconscious" (1916), p. 230.
[9] Ibid., p. 173.
[10] "On the Psychology of the Unconscious" (1917), p. 110.
[11] Ibid.
[12] "The Relations Between the Ego and the Unconscious," p. 221.

conscious and unconscious impulses, whether he was dealing with the dualism between primary and secondary processes, between censor and sexual drive, or between ego and id. Even when he attempted an anthropological approach (1933), which proceeded from the opposition of the structures of ego and id, the concept of a core in the individual as a whole is missing. Instead, Freud credited the ego with a partial function in organizing the psyche.[13]

But when Jung explored the energic laws governing the psyche—as we will see later on—his approach by no means excluded the assumption of a self-regulating principle.[14] On the contrary, he recognized the self-regulating system as the basis of the interplay between conscious and unconscious as well as the transformation process of the personality.

Jung already stressed in 1921 that these events occurred in close connection with the differentiation of consciousness and individuation. (The first English translation, in 1923, was expressly titled: *Psychological Types, or The Psychology of Individuation*.)[15] In contrast to Freud, who primarily traced psychic dynamics to psychic mechanisms or elementary facts, Jung always presupposed the indivisible unity and totality of the human personality. He saw a "virtual center" between consciousness and the unconscious, which was basically different from the ego.

> This would be the point of new equilibrium, a new centering of the total personality, a virtual centre which, on account of its focal position between conscious and unconscious, ensures for the personality a new and more solid foundation.[16]

This center was the beginning as well as the end; it not only developed in the course of life but existed from the very outset as a specific entity. Seen from this perspective, it becomes apparent how Jung could describe the human personality as the "supreme realization of the innate idiosyncrasy of a living being,"[17] or again as "the optimum development of the whole individual human being."[18] Indeed, this concept served principally as an ideal or guidepost. Although Jung took the greatest care to enlarge gradually upon his thoughts on the psychic totality, they were the basis of his entire psychological work, expressing the outermost experiences of the human condition. This

13 Freud, *New Introductory Lectures on Psycho-Analysis* (1933), pp. 75-76.
14 Jung, "On the Psychology of the Unconscious," p. 61.
15 C. A. Meier kindly pointed this out.
16 Jung, "The Relations between the Ego and the Unconscious," p. 221.
17 "The Development of the Personality" (1932), p. 171.
18 Ibid.

"center," which Jung also designated as "self," will be discussed in detail in a later chapter.

Jung himself understood clearly that his psychological approach embracing the total personality, with its unavoidable metaphysical premises (see App. I.2), came close to a realm which up to that time had been left almost entirely to the domain of religion and metaphysical philosophy. Jung had in mind the realization of a center which in part transcended the confines of empiricism, that is, a unity extending beyond the multitude of psychic phenomena; it represented not only the indiscernible beginning of human development but also the equally imperceptible points of reference and orientation. Jung's statement in 1936 follows a similar trend:

One absolutely essential field of experience, the human psyche itself, remained for a very long time the preserve of metaphysics, although increasingly serious attempts were made after the Enlightenment to open it up to scientific investigation. They began, tentatively, with the sense perceptions, and gradually ventured into the domain of associations. This line of research paved the way for experimental psychology, and it culminated in the "physiological psychology," of Wundt. A more descriptive kind of psychology, with which the medical men soon made contact, developed in France. Its chief exponents were Taine, Ribot, and Janet. It was characteristic of this scientific approach that it broke down the psyche into particular mechanisms or processes. In face of these attempts, there were some who advocated what we today would call a "holistic" approach—the systematic observation of the psyche as a whole. It seems as if this trend originated in a certain type of biography, more particularly the kind that an earlier age, which also had its good points, used to describe as "curious lives." In this connection I think of Justinus Kerner and his *Seeress of Prevorst*, and the case of the elder Blumhardt and his medium Gottliebin Dittus. To be historically fair, however, I should not forget the medieval *Acta Sanctorum*.

This line of research has been continued in more recent investigations associated with the names of William James, Freud, and Théodore Flournoy. James and his friend Flournoy, a Swiss psychologist, made an attempt to describe the whole phenomenology of the psyche and also to view it as a totality.[19]

[19] "Psychological Typology" (1936), pp. 546–47.

C. FROM THE PERSONAL
TO THE COLLECTIVE CONTENTS
OF THE PSYCHE

I. THE PSYCHOLOGY OF FANTASY

1. Fantasy as Distortion and Wish-Fulfillment (Freud)

Freud started to investigate fantasies in the 1890's, emphasizing the study of hysterical fantasies.[1] In his first attempt at an explanation he stated that hysterical fantasies could be traced back to painful childhood memories, that is, to seduction and sexual abuse. But this attempt ended in disappointment. (As Jones stressed, this disappointment was a turning point in Freud's scientific career, since he felt compelled to uphold the significance of such fantasies.)[2] The theory of the sexual childhood trauma proved to be untenable, because in only very few cases could any actual scenes of seduction be uncovered. In spite of the "general collapse" of his theory,[3] Freud continued to place importance on the etiology of memory traces in developing fantasies. Whether they were related to actually experienced scenes or not, he considered them to be fantastic transformations of memories, which were never without infantile or erotic characteristics. Freud initially emphasized the aspect of distortion which formed the basis for fantasies to culminate in tendentious falsifications of memory.[4] Later, in connection with his dream studies, fantasies increasingly appeared to express a tendency to wish-fulfillment. In each case, they revealed a process which veiled reality and substituted for the absence of satisfying experiences. From the findings in dream material, Freud also gained insight into the fantasies occurring during puberty, such as "overhearing the parents in sexual intercourse," "seduction at an early age by a loved one," and primarily, "fantasies of being in the womb."[5] Both in nocturnal and day dreams, these fantasies showed the need to replace a missing drive-fulfillment by an imagined experience. Early in his self-analysis[6] Freud had recognized the presence of such incestuous fantasies (the term he used for fantasies tracing back to sexual desires of infancy),[7] that is, feelings of hatred toward the father and sexual desire toward the mother.[8] Regression into infancy was typical of these fantasies as well as accentuation of the nuclear complex, the Oedipus complex.

[1] Freud, *The Origins of Psycho-Analysis* (1887–1902), p. 193.
[2] Jones, *The Life and Work of Sigmund Freud*, Vol. I (1953), p. 265.
[3] Freud, *Origins*, p. 218.   [4] "Screen Memories" (1899), p. 322.
[5] "Three Essays on the Theory of Sexuality" (1905), p. 226, n. 1.
[6] *Origins*, p. 223.   [7] "Three Essays," p. 227.
[8] Ibid.

In a similar vein, Freud perceived the fantasies of the creative writer as products arising from yearning and privation and, in a certain sense, forming "a continuation of, and a substitute for, what was once the play of childhood."[9] Upon closer examination the creative writer could be seen without his cocoon to be a day-dreamer who had the talent to give his childhood memories the imprint of a whole era as well as the power to disguise real events so artfully that they yield pleasure for the reader.[10] Turning from the outside world was always a characteristic trait, for fantasy appeared as a compromise-formation between wish and reality. Later, under the influence of Jung, Freud viewed fantasies also as a product of introversion[11] and not necessarily as a pathological phenomenon.

In general, Freud was of the opinion that unfulfilled wishes motivated fantasy-formation in sick as well as healthy subjects.

> The motive forces of phantasies are unsatisfied wishes, and every single phantasy is the fulfillment of a wish, a correction of unsatisfying reality. . . . They are either ambitious wishes, which serve to elevate the subject's personality; or they are erotic ones.[12]

Without fail, neurotic or even psychotic symptoms appeared hand in hand with luxuriant fantasies. A predominance of fantastic reveries could be due to the attraction of foci of libidinous fixation—particularly the primal scenes—or to external deprivation, but in every case regression of the libido toward these relinquished foci was apparent.

2. Fantasy as Creative Formation (Jung)

This brief outline gives the essentials of the psychological situation in which Jung found himself at the time he discovered the creative basis of fantasy activity. Up to that time (1908), he had been more or less under the spell of Freud's *Dream Interpretation* or, more precisely, the theory of wish-fulfillment which conceived fantasy images as compensation for what was unfulfilled in a person's life. For example, he attempted in his doctoral thesis to trace the fantasies of a somnambulistic medium and the fanciful dreams of hysterical subjects to "sexual wish-fulfillment."[13] The concept of wish-fulfillment stood out with particular clarity in Jung's *Psychology of Dementia Praecox*. In this

9 "Creative Writers and Day-Dreaming" (1908), p. 152.
10 Ibid., p. 153.
11 *Introductory Lectures on Psycho-Analysis* (1915–17), p. 374.
12 "Creative Writers," pp. 146–47.
13 Jung, "On the Psychology and Pathology of So-Called Occult Phenomena" (1902), p. 70.

work he described the fantasies experienced by a patient with dementia praecox as dream-like formations which conveyed her unfulfilled wishes and hopes.[14] To be sure, these formations differed from those of normal subjects in that they extended throughout the entire waking state and occasionally completely replaced it, sometimes with great damage to the "fonction du reél."[15] Above all, Jung was impressed by the finding that in a psychotic the conscious life exhausted itself in the production of wishful images while the unconscious was influenced by conflicting complexes, that is, compensatory processes—to use a term of a later period (1914).

> The conscious psychic activity of the patient, then, is limited to a systematic creation of wish-fulfillments as a substitute, so to speak, for a life of toil and privation and for the depressing experiences of a wretched family milieu. The unconscious psychic activity, on the other hand, is entirely under the influence of repressed, contradictory complexes—on one side the complex of injury, on the other the remnants of normal correction.[16]

These remarks have a certain historical importance; they were the first indication of the function of compensation and of the significance of such compensatory maneuvers. It is also interesting that simultaneously Jung and Adler (whom Jung liked to call the creator of the theory of compensation) drew attention to compensating (contradictory) complexes.

One of Jung's outstanding achievements was to be the first in medical psychology to pose the question of the meaning of psychotic formations; he also saw that the goal of therapy depended on understanding this significance. In the years immediately following, he made many more observations on the essence of psychotic formations which went beyond the assumption of personal wish-formations and personal motivations in general. Among his most productive experiences were the findings that the fantasies of psychotics not only revealed a meaning but, more than that, an impersonal meaning. Jung discovered that in spite of the patient's unusual mode of reaction to emotional problems, these "are in no wise foreign to ourselves."[17] The realization that there is a deeper, hidden "method in the madness,"[18] a meaning based in the "still unknown depth of the psyche," finally brought him to the recognition that psychotic formations, like those of normal subjects, were

[14] "On the Psychology of Dementia Praecox" (1907), p. 144.
[15] Ibid., p. 145.   [16] Ibid., pp. 145–46.
[17] "The Content of the Psychoses" (1908), p. 165.
[18] Ibid.

derived from a foundation common to all human beings. Jung described his response to the discovery of the profound basis of fantasies in stirring words:

> Even the most absurd things are nothing other than symbols for thoughts which are not only understandable in human terms but dwell in every human breast. In insanity we do not discover anything new and unknown; we are looking at the foundations of our own being, the matrix of those vital problems on which we are all engaged.[19]

On the strength of this evidence Jung established a connecting link between the psychic life of psychotics and that of normal and healthy people; but he also gained a new approach to psychotherapy. Instead of dismissing the systematized fantasies of demented persons as bizarre and nothing more, he found it more appropriate to arouse in the patient a feeling that his fantastic formations had a meaning common to all humans.

The problem of the mental content of psychotic creations also led Jung to the detection of their teleological significance. As early as 1908 he had pointed out the "silent activity of the unconscious"[20] in psychotic products. A few years later (1911), he drew attention to the phenomenon of the "prophetic significance of dreams."[21] However, under the strong influence of Freud's personality Jung set aside these ideas and resumed them to their full extent only in the years 1913–14. We will return to this subject a little later (see C.III).

The book *Transformations and Symbols of the Libido* was destined to initiate a new epoch in the development of Jung's thought. In this work he demonstrated that the unconscious foundations of dreams and archaic fantasies were objective sources of creativity, largely independent of personal motivations.

With Théodore Flournoy's permission Jung based his book on fantasies of an American girl, which Flournoy had published under the woman's name (Miss Frank Miller) in 1906.[22] Miss Miller was in the prodromal stage of schizophrenia, and Jung attempted to elucidate her personal problems as well as the background common to humanity. In equal measure, he examined her conscious impressions and her dreams and fantasies. For the first time he applied a new method, that is, drawing on historical parallels and mythical motives

---

[19] Ibid., p. 178.   [20] Ibid., p. 170.
[21] *Psychology of the Unconscious* (*Transformations and Symbols of the Libido*, 1912), p. 493.
[22] "Quelque faits de l'imagination créative subconsciente" (Tr. Flournoy; 1906).

in order to enlarge and deepen the significance of autonomous forma-tions. Jung described his method in the preface to the second edition (1924):

> If, in this work, various mythologies are shown in a light which makes their psychological meaning more intelligible, I have men-tioned this insight simply as a welcome by-product, without claiming to propound any general theory of myths. The real purpose of this book is confined to working out the implications of all those histori-cal and spiritual factors which come together in the involuntary products of individual fantasy.[23]

In spite of this remarkable beginning, with its penetrating inquiry into the spiritual content of fantasies, Jung—initially still strongly influenced by Freud's thoughts—only gradually divulged his own intuitions.

It is fascinating as well as moving to follow the inner conflict which Jung underwent in his endeavor to do justice to the discoveries of Freud and at the same time to remain faithful to his inner daemon. The first part of *Transformations and Symbols of the Libido* exhibits distinct traces of this inner discord, while in the second part, published a year later, his increasing distance from Freud became more apparent. Jung's positive reaction to Freud's earlier writings had been quite as strong as were his later reservations toward the theory of sexuality (1905)[24] and the writings based on this theory. In particular Jung's thinking was opposed to Freud's statement that fantasies were not only unreal and distorted but were also of an incestuous nature,[25] a com-promise between infantile incestuous wish and the barrier against incest imposed by society.[26] Incestuous fantasies will be discussed again in a later chapter.

Jung, aiming to bridge the differences that separated him from Freud, initially outlined a description of fantasy similar to Freud's concept (1911), which was largely characterized by personal and in-fantile traits and by distortion. Without using explicit terms such as self-deception or substitute-formation, Jung nevertheless described the view arising from "fantastic thinking" (associative thinking) as "an overwhelmingly subjective and distorted picture of the world."[27] Likewise, some remarks traced fantasy formations to "not-recognized wishful tendencies of the psyche," primarily to sexuality—concepts

---

23 See *Symbols of Transformation* (1952), p. xxix.
24 Freud, "Three Essays," p. 228.   25 Ibid., p. 227.
26 "Delusions and Dreams in Jensen's *Gradiva*" (1907), pp. 52, 58.
27 *Psychology of the Unconscious*, p. 36.

which Jung would not only correct and complete in the second part of *Transformations and Symbols of the Libido*, but would refine still more in the 1952 revision.

Jung's revisions of the above-mentioned passages, which appeared in the fourth edition, entitled *Symbols of Transformation*, are of particular interest. The expression "subjective thinking" had been modified by adding "which is actuated by inner motives."[28] In the same way, he not only spoke of "distortion of the objective world-picture" but questioned whether these fantasy processes were not guided by an inner motive, which is itself "an objective fact."[29] Finally, Jung was no longer thinking primarily of "infantile reminiscences" but of "archaic thought-forms."

> The unconscious bases of dreams and fantasies are only apparently infantile reminiscences. In reality we are concerned with primitive or archaic thought-forms, based on instinct, which naturally emerge more clearly in childhood than they do later.[30]

This distinction should by no means be understood as if Jung had fundamentally devaluated either the personal or the primitive-archaic aspect of fantasy (as we will see later). As with complexes, Jung had always recognized the significance of formations based on personal reminiscences, impressions, and experiences which were related to events in the history of the subject's life. In this respect, Jung always referred to the remarkable discoveries of Freud. But he could not agree with the limitation to exclusively personal factors because, during his research on the history of religion and on mythology,[31] he had been impressed by the significance of impersonal motives.

From this perspective we can understand his leanings toward abandoning the basic premises of the Freudian system, a tendency already noticed in the first part of *Transformations and Symbols of the Libido*. Jung discovered ageless motives in myths, in fairy tales, and in folklore—and ever-repeated motives—which pointed to the existence of symbols common to all humanity and to the so-called primordial images (a term which first appeared in the second part of *Transformations and Symbols of the Libido*; cf. C.IV). Such observations led Jung to assume that there were impersonal nuclear processes in the unconscious psyche—an assumption which he later was able to confirm on the basis of collective archaic patterns, the archetypes (cf.

28 *Symbols of Transformation*, p. 28.   29 Ibid., p. 28.
30 Ibid., pp. 28–29.
31 In *The Freud/Jung Letters*, see Jung's letters to Freud of 15 Nov. 09, 10 Jan. 10, and 30 Jan. 10.

C.V). Jung observed "attempts at myth-making" in children[32] and on this basis originated the hypothesis of a creative urge toward mythology[33] in the psyche, a conclusion which Freud always declined.

Jung's discovery of the symbolic significance of fantasy during this period of transition was an achievement anticipating later developments. He made a distinction between a "lower and higher meaning,"[34] thus recognizing a double meaning in everything in the psychic sphere; he also demonstrated a general polarization of primordial ideas. The finding of a pronounced tension of opposites in the meaning of symbols was enlightening to Jung and made a deep impression on him. He saw it operating in religious basic thoughts[35] as well as in concepts of God (god and devil).[36] In a dynamic context this gradient led to transcending the opposites, while in considering content the presence of analogies facilitated symbol formation (see E.III.5). Because of these and similar observations, Jung finally found himself unable to accept Freud's hypothesis that fantasy was a distorted and falsified phenomenon.

[32] *Symbols of Transformation*, p. 24. [33] Ibid., p. 20.
[34] Ibid., p. 50. [35] Ibid., p. 60.
[36] Ibid., p. 56.

II. ARCHAIC FANTASIES

Looking back, Jung stated that the actual breakthrough of the new world view occurred while working on the second part of *Transformations and Symbols of the Libido*. The new outlook was destined to liberate him from the "narrowness of the materialistic concretism" of the nineteenth century. In the foreword to the fourth edition (1952), Jung wrote:

> The whole thing came upon me like a landslide that cannot be stopped. The urgency that lay behind it became clear to me only later: it was the explosion of all those psychic contents which could find no room, no breathing-space, in the constricting atmosphere of Freudian psychology and its narrow outlook. I have no wish to denigrate Freud, or to detract from the extraordinary merits of his investigation of the individual psyche. But the conceptual framework into which he fitted the psychic phenomenon seemed to me unendurably narrow.[1]

This outbreak should not be understood to mean that Jung had ever disavowed the archaic and primitive aspects of fantasy (which Freud had stressed so much), nor that he denied regression to archaic layers of the psyche. Quite the contrary! It was precisely the archaic layers of fantasy-formation which became the starting point for Jung's new discoveries. What he had found in the archaic images was a "plain objective fact and is no more dependent upon individual experience or personal choice than is the inherited structure and functioning of the brain or any other organ,"[2] as he stated in retrospect. In the regression of fantasy activity to archaic images, though initially individual and subjective in character, Jung discovered a process which, suitably approached, brought to light traits common to all human beings. To Jung it was fundamental that a primitive mind with its peculiar contents would be ultimately manifested in creative fantasy, just as the mythical creations of people have revealed from time immemorial. In the preface to the second edition of *Transformations and Symbols of the Libido* (1924), he wrote:

> Besides the obvious personal sources, creative fantasy also draws upon the forgotten and long buried primitive mind with its host of

1 *Symbols of Transformation* (1952), p. xxiii.
2 Ibid., p. 29.

images, which are to be found in the mythologies of all ages and all peoples.[3]

In archaic fantasy-formations Jung also discovered the historical aspect of the unconscious. It became evident to him that the unconscious psyche rested on a "condensation of the average run of historical experience"[4]—a finding which he could also confirm in the dream-unconscious. In the dream, "historical layering"[5] manifests itself in the blending of personal and collective contents and in the contamination of motives which originated in the most recent as well as the most ancient times. All these data showed with increasing clarity that the background of the psyche was not only personal but also had characteristics common to all humans, even of an impersonal and objective nature.

A reversal of approach was indeed called for, if such objective, perennial phenomena, which originally were not assimilated into the ego, were to be verified in the material of the unconscious. Instead of deducing the meaning of a fantasy from material already known—as typically in Freudian psychology (see C.I.1)—Jung emphasized a method of "questioning" the fantasy-formation so as to determine its still unknown nuclear significance. This approach not only presupposed an attitude which accepted the unconscious contents as substantial and factual; it also required a technique of searching for analogies and an attempt to understand motives and thought structures from a wider aspect. Only such a method—Jung called it *hermeneutic* (see G.II.4)—guaranteed an adequate understanding of the meaning of fantasy-formations. As Jung always emphasized, this understanding was bypassed if, following Freud's lead, fantasy was reduced to a mere striving for wish-fulfillment and was made a substitute for unsatisfactory reality. One was then unable to discern in the formations of the unconscious psyche what was authentic and genuine, what surpassed man's personal horizon, lifted him above an existence limited to mere drives, and gave an inkling of the depth of the background of his psyche.

Jung never claimed any priority for the discovery of phylogenetic motives within fantasies. On the contrary, as early as 1911 he referred to Nietzsche's statement that an "atavistic element in man's nature still manifests itself in our dreams."[6] He also mentioned at that time that rather disputable concept of Freud, who saw in the myth "dis-

---

[3] Ibid., p. xxix. [4] Ibid., p. 49.
[5] Ibid., pp. 22-25.
[6] Ibid., p. 23, citing *Human, All-Too-Human*, Vol. I, pp. 24f.

torted vestiges of the wish-phantasies of whole nations."[7] Furthermore, Jung cited a work by Abraham dealing with the connection between dream and myth, but the statement that the myth is "a fragment preserved from the infantile psychic life of the race"[8] was incompatible with Jung's thinking. Interestingly, Freud referred several years later (1915) to the appearance of primal fantasies[9] in the dreams and fantasies of his patients; still, this remark should not mislead one as to the considerable difference in the basic assumption of the two investigators. While Freud drew attention to the fact that such phylogenetic motives characteristically repeat themselves, he also emphasized that the individual "replaces occurrences in his own life by occurrences in the life of his ancestors. . . . He fills in the gaps in individual truth with prehistoric truth."[10] However, in the context of Freud's causalistic-reductive thinking such remarks have an entirely different meaning than Jung's observations. As we will enlarge upon in a later chapter, Freud found that phylogenetic motives originated in the experiences of earlier generations. He could not do otherwise than assume the existence of traces of collective memories, going back ultimately to concrete experiences which at some time had been real events in the lives of remote ancestors.

Contrary to Freud, Jung saw in archaic fantasies spontaneous manifestations of fantasy activity and also formations of an impersonal, even timeless character. The proper meaning hidden in such formations of "ancient humanity" seemed to him to rest in objective data which—independent of individual opinion and historical events—originated in the collective primal foundation. We will return to the differences between the two investigators when discussing incest fantasies (see E.III.5), particularly Freud's "archaic inheritance" (see D.III).

[7] Ibid., p. 24, citing "Creative Writers and Day-Dreaming" (1908), p. 152.
[8] Ibid., citing Abraham, *Dreams and Myths* (1909), p. 72.
[9] "A Case of Paranoia Running Counter to the Psycho-Analytic Theory of the Disease" (1915), p. 269.
[10] "From the History of an Infantile Neurosis" (1918), p. 97.

III. GOAL-DIRECTEDNESS IN THE PSYCHE

Closely connected with the meaning of fantasy was the question of a possible prospective content. Again, his investigations of the delusional fantasies of psychotics enabled Jung to determine not only the meaning of fantasies but the directing and anticipating tendencies within the psyche of psychotics as well. A first hint could be detected in 1908: In the regressive fantasies of the psychotic, Jung recognized a flight into childhood memories and also meaningful germs of new solutions to largely insoluble problems. Because of the loss of reality, such attempts at a solution could seldom be utilized productively.

The world of reality [is] that of unsolved problems. . . . His [the insane person's] solutions are unsatisfying illusions, his cure a temporary relinquishing of the problem, which yet goes on working unsolved in the depths of the unconscious, and at the appointed time rises again to the surface and creates new illusions with new scenery—the history of mankind writ small.[1]

What did Jung understand by "anticipation"? I would just like to mention here that Jung—agreeing with Maeder,[2] who very early examined prospective tendencies—saw in the prospective and anticipating activity of the psyche a tendency toward a "preliminary exercise or sketch, or a plan roughed out in advance. Its symbolic content sometimes outlines the solution of a conflict."[3]

From these early conjectures, convincing insights gradually developed. In 1909 Jung already recognized the extraordinary importance of the father-figure in *shaping the destiny* of his children. This resulted from observations on the fateful effects of the entanglements and dependencies between parents and children. In contrast to Freud's causal approach—which took the "family romance"[4] as the cause of neurotic symptoms in young people—Jung posed the question of the prospective significance of the father in the child's future life, which was hidden in the symptom. It became evident to him that not only unconscious phenomena but also the statements of neurotic children indicated a goal-directedness immanent in life.

[1] Jung, "The Content of the Psychoses" (1908), p. 170.
[2] Maeder, "Über die Funktion des Traumes" (1912); "Zur Frage der teleologischen Traumfunktion" (1913).
[3] Jung, "General Aspects of Dream Psychology" (1916/1928), p. 255.
[4] Freud, *The Origins of Psycho-Analysis* (1887–1902), p. 256 (20 June 1898).

The parental influence . . . sinks into the unconscious, but is not eliminated; by invisible threads it directs the apparently individual workings of the maturing mind. Like everything that has fallen into the unconscious, the infantile situation still sends up dim, premonitory feelings, feelings of being secretly guided by other worldly influences. . . . These are the roots of the first religious sublimations.[5]

However, this did not mean that the directing tendencies always had a positive effect. Neurotic conflict resulted only too readily from the clash between the "infantile constellation" (the persistent effect of the father-imago)[6] and the "urge towards individualization"[7] (self-realization). Nevertheless, it seemed to Jung that the outbreak of neurosis was often more wholesome than a torpid clinging to infantile fantasies.

Jung took a further step in the paper "Psychic Conflicts in a Child" (1910)[8] which was intended as a counterpart to Freud's "Analysis of a Phobia in a Five-Year-Old Boy" (Little Hans) (1909). Several years later (1915), Jung stated in retrospect that Freud's paper, which had originally been intended to confirm his sex theory and his view of causality, was in fact a convincing demonstration of the prospective method and its significance for psychotherapy. Primarily, the fabric of fantasies, derived from the craving for knowledge and sexual curiosity, afforded him insight into the development of a child's mind. Even though Jung in no way contested Freud's concept that both birth and death fantasies were related to the sexual function, the material served him mainly as confirmation of his assumption that the sexual function is the seed of higher spiritual functions. In the foreword to the second edition of "Psychic Conflicts in a Child" (1915), Jung wrote:

While perceiving in infantile sexuality the beginnings of a future sexual function, I also discern there the seeds of higher spiritual functions.[9]

With this paper Jung began to see the prospective significance of the resistance of children against their parents and environment, to which Freud had given only a negative value. For Jung, not only the child's stubbornness and distrust but also his obstinate questioning

---

[5] Jung, "The Significance of the Father in the Destiny of the Individual" (1909), pp. 320–21.

[6] Ibid., p. 320.

[7] "Some Crucial Points in Psychoanalysis: A Correspondence between Dr. Jung and Dr. Loÿ" (1914), p. 284.

[8] Given as lecture 1909, published 1910.   [9] "Psychic Conflicts in a Child," p. 5.

were expressions of his anxious search, of his attempt to orient himself in the world; in other words, they revealed the starting point of intellectual development.

The investigation of the fantasies of Miss Miller (in *Transformations and Symbols of the Libido*) threw further light on the problem. Here, Jung became certain that the products of fantasy which Freud usually interpreted as a "return of the libido to an infantile state" were not exhausted in regression to an earlier level or even in stagnation, but held out the possibility of renewal. Jung could no longer overlook the fact that fantasy should never be regarded as a mere relic of a causal nexus; in so far as, "in this subliminal material, combinations of future events"[10] could be recognized, fantasy presented a meaningful bridge from the present to the future. Although fantasy-oriented traits that substituted paradisiac ideas for stern and forbidding reality were often encountered, still the patient's fantasies showed germs of an intellectual development and new possibilities.

The prospective approach proved extremely productive in understanding neurotic symptoms. Jung was able to establish that their meaning was not restricted to discovering causes, but that they also could be understood as attempts at a *new* synthesis of life.

The symptoms of a neurosis are not simply the effects of long-past causes, . . . they are also attempts at a new synthesis of life—unsuccessful attempts, let it be added in the same breath, yet attempts nevertheless, with a core of value and meaning.[11]

Jung also observed that dreams, particularly the dreams of neurotic subjects, reveal anticipating tendencies when approached correctly. He established that "in certain cases of long-standing neurosis a dream, often of visionary clarity, occurs about the time of the onset of the illness or shortly before, which imprints itself indelibly on the mind and, when analyzed, reveals to the patient a hidden meaning that anticipates the subsequent events of his life."[12]

Jung also used dreams to develop the function of self-regulation[13] (discussed more fully later). This discovery most beautifully confirmed the hypothesis of a goal-directedness inherent in the psyche.

These remarks are not intended to suggest that Jung was the first to ascribe the quality of goal-directedness to the psyche. Theodor Lipps[14] had already based his philosophically oriented psychology on

10 "The Theory of Psychoanalysis" (1912), p. 201.
11 "On the Psychology of the Unconscious" (1917), p. 46.
12 *Symbols of Transformation*, p. 51 (also in 1911–12 edn.).
13 "On the Psychology of the Unconscious," p. 61.
14 In, e.g., *Leitfaden der Psychologie* (1903).

"endeavors" and noticed a tendency to the unification of psychic processes as well as to their dissociation.

What is more important, Freud had already discovered a goal-directed mechanism in the phenomenon of wish, desire, and drive. While the causal approach was always typical of his investigations, he nevertheless thought of these causes in relation to aims; in other words, he also understood causes as goal-directed impulses. However, in contrast to Jung's concept of a purely psychic motivation, based on emotion, value, and meaning, according to Freud pleasure and displeasure were the exclusive regulating mechanisms of the psyche. This approach was not changed even by the introduction of the reality principle, which Freud saw as avoidance of displeasure. Since he found the motives of wish-fulfillment and avoidance of displeasure closely connected to the sexual function and thereby to bodily functions, the goals described by him were ultimately derived from somatic impulses and instinctual needs. A biological goal-directedness was also the basis of Freud's dream psychology, since he considered preservation of sleep as the principle function of the dream.

In contrast to this hedonistic definition of the goals of psychic events, Jung stressed the importance of purely psychic motives, goals being regulated by certain tendencies toward value and meaning. What Jung understood by this was described in a passage elaborating Maeterlinck's concepts:

There is no doubt that the unconscious contains psychological combinations which do not reach the threshold of consciousness. Analysis dissolves these combinations back into their historical determinants. It works backwards, like the science of history. . . . History, however, knows nothing either of that which is hidden in the past or of that which is hidden in the future. . . . Thus, in so far as tomorrow is already contained in today, and all the threads of the future are already laid down, a deeper knowledge of the present might render possible a moderately far-sighted prognosis of the future. . . . Just as memories that have long since fallen below the threshold are still accessible to the unconscious, so also are certain very fine subliminal combinations that point forward, and these are of the greatest significance for future events in so far as the latter are conditioned by our psychology. But no more than the science of history bothers itself with future combinations of events, which are rather the object of political science, can the forward-pointing psychological combinations be the object of analysis; they would be much more the object of a refined psychological syntheticism that knew how to follow the natural currents of libido. This we cannot do, or only badly; but it happens easily enough in the unconscious, and it seems as if from time to time, under certain conditions, important fragments of this work come to light, at least in dreams, thus accounting for the prophetic significance of dreams long claimed by superstition.[15]

In the course of time, Jung came to prefer the term "finalistic" to describe the anticipating and prospective tendencies of the psyche in order to preclude any misunderstanding that they might be taken as tantamount to "prophetic." The new term was intended to indicate a psychic tendency, related solely to the goal and purpose of events.

It would, also, be a grave error to try to trace Jung's assumption of the finality and goal-directedness of the psyche to a "pre-existent fixation of a final end" or even to a "philosophical teleology." Jung has spoken out strongly against making such parallels, as shown in the following remark:

This is not to say that the final meaning, in the sense of an end given *a priori*, pre-existed in the preliminary stages of the phenomenon we are discussing. According to the theory of knowledge it is evidently not possible, from the indubitably final meaning of biological mechanisms, to deduce the pre-existent fixation of a final end. But while thus legitimately abandoning a teleological conclusion it would be weak-minded to sacrifice also the point of view of finality. All one can say is that things happen as if there were a fixed final aim. In psychology one ought to be as weary of believing absolutely in causality as of an absolute belief in teleology.[16]

Having demonstrated an immanent goal-directedness in the unconscious psyche, Jung gained a new approach to the understanding of the human psyche. It included highly productive possibilities for psychotherapy—possibilities which above all fostered adaptation to the inner man, facilitating a better understanding of one's self as well as achieving a realization of predispositions within the framework of the whole.

[15] *Symbols of Transformation*, pp. 50–51, n. 18 (also in 1911–12 edn.).
[16] "The Structure of the Unconscious" (1916), p. 295.

IV. THE PRIMORDIAL IMAGE

In his work on creative fantasy and impersonal complexes Jung had gained a new perspective: the primordial mind of man, which found expression in characteristic images. During the years 1908–10, when Jung encountered unconscious contents which stubbornly resisted integration into consciousness, his attention was drawn to the existence of nuclei of meaning situated at a deeper level. He saw that in back of everything that was important in the psyche there were archaic psychic nuclei, primordial images, which had not only a fascinating, but also a constellating effect upon consciousness. (Jung took the term "primordial image" from a letter of Jacob Burckhardt to his student Albert Brenner [1855, published in 1901] in which *Faust* and other "genuine myths" were designated as primordial images.)[1]

It might be worth mentioning at this point that in *Transformations and Symbols of the Libido* Jung replaced the expression "unconscious complex" by the technical term "imago." He was motivated by the wish to throw into relief the quality of a "living independence in the psychic hierarchy, i.e., . . . that autonomy which wide experience has shown to be the essential feature of feeling-toned complexes."[2] To be sure, in the revised edition *(Symbols of Transformation,* 1952), he emphasized that the term "imago" was insufficient, too, because it paid too little heed to the collective basis of all things psychic. In this connection Jung also stated that the concept of the archetype was more fertile, because it helped to stress the impersonal, collective aspects of certain contents which transcended individual experience.[3]

In the primordial image Jung was first of all impressed by the high degree of emotionality, which appeared to be beyond the subject's reach and was woven about by the secret of the *numinosum.* The inner images were seen not only as centers of great intensity of energy, but were also important as "a self-acting organism," affording "a *co-ordinating and coherent meaning.*"[4] To Jung they represented no less than the expression of a specific formative principle of life in general—an "image-creating mind"[5] inherent in the psyche (a term which came

---

1 Jung, *Symbols of Transformation* (1952), p. 32, n. 45 (in 1911–12 edn.).

2 *Psychology of the Unconscious (Transformations and Symbols of the Libido,* 1912), p. 492.

3 *Symbols of Transformation,* p. 44, n. 4.

4 *Psychological Types* (1912), pp. 447, 445.

5 "Psychological Commentary on the *Tibetan Book of the Great Liberation*" (1939), p. 490.

into use much later, 1939). Like the feeling-toned complex, the primordial image, too, referred to an individual constellation which included *feeling as well as intellectual idea*[6]—an insight which led Jung to further fundamental discoveries concerning the nature of psychic formations. It not only confirmed his earlier finding of "a *lower and a higher meaning*"[7] of everything psychic, but also corroborated his concept that the psychic event in general presents a tension of opposites between nature and mind. This idea was destined to elucidate the question of the origin of symbol formation and was to become one of the essential foundations of the theory of psychic energy.

The primordial images had, as noted earlier, their own *autonomy* and accordingly were detached from individual volition and, generally, from all personal traits. A striking fact is the undoubted relationship of the image to the "psychic situation as a whole."[8] The image therefore represented a concentrated expression of the individual's particular situation and his psychic contents, whether constellated by consciousness or the unconscious. Whatever was constellated at a given time was "the result of the spontaneous activity of the unconscious on the one hand and of the momentary conscious situation on the other, which always stimulates the activity of relevant subliminal material and at the same time inhibits the irrelevant."[9]

One of the deepest insights into the essence of primordial images was that they were exponents of the inner reality, namely of the psychic values "representing an inner reality which often far outweighs the importance of external reality."[10] What fascinated Jung above all was the fact that a kind of "subjective readiness" for inner experiences was demonstrated in the primordial image. In contrast to perception, which depended largely on the material of experience, the image indicated the subjective aspect of experience. It showed the manner in which the world was at all times reflected within the psyche.

Setting aside the effect of the primordial images on the deeper layers of the psyche and their kinship with archaeological formations as well as those related to the history of religion, Jung was deeply impressed by the typical basic figures which appeared within the recurrent motives. The psychotherapeutic experience revealed that archaic images could be detected in the dreams, symptoms, and fantasies of patients and presented a surprising constancy in the choice of motives. In addition, there was a constantly renewed projection of archaic motifs— for example, transferring the figure of the medicine man or magician

[6] "On the Psychology of the Unconscious" (1917), p. 119.
[7] *Psychology of the Unconscious*, p. 63.   [8] *Psychological Types*, p. 442.
[9] Ibid., p. 443.   [10] Ibid., p. 442.

to the physician. Such findings indicated the existence of impersonal factors within the psyche as well as primordial ideas which always repeated themselves in similar ways.

The various qualities of primordial images which Jung had established—repetitions, constancy, fascinating effect, and regularity—led him to assume that they were the dominants of the superpersonal psyche.

> The archetypes or dominants . . . are the ruling powers, the gods, images of the dominant laws and principles, and of typical, regularly occurring events in the soul's cycle of experience.[11]

Up to about 1921 Jung referred to the archaic image as "primordial image." From then on, he also used the term "archetype" or archetypal image—an expression which was adopted with increasing frequency. The term "archetype" appeared for the first time in "Instinct and the Unconscious" (1919).[12] In later years, Jung distinguished between archetypal image and "archetype." The latter he understood as indicating universal patterns of perception, while he restricted the term "archetypal images" to mean symbolic manifestations and the pictorial expression of the "archetype."

Although Jung used both terms synonymously for quite some time, noticeable differences in meaning began to appear. This brought about a constant expansion of the meaning of the psychic image. Originally, the concept of the primordial image grew out of the necessity to reflect the superpersonal and numinous aspects of some fantasy images as well as the way they conformed to well-known mythological motives. But with the term "archetype" a new psychic aspect—*karma* or destiny—was introduced into the field of psychological research.

> The reader will note the admixture here of a new element in the idea of the archetypes, not previously mentioned. This admixture is not a piece of unintentional obscurantism, but a deliberate extension of the archetype by means of the *karmic* factor, which is so very important in Indian philosophy. The *karma* aspect is essential to a deeper understanding of the nature of an archetype.[13]

This perspective of a new dimension had further implications: In the term "archetype" the emphasis was not only on the root (*arche* = beginning or primary cause) but also on the last syllable (*type* = im-

11 "On the Psychology of the Unconscious," p. 95.
12 See p. 133, editorial comment in n. 7.
13 "On the Psychology of the Unconscious," p. 77, n. 15.

print). Accordingly, the type could be conceived as "an imprinted effect" and also as the symbol of an as yet unknown meaning.

The religious point of view understands the imprint as the working of an imprinter; the scientific point of view understands it as the symbol of an unknown and incomprehensible content.[14]

In addition, the regularity and conformity to rules as well as the repetitive tendency of primordial images suggested that preformed structural elements and functional potentials existed, even preconscious categories which channeled thought and action into definite shapes. Furthermore, the selection of the new term perhaps originated from the presentiment of a *nonpsychic* factor in the background of the psyche, a realm inaccessible to experience (cf. App. II.2.a,d).

[14] *Psychology and Alchemy* (1944), p. 17.

V. THE ARCHETYPE AS STRUCTURAL ELEMENT
AND AS FORMATIVE PRINCIPLE

The phenomenon of the primordial image revealed the universal occurrence and the repetitive tendency of certain motives, but the glimpse of the archetypal background brought an essentially unconscious tendency of the psyche into view.[1] This unconscious trait was manifested not only as a preformed and innate factor but also as a functional disposition. These concepts, however, matured gradually. At first, Jung saw in the archetypal image, just as in the primordial image, "a typical basic form of certain ever-occurring psychic experiences."[2]

In his attempt to elaborate the general formal structure of the archetype, Jung was initially inspired by Plato. He understood the archetypal images as a kind of prefigurative potentiality for forming ideas, which drove a person's experience in a certain direction.

> They are ideas *ante rem*, determinants of form, a kind of pre-existent ground-plan that gives the stuff of experience a specific configuration, so that we may think of them, as Plato did, as *images*, as schemata, or as inherited functional possibilities which, nevertheless, exclude other possibilities or at any rate limit them to a very great extent.[3]

The assumption of prefigurative dispositions naturally led to the question of their possible hereditary transmission. Jung had no choice but to see in the archetypes or archetypal images inherited psychic structures which pointed to a definite physiological and anatomical predisposition.[4] The archetypes not only interacted constantly with environmental situations but also unfolded according to definite laws inherent in all living matter. What Jung had already recognized in 1921, he formulated twenty years later (1940) in a very graphic way:

> It is not the world as we know it that speaks out of his [the Australian aborigine's] unconscious, but the unknown world of the psyche, of which we know that it mirrors our empirical world only in part, and that, for the other part, it moulds this empirical world in accordance with its own psychic assumptions. The archetype does not proceed from physical facts; it describes how the psyche experiences the physical fact . . .[5]

[1] Jung, "The Psychology of the Child Archetype" (1940), p. 153.
[2] *Psychological Types* (1921), p. 444.   [3] Ibid., pp. 304–5.
[4] Ibid., p. 444.   [5] "Child Archetype," p. 154.

94

His research into mythology and his experience with patients having psychological and psychopathological problems made it increasingly more evident to Jung that the archetypes were "psychic forms which, like the instincts, are common to all mankind." Their numinous effect seemed to result from the fact that they represented "typical situations in life."[6] At about the same time (1935), Jung even ventured so far as to describe the archetypes as follows:

> The archetypes are, so to speak, organs of the prerational psyche. They are eternally inherited forms and ideas which have at first no specific content. Their specific content only appears in the course of the individual's life, when personal experience is taken up in precisely these forms.[7]

Because of the universal effect of the archetypes, Jung suspected that they might have a relationship to the "general similarity of brain structure." In other words, they seemed to be a repetition of "the precipitate of the psychic functioning of the whole ancestral line."[8] This analogy of a "universal function of the mind" to the modes of brain function brought Jung quite early (1921) to the recognition of factors in the archetypes which regulate psychic functioning. Subsequently, Jung again took up this idea and completed it in connection with his investigations of synchronicity. His last writings show a revival of his doubts of the earlier concept of a connection between archetype and brain structure. On the one hand, he expanded the hypothesis of a cerebral function by taking the sympathetic nervous system into account;[9] on the other hand, he questioned that the psychic experience might be tied to the biological substrate.[10] In spite of this, Jung still maintained that "the archetype is an element of our psychic structure and thus a vital and necessary component in our psychic economy."[11]

1. The Archetypal Image as Creative Center

Jung showed that the archetype was not only the focal point of ancient pathways but also the center from which new creative endeavors emanated. This discovery pointed to a drastic change and paved the way for a host of new discoveries. Because of its signal importance this decisive passage is quoted in its entirety:

[6] "Psychological Factors Determining Human Behaviour" (1936), p. 122.
[7] "Psychological Commentary on *The Tibetan Book of the Dead*" (1935), p. 518.
[8] *Psychological Types*, p. 400.
[9] "Synchronicity: An Acausal Connecting Principle" (1952), p. 510.
[10] Ibid., pp. 509–10.   [11] "Child Archetype," p. 160.

The archetype is a kind of readiness to produce over and over again the same or similar mythical ideas. Hence it seems as though what is impressed upon the unconscious were exclusively the sub-jective fantasy-ideas aroused by the physical process. We may there-fore assume that the archetypes are recurrent impressions made by subjective reactions. Naturally this assumption only pushes the problem further back without solving it. There is nothing to pre-vent us from assuming that certain archetypes exist even in animals, that they are grounded in the peculiarities of the living organism it-self and are therefore direct expressions of life whose nature cannot be further explained.[12]

The archetypes, then, being inherent in the life process, represented forces and tendencies which not only repeated experiences but also formed creative centers of numinous effect. The molding and reshap-ing character of the archetype, primarily manifested in the tendency toward creative metamorphosis of earlier imprints, stands out more and more in Jung's work. It took only a small step further to show the concept of the archetype as a primary model in the background of the psyche, which had its roots in the transcendental and nonpsychic realm (see App. II.1). For the time being, however, Jung still limited himself to the image aspect of the archetype, emphasizing its imper-sonal character, withdrawn from the arbitrary action of the ego.

2. Archetypal Image and Consciousness

Jung regarded the capacity of the archetypal image to stir and trans-form the conscious ego as one of its most significant qualities. To realize this aim, however, required the cooperation of the ego.

The archetypal images, originating in the collective unconscious, "the matrix of experience"[13] itself, represented, on the one hand, the self-manifestation of the unconscious and, on the other hand, a spon-taneous reaction of the psyche to a specific crisis in the individual's life or a collective threat due to the spirit of the time. The archetypal image had not only a constellating effect but was also itself highly con-stellated. In each instance it represented an inner opposite to the ego, which was prominently characterized by a challenge for self-reflection. Such a demand, however, called for a responding subject, namely the conscious ego-personality. The image was only the raw material which needed to be translated into the language of a specific era.

12 "On the Psychology of the Unconscious" (1917), p. 69.
13 "Analytical Psychology and Weltanschauung" (1927), p. 380.

Nevertheless, it would be a misunderstanding to suppose that the fantasy-images of the unconscious can be used directly, like a revelation. They are only the raw material, which, in order to acquire a meaning, has first to be translated into the language of the present.[14]

Without the response of the ego, without its active cooperation, no experience of the opposite and therefore no personality transformation was possible. Even Jung recognized that the individual's capacity to understand was an equally important prerequisite for a vital experience of the inner reality. This process depended on reciprocity: On the one hand, spontaneous effects emerged from the unconscious; on the other hand, shaping by the conscious psyche occurred. The experience of an image depended on "the harmony of the experiencing subject with the object experienced."[15]

Just as the archetypal modes of experience demanded shaping by the ego in order to approach the human sphere, so consciousness needed the depth of the psyche for creative thought. While the expansion of consciousness was tied to the creative opposite, contrariwise, the realization of the "self" was dependent on intellectually and morally integrating the potentialities of the image into consciousness. Only in such cooperation of conscious and unconscious factors did the individual experience the deepening of his vital feeling as well as his self-understanding.

The psychological understanding of the archetypal image as a creative center, from which formative effects go forth, opened new approaches to psychotherapy for Jung. The perspective of higher and impersonal elements in the psyche, as well as creative and balancing forces inside the person, was suited to expand the personalistic point of view. From this angle symptoms could be traced to the individual's life history by including the impersonal structural elements of the psyche. Jung thus gained a tool which effectively liberated the neurotic from his personal entanglements, rescued him from his isolation, and directed his gaze into the impersonal forces in life. This tool, to be sure, was productive and helpful only in the hands of one who had a subtle ability to discern between the contents which belonged to the personal psyche and those which had to be attributed to the impersonal.[16]

---

[14] Ibid.   [15] Ibid.
[16] "On the Psychology of the Unconscious," p. 93.

D. FROM THE UNCONSCIOUS DRIVE TO THE COLLECTIVE UNCONSCIOUS

D. FROM UNCONSCIOUS DRIVE TO COLLECTIVE UNCONSCIOUS

The empirical demonstration of a suprapersonal and spiritual dimension in the unconscious psyche was one of Jung's discoveries which increased the chasm between his psychological concepts and those of Freud. Both investigators were prominently empiricist in approach and made many similar observations; nevertheless, they pursued entirely different goals and methods in explaining, understanding, and interpreting unconscious material. Many attempts have been made to trace Jung's basic concept of the unconscious back to corresponding concepts of Freud. For example, some writers have tried to equate Freud's idea of the repressed with Jung's personal unconscious, or to parallel primal repression and "archaic inheritance" with the collective unconscious. To my mind all such attempts are lopsided. Upon closer examination, the corresponding concepts are so different and, above all, must be understood in such a dissimilar context that treating them alike is hardly justified. Their differences in forming ideas not only arose from a dissimilar choice of problems and goals but also from a basic divergence in the intellectual approach of the two psychologists. Freud, always absorbed with surface phenomena, was most interested in the neuroses, while Jung concentrated on the deeper understanding of all phases of psychic life.

Both investigators shared a common interest in attempting to break through the attitude of medical psychology, which at that time usually identified consciousness with psyche. Both fought for the acceptance of unconscious phenomena and, from their effects, aimed at drawing conclusions as to the nature of the psyche. The dynamic aspect, that is, the interplay between conscious and unconscious phenomena, was the particular focal interest of both. Freud's extraordinary achievement was the empirical demonstration of unconscious phenomena as meaningful and linked-up connections of memory traces, the interpretation of which, of course, had to be revealed by the psychoanalytic method. In contrast, Jung's research centered more and more on the discovery of non-representable dominants in the background of the psyche. His investigations encompassed a field which was destined to reach from the unconscious complex to the indiscernible basic forms of the psychoid-unconscious. He thus painted a picture of the unconscious psyche as he had dimly perceived it from his earliest years, namely, the image of something unknown and greater, which transcended consciousness in all directions.

I. FREUD'S CONCEPT OF CONSCIOUSNESS
AND THE UNCONSCIOUS

The conceptual grasp of Freud's basic ideas is complicated, as Rapaport[1] has stressed, because he repeatedly changed "the level of analysis." His concept of the unconscious developed in connection with his principal interest, which at all times was focused on the psyche of his patients. (Since Freud's concept of the unconscious developed gradually from his ideas of trauma and defense—discussed in earlier chapters—some repetitions are unavoidable.) Freud's first attempt to understand neurosis was based on the discovery of a psychological dynamism between traumatic experiences, on the one hand, and the censuring ego, on the other. Because these two poles were incompatible, he established the mechanism of defense. This process was characterized by the dissociation of the experience complex and was accompanied by displacement of the affect, the idea becoming unconscious, and it finally led to symptom formation. A group of ideas resulted, separated from the ego and presenting a nucleus[2] or point of crystallization. It was essential to Freud's hypothesis that an idea when rejected from consciousness could not return over the threshold of consciousness in spite of increased tension and intensity of excitation. The idea left a trace which was at once operative and yet unconscious. As a memory trace of trauma the repressed idea represented the basis of unconscious events (1896).

The Interpretation of Dreams already referred to a layer of contents relatively close to consciousness. This layer of the latent-unconscious had been mentioned earlier by Freud's predecessors. The latent-unconscious, according to Freud, incorporated those ideas which could temporarily disappear from consciousness but were essentially admissible to consciousness. This assumption he based on well-known experiences, such as the observation of an unexpected emergence of solutions to mathematical problems during sleep, the posthypnotic performance of suggested acts (Bernheim), and similar phenomena.

By distinguishing latent contents (admissible to consciousness) from repressed contents (inadmissible to consciousness), it was possible to make a parallel assumption of layering the psyche into the repressed-unconscious, the latent-unconscious (preconscious), and consciousness. This division was underlined by the fact that in each instance a censor-

---

[1] "The Structure of Psychoanalytic Theory: A Systematizing Attempt" (1959), p. 66.
[2] Breuer and Freud, *Studies on Hysteria* (1893–95), pp. 288ff.

ship existed which separated the different areas. As early as 1900 Freud wrote:

> Thus there are two kinds of unconscious, which have not yet been distinguished by psychologists. Both of them are unconscious in the sense used by psychology; but in our sense one of them, which we term the *Ucs.*, is also *inadmissible to consciousness*, while we term the other the *Pcs.* because its excitations—after observing certain rules, it is true, and perhaps only after passing a fresh censorship, though nonetheless without regard to the *Ucs.*—are able to reach consciousness.[3]

In contrast to the character of an idea, whether conscious or unconscious, Freud conceived the term unconscious as covering an entire system, "the single acts forming part of it [being] unconscious."[4] This definition was first formulated in 1912, but it had always guided his thinking.

A further attempt to comprehend the unconscious was also connected with *The Interpretation of Dreams*, in which Freud's point of view changed from exterior events to the inner psyche. Instead of beginning with traumatic excitations, his dream theory now started from repressed wish strivings in the background of the psyche. He was aided by his self-analysis, which led him back not only to infantile and sexual traits but also to the archaic component of dream life. His now-famous statement was:

> We find the child and the child's impulses still living on in the dream.[5]

Freud discovered that the dream held an extremely important key for understanding the unconscious: The laws governing the unconscious were essentially different from those of the preconscious. Two forms of processes governing psychic events were revealed: the primary and the secondary.[6] Freud recognized in them a difference in the operation of forces in the unconscious and in the preconscious, which became an essential part of his theory. Working from Breuer's theories (tense, intra-cerebral excitation, and relatively quiet excitation),[7] Freud established the opposition of "free-floating" and "tonically bound" states of excitation. While he saw only primary processes operating in the un-

[3] Freud, *The Interpretation of Dreams* (1900), pp. 614–15.
[4] "A Note on the Unconscious in Psycho-Analysis" (1912), p. 266.
[5] *Interpretation*, p. 191.
[6] "Project for a Scientific Psychology" (1895), *The Origins of Psycho-Analysis*, pp. 386–89. See also *Interpretation*, pp. 588–609.
[7] *Studies on Hysteria*, p. 194, n.

conscious which acted according to the pleasure principle, the conscious system, or more precisely the preconscious, was "tied up in structures,"[8] as Rapaport correctly observed. Freud was thinking of such things as systematic thought, controlled effects, goal-directed behavior, and logical reasoning as well as the reality principle. Basically the unrestrained, unconscious desires were placed in opposition to a well-developed system of inhibiting influences—a dualism which was also essential for understanding Freud's concept of the repressed. Inasmuch as Freud very early equated the unconscious processes with repressed memory traces, all his statements regarding the unconscious applied also to the repressed. Accordingly, the unconscious as well as the repressed idea was in a state of free-floating energy.

In the dualism of this dynamism Freud recognized a further law, which he described as the "mobility of cathexes."[9] He understood cathexis as the quantum of energy flowing to the memory traces. He was of the opinion that a change in cathetic energy took place each time during the transition of ideas from the preconscious to the unconscious and vice versa, that is, in the process of repression or in the release of the repressed. In the transition from the preconscious to the unconscious, he observed a withdrawal of preconscious cathexis, while with the lifting of the repressed and its entrance into the preconscious, the cathetic energy became structured and bound. These were not the only principles Freud established. He assumed, furthermore, a difference in the mode of binding cathexis to objects. While only thing-cathexes were present in the unconscious, they were accompanied in the preconscious by word-representations of objects.[10] Even though these deviations may seem unimportant at first glance, Freud recognized therein the criterion for differentiating between hysteria and schizophrenia: characteristically, in hysteria thing-cathexes predominated, while in schizophrenia word-representations were preponderant.[11] With such premises Freud was enabled to discriminate between the unconscious, that is, the repressed—as a psychic sphere subject to genuine, specific dynamics (free-floating)—and the preconscious with its specific qualities (thing-cathexes), its bound-down energy and word-representation.

The theory of sexuality[12] led Freud to discover a rich source of important data concerning the nature of the unconscious. After his hypothesis of childhood traumata as the cause of hysteria had collapsed, his physiological investigations and his self-analysis brought about the

8 Rapaport, p. 126.   9 "The Unconscious" (1915), p. 187.
10 Ibid., p. 202.   11 Ibid., p. 203.
12 "Three Essays on the Theory of Sexuality" (1905).

recognition of the significance of the sexual function in psychic life—an unexpected illumination. He saw that the sex drive was a power of extraordinary effectiveness which operated continuously from earliest childhood because of an endosomatic source of irritation, prior to any traumatic effects or scenes of seduction. The problem of drawing a boundary line between the psychic and the somatic was difficult. Freud resolved it at first by conceiving the instinct as "the psychical representative of an endosomatic, continuously flowing source of stimulation";[13] however, he constantly put greater emphasis on the biological aspect. The instincts accordingly were forces which represented "the somatic demands [i.e., of the body] upon the mind."[14] Starting with the sex theory, Freud built the psychology of the unconscious essentially on the basis of instinctual factors, particularly sexual drives: Drive impulse, craving, tension of needs, and satisfaction were the specific motor forces of psychic events. The ideas arising from these drives—instinct representatives—made up the nucleus of the unconscious.

Freud developed a parallel to this dynamic dualism by distinguishing two groups of drives: the ego-instinct, which served to preserve the individual, and the sexual drives, which aimed at continuing the species. Freud abandoned this concept for a short time, in 1914, and replaced it with a monistic system of the libido (sexual instinct), which comprised the object-libido as well as the ego-libido.[15] Six years later, he opposed the vital drive (eros) to the death drive, or destructive drive.[16] Thus, while his findings of destructive impulses in the unconscious were of great interest, he formulated them in a highly debatable way.

Up to the year 1923, Freud maintained the concept that the unconscious was correlated with the repressed.[17] To be sure, this did not preclude, in the course of time, his extending the area of unconscious ideas beyond the repressed in the narrow sense. His investigations of neuroses and dreams prompted him to consider the manifold derivatives of the repressed, which appeared not only in fantasies and dreams but also in substitute- and compromise-formations of neurotic symptoms. Above all, his basic concept of the unconscious changed, and he no longer saw it as a rudimentary organ, as something defunct, but rather as a viable entity capable of development.[18]

The most incisive change in Freud's concept of the psyche occurred

13 Ibid., p. 168.
14 "An Outline of Psycho-Analysis" (1938), p. 148.
15 "On Narcissism: An Introduction" (1914), p. 76.
16 "Beyond the Pleasure Principle" (1920), p. 53.
17 "Repression" (1915), p. 148.   18 "The Unconscious" (1915), p. 190.

in 1923, when he made the first attempt to arrive at an anthropological view of psychology. He saw himself "forced" not only to discontinue equating the repressed and the unconscious but to reconstruct entirely his concept of the unconscious. Instead of the unconscious, the concept of the "id" became increasingly more important.

With his anthropological psychology, particularly his formulation of ego psychology, Freud made a decisive advance into general psychology. Although he had demonstrated earlier the productivity of psychoanalysis in ethnology, literary criticism, mythology, etc., his statements had always been derived from his experiences in psychopathology. In "The Ego and the Id"[19] Freud for the first time took the point of view of the totality of the individual and, breaking through the hitherto prevailing personalistic approach, began to see human beings from a wider and higher perspective. Not only the interplay between the three agencies—ego, superego, and id—drew his major interest, but also the view of a deep layer in the human psyche which transcended everything personal. In the id Freud recognized an area which was more encompassing than the unconscious, and which also contained drives which did not need to be repressed. Everything which he had formerly assumed to be characteristic of the unconscious was equally valid for the id. But beyond that, the id opened a vista of the impersonal phylogenetic background of the psyche. Fundamentally, it represented the "dark, inaccessible part of our personality."[20] Because of this inherent inaccessibility, Freud saw the id as an area which, on the one hand, was open to somatic influences and from it "is filled with energy"[21] but, on the other hand, acted as the bearer of a secret which had been lost in the dark and unfathomable backwater of the phylogenetic or archaic inheritance of ancestors. As in biology, Freud connected the drives with tendencies inherent in life itself, which might be constructive as well as harmful, and might even have a destructive-aggressive character.

The perspective of the phylogenetic background deepened the basic concepts of Freud's psychology. The id was considered important not only as the fountainhead of the drives which constellate all destiny, but also as the origin of the formations of ego and superego. Freud designated the id "as the great reservoir of libido"[22] which preserved all the residues of earlier ego-configurations, of religious, moral, and even social attitudes. His impulse to substitute the term "id" where "unconscious" had formerly been used came from the discovery that the

19 "The Ego and the Id" (1923), pp. 15–17.
20 "New Introductory Lectures on Psycho-Analysis" (1933), p. 73.
21 Ibid.   22 "Ego and Id," p. 30, n. 1.

superego contained an unconscious part of the ego which had not been repressed. The superego, although not repressed, was, however, the cause of all repression activity. Equating the unconscious and the repressed was decidedly no longer possible.

> We recognize that the *Ucs.* does not coincide with the repressed; it is still true that all that is repressed is *Ucs.*, but not all that is *Ucs.* is repressed. A part of the ego, too—and Heaven knows how important a part—may be *Ucs.*, undoubtedly is *Ucs.*[23]

The superego, that unconscious part of the ego, in the first place, seemed important to Freud because essential functions of the individual—such as the stirrings of conscience, striving for improvement, or the emergence of guilt feelings—originated in the unconscious or operated out of the unconscious. While investigating narcissism, Freud had encountered the "ideal,"[24] which embodied unconscious longing to realize the paternal guiding image. In turn, he recognized in the superego the moral resistance against infantile sexual desires, produced by introjection of paternal prohibitions.

With the conception of the superego Freud took a decisive step from, almost exclusively, considering the libidinous object, to an appraisal of the subject. In the first place, he connected this inner agency with the qualities of the categorical imperative, the demands of morality *per se*, and the striving for perfection.[25] Moreover, he went even further. The question of the phylogenetic deep layer of the psyche paralleled the problem of general morality standards and the authority imposing them. Such ideas, in principle, put Freud beyond the confines of a prevalently personalistic point of view.

The psychology of the superego developed hand-in-hand with an increasing darkening in Freud's view of the world. This outlook was related to his connecting this agency with the aggressive drives. Just as, in working on the psychology of instincts, he pursued the drives up to the destructive aspect of the repetition compulsion, his ego-psychology developed to the point where the superego evoked the appearance of a demonically inexorable authority, inimical to life. In applying this concept to the criticism of civilization, it ultimately culminated in the principle of renunciation of instinctual wishes. Although Freud saw the superego mainly as an aggressive and self-destructive power which in its role of introjecting parental authority included all the aggression accumulated since the days of the first progenitor, he should neverthe-

23 Ibid., p. 18.   24 "On Narcissism," p. 93.
25 "New Lectures," p. 61.

less be given extraordinary credit for filling the gap in his psychology with an understanding of moral values.

While the plan of this book is limited principally to the basic aspects of the unconscious, it may serve to make a more coherent presentation by touching briefly on the psychology of the conscious system of the psyche.

Together with the discovery of the unconscious part of the ego went a clearer understanding of the (pre)conscious part, the so-called reality-ego. Freud earlier conceded to the ego the tasks of the reality principle, of control and repression. This hypothesis was further confirmed by the discovery of the roots of the ego in the deep layers of the id. Freud determined that the (pre)conscious ego "is that part of the id which has been modified by the direct influence of the external world"[26] and has become an organizing center. Freud more and more saw the superego as the agency which put an obstacle in the way of the wish-fulfillment urge of the drives and protected the individual from the threatening perils of the id. After Freud had allotted the moral function to the superego and separated it from the total ego, the ego in the narrower sense retained the vital functions of reality testing and of protecting the individual from the dangers lurking both inside and out. Since the ego was also assigned the agencies of thinking, reasoning, and prudence,[27] this made it "a poor creature owing service to three masters," protecting the individual "from the external world, from the libido of the id, and from the severity of the superego."[28] Thus, the ego was confined and oppressed to such a degree that it also became "the actual seat of anxiety."[29]

Freud distinguished three types of anxiety, corresponding to the service to "three masters": realistic anxiety in the face of a threatening external danger, neurotic anxiety due to the excessive demands of the libido (fear of castration, fear of loss of love)[30] and, finally, moral anxiety, caused by the exactions of the superego which entangle the individual in reproach and guilt-feelings. Freud recognized anxiety as a means of protection, "as a signal announcing a situation of danger."[31]

In summary, Freud wrote about the ego in 1923, as follows:

It is entrusted with important functions. By virtue of its relation to the perceptual system it gives mental processes an order in time and submits them to "reality-testing." By interposing the processes of thinking, it secures a postponement of motor discharges and controls

26 "Ego and Id," p. 25.   27 Ibid., p. 26.
28 Ibid., p. 56.   29 Ibid., p. 57.
30 "New Lectures," p. 88.   31 Ibid., p. 85.

the access to motility. . . . All the experiences of life that originate from without enrich the ego; the id, however, is its second external world, which it strives to bring into subjection to itself. It withdraws libido from the id and transforms the object-cathexes of the id into ego-structures. With the aid of the superego, in a manner that is still obscure to us, it draws upon the experiences of past ages stored in the id.[32]

In the area of psychotherapy, Freud assigned an increasingly major importance to the ego, chiefly in the adjustment to reality and control of the drives. He expressed this in the remarkably concise sentence "Where id was, there ego shall be."[33]

In contrast, the role of consciousness remained shadow-like. From the beginning to the end of his work he maintained his position of reducing consciousness to a mere process of observation—both of internal and external events. In addition, he conceived this "superficial part of the psychic apparatus"—as he had already pointed out in *The Origins of Psycho-Analysis*—as a "highly fugitive state," which does "not leave behind any permanent change . . . but expire(s), as it were, in the phenomenon of becoming conscious."[34] He even went so far as to assert that consciousness and memory were on the whole "mutually exclusive"; in other words, there was a complementary relationship between consciousness and traces of excitation.[35] In the process of perception the memory trace was supposed to have slipped into the preconscious and only from there became accessible to ego and consciousness. Apparently, this conclusion meant only that the function of becoming conscious was in fact dependent on the preconscious and reserved for the preconscious ego. From this, Freud derived the premise that bringing to consciousness was the same as bringing to preconscious awareness!

The question, "How does a thing become conscious?" would thus be more advantageously stated: "How does a thing become preconscious?" And the answer would be: "Through becoming connected with the word-presentations corresponding to it."[36]

It would, however, be rash to conclude that Freud devalued the function of consciousness simply because he traced the process of becoming conscious to the word-representations in the preconscious. Everything depended on how he understood the term "word-represen-

32 "Ego and Id," p. 55.   33 "New Lectures," p. 80.
34 "Beyond the Pleasure Principle," p. 25.
35 *The Interpretation of Dreams*, p. 615.   36 "Ego and Id," p. 20.

tations." It is indeed surprising that, owing to their "association with residues of speech,"[37] Freud ultimately deduced a relationship to the residues of perception and, consequently, to consciousness. Word-representations were nothing less than "residues . . . from auditory perceptions."[38] Truly, a vicious circle! At any rate, it follows from all of this that the ego could not bring anything to consciousness which had not at an earlier time been conscious.

> . . . only something which has once been a Cs. perception can become conscious, and . . . anything arising from within (apart from feelings) that seeks to become conscious must try to transform itself into external perceptions: this becomes possible by means of memory-traces.[39]

This statement, which is one of the most problematical that Freud made about the relationship of the two systems, amounts to an outright admission that everything that can be known is derived from the perceptual world and its mnemonic traces.

> It is like a demonstration of the theorem that all knowledge has its origin in external perception.[40]

Freud's absolute commitment to the psychology of consciousness became intensified during the following years until in 1927 he wrote an unequivocal glorification of the intellect, the logos:

> We may insist as often as we like that man's intellect is powerless in comparison with his instinctual life, and we may be right in this. Nevertheless, there is something peculiar about this weakness. The voice of the intellect is a soft one, but it does not rest till it has gained a hearing. Finally, after a countless succession of rebuffs, it succeeds.[41]

Even though Freud continued to maintain that the psyche was more comprehensive than consciousness, he saw the latter ever more surely as the only light which illuminated the darkness of the psyche.

But none of this implies that the quality of being conscious has lost its importance for us. It remains the one light which illuminates our path and leads us through the darkness of mental life. In conse-

---

[37] "An Outline of Psycho-Analysis," p. 199.
[38] "Ego and Id," p. 20.   [39] Ibid.
[40] Ibid., p. 23.
[41] "The Future of an Illusion" (1927), p. 53.

quence of the special character of our discoveries, our scientific work in psychology will consist in translating unconscious processes into conscious ones, and thus filling in the gaps in conscious perception.[42]

One might justly ask which was Freud's greater object of love: the whirling passions of the id, or consciousness?

[42] "Some Elementary Lessons in Psycho-Analysis" (1938), p. 286.

II. CONSCIOUSNESS AND THE UNCONSCIOUS
IN JUNG'S PSYCHOLOGY

1. The Totality of Consciousness and the Unconscious

Freud did not give attention to the structure of the personality until he made an attempt at anthropological psychology in 1923. In contrast, Jung started very early to work on the totality of conscious and unconscious processes. He used the terms "unity" and "totality" or "wholeness" for the first time in 1913,[1] and he understood this "total reaction"[2] as a developmental process which comprised all aspects of the human personality. From then on, he was consistently occupied with the idea of a "total personality." The concept of "the personality as a whole"[3] seemed to be indispensable to him. Because this totality essentially included conscious as well as unconscious contents, everything depended on establishing a productive relationship between the ego and the unconscious. Such a relationship promoted the creative powers of the psyche and the understanding of its formations, and particularly, facilitated the ego and the unconscious to come to terms; this culminated in the "confrontation of the two positions [which] generates . . . a third thing . . . the transcendent function."[4] The mediation of the opposites of conscious and unconscious was the prerequisite for "individuation," that "process of differentiation having for its goal the development of the individual personality."[5] This always included the complementation of the ego-personality by the counterfunction, "the greater personality"—a process which Jung later exalted in the concept of self-realization (1928).[6]

Conscious and unconscious, therefore, were not necessarily in a conflicting opposition, which was largely the case with Freud's view until the third decade of the century. While the attitude of "defense" played a part in Jung's psychology—for example, in suppression of unconscious impulses and complexes by the ego—he put much more emphasis on an attitude open toward the interplay between consciousness and the unconscious.

Conscious and unconscious do not make a whole when one of them is suppressed and injured by the other. . . . Both are aspects of life.

---

1 Jung, "General Aspects of Psychoanalysis" (1913), p. 241.
2 "The Transcendent Function" (1916), p. 89.
3 Ibid., p. 88.   4 Ibid., p. 90.
5 *Psychological Types* (1921), p. 448.
6 "The Relations Between the Ego and the Unconscious" (1916/1928), p. 136.

Consciousness should defend its reason and protect itself, and the chaotic life of the unconscious should be given the chance of having its way too—as much of it as we can stand. This means open conflict and open collaboration at once.[7]

The basic anthropological assumption of a *total personality*, in spite of verging on the outer limits of comprehension, was extremely important for the understanding of psychology. It included an attitude which enabled the individual to guard against overestimating either the ego or the unconscious. In his youth, Jung had put greater stress on the necessity of a psychology of the unconscious than a psychology of consciousness, which was at that time the fashion; yet later, he just as strongly opposed the romantic overevaluation of everything creative, prophetic, and eternal in the background of the psyche in order to uphold the point of view of the ego.

This review makes it evident that Jung did not equate the psychic totality either with the ego or with the unconscious, but always considered it as encompassing both. In the following sections all references to the ego or to the unconscious should be understood in the sense that they form merely parts of a whole, which is governed by the principle of self-regulation.

2. *Ego and Consciousness*

This principle applied particularly to the ego, which in spite of its frequent overevaluation, formed only one complex—albeit a very important one—of the human personality.

The ego is a complex that does not comprise the total human being. . . . The ego can therefore be only a fragmentary complex. Is it perhaps that peculiar complex whose inner cohesion amounts to consciousness?[8]

As a psychic complex the ego presented a feeling-tone as well as a stable nucleus, which Jung pointed out as early as 1907.[9] The feeling-tone was kept alive by the presence of the biological substrate and also by the constant background of memories and sensations; the nucleus of the complex presented a "virtual focusing-point," characterized both by its own identity and by a high degree of continuity. Like Freud, Jung attributed to the ego the power of self-preservation, protecting

7 "Conscious, Unconscious, and Individuation" (1939), p. 288.
8 "Spirit and Life" (1926), p. 324.
9 "The Psychology of Dementia Praecox" (1907), p. 40.

the individual against assaults from without and within, but he did not see it as the seat of anxiety nor as a signaling apparatus.

Jung's idea of the ego differed completely from Freud's concept due to its unique connection with consciousness. Jung recognized in the ego the point of reference of all conscious actions. In this quality he saw a further confirmation of the structure of the ego as a complex, inasmuch as the ego also exerted an attracting and assimilating effect on ideas; consequently, the ego was not only the center of the field of consciousness, but also "the subject of all conscious actions of the individual."

> By ego I understand a complex of ideas which constitutes the centre of my field of consciousness and appears to possess a high degree of continuity and identity.[10]

In sharp contrast to Freud, who recognized in the superego an unconscious part of the ego, Jung had always maintained that "consciousness . . . seems to be the necessary precondition for the ego";[11] however, the converse of this statement—that is, that "without the ego, consciousness is unthinkable"[12]—is not equally valid. Only through consciousness did the ego possess that quality which always stimulated the comparison with the luminous body of the sun. With this faculty the ego became the specific opposite of the unconscious, the agency which was able to decide conflicts and *assume decisions and responsibilities.*

Even though the personality's highest degree of brightness was reflected in the ego, the quality of consciousness was not equivalent to that of the personality as a whole. Also, certain structures in the unconscious, split-off complexes or unconscious fragments, personifications in dreams, etc., were able to assume characteristics of personality. But in contrast to the assumptions of the French psychopathologists, Jung could hardly attribute to these structures the quality of an ego.[13] In distinction from the ego, they were "masklike, wraithlike, without problems, lacking self-reflection, with no conflicts, no doubts, no sufferings."[14] As Jung admitted in later years, these structures might at best be ego-like centers, because, in spite of a certain degree of brightness, they lacked the qualities of continuity and self-determined reproducibility.

10 *Psychological Types*, p. 425.   11 "Spirit and Life," p. 323.
12 Ibid.
13 "A Review of the Complex Theory" (1934), p. 97.
14 "Consciousness, Unconscious, and Individuation," p. 286.

In the same way, Jung did not attribute to the dream-ego the characteristics of the ego when awake.

> In a dream, consciousness is not completely extinguished; there is always a small remnant left. In most dreams, for instance, there is still some consciousness of the ego, although it is a very limited and curiously distorted ego known as the dream-ego. It is a mere fragment or shadow of the waking ego. . . . The difference between psychic activity in the waking and in the sleeping state seems, therefore, to be an important one.[15]

Jung, accordingly, conceived of the dream-ego as the archetypical prerequisite of the conscious ego, never as equivalent with it.

It now becomes clear that Jung's ideas of the ego as a "center which is conscious of something" neither coincided with Freud's (pre)conscious ego nor with his superego. Regarding the preconscious ego, it remained unclear how the ego was able to carry out the functions of adaptation to reality or thinking without being bestowed with consciousness; in the case of the superego, it was extremely questionable how, as an essentially unconscious agency, it could fulfill the functions which Freud ascribed to it. What Freud attributed to the superego appeared to Jung much more like the image of a representative of the collective consciousness, of the "conventional morality, the creation of curmudgeonly *praeceptores mundi*."[16]

As opposed to Freud's assumption of a basically unconscious origin of the superego (by introjection of moral rules and paternal authority), Jung saw in the superego a conscious acquisition which largely coincided with the moral code, passed on mainly by education, even though in some particular case it might sink back into the unconscious. When the individual was completely unconscious as far as intellectual and moral prerequisites were concerned, even the psychic image of God could be reduced to the superego! The superego then became an agency with absolute binding force, overshadowing the relationship to the individual's inner being.

One of the latest statements of Jung was made in 1958:

> The superego is a patriarchal legacy which, as such, is a conscious acquisition and an equally conscious possession. . . . To that extent it is identical with what we call the "moral code." The only peculiar thing about it is that one or the other aspect of the moral tradition proves unconscious in the individual case.[17]

15 "The Psychological Foundations of Belief in Spirits" (1920), p. 306.
16 "Sigmund Freud in His Historical Setting" (1932), p. 35.
17 "A Psychological View of Conscience" (1958), pp. 439-40.

What Jung missed in the concept of the superego was the presence of an intellectual, suprapersonal authority to challenge the individual. Conscience, according to Freud, was an indisputable force, imposed by moral law, which recognized man as an ethical being only so far as he is conditioned by the moral demands of contemporary civilization. As Jung understood, Freud did not recognize moral feelings which were warranted by the deeper structures of the unconscious, such as the archetypal ideas and numinous images, particularly the image of God.

Jung's all-inclusive point of view also became evident in his concept of the origin of the ego. He saw the ego as the result of a developmental process in which the individual gradually grew from a state of complete dependence on the background of the psyche to firmness, constancy, and continuity. For him, this process was the expression of something greater in the individual which tended to concentrate the initially uncentered realm of the psyche into a virtual focusing-point. He saw the ego as an unfathomable mystery encompassing the greatest darkness—even though it seemed to be the most familiar. On the one hand, the ego was felt to be the area of a (relative) freedom from the unconscious, the site of deciding conflicting situations, but, on the other hand, it was an outgrowth of the "darkness of the psyche."[18] Jung even went so far as to see in the ego "a relatively constant personification of the unconscious itself."[19] He expressed this idea further by ascribing to the ego the role of an opponent of the self. It might be that the ego not only was subordinated to the self (in a relationship of *patiens* to *agens*), not only was cooperative, but also soared above the greater agency, conjuring up the danger of hybris. Jung expressed this paradox in the striking statement: "In reality both are always present: the supremacy of the self and the hybris of consciousness."[20]

Thus, the psychic destiny of the individual depended largely on the exact relationship of the ego to the self. It was quite as possible to come to a standstill and be overwhelmed as to change and transform the individual. These insights resulted from viewing the personality as a totality.

Although Jung asserted that consciousness is the most essential quality of the ego, it might be worthwhile to consider the typical characteristics of consciousness apart from and independent of the ego. In general, Jung understood the term "conscious" as indicating the presence of a certain brightness of psychic processes signified by expressions like "conscious motivations" or "conscious intentions."

[18] *Mysterium Coniunctionis* (1955), p. 108.
[19] Ibid., p. 107.
[20] "Transformation Symbolism in the Mass" (1940/1941), 1958, pp. 259–60.

Except for occasional side remarks, in which he conceived consciousness in a spatial sense and spoke of something "above" or "below" consciousness, Jung saw consciousness as primarily characterized by the qualities of lighting up or illuminating—qualities founded on the capacity to discriminate.

> ... the whole essence of consciousness is *discrimination*, distinguishing ego from non-ego, subject from object, positive from negative, and so forth. The separation into pairs of opposites is entirely due to conscious differentiation; only consciousness can recognize the suitable and distinguish it from the unsuitable and worthless. . . . But, where no consciousness exists, where purely unconscious instinctive life still prevails, there is no reflection, no *pro et contra*, no disunion, nothing but simple happening, self-regulating instinctivity, living proportion.[21]

The development of consciousness, the ability to discriminate ego and non-ego and, generally, the separation of opposites were values which could wrench man out of his primitive state and bestow on him the special dignity of a human being. Neither psychotherapy nor education could dispense with them. The patient could only achieve a distance from his symptoms through his ability to discriminate; not only that, but his development of new potential values was tied to recognizing unconscious strivings. Furthermore, Jung realized that the deeper meaning of becoming conscious became apparent only when some light was thrown on the goals immanent in life. Bringing to consciousness tendencies inherent in the background of life took the place of bringing into preconsciousness the data which had formerly been conscious, as proposed by Freud. Becoming conscious was a creative process which opened up new possibilities and could never be limited to the reproduction of perceptions of the world around us or to memory traces.

From earliest times the creative significance of the process of becoming conscious was the subject of heroic myths. Always in some novel manner they describe the hero's fight against the powers of darkness which threaten to annihilate him. He is a human being equipped with supernatural strength ("endowed with more than mere human qualities"), who is driven by the desire for psychic rebirth to attempt the hazardous venture, to conquer the fatal pull of the unconscious which confronts him in the guise of the paralyzing and poisonous power of the mother. By liberating himself from the dangerous ties to the parents, he gains the precious thing which is so difficult to attain,

21 *Psychological Types*, p. 112.

that is, the secret of a new life and of a new light. This is what Jung had described earlier in *Transformations and Symbols of the Libido* as winning a new life and the "food of immortality."[22]

> His [the hero's] ascent signifies a renewal of the light and hence a rebirth of consciousness from the darkness, i.e., from regression to the unconscious.[23]

3. The Unconscious

When we turn to the concept of the unconscious in Jung's psychology, we find three epochs—just as in Freud's development. Jung's first phase was connected with the opposition of personal and impersonal memory traces; the second phase was founded on the recognition of archetypal dominants as the structural elements of the background of the psyche. Because of this Jung was able to distinguish the personal and the collective unconscious, a finding which was extremely important for understanding his psychology. Finally, a third phase led to the discovery of the archetype-as-such. Under this term Jung understood a structural framework which culminated in the idea of a basic form of the unconscious psyche which was non-representable, that is, psychoid. Since this last phase occurred during the period after Freud's death, it will be evaluated in the Appendix.

A. THE PERSONAL UNCONSCIOUS

In his early work dealing with the unconscious background of the psyche, Jung was guided to a large degree by the prevailing concepts of his time. In the first place, he clarified his position toward the findings of the French psychopathologists. Like Janet and Freud, he studied the phenomena of hysteria and somnambulism in order to find his own solution. From his doctoral thesis, it became evident that he faced the unconscious psyche not only in the form of various automatisms—hyperesthesia, hypermnesia, hallucination, and fantasy—but also in the shape of split personalities, double personalities, or separate personalities. From these observations Jung gained the decisive insight that the unconscious psyche was capable of heightened performance during sleeping or somnambulistic states. In other words, he felt it necessary to propose the hypothesis of "unconscious heightened performance."[24]

---

[22] *Psychology of the Unconscious* (*Transformations and Symbols of the Libido*, 1912), p. 185.

[23] *Symbols of Transformation* (1952), p. 359 (also in 1911–12 edn.).

[24] "On the Psychology and Pathology of So-Called Occult Phenomena" (1902), p. 87. (Also see B.III.2.b.)

D. FROM UNCONSCIOUS DRIVE TO COLLECTIVE UNCONSCIOUS

Jung's concept that a form of "higher intelligence," an intellectual principle, was active in the unconscious, was his first divergence from Freud, who (in 1895) had denied unconscious "intelligence."[25] Equally original was Jung's conjecture that the coherence of unconscious events depended on a superimposed, unconscious unifying factor. It would not be amiss to read into such statements the insignificant-looking birth of his later recognition of the self and its regulating activity. Even though (under the strong impact of Freud's personality) Jung did not follow up his early intuitions, still, they remained as guideposts for his later work.

In his *Studies in Word-Association*, which in part confirmed Freud's theories, the concept of the feeling-toned complex was the principal source of fundamental insights into the character of the unconscious. Jung used it to demonstrate that not only objective factors, independent of consciousness, were present, but also that they represented centers of great emotional significance. Observation of the complexes drew Jung's attention to higher units in the unconscious psyche, always characterized by a dynamic and a content aspect. Twenty years later, this assumption led to the recognition of a connection between instinct and archetype. In his investigations of the complex—at least those dealing with acute complexes due to the affect of fright—Jung found a confirmation of Freud's hypothesis of repression, that is, the dissociation of intensive affects from consciousness (cf. B.III.2).

Unquestionably, until 1910 the focus of Jung's interest was on the investigation of the patient's complex-connected personal memories of his life history, as they had been imprinted since childhood upon the unconscious psyche. A turning point occurred with his study of the fantasies of psychotics. In their archaic fantasy and dream formations Jung recognized not only the quality of autonomy and the potential for creative new formations within the unconscious psyche, but also the presence of deeper meaning, for the most part beyond the confines of consciousness. However, these findings left intact his observation that the permanent storehouse of the unconscious contained forgotten contents which had remained unnoticed as well as those which had not yet been perceived and were incompatible with consciousness. In addition, Jung identified impressions in the background of the psyche which were not yet capable of being perceived because their energy was too feeble to reach consciousness. In such cases, the contents usually had only begun to take shape and to become distinct in the unconscious psyche, while the conscious personality had not been able to

25 *Studies on Hysteria* (1893–95), p. 292.

bridge the gap through associations. Hence, they remained relatively inaccessible to consciousness in spite of their potential significance. This discovery, which was a substantial supplement to Freud's hypothesis of repression, led Jung to recognize a very important premise for his psychology—that there are two groups of contents in the personal unconscious: on the one hand, contents which at some time had been conscious, but now were subliminal or repressed; on the other hand, contents which because of the absence of conscious understanding could not yet be perceived, even though, in principle, they were capable of being perceived. The phenomena of the first group were relatively similar to contents of consciousness, but those of the second group appeared rather strange and unknown. As early as 1917, Jung had attempted to distinguish between personal memories and the "manifestations of a deeper layer of the unconscious where the primordial images common to all humanity lie sleeping."[26] However, only in 1919 do we find his first description of the personal unconscious:

> The personal unconscious . . . includes all those psychic contents which have been forgotten during the course of the individual's life. Traces of them are still preserved in the unconscious, even if all conscious memory of them has been lost. In addition, it contains all subliminal impressions or perceptions which have too little energy to reach consciousness. To these we must add unconscious combinations of ideas that are still too feeble and too indistinct to cross over the threshold. Finally, the personal unconscious contains all psychic contents that are incompatible with the conscious attitude. This comprises a whole group of contents . . .[27]

How does Jung's concept of the personal unconscious compare with Freud's idea of the unconscious? We must remember that, as early as the turn of the century, Freud distinguished between the purely descriptive concept of the latent unconscious, which is separated from consciousness only by an insignificant censor, and the so-called dynamic unconscious, that is, the repressed contents. It can readily be seen that the latent unconscious largely coincided with the "fringe of consciousness" (see App. II.2.d), which is close to consciousness, and, at the same time, with the chiaroscuro of the fringe phenomena of consciousness—an idea which Jung had borrowed from William James. On the other hand, only with great reservations can the repressed unconscious be considered as equivalent to the corresponding contents of Jung's

[26] Jung, "On the Psychology of the Unconscious" (1917), p. 65.
[27] "Belief in Spirits" (1920), p. 310.

personal unconscious. The repressed in Freud's and in Jung's psychology conformed only in part, as we have already mentioned, since as far as Freud was concerned, the unconscious constituted an essentially different agency than the (pre)conscious. It obeyed other laws (free-floating energy, mobility of cathexis, mechanisms of dissociation between affect and idea) as well as different motives (pleasure vs. displeasure principle). In contrast, Jung could not see a basic difference between the two spheres of consciousness and the personal unconscious, that is, the repressed. Granted that the contents of the personal unconscious were only relatively reproducible and correctible and the unconscious structures (complexes and personality fragments) had no ego nucleus and were at best similar to the ego, still, these differences were never so great as to force Jung to maintain an essential incompatibility of the two spheres. (In passing it should be mentioned that Glover's distinctions were partly incorrect, partly confused.)[28] Above all, such an assumption was militated against by the fact that unconscious data, from the point of view of content, could in no way be demarcated from conscious material. Both spheres—consciousness as well as the personal unconscious—presented feelings, images, ideas, and thoughts.

A study of the theory of repression as developed by Freud should make it abundantly clear that Jung's repeated statement reducing Freud's repressed-unconscious to nothing other than "a subliminal appendix to the conscious mind"[29] did not do justice to the theoretical concepts of Freud. Jung's remark that the unconscious as described by Freud represented "nothing but the gathering place of forgotten and repressed contents"[30] likewise was not quite fair to Freud's basic concept. Not only the superego, which was unconscious but not repressed, but primal repression as well clashed with Jung's assumption. Primal repression seemed to outline an area of variability in primary affects, which had taken place in earliest childhood prior to the formation of the ego and, therefore, had not been conscious at any time. If I understand Freud correctly, the material of primal repression was on principle inadmissible to consciousness, even though it was constantly on the verge of manifesting itself in attacks of anxiety or in affective repetition compulsion; on the other hand, its fundamental power to attract consciousness favored secondary repression. These statements show that without any doubt the unconscious as understood by Freud could not always be traced back to contents which at one

28 Glover, *Freud or Jung* (1950), pp. 24–25.
29 Jung, "On the Nature of the Psyche" (1946), p. 179.
30 "Archetypes of the Collective Unconscious" (1934/1954), p. 3.

time had been conscious but were subsequently repressed. Primal repression also could not in every instance be coordinated with the personal unconscious. Just as primal repression could not be ascribed to the personal unconscious, it was not possible to attribute it to the collective unconscious. In that respect it lacked creative qualities as well as traits of the archetypes.

In later life Jung came to see the unconscious as an agency which differed from consciousness. This seeming contradiction to his earlier statements might be only the consequence of his placing the dividing line between the two agencies deeper than before (that is, between consciousness and the collective unconscious), while at the same time, accentuating their differences in content. Jung continued to grow more aware that the collective unconscious was a deep layer of the psychic background which was only quasi-psychic and could not be represented; thus, in the final analysis, it was incapable of becoming conscious. For this part of the background of the psyche Jung used the term psychoid-unconscious (see App. II.2.d). He conceived of it as so essentially different from the personal unconscious—and still more at odds with consciousness—that the two entities had hardly anything in common. In fact, they differed from each other as much as the psyche from the non-psyche.

B. THE COLLECTIVE UNCONSCIOUS

In the course of his investigations Jung became more and more convinced that the unconscious basis of the psyche was anything but an *affaire scandaleuse* or "mud from the depths," but rather something greater, transcending the individual, able to intervene autonomously in psychic events. As a result of his studies on the psychology of religion and mythology, Jung could not be satisfied with limiting unconscious motivation to infantile, sexual, or merely personal drives. Likewise, he could not agree with reducing unconscious motives to wish and wish-fulfillment. It was primarily his work on primordial images (see C.IV),[30a] and his observation of their often overpowering numinosity and suprapersonal meaning which led Jung to discover the particular life of the psyche. Through this discovery it became obvious that individual consciousness was not without predetermining factors—as had often been assumed—but, on the contrary, was directed by significant powers within the psyche. These predetermining factors he found in the idea of the collective unconscious.

Jung had already taken such factors into consideration in *Transformations and Symbols of the Libido*, even though the collective un-

30a In *The Freud/Jung Letters*, see Jung's letter to Freud of 29 July 13.

conscious was at first only a dim concept, and no definite term for it had as yet been established. A number of statements in this book pointed to collective factors; one was the finding that the unconscious contained "remnants of the undifferentiated archaic psyche,"[31] and another was the recognition that "the unconscious . . . is universal: it not only binds individuals together into a nation or race, but unites them with the men of the past and with their psychology."[32] Unlike Freud, to whom the unconscious consisted essentially of repressed infantile sexual wishes,[33] Jung saw in it also "a collective psychic disposition, creative in character."[34] The term "collective unconscious" appeared for the first time in 1917, as a description not only of the archaic, but also of the universal and ubiquitous deep layer of the psyche.

> The collective unconscious, being the repository of man's experience and at the same time the prior condition of this experience, is an image of the world which has taken aeons to form.[35]

The collective unconscious, accordingly, was an objective fact, always existent and forming the constantly vital background of psychic events. It embodied the maternal soil of consciousness, the old pathways which always endeavored to lead conscious processes back to the source; in it the ancestral experience remained alive, as far back as the earliest beginnings.

> The personal layer ends at the earliest memories of infancy, but the collective layer comprises the pre-infantile period, that is, the residues of ancestral life.[36]

By the end of the first decade of the twentieth century, Jung had emphasized that the collective unconscious was founded not only on collective ideas but also on "vital drives," on "subliminal vestiges of archaic functions . . . [and] subliminal combinations in symbolic form."[37] Similarly, he stressed somewhat later that the collective unconscious was composed of the "sum of instincts and their correlates, the archetypes." It took only one step further to arrive at the assumption of collective, inherited psychic structures. In 1928 Jung described the collective unconscious as containing *"the whole spiritual inherit-*

---

31 *Psychology of the Unconscious*, p. 198.   32 Ibid., p. 199.
33 Freud, "Three Essays on the Theory of Sexuality" (1905).
34 Jung, "Yoga and the West" (1936), p. 537.
35 "On the Psychology of the Unconscious," p. 95.
36 Ibid., p. 77.
37 "The Structure of the Unconscious" (1916), pp. 303-4.

ance of mankind's evolution, born anew in the brain structure of every individual."[38] From the uniformity of brain structure, which found its expression in common traits, universality, and in the widespread conformity of motives, Jung deduced the premise that man's collective unconscious "contains all the patterns of life and behaviour inherited from his ancestors."[39] Accordingly, all functions of the conscious psyche were pre-formed by unconscious structures.

The hypothesis proposing a potential of inherited archetypal ideas should not be understood as an inheritance of distinct thoughts, as Jung again and again stressed. What he had in mind was the assumption that the primordial images as well as the instincts were pre-formed in the brain, that is, they existed as pathways, as *Anlage.*

The collective unconscious, as a deposit of ancestral life, sheltered not only the individual experiences of father, mother, child, man, and wife, but also the totality of *psychic traces* which had originated under the influence of instincts, particularly hunger and sexuality. For Jung, the collective unconscious was the source of drives and instincts, yet also the fountainhead of the basic forms of human thought and feeling, combining creative impulses and collective primordial images.

It [the collective unconscious] is not just a gigantic historical prejudice, so to speak, an *a priori* historical condition; it is also the source of the instincts, for the archetypes are simply the forms which the instincts assume. From the living fountain of instinct flows everything that is creative; hence the unconscious is not merely conditioned by history, but is the very source of the creative impulse. It is like Nature herself—prodigiously conservative, and yet transcending her own historical conditions in her acts of creation.[40]

It was characteristic not only for events in the collective unconscious to be detached from personal experiences and to display ubiquitous contents, but also for the form in which they were perceived to be specific. The individual's experience of such contents always took place in the form of images. In the collective unconscious the world manifested itself as an "interior spiritual world,"[41] which was moved and supported by potent impulses. Its experience had from times immemorial been accomplished in the form of images and could always rise anew in the same manner. It embraced the world as historically known, the historical past, now internally experienced.

---

[38] "The Structure of the Psyche" (1928), p. 158.
[39] "Basic Postulates of Analytical Psychology" (1931), p. 349.
[40] "The Structure of the Psyche," p. 157.
[41] "On the Psychology of the Unconscious," p. 77.

D. FROM UNCONSCIOUS DRIVE TO COLLECTIVE UNCONSCIOUS

The collective unconscious contains, or is, an historical mirror-image of the world. It too is a world, but a world of images.[42]

While the images of the personal unconscious presented a kind of reflection of personal experiences, the forms of the collective unconscious were of an impersonal nature—Jung intending "impersonal" to mean forms not individually experienced.

Whereas the memory-images of the personal unconscious are, as it were, filled out, because they are images personally experienced by the individual, the archetypes of the collective unconscious are not filled out because they are forms not personally experienced.[43]

Because of this character of the archetypes, Jung conceived of collective images as a kind of raw material which to be understood needed to be rendered into the specific language of a certain period. In the process of such a translation Jung certainly did not think of an intellectual formulation; he felt the figurative representation, expressed in symbolic forms, was more powerful. Bringing collective images to life by performing a deed or a ritual was also effective.

If this is successful, then the world as we perceive it is reunited with the primordial experience of mankind by the symbol of a *Weltanschauung*; the historical, universal man in us joins hands with the newborn, individual man. This is an experience which comes very close to that of the primitive, who symbolically unites himself with the totem-ancestor by partaking of the ritual feast.[44]

Whenever the individual experienced the deeper significance of collective images and the connection with the existing store of experiences had been established, it was equivalent to a reunion with the source of life. The individual felt himself as one with the greater in his psyche. What he experienced was the mystery of again putting together what had been separated.

Jung described the character of this new view of the world and of life, which incorporated the collective unconscious, as follows:

. . . the collective unconscious is in no sense an obscure corner of the mind, but the mighty deposit of ancestral experience accumulated over millions of years, the echo of prehistoric happenings to which each century adds an infinitesimally small amount of variation and differentiation. Because the collective unconscious is, in the

---

42 "The Structure of the Psyche," p. 298.
43 "On the Psychology of the Unconscious," p. 77.
44 "Analytical Psychology and *Weltanschauung*" (1927), p. 380.

last analysis, a deposit of world-processes embedded in the structure of the brain and the sympathetic nervous system, it constitutes in its totality a sort of timeless and eternal world-image which counterbalances our conscious, momentary picture of the world. It means nothing less than another world, a mirror-world if you will. But unlike a mirror-image, the unconscious image possesses an energy peculiar to itself, independent of consciousness. By virtue of this energy it can produce powerful effects which do not appear on the surface but influence us all the more powerfully from within. These influences remain invisible to anyone who fails to subject his momentary picture of the world to adequate criticism, and who therefore remains hidden from himself. That the world has an inside as well as an outside, that it is not only outwardly visible but acts upon us in a timeless present from the deepest and apparently most subjective recesses of the psyche—this I hold to be an insight which, even though it be ancient wisdom, deserves to be evaluated as a new factor in building a *Weltanschauung*.[45]

45 Ibid., p. 376.

III. ARCHAIC INHERITANCE AND
COLLECTIVE UNCONSCIOUS

Turning again to Freud's psychology, we must ask whether we can recognize in it any ideas which were analogous to the collective unconscious. The phylogenetic factors which we were able to detect were essentially related to archaic motives, primordial fantasies, and typical complexes, such as the Oedipus and the castration complexes. Initially, Freud had been interested only in their ontogenesis in tracing phylogenetic motives back to the prehistory of childhood and infancy. As time went on, he could hardly fail to pay heed to the fact that these phenomena presented contents common to all of humanity—that they were not only tied to the individual's constitution but could be traced back to the remote antiquity of the race. He had no choice but to assume a "phylogenetic heritage,"[1] an expression which he used in "From the History of an Infantile Neurosis" (1918). The date and purpose of this work is significant. Freud wrote:

> This case history was written down shortly after the termination of the treatment, in the winter of 1914–1915. At that time I was still freshly under the impression of the twisted re-interpretations which C. G. Jung and Alfred Adler were endeavouring to give to the findings of psycho-analysis. This paper is therefore connected with my essay "On the History of the Psycho-Analytic Treatment" which was published in the *Jahrbuch der Psychoanalyse* in 1914. It supplements the polemic contained in that essay, which is in essence of a personal character, by an objective estimation of the analytic material.[2]

Later, Freud described these archaic tendencies and motives as "elements with a phylogenetic origin," that is, "things that were innately present in him [the individual] at his birth."[3]

We may justifiably ask whether Freud, in advancing the hypothesis of an "archaic heritage,"[4] actually thought of primordial experiences or inherited dispositions of the psyche. This question, however, is difficult to answer because Freud's statements are contradictory and not uniform. At first, it appeared that he affirmed psychic dispositions,[5]

---

[1] Freud, "From the History of an Infantile Neurosis" (1918), p. 97.
[2] Ibid., p. 7, n.
[3] "Moses and Monotheism: Three Essays" (1939), p. 98.
[4] "Analysis Terminable or Interminable" (1937), p. 240.
[5] "Moses and Monotheism," p. 98.

which served to rekindle inherited contents[6] or "phylogenetically inherited schemata." Still, in his "History of an Infantile Neurosis" he stated that "phylogenetically inherited schemata . . . like the categories of philosophy, are concerned with the business of 'placing' the impressions derived from actual experience."[7] Freud resumed this idea in the late work *Moses and Monotheism* (1939). Here, he expressed the thought that the archaic formations were more than merely "specialized precipitates left by early human development."[8] He recognized specific modes of reaction and dispositions which force psychic processes to take a certain direction. He saw such dispositions "in the capacity and tendency . . . to enter particular lines of development and to react in a particular manner to certain excitations, impressions and stimuli."[9]

When Freud spoke of psychic dispositions, he thought of a kind of heritage which in each instance needed to be reawakened by the individual. Among these dispositions he counted certain tendencies in the id, for example, intellectual dispositions and historically acquired thought-connections between ideas, established during the earliest development of speech;[10] he also included individual dispositions and trends in the ego.[11] According to Freud, these dispositions seemed in every case to determine the individual's development and to steer him into a particular direction.

At first glance, Freud's idea of the "archaic inheritance" reminds one to a surprising degree of Jung's concept of archetypal structures—and no wonder, in view of the impression made on him by Jung's early work *Transformations and Symbols of the Libido*. Upon closer examination, there appear profound differences. It is true that Freud's assumptions of experiences of former generations as still operative and of constitutionally fixed dispositions seemed to be based on observations similar to those that Jung made in regard to the archetypes. However, when one is searching for the character of the inherited experiences, the gap between the two thinkers becomes unmistakably clear. When referring to inherited dispositions, Freud by no means had in mind systems of predetermined channels or pathways (Jung) but "memory-traces of the experience of earlier generations."[12] By thinking only in concrete terms, Freud went so far as to ascribe such memory-traces to the after-effect of prehistoric events. His concept culminated

6 "An Infantile Neurosis," pp. 21–22.   7 Ibid., p. 119.
8 "Analysis Terminable or Interminable," p. 241.
9 "Moses and Monotheism," p. 98.   10 Ibid., p. 99.
11 "Analysis Terminable or Interminable."
12 "Moses and Monotheism," p. 99.

in the hypothesis that all such memories, in the final analysis, pointed to a legendary episode concerning the primal horde and the killing of the primal father[13]—a hypothesis which Freud had mentioned for the first time in *Totem and Taboo* (1913).

Thus, Freud explained the motive of parricide as a fantastic repetition of a homicide that occurred in the dark dawn of history—the actual murder of the father by his own sons. He also saw the incest conflict as a repetition of a primeval conflict of humanity. Against such incestuous impulses, the "oldest and strongest longings of man," he opposed an equally strong or even stronger prohibition, which he described as the "unremitting prohibition of the primal father." Freud conceived these taboos as expressions of the father's castrating authority, and to them he traced the renunciation of drives so often demanded by civilization. The religious symbol, too, was not exempt from Freud's reductive approach. For him it was always a mere mnemonic symbol of the historical murder of the primal father. He proposed, for example, that in the idea of an almighty deity "the supremacy of the father of the primal horde was re-established."[14] Similarly, Freud always understood the changing conceptions of God as a replacement, a distortion, and a final restitution of the myth of the primal father. In his system there was fundamentally no place for the recognition of psychic traces or archetypal structures. In the final analysis, Freud acknowledged nothing other than mnemonic traces of events that took place in remote times, or repetitions of such traces. He assumed that these traces were revived by similar events happening in the present, but he did not exclude the possibility of a spontaneous repetition of unconscious memory traces, as might occur on momentous occasions.

1. Archaic Inheritance and Instinct

It is odd that Freud always hesitated to hypothesize an instinctive disposition in man, even in the context of his biological considerations. Such an instinctive inheritance seemed to be more or less demonstrated in animals and was also highly probable in the child. Surprisingly, Freud could never bring himself to assume an inherited store of behavioral modes or an instinctive knowledge similar to that of animals, even though he could not avoid certain conjectures, such as when he published in 1918:

> If human beings too possessed an instinctive endowment such as this, it would not be surprising that it should be very particularly con-

13 Ibid., p. 82. 14 Ibid., p. 133.

cerned with the processes of sexual life, even though it could not be by any means confined to them. This instinctive factor would then be the nucleus of the unconscious, a primitive kind of mental activity, which would later be dethroned and overlaid by human reason, when that faculty came to be acquired, but which in some people, perhaps in everyone, would retain the power of drawing down to it the higher mental processes. Repression would be the return to this instinctive stage, and man would thus be paying for his great new acquisition with his liability to neurosis, and would be bearing witness by the possibility of the neuroses to the existence of those earlier, instinct-like, preliminary stages. The significance of the traumas of early childhood would lie in their contributing material to this unconscious which would save it from being worn away by the subsequent course of development.[15]

Such ideas as an "instinctive endowment," or the "nucleus of the unconscious"—even the idea of neurosis as a price for the new acquisition of reason—may be very fascinating; such ideas may even lean toward an approximation of Jung's hypothesis of the archetypal modes of behavior; still, Freud's ultimate retreat to the etiology of memory traces of earlier generations[16] relegated such intuitive feelings to the realm of mere speculations.

2. Fantasies and Primal Scenes

Freud not only shifted his course in questioning the nature of the archaic inheritance, but in psychotherapeutic practice he also changed his emphasis on whether greater weight should be attached to the so-called primal scenes (actual experiences during childhood) or to phylogenetic schemata. On the whole, Freud's attitude fluctuated with the emphasis he placed at various times on ontogenesis or phylogenesis. The following passage, published in 1918, may clarify the problem:

> I fully agree with Jung in recognizing the existence of this phylogenetic heritage; but I regard it as a methodological error to seize on a phylogenetic explanation before the ontogenetic possibilities have been exhausted. I cannot see any reason for obstinately disputing the importance of infantile prehistory while at the same time freely acknowledging the importance of ancestral prehistory. Nor can I overlook the fact that phylogenetic motives and productions themselves stand in need of elucidation, and that in quite a number of

15 "An Infantile Neurosis," p. 120. (Written 1914–15.)
16 "Moses and Monotheism," p. 100.

instances this is afforded by factors in the childhood of the individual. And, finally, I cannot feel surprised that what was originally produced by certain circumstances in prehistoric times and was then transmitted in the shape of a predisposition to its re-acquirement should, since the same circumstances persist, emerge once more as a concrete event in the experience of the individual.[17]

As becomes clear from these remarks, Freud's consideration of infantile prehistory ultimately got the upper hand over the ancestral prehistory. Similarly, he emphasized (with an oblique reference to Jung) that the psychotherapist should apply the phylogenetic approach only after clarifying and working through what had been acquired by the individual. Freud maintained that whenever the child's personal experiences or traumatic impressions deviated from the hereditary schema (or in instances in which "experiences fail to fit in with the hereditary schema"),[18] they "become remodelled in the imagination";[19] nevertheless, in doubtful cases he opted for the priority of infantile primal scenes.

In his argument with Jung's discovery that fantasies created childhood memories, that is, memories of the primal scene, Freud was increasingly pushed into the opposite position. According to his experience, the situation was reversed: primal scenes were the basis of the fantasies. In considering the formation of infantile fantasies he could not help but grant primary importance to early experiences in childhood, such as experiences in the parental bedroom.

. . . it seems to me more probable that the phantasy of re-birth was a derivative of the primal scene than that, conversely, the primal scene was a reflection of the phantasy of re-birth.[20]

The following remark is noteworthy:

I admit that this is the most delicate question in the whole domain of psycho-analysis. I did not require the contributions of Adler or Jung to induce me to consider the matter with a critical eye, and to bear in mind the possibility that what analysis puts forward as being forgotten experiences of childhood (and of an improbably early childhood) may on the contrary be based upon phantasies created on occasions occurring late in life. According to this view, wherever we seemed in analyses to see traces of the after-effects of an infantile impression of the kind in question, we should rather have to assume that we were faced by the manifestations of some con-

[17] "An Infantile Neurosis," p. 97.
[19] Ibid.
[18] Ibid., p. 119.
[20] Ibid., pp. 102–3.

stitutional factors or of some disposition that had been phylogenetically maintained. On the contrary, no doubt has troubled me more; no other uncertainty has been more decisive in holding me back from publishing my conclusions. I was the first—a point to which none of my opponents have referred—to recognize both the part played by phantasies in symptom-formation and also the "retrospective phantasying" of late impressions into childhood and their sexualization after the event.[21]

3. Phylogenetic Inheritance and Historical Repression

Freud found his assumption of a memory-trace preserved in each individual[22] to be a fertile idea for further speculation. It might bridge the gap between individual and group psychology, since he considered repressed memory-traces to be the connecting link. Just as he conceived the repressed contents of each individual to be something which will never be extinguished in the unconscious psyche but has only become inadmissible to consciousness, he saw that which was repressed in a people's history as something buried in darkness.

> Here I am not using the term "the repressed" in its proper sense. What is in question is something in a people's life which is past, lost to view, superseded and which we venture to compare with what is repressed in the mental life of an individual.[23]

Similarly, the "return of the repressed" in individual psychology (the event which loosens the grip of neurosis) corresponded to a phenomenon in collective psychology. According to Freud, the entire historical development, beginning with the myth of the primal father, could easily be understood as a successive repetition of the "return of the repressed"—longing for the father and hate for him, murder of the primal father and guilt-feeling (for example, Judaism and Christianity). Still, Freud energetically protested that applying his concept of the repressed to the psychology of the group was in no way a concession to the collective unconscious as used by Jung.

> It is not easy for us to carry over the concepts of individual psychology into group psychology; and I do not think we gain anything by introducing the concept of a "collective" unconscious. The content of the unconscious, indeed, is in any case a collective, universal property of mankind.[24]

21 Ibid., p. 103, n. 1.
23 Ibid., p. 132.
22 "Moses and Monotheism," p. 94.
24 Ibid.

D. FROM UNCONSCIOUS DRIVE TO COLLECTIVE UNCONSCIOUS

The passages quoted above may suffice to clarify the unbridgeable chasm between Freud's concepts and those of Jung. The rift became apparent in Freud's putting historical and mythical events into categories applied in individual psychology, and it was also quite generally evident in his assuming that collective memories of historical events were the basis of the phylogenetic heritage. At the decisive point Freud always slipped into an approach geared to individual psychology and concrete factors, while Jung envisaged impersonal features and aspects common to mankind.

E. FROM LIBIDO TO
PSYCHIC ENERGY

I. FREUD'S SEXUAL THEORY

After Freud's hypothesis of sexual trauma during childhood had collapsed, it was almost impossible to avoid the question of whether infantilism and sexuality had any etiological significance in the symptomatology of the psychoneuroses. It was an unexpected sidelight that, through his physiological observations and his self-analysis,[1] Freud chanced upon the significance of the sexual function in the development of neurosis. Initially, he became aware of the importance of the erogenous zones, and somewhat later (1897) he formulated the Oedipus complex, which had a fundamental role in psychoanalysis.[2] He recognized that the sexual drive was a force of extraordinary activity, which operated in man from earliest childhood. It was sexuality which decided between health and disease, and determined the development and destiny of the individual. Freud stated in retrospect that his early assumption regarding the etiology of neurosis was by no means untenable: What he formerly had called infantile sexual trauma reappeared in a modified form as the infantilism of sexuality. (The term "sexual theory" appeared for the first time in a letter to Fliess, October 11, 1899.)[3]

With the sexual theory,[4] Freud based his psychology principally on the factors of drive and instinctual desire. Tension due to needs and gratification formed the framework of his sexual theory, and the process of channeling stimulation was regulated essentially by the pleasure-displeasure principle. In 1911 Freud took the "momentous step" of supplementing the pleasure principle with the reality principle[5]—a step which prompted Jones to write:

> It was this distinction on which rests Freud's chief claim to fame: even his discovery of the unconscious is subordinate to it. . . . Now it is no longer what is pleasurable that counts but also what is real.[6]

In the sexual drive, Freud distinguished between its organically determined "sexual power" and its psychic manifestation, the libido. Occasionally, however, he used both terms indiscriminately. He conceived the libido as a specifically sexual drive in contrast to the hunger drive and self-preservation drive (ego-drive). The libido was, according

[1] Freud, *The Origins of Psycho-Analysis* (1887–1902), p. 218.
[2] Ibid., p. 223.   [3] Ibid., p. 300.
[4] "Three Essays on the Theory of Sexuality" (1905).
[5] "Formulations on the Two Principles of Mental Functioning" (1911), p. 219.
[6] Jones, *The Life and Work of Sigmund Freud*, Vol. II, p. 313.

to him, essentially of psychosexual nature,[7]—on the one hand, biologically anchored; on the other, regulated by the psychic factors of pleasure and displeasure.

Freud's theory of drives underwent two fundamental changes. The
first took place in 1914 with the introduction of the concept of narcissism, the second one six years later with the discovery of the destructive
and aggressive instincts in the unconscious. The assumption of a
narcissistic libido, that is, an *original libidinal cathexis of the ego*,[8]
was the result of Freud's observations of megalomania and feelings of
omnipotence in certain psychoses; in addition, it was a reaction against
Jung's rejection of the application of the libido theory to dementia
praecox.[9] As Jones pointed out, Freud's hypothesis of a cathexis of the
ego with libido was extremely "confusing" and could open the door
for his opponents' statements that psychoanalysis proposed an absolute
role of sexuality. However, Jones also pointed out that, in fact, Freud
had never had in mind sexualization of the entire ego but only of its
regressively affected portion.

Freud's second attempt to supplement the theory of drives with the
introduction of the aggressive drives (1920) was questioned by most of
his fellow-workers. He based it on observations of a constantly recurring "compulsion to repeat"[10] repressed material. The discovery of the
aggressive drives led Freud to distinguish between Eros and a death
instinct—the one conceived as gathering the living substance into
progressively higher units, the other understood as an entrenched and
regressive tendency in the psyche, which resulted in repetition of earlier
attitudes and virtually strove toward a dissolution into the inorganic
state.

Freud's concept of depth psychology as based on drives focused
scientific discussion on four crucial problems: the overall determination of psychic events by drives; the predominant importance of sexuality in understanding disturbances of development; the relationship
between psychology and biology; and recognition of the teleological
structure of the psychic world, that is, of a goal-directed factor extending into the realm of unconscious feelings and physical processes.

Jung's investigations of the complex and fantasy necessarily led
him to an intensive and profound controversy with Freud's sexual
theory. From the very beginning, Jung felt slightly uncomfortable with
Freud's "extreme position." He could not agree with Freud's attempt

---

[7] "Three Essays," p. 217.

[8] "On Narcissism: An Introduction" (1914), p. 75.

[9] Jung, *Psychology of the Unconscious* (*Transformations and Symbols of the Libido*, 1912), pp. 141f.

[10] "Beyond the Pleasure Principle" (1920), p. 19.

to trace neurosis to repression of sexual, ego-incompatible factors and (in 1907) refused to "attribute to the infantile sexual trauma the exclusive importance that Freud apparently [did]."[11] However, he found it extremely important to scrutinize carefully psychoanalytic findings and to outline the limits within which they were valid. Jung was too much the empiricist to close his eyes to the great influence of sexuality in human life.

Jung, too, recognized sexuality as one of the basic factors of life, and he also saw it as an important causative factor in the development of neurosis. The abundance of sexual symbols in the fantasies of diseased as well as healthy people again emphasized the role of sexuality. The social aspect, too, appeared to him to be essential, because it is sexuality that "drives the individual away from his family and forces him to achieve independence"[12] and to become involved in the world.

In spite of the powerful emotional impact behind the sexual drive, Jung stressed that it should not be understood as the sole foundation of human life. Not even at the time of his greatest fascination with Freud was it possible for Jung to trace all human activities back to changes and disturbances of the sexual function. Such an attempt, in his opinion, amounted to a complete misinterpretation of human nature. He mainly rejected the avowal of a "sexual myth," or—as he formulated it as late as 1929: "the Freudian tendency to derive everything from sexuality and other moral incompatibilities."[13]

This remark, however, should not lead one to assume that Jung did not recognize the importance of drive and instinct in the life and destiny of man. As early as 1907 he declared, "The essential basis of our personality is affectivity."[14] This also applies to emotion, the feeling-tone of complexes, and the stirring of the drives. In 1952 Jung wrote:

. . . the instincts . . . , which are the vital foundations, the laws governing all life.[15]

Even though Jung confessed that he did not know what was the basic nature of the drive—any more than Freud did—he still described instinct as "a very mysterious manifestation of life, partly psychic and partly physiological by nature. It is one of the most conservative functions in the psyche. . . ."[16] (Compare the "partie inférieure de la

11 Jung, "The Psychology of Dementia Praecox" (1907), p. 4.
12 "The Theory of Psychoanalysis" (1913), p. 154.
13 "Some Aspects of Modern Psychotherapy" (1929), p. 30.
14 "Dementia Praecox," p. 38.
15 Symbols of Transformation (1952), p. 180.
16 Ibid., p. 139.

fonction" of Janet.) In contrast to Freud, one fact was certain as far as Jung was concerned: the character of the drive was never totally described by attributing to it a goal and coordinating it with an object. As we will see later, a spiritual aspect, a "meaning," was also coordinated with the drive—a thought which Jung formulated for the first time in 1919:

> The primordial image might suitably be described as the *instinct's perception of itself*, or as the self-portrait of the instinct.[17]

Twenty-seven years later (see Appendix), Jung returned again to the subject and described the archetype as "the meaning of the instinct."[18]

From this point of view, one can understand Jung's objections to Freud's distinction between Eros and death-instinct. He was able neither to equate Eros with the life principle *per se*, nor to conceive the death-instinct as the ultimate source of what is evil, destructive, and deadly. Both drives contained within themselves the other side, too—Eros, the psychic principle of relatedness; the death-instinct, a spiritual aspect.

> This fact led my pupil Dr. Spielrein to develop her idea of the death-instinct, which was then taken up by Freud. In my opinion it is not so much a question of a death-instinct as of that "other" instinct (Goethe) which signifies spiritual life.[19]

Jung's comprehensive approach, which attempted to include the drive as well as its meaning, called for a demarcation between psychology and biology. Jung admired Freud for his achievement in incorporating biologic data into psychology, thereby supplementing the intellectualism of French psychology and psychopathology with the findings of natural science. However, he firmly rejected the mixture of psychological and biological categories as well as the attempt to reduce the unconscious to "instinctive sexuality," that is, to the merely biological aspect of drive and desire.

After this introduction, we can examine the arguments which Jung raised in regard to Freud's sexual theory. His earliest critical remarks came from the period between 1906 and 1912. I am thinking particularly of his statements concerning the "universality of sexuality" which he seemed to detect in Freud's psychology and other references to the reification of sexuality. In the foreword to *The Psychology of Dementia Praecox* Jung wrote:

17 "Instinct and the Unconscious" (1919), p. 136.
18 "On the Nature of the Psyche" (1946), p. 201.
19 *Symbols of Transformation*, p. 328, n. 38.

If I, for instance, acknowledge the complex mechanisms of dreams and hysteria, this does not mean that I attribute to the infantile sexual trauma the exclusive importance that Freud apparently does. Still less does it mean that I place sexuality so predominantly in the foreground, or that I grant it the psychological universality which Freud, it seems, postulates in view of the admittedly enormous role which sexuality plays in the psyche.[20]

In spite of these and similar remarks, Jung's early psychopathologic investigations confirmed the sexual determination of neurotic symptoms and the sexual character of patients' ideas. Above all, the sexual character of the affects and the infantile-sexual aspect of ideas seemed to him to be in the foreground of hysteria. However, Jung explained the corresponding phenomena on an entirely different basis than Freud. As early as 1908, he implied that the tendency to cast products of fantasy into sexual images should be interpreted as an expression of the archaic-sexual character of the background of the psyche and its figures of speech. Jung observed that the sexually-toned fantasies of patients had a great kinship with the motifs in myths and in poetic productions[21]—a finding which gained still more prominence in his later investigations. In *Transformations and Symbols of the Libido* he pointed out that the "analogy of the sexual act"[22] encountered in symbolic expressions must be understood in the context of the fantasy activity of the individual and its regression to the archaic world of images, rather than in a literal sense. On the contrary, over the years he became increasingly aware that the correct meaning of the primitive-sexual expression was the symbolic content of the image which hinted at something still undeveloped, not understood, and, most of all, unknown.

Jung took another step forward in *Psychological Types*. Here, he attempted to understand the sexualization of ideas as a consequence of insufficient differentiation of psychic functions or, in other words, the inferior function fusing with sexual sensations.[23] The inferior function, connected as it was with socially repressed values, was particularly likely to be contaminated by sexuality.

Jung made a further concession to Freud in a paper of 1909, in which he dealt with the significance of the father in constellating the future life of the child. At that time, Jung still agreed with Freud to such an extent that he declared, "in essence our life's fate is identical

20 "Dementia Praecox," p. 4.
21 "The Freudian Theory of Hysteria" (1908), p. 23.
22 *Psychology of the Unconscious*, p. 176.   23 *Psychological Types* (1921), p. 424.

with the fate of our sexuality"[24]—a comment he pointedly eliminated in the 1948 edition!

Jung also discussed the importance of sexual interest in developing intellectual potentialities in the lecture "Psychic Conflicts in a Child (1909)" which was a reaction to Freud's "Analysis of a Phobia in a Five-Year-Old Boy (1909)." In the foreword to the 1916 edition, Jung interpreted the material which he had at first accepted according to Freud's sexual theory in an entirely different way.

In the first part of *Transformations and Symbols of the Libido* Jung followed Freud's ideas for the last time before separating from him (1913). But, in the second part of this book, Jung already retracted many of his earlier concessions to the causal method and to the theory of infantile sexuality, as proposed by Freud. Instead, he posed the question of the meaning and symbolism of unconscious contents.

An objective examination of Jung's earlier works gives one the impression that he always had reservations, even though out of respect they were couched in veiled terms. He held back his own views until he was able to test them empirically in his investigations. His work on the concept of libido was destined to become the decisive turning point. Through these observations he gained the support he needed for the formulation of his own discoveries. What concerned him above all was to find a point of view which permitted him to express adequately the dynamics of the unconscious.

Jung's struggle with Freud's ideas was of inestimable value. His confrontation with the sexual theory amounted virtually to a milestone in his own growth and development. Out of this, he originated not only the concept of psychic energy and the principle of equivalence but also the idea of the tension between the opposites. Furthermore, he found that this confirmed his concept of the etiology of regressive fantasy activity and the importance of an actual conflict situation in the development of neurosis. Finally, Jung's own understanding of the symbolic approach was enhanced by his opposition to Freud's concrete thinking in formulating the incest theory.

In 1913, the year after publication of *Transformations and Symbols of the Libido*, Jung saw himself faced with the task of devising an approach fundamentally at odds with Freud's libido theory. He detailed his essential criticisms regarding infantile sexuality, incest fantasies, and Freud's concept of the libido (to mention only a few of the more important issues) in a remarkable series of lectures, which unfortunately are often overlooked. These were published in English under the title *The Theory of Psychoanalysis*.

[24] "The Significance of the Father in the Destiny of the Individual" (1909/1948), p. 320, n. 21.

II. INFANTILE SEXUALITY AND THE
ORGANIZATION OF THE LIBIDO

1. Freud's Concept of Infantile Sexuality: Polymorphous
Perverse Disposition and the Diphasic Process of Sexuality

Freud's recognition that libidinous experiences during childhood were among the basic events of psychic life was destined to have immeasurable impact on psychoanalysis. Such childhood experiences had a deep basis in man's constitution and were to throw a light on the dynamics of human development. They were not only the starting point for the normal unfolding of life, but also for various infantilisms and perversions, as well as the entire symptom complex of neurosis.

It was characteristic of Freud to deduce his fundamental hypotheses regarding infantile sexuality from observations in neurotic adults. Generally, these findings referred to numerous sporadic sexual experiences during childhood, and from these data Freud not only arrived at bold conclusions regarding the etiological role of infantile sexuality, but he also used this material as his basis for asserting that the *innate disposition of children's psychic life was essentially of a polymorphously perverse disposition.*[1] According to this theory, all children were inclined toward "perverse" tendencies—perverse, according to Freud, denoting sexual activity without inhibitions. Infantile sexuality was "polymorphously perverse" because it hinted at a primary, completely uncentered multiplicity of partial drives, functioning entirely independently of each other. Essentially, such polymorphous perverse sexuality coincided with attempts at erotic gratification.

Freud postulated an equally important cause of disturbance in the diphasic onset of sexual development.[2] This, too, was a congenital tendency and was related to the interruption of sexual development by the latency period,[3] that is, a temporary arrest or even a return to sexual impulses of the early infantile period. Since man alone, among all living creatures, showed this diphasic onset of sexual growth, it seemed to Freud to be "the biological determinant of his predisposition to neurosis."[4] Because the latency period—the phase intervening between infantile and mature sexuality—served not only in the unfolding of the ego but at the same time required adaptation to the increased demands of society, it represented a critical time, embracing the

---

[1] Freud, "Three Essays on the Theory of Sexuality" (1905), p. 191.
[2] Ibid., p. 234.   [3] Ibid., pp. 176ff.
[4] "An Autobiographical Study" (1925), p. 37.

prerequisites for incisive blocks and disturbances of development. On the one hand, early infantile sexuality was exposed to certain types of repression, on the other, it was confronted with fixation to them and perseveration of earlier experiences. Fixation and repression acted along similar lines: In both instances, the free-floating energy characteristic of infancy was *inhibited* and *tonically bound.*[5] Just as repression always indicated a *weak point in the development of the ego,* fixation invariably suggested a very *sensitive point in sexual development.* In each case disturbances of development resulted; certain parts of the drives participated in development, while other parts remained infantile, with consequent retardation in making the transition to the goals of civilization.

Freud recognized in childhood experiences the most significant causes of conflicts in adults as well as in children. Because of this, the success of psychotherapy depended largely on the possibility of reviving childhood memories. This, however, was not an easy task. Freud had noted as early as 1897 that the credibility of childhood memories[6] was doubtful, because fantasies and imaginary bits of recollection veiled and distorted the true facts. He formulated his experiences with utter clarity:

> It may indeed be questioned whether we have any memories at all *from* our childhood: memories *relating to* our childhood may be all that we possess. Our childhood memories show us our earliest years not as they were but as they appeared at the later periods when the memories were aroused.[7]

Freud became convinced that so-called childhood memories were always the result of *falsification and misrepresentation* due not only to fantasy but also because of a censoring agency. Notwithstanding this new difficulty, Freud clung to the possibility of dissolving these misrepresentations and of penetrating to the true events. The recognition of a "constant aetiological relation"[8] between psychic contents (childhood experiences and distorting fantasy as well as the repressing censor and symptom) seemed to guarantee that the traumatic childhood experience could be uncovered provided the analysis was competent.

2. Freud's Organization of the Libido and the Oedipus Complex

Freud's discovery of the hereditary pregenital phases in the development of sex represents the crowning achievement of his theory of in-

---

5 "The Unconscious" (1915), p. 188.
6 *The Origins of Psycho-Analysis* (1887–1902), p. 215.
7 "Screen Memories" (1899), p. 322.
8 "Heredity and the Aetiology of the Neuroses" (1896), p. 149.

fantile sexuality. The hypothesis of fixations and of the regression of the libido to them were to have extraordinary significance in the choice and development of neuroses. The importance of these hypotheses in the further course of psychoanalysis justifies a closer consideration of the subject.

Freud's investigations led him to make the crucial distinction between oral,[9] anal,[10] and genital[11] eroticism. However, only much later was he able to complete these contrasts in a satisfactory manner by introducing the concepts of narcissism (1914) and the phallic phase (1924).

Originally, Freud had disclosed problems connected with incorporation (the oral phase) and usurpation (the anal phase), but only the discovery of the phallic phase—that is, the phase of overestimating maleness—permitted him to come closer to the problems of masturbation and the Oedipus complex.[12] By introducing a primary phase of narcissism (1914)[13]—the attitude in which the individual seeks himself as a love-object and the ego is cathected with libido—Freud attempted to explain paranoid symptoms of megalomania and ideas of omnipotence.[14] Jung had earlier (1907) traced such symptoms back to the loss of a sense of reality[15] and explained them by his libido theory. Freud described the genital phase as the end of infantile organization of the libido, in which he recognized that the partial drives became subordinated to "genital primacy." Concurrently, the transition from autoeroticism to object love took place.

Of all the stages in the differentiation of the libido, Freud attributed to the phallic phase the greatest importance in the later development of sexuality (1923). He regarded certain characteristics which he had observed as early as 1909[16] as indicative of the phallic phase: the cult of the phallus, which went hand-in-hand with an overevaluation of the male; inquisitiveness; increased masturbation, as well as an increased tie to the parents. The phallic phase reached its culminating point in the Oedipus complex, in which the conflict can be summarized in these few words: "The antithesis here is between having a *male genital* and being *castrated*."[17] With the phallic phase, a breakthrough was made in the prevalently autoerotic need-gratification of the early infantile period. Likewise, the narcissistic object-choice was superseded by object-

[9] "Three Essays," p. 179.   [10] Ibid., p. 185.   [11] Ibid., p. 187.
[12] "The Infantile Genital Organization" (1923), p. 144.
[13] "On Narcissism: An Introduction" (1914), p. 92.
[14] "Psycho-Analytic Notes on an Autobiographical Account of a Case of Paranoia (Dementia Paranoides)" (1911).
[15] Jung, "The Psychology of Dementia Praecox" (1907), p. 94.
[16] Freud, "Analysis of a Phobia in a Five-Year-Old Boy" (1909), p. 214.
[17] "The Infantile Genital Organization," p. 145.

love, that is, a tie to persons in the outside world, mainly the parents. Freud was fascinated, and at the same time amazed, in following the maturation of the child to observe the progress of object-choice from a narcissistic-autoerotic frame of reference to the climax where "love of the mother and jealousy of the father"[18] takes over. The Oedipus complex, modeled on the Greek myth, culminated in the incestuous wish, as seen from the boy's side, to marry the mother and kill the father; conversely, the young girl reversed the roles. A letter which Freud wrote to Fliess on October 15, 1897, contained this passage:

> I have found love of the mother and jealousy of the father in my own case too, and now believe it to be a general phenomenon of early childhood. . . . If that is the case, the gripping power of *Oedipus Rex*, in spite of all the rational objections to the inexorable fate that the story presupposes, becomes intelligible, and one can understand why later fate dramas were such failures . . . the Greek myth seizes on a compulsion which everyone recognized because he has felt traces of it in himself.[19]

In the Oedipus complex Freud by no means saw only a neurotic condition, but an event occurring in early childhood common to all men and phylogenetically determined. The complex varied in impact, depending on the strength of parental ties, the intensity of repression beginning in the latency period, and, particularly, the degree of regression to the point of fixation.

The activity of the Oedipus complex was accentuated by the "constitutional bisexuality of each individual"[20] as well as by the triangular character of the relationship between parents and child; both factors gave rise to complicated mechanisms of attachment, identification, introjection, and ambivalence. All these entanglements induced Freud to regard the Oedipus complex not only as the most important childhood complex, but also as the nuclear complex of neurosis *par excellence*. He tended increasingly to see the difficulty in overcoming the Oedipus complex as due to the long-lasting dependency of the child on the parents, because of physiological conditions and the relatively late maturation of the ego. These circumstances retarded separation from infantile attachments, adequate object-choice, the overcoming of masturbation, and finally the child's integration into the mores of civilization.

The Oedipus complex became truly tragic because of what replaced it in the subsequent phase of development—a change determined

---

[18] *Origins*, p. 223.   [19] Ibid.
[20] "The Ego and the Id" (1923), p. 31.

equally by heredity and an innate program. This was the castration complex, the true exponent of the latency period, on which the Oedipus complex was bound ultimately to founder.

By the postponing of sexual maturation, time has been gained in which the child can erect, among other restraints on sexuality, the barrier against incest, and can thus take up into himself the moral precepts which expressly exclude from his object-choice, as being blood-relations, the persons whom he has loved in his childhood. Respect for this barrier is essentially a cultural demand made by society. Society must defend itself against the danger that the interests which it needs for the establishment of higher social units may be swallowed up by the family.[21]

Freud drew an interesting inference from the concerted action of both complexes. As early as August 1, 1899, he reported to Fliess the discovery of a highly complex conjunction of four components:

Now for bisexuality! I am sure you are right about it. And I am accustoming myself to the idea of regarding every sexual act as a process in which four persons are involved.[22]

Freud expanded this idea in 1923 as the combined action of innate bisexuality with an ambivalent attitude toward the object of love.[23] This subject will be further dealt with in the chapter on Freud's concept of neurosis.

The clash between the Oedipus and the castration complexes became manifest in the battle between incest-wish and incest-anxiety. This battle not only retarded growing out of the Oedipus complex, but also entangled the individual in guilt-feeling and anxiety toward paternal authority.

Even the normal course of development—proceeding from autoerotic partial drives to fixations, phases of the libido, and particularly the Oedipus complex—was always beset by many dangers. The individual might not be able to pass through all phases equally well and overcome them; for instance, certain elements of function might be permanently arrested in some phase or at some point of fixation. Again, extraneous impediments, frustrations in sex life, or disappointments in love affairs might lead to regression of the libido. In Freud's opinion, the *pathology of neurosis* was connected with four factors: denial, fixation, repression, and regression.[24]

21 "Three Essays," p. 225. 22 *Origins*, p. 289.
23 "The Ego and the Id," p. 33.
24 *Introductory Lectures on Psycho-Analysis* (1915–17), pp. 347f.

E. FROM LIBIDO TO PSYCHIC ENERGY

The discovery of regressive tendencies in the psyche was among the earliest observations which Freud and Breuer had made together.[25] Freud used the expression "regressive direction" for the first time in a letter to Fliess (November 14, 1897),[26] but he subsequently modified the term considerably. It was a long road from the discovery of retrograde revivification of traumatic experiences during hypnosis to the findings brought out in the dream theory. As to regression in dreams, Freud stressed the characteristic of the reawakening of older and more primitive modes of action, with infantile and archaic traits coming to the fore. In the regression of libido, he recognized the more comprehensive fact of "a return to the objects first cathected by the libido,"[27] that is, the return to points of fixation. In contrast to regression in dreams—which he increasingly felt to be a normal psychic process—Freud considered the regressive movement of the libido in the development of neurosis as decidedly pathological and culminating in the return of the sex drive to earlier incestuous objects and even to abandoned phases of sexual organization.[28] As Nunberg so excellently expressed it, the retreat of the libido to former positions and its renewed cathexis to formerly cathected situations was characteristic.[29]

In normal individuals, frustration could lead to a renunciation of drives or to an enhanced cultural achievement and ultimately to a process of intensified experiencing. In neurosis, however, regression of the libido meant a return to the phallic, anal-sadistic, or oral-narcissistic phase, depending on the points of fixation. The related strivings and object fixations would be repeated according to the specific phase of libido organization.[30] While, for example, genital striving and the ties to parental figures were activated upon retreat to the phallic phase, continued regression resulted mainly in increased aggressive tendencies. When aggression was augmented by regression to the anal phase, sadistic impulses might break through, but regression to the narcissistic phase (schizophrenia) could lead to pronounced negativistic tendencies, combined with a hostile attitude toward people close to the subject. In contrast to repeated statements of others that Freud had postulated a necessary connection between frustration and aggressive reaction, I would propose—following the suggestion of Nunberg—that such reactions could be observed only in neuroses or

[25] Breuer and Freud, "On the Psychical Mechanism of Hysterical Phenomena: Preliminary Communication" (1893), in *Studies on Hysteria*, pp. 3–17.
[26] *Origins*, p. 233. [27] *Introductory Lectures*, p. 341.
[28] Ibid., p. 343.
[29] Nunberg, *Principles of Psychoanalysis* (tr., 1955), p. 103.
[30] Ibid., pp. 104–11.

narcissistic psychoses. They always presupposed a regression of the frustrated libido to aggressively toned, infantile points of fixation.

3. Infantile Sexuality According to Jung

Jung's preoccupation with the hypothesis of sexuality reached its high point at the time of his separation from Freud. It concerned not only the reliability of childhood memories and the productivity of the concept of infantile sexuality but also the Oedipus complex, which was for Freud the most important complex of sexual organization in early childhood. None of these problems, which played such an eminent role in Freud's theory, was considered of equal value in Jung's psychology. In the second edition of *Transformations and Symbols of the Libido* (1925), he attributed neurotic symptoms to infantile memories and erotic substitutes[31] and traced the state of "fantasy-thinking" to the characteristics of "infantilism" and "distortion."[32] However, after his parting from Freud, Jung revised this point of view more and more. Primarily, he brought two problems into discussion: the questions of the sexual character of autoerotic activities of children and the reliability of childhood memories.

Even though Freud had already decided that memories of the early infantile period were only relatively valid because of the distorting activity of fantasy, they nevertheless retained a prominent place in his system as important factors in neurosis. Jung, in contrast, took an essentially different position. In situations of neurotic conflict, he put less and less emphasis on the value of childhood impressions in reporting actual events. The current situation seemed to Jung more essential than past events and the psychic attitude of the individual more fundamental than the actual event. Lastly, the symbolic significance of reminiscences was more important than what had actually occurred during childhood. Unpredictably, this question of the etiological value of memories from early childhood turned full circle: the traumatic childhood experience no longer seemed essential in the development of neurosis, but was superseded by fantasy activity which regressively seized upon memory remnants, exaggerating them and invigorating them erotically. What Freud had understood as an after-effect of memory traces, Jung considered rather the result of an exorbitant fantasy activity which regressive imagination produced as childhood experiences (see D.III.2 and E.II.3.c).

31 *Wandlungen und Symbole der Libido* (2nd edn., 1925), p. 61.
32 *The Psychology of the Unconscious (Transformations and Symbols of the Libido*, 1912), p. 36.

In spite of Jung's evaluation of childhood memories as only relatively trustworthy, there is no justification for assuming that he had failed to recognize the importance of the past in the individual's development. The subject's past, that is, his life history, was not tantamount to his memory thereof. Even though childhood memories were highly unreliable, the fact that each moment of life contained the whole prehistory was not changed. The specific impressions during his lifetime and his distinct modes of experiencing and working-over accounted for what became of the individual. However, this did not mean that actual conflicts could be resolved by reproducing the life history, particularly not by the highly questionable reproduction of childhood memories.

Freud had always seen the nucleus of the neurotic conflict in childhood experiences, and the conflict taking place in adult life was nothing other than the revival of the childhood conflict; Jung, however, rejected this concept. At no time did he consider the past to be more important than the present, "yesterday" more essential than "today." Regarding the development of neurosis, particularly, he emphasized: ". . . the cause of the pathogenic conflict lies mainly in the present moment."[33]

Instead of an analysis of childhood difficulties, Jung considered it far more appropriate to concentrate on the actual tension between the adult personality and the personality formed by the infantile milieu.[34] Accordingly, he saw the infantilisms of the neurotic less as the consequence of burdensome childhood impressions than as an indication of "retarded affective development,"[35] or a carry-over of infantile emotions. This might be expressed in infantile clinging to father, mother, and siblings. Jung recognized in this phenomenon the cause of separation anxieties and attempts to escape from the demands of the outside world. As Jung saw it, the neurotic adult met defeat because he retained an infantile approach; his attitude toward performing obligations was wrong and he had difficulty in adapting to the demands of daily life. Jung expressed his concept in these words:

What is the task which the patient does not want to fulfil? What difficulty is he trying to avoid?[36]

In Jung's mind the moral approach to the theory of neurosis seemed to be at least as valid as the genetic approach.

We cannot overlook the realm of archetypal images when considering how important childhood impressions may be in the later develop-

33 "The Theory of Psychoanalysis" (1913), p. 166.   34 Ibid., pp. 137–38.
35 Ibid., p. 130.   36 Ibid., p. 182.

ment of the individual, because this was such a significant force in the framework of Jung's psychology. Jung never placed the principal emphasis on the concrete event, the actual behavior of the parental figures. Rather than stressing the part played in adult life by fixation on particular environmental influences occurring in early childhood, Jung insisted that the individual was tied at least as firmly to the archetypal images in the background of the psyche, which had been set in motion by concrete experiences. In other words, what fascinated the human mind and made it cling to the past were not only the concrete events of the individual's life history but also the primal images (such as sun, light, cave, temple, and so on) which shone through these incidents. At this time, we want merely to indicate that this more profound view led to a deeper method of understanding (see F.II.2).

A. POLYVALENT AND POLYMORPHOUS PERVERSE DISPOSITION

Jung repeatedly emphasized that from his observations he was unable to demonstrate either a multiplicity of partial drives (that is, a polymorphous perverse disposition) or a diphasic development of the sexual function. Both hypotheses seemed to him to be ideas gained from psychological observations of adult neurotics and retrospectively projected into child psychology as actual events.[37] Jung definitely accepted Freud's hypothesis that numerous independently functioning libido components were present during childhood. He, too, recognized a polymorphism of modes of action during early childhood, such as sucking, nail biting, and so on. Being first of all an empiricist, he could not fail to observe the common occurrence of autoerotic play and infantile habits which later continued as sexual games. Recognition of the polymorphism of modes of action during early childhood, however, by no means meant that they were always of a sexual character. On the contrary, Jung refused to extend the concept of sexuality to these autoerotic childhood activities. Sexual games during childhood were essentially different from those of adult years. They were far less locally determined, not related to specific bodily areas, and the mode of gaining pleasure was essentially different. According to Jung, striving for pleasure was not identical with sexual gratification. However, he was misled in thinking that this was Freud's assumption, as Karl Abraham[38] pointed out in a critique of *The Theory of Psychoanalysis.*

All of this made it apparent that what Freud had described as

37 Ibid., p. 132.
38 A review of Jung's "Versuch einer Darstellung der psychoanalytischen Theorie" (Attempt at a Representation of Psychoanalytic Theory) (1914), p. 104.

sexuality of early childhood, proposing the term "perverse," was for Jung only a preliminary step toward true sexuality in adult life. Rather, he saw in the so-called perverse activities that "the libido gradually sloughs off the character of the nutritive instinct and assumes that of the sexual instinct."[39] What he had observed was definitely not a universality of the sexual function, but instead a step-by-step development of the libido from a first, presexual stage, characterized by the functions of nutrition and growth, then a second stage of germinating sexuality (the prepubertal stage), ending in the period of sexual maturity.[40] In early autoerotic habits, Jung saw merely the germs of later sexuality, but never considered them to be manifestations of an already developed sexual function. He recognized with increasing clarity that this *Anlage* in childhood had to be considered a preliminary step in the development of the psyche. Polymorphism found its expression in the fact that the beginnings of developing intellectual faculties could be traced back to the earliest periods of life. Based on matters he had considered since 1913, Jung decided to replace Freud's term of "perverse disposition" with polyvalent germinal disposition. He arrived years later (1938) at the following formulation:

> To document the polyvalent germinal disposition of the child with a sexual terminology borrowed from the stage of fully fledged sexuality is a dubious undertaking. It means drawing everything else in the child's make-up into the orbit of sexual interpretation, so that on the one hand the concept of sexuality is blown up to fantastic proportions and becomes nebulous, while on the other hand spiritual factors are seen as warped and stunted instincts.[41]

The hypothesis of a polyvalent germinal disposition in the child was later to assume extraordinary significance not only for evaluating the development of concept formation during the individual's early years, but also for Jung's subsequent investigations into the connection between drive and archetype.

Opposed to Freud's concept that the child's interest in knowing and exploration had a derivative nature, Jung emphasized the genuine character of such activities. According to Freud, the child's curiosity was based on his attempt to explain vexing, sexually toned experiences; Jung, however, arrived at the conviction that intellectual curiosity was not only autoerotically determined, but aimed at a meaning and

[39] Jung, "The Theory of Psychoanalysis," pp. 127–28.
[40] Ibid., p. 117.
[41] "Psychic Conflicts in a Child" (1909/1938), foreword to the 3rd edn., p. 7.

purpose which was basically different from sexual motives. In December 1915, he wrote:

> It should be sufficiently clear . . . that the initial sexual interest strives only figuratively towards an immediate sexual goal, but far more towards the development of thinking.[42]

While Freud, concentrating on the elucidation of neurosis, primarily outlined the pathological consequences of an exaggerated inquisitiveness during early childhood, Jung investigated the general significance of the inquiring mind in the development of the intellectual faculties of the individual. It is true, Freud had recognized infantile sexual searches as "a first step towards taking an independent attitude in the world,"[43] but this did not preclude an evaluation which was essentially different from that of Jung. What interested Freud was how this drive could actually become the cause of later damage to development. He found proof in an insufficient mental apparatus during the early phase of life and also in the successive attempts at repression which are so characteristic of the latency period.[44] Both factors worked against a positive development of the drive for knowledge and for investigation. Jung differed radically from the hypothesis proposed by Freud. He took precisely the opposite position and thought of disturbed psychic development as a consequence of impeded concept-building. This idea was completely compatible with Freud's hypothesis that what he called the stage of infantile sexuality quite generally represented the start of human development. Jung merely added that this period was not characterized by sexual traits, nor was its significance limited to the beginnings of sexuality. It was Jung's great achievement that he recognized in the polyvalent disposition not only the beginnings of later sexual functions but also the beginnings of higher spiritual functions.

> As these reflections show, I do not regard the thinking function as just a makeshift function of sexuality which sees itself hindered in its pleasurable realization and is therefore compelled to pass over into the thinking function; but, while perceiving in infantile sexuality the beginnings of a future sexual function, I also discern there the seeds of higher spiritual function.[45]

Jung's observation of "the importance of concept-building for the solution of psychic conflicts"[46] went in the same direction. He expanded

---

[42] Ibid., foreword to the 2nd edn., p. 4.   [43] Freud, "Three Essays," p. 197.
[44] "Leonardo da Vinci and a Memory of His Childhood" (1910), pp. 131–32.
[45] Jung, "Psychic Conflicts," 1915 foreword, p. 5.
[46] Ibid., p. 4.

this line of thought to show that the infantile germinal state contained the beginnings of the pattern of later life, the germ of the "entire later human being," as well as the precipitate of the total archetypal inheritance. According to this view, the polyvalent character of the disposition referred to the totality of drives and instincts.

> Out of the infantile germinal state there develops the complete adult man; hence the germinal state is no more exclusively sexual than is the mind of the grown man. In it are hidden not merely the beginnings of adult life, but also the whole ancestral heritage, which is of unlimited extent. . . . If now, by means of a reductive procedure, we uncover the infantile stages of the adult psyche, we find as its ultimate basis germs containing on the one hand the later sexual being *in statu nascendi*, and on the other all those complicated preconditions of the civilized being.[47]

Jung became increasingly convinced that the infantile germinal state was the source of natural drives as well as "the mind *in nuce*."[48] In 1928, he even went so far as to fuse the mind with the drive component. Empirically, both qualities of the psyche seemed to be connected in such a way that the "spiritual appears in the psyche also as an instinct."[49] The spiritual quality was not only "a specific and necessary form of instinctual power"[50] but, in addition, the ultimate formative principle of the drive.

After another eighteen years (1946), Jung was able to clarify this hypothesis by describing one aspect of the archetype as a spiritual factor, another as representing the *meaning of the instinct*.[51] He assumed a primary connection between spiritual and natural principles, which was present in the psyche of the child from the very beginning. This statement is important because the hypothesis of coupling both principles was going to become the origin of the basic awareness of a tension of the opposites immanent in every human being (see E.III.3). The recognition of this was fundamental to Jung's psychology. The assumption of an inherent opposition between drive and spirit demonstrated anew that the gap between Freud and Jung could not be bridged.

B. THE LATENCY PERIOD AS THE BEGINNING OF SEXUALITY

Jung rejected Freud's premise that a latency period interrupted the early infantile sexual development. This attitude was similar to his

---

47 "On Psychic Energy" (1928), pp. 51–52.
48 Ibid., p. 52.   49 Ibid., p. 58.   50 Ibid.
51 "On the Nature of the Psyche" (1940/1954), p. 182.

criticism of Freud's concept of the polymorphous perverse disposition. Jung had observed—as Freud did—that between the third and fifth years of life certain early infantile strivings disappeared, but he interpreted this phenomenon in an entirely different manner. He saw the latency period neither as indicating an interruption of sexual activity nor as a time of stagnation; he saw it rather as an event related to the progression from presexual to sexual libido. What Freud had described as the "disappearance" of early infantile sexual activity or as a "period of sexual latency," Jung understood as *the real beginning of sexuality.*[52] Just as he saw Freud's concept of a latency period to be founded on the erroneous hypothesis of early infantile sexuality, Jung also believed that Freud's attempt to explain the amnesia of childhood experiences was the consequence of a wrong assumption. While Freud traced this amnesia to sexual repression (based on his model of neurosis), Jung recognized its cause in the imperfection of a child's ability to remember, traceable to the characteristics of developing consciousness. Only neurotic amnesia seemed to him to be of pathological significance.

A neurotic amnesia is punched out, as it were, from the continuity of memory, whereas memory in early childhood consists of single islands in the continuum of non-memory.[53]

C. THE OEDIPUS COMPLEX AS AN ARCHETYPAL IMAGE

Jung took a definite position in regard to the Oedipus complex. That which Freud characterized as an incestuous tie, Jung also recognized as an important aspect of childhood. However, he described the phenomenon differently and drew other conclusions from the child's attachment to the personalities of his parents. He considered the Oedipus complex, in the first place, to be a total complex of all feeling-toned dependencies in the child. Its principal components were stirrings of possessiveness, of clinging, jealousy, and envy rather than sexually relevant fixation. Very early (1913), Jung became convinced that the Oedipus complex was merely a formula, although a most important formula, for the child's general desires directed toward the parents.

If I now say that the Oedipus complex is in the first place only a formula for childish desires in regard to the parents and for the conflict which these desires evoke—as every selfish desire must—the matter may seem more acceptable.[54]

[52] "The Theory of Psychoanalysis," p. 165.
[53] Ibid., p. 164.   [54] Ibid., p. 153.

Jung saw a fallacy in the sexual implication of emotional ties—although often very tenacious—between parents and children, because such relationships could also be observed between foster parents and children, where incestuous attachment, of course, was ruled out. As far as he was concerned, the chief characteristic of emotional fixation was connected with the psychic function of father and mother—the mother having the role of tender care and protection, while the father had the authority, made the decisions, and provided moral support. As the first strong impressions in the child's life, they had lasting influence on his development.

> The parents are not just "sexual objects" or "pleasure objects" to be dismissed out of hand; they are, or they represent, vital forces which accompany the child on the winding path of destiny in the form of favourable or dangerous factors, from whose influence even the adult can escape only in limited degree . . .[55]

The rejection of the concept of parents as objects of pleasure and sexual desire, however, made up only a very small part of Jung's doubts concerning the Oedipus complex. His criticism developed in several steps. In 1913 he merely disputed the sexual nature of the emotional ties of small children.[56] As the years went on, he began to question the concept that the parents' main role during childhood was as objects.[57]

Jung felt that, above all else, natural parents were significant as *image bearers*. At least as important as the immediate impact of the parents, were the images they embodied for the child—for example, the image of being nourished or being loved and, similarly, the image of being a child and wanting to stay a child.

> The simple soul is of course quite unaware of the fact that his nearest relations, who exercise immediate influence over him, create in him an image which is only partly a replica of themselves, while its other part is compounded of elements derived from himself. The imago is built up of parental influences plus the specific reactions of the child; it is therefore an image that reflects the object with very considerable qualifications. . . . The image is unconsciously projected, and when the parents die, the projected image goes on working as though it were a spirit existing on its own.[58]

[55] "Analytical Psychology and Education" (1924/1946), p. 84.
[56] "The Theory of Psychoanalysis."
[57] "The Relations Between the Ego and the Unconscious" (1916/1928); "The Psychology of the Transference" (1946); *Symbols of Transformation* (1952), p. 419.
[58] "The Relations between the Ego and the Unconscious," p. 186.

It often seemed as if the images of children literally forced the parents into their roles of father or mother. Jung often came back to the thought that the Oedipus complex was founded on images essential for maintaining life; finally, he understood the Oedipus complex as an expression of congenital modes of function or, in other words, of regulating factors of hereditary origin. As such, they exerted a fascinating and overpowering effect. His formulation in 1952 was particularly enlightening:

> Interpretation in terms of the parents is, however, simply a *façon de parler*. In reality the whole drama takes place in the individual's own psyche, where the "parents" are not the parents at all but only their imagos: they are representations which have arisen from the conjunction of parental peculiarities with the individual disposition of the child.[59]

This perspective of the archetypal basis of the Oedipus complex permitted Jung to introduce an entirely new point of view into psychology: The numinous characteristics of images invested the parents with an "incestuous" quality arising from the deep layer of the psyche, and, retrospectively, this made them appear as the objects of "incestuous desires." In the course of his investigations, Jung discovered the overwhelming importance of fantasies, particularly those regressing into childhood. This fantasy preserved in the adult the attachment to family and created the imagined childhood as a paradise lost in which love, tender care, and protection abounded. This infantile frame of mind (or to use Jung's words: "an anachronistic clinging to the infantile attitude"),[60] combined with a longing for the past, were frequently the origin of the incestuous image in relation to the parents. On such a background, the idea of love and veneration flourished or, conversely, feelings of resistance, aversion, and hatred which left the neurotic adult fixated to images of the past. A little step further brought the recognition that in religious regression, too, similar archetypal processes were at work.

> Religious regression makes use of the parental imago, but only as a symbol—that is to say, it clothes the archetype in the image of the parents.[61]

As Jung repeatedly emphasized, the regressive tendency of the individual "is not just a relapse into infantilism, but a genuine attempt

---

[59] *Symbols of Transformation*, p. 328.
[60] "The Theory of Psychoanalysis," p. 168.
[61] *Symbols of Transformation*, p. 90.

to get at something necessary";[62] it "means that the patient is seeking himself in his childhood memories."[63] The combination of infantile attitude and regressive fantasy led Jung to an entirely different interpretation of sexual trauma and "primal scenes," than that assumed by Freud. It became a highly controversial issue whether the primary etiological significance in the development of neurosis should be attributed to the "primal scenes" or to the subsequent activity of fantasy. While Freud, after long vacillation, finally decided that such fantasies were essentially "a derivative of the primal scene,"[64] he noted that Jung, conversely, maintained that "forgotten experiences of childhood . . . may . . . be based upon phantasies created on occasions occurring late in life."[65] Jung considered it indisputable that in the majority of cases fantasy conceived the incestuous experiences and presented them as real occurrences.

Just as Jung rejected Freud's hypothesis of a primary incestuous wish (and traced it to the work of fantasy), he also repudiated Freud's hypothesis that the prohibition of incest was necessarily related to the castration complex. What Freud had understood as the result of an antagonism between incest-desire and castration complex (or demands of society), Jung conceived as an immanent potential in the individual to develop. In his view, resistance against the incest tendency was motivated from within, and, therefore, the incest taboo was anything but the result of mere repression, particularly not repression of incestuous drives. It was, rather, a restriction on instinctual drives imposed from within and assuming the character of transformation. Only a voluntary sacrifice of the primordial state of dependency—not a prohibition—could bring about the transformation which created the self-conscious individual.

> It was only the power of the "incest prohibition" that created the self-conscious individual, who before had been mindlessly one with the tribe.[66]

Jung took the decisive step beyond Freud with the introduction of the symbolic point of view. Instead of reducing incestuous desire to a wish to cohabit with the partner of the opposite sex, Jung raised the question of a possible symbolic meaning, hidden in the image of incest (see H.II.1). To be sure, he did not see a symbol in the incest fantasy

---

[62] "Some Aspects of Modern Psychotherapy" (1929), p. 32.
[63] Ibid., p. 33.
[64] Freud, "From the History of an Infantile Neurosis" (1918), p. 103.
[65] Ibid.
[66] Jung, *Symbols of Transformation*, p. 271.

per se, but found that it could become the impetus for symbolic transformation within the overall framework of antagonistic tendencies. Because the understanding of the symbol is intimately related to that of the concept of energy—which Jung opposed to Freud's concept of libido—we will continue the discussion of the symbol only after a review of the concept of energy.

III. THE LIBIDO AS UNDIVIDED
VITAL ENERGY (JUNG)

Freud's ultimate theory of the libido grew out of his investigations into the dynamism of psychic processes and his work on the organization of the libido. Jung was opposed to this theory because he felt the need for a concept of psychic energy which would be independent of the specific manifestations of the libido. Although the first hints of a new concept of energy could already be seen in *The Psychology of Dementia Praecox*, the breakthrough to an abstract concept of energy took place only in the years 1911–1913.

Basically, Jung criticized two points: In the first place, it seemed to him that Freud's libido theory did not sufficiently demarcate vital energy from psychic energy, which resulted in its limited usefulness. To understand the mechanisms of psychic energy required a differentiation from biological energy. Jung therefore proposed the term *life-energy*[1] as a concept of wider scope, encompassing psychic as well as biological energy.

Secondly, Jung became convinced that a concept of energy founded mainly on concrete phenomena (such as the aggressive or sexual drives) was not suited to convey the dynamic changes of the libido in an adequate way. He, therefore, searched for a concept of libido which would permit an understanding of the vicissitudes and displacements of the libido as arising from a unified principle. His aim was to find an expression of the total psychic activity which would permit one to understand particular psychic events as manifestations of one and the same form of energy. His goal was to establish an abstract concept of the libido based on quantitative determinations.

In his attempt at a quantitative determination of the libido, Jung partially agreed with Freud, who—owing to his bent for natural science—always pursued the ideal of a universal determinism and measurability of all phenomena. Freud, however, was limited by restricting the libido concept to the assessment of sexual drives and their dynamic relationships. Consequently, psychic mechanisms were always understood only as transformations of sexual energy or of sexually determined qualities. According to Freud, libido was "a quantitatively variable force which could serve as a measure of processes and transformations occurring in the field of sexual excitation."[2] He

---

[1] Jung, "On Psychic Energy" (1928), p. 17.
[2] Freud, "Three Essays on the Theory of Sexuality" (1905), p. 217.

postulated "the idea of a quantity of libido . . . whose production, increase or diminution, distribution and displacement should afford us possibilities for explaining the psychosexual phenomena observed."[3]

In spite of seemingly similar efforts, Jung's concept of psychic energy differed fundamentally from Freud's theory of libido. He believed that Freud completely missed the point by tying the concept of libido so closely to sexuality, particularly to infantile sexuality.

Jung felt compelled to extend the concept of libido in two directions: He became aware of the shortcomings of the libido concept when Freud declared that archaic religious ideas were nothing more than products of sexual sublimation and incest images; he also took exception to Freud's theory of paranoia. In both cases, Freud reduced these phenomena to primary sexual drives and thus made it impossible to discern subtle differences. Jung could no more accept Freud's concept that religion was "the universal obsessional neurosis of humanity"[4] than his explanation of incest images by purely libidinous processes. Such an approach, in Jung's eyes, amounted to a distortion of psychic phenomena, which disregarded the reality of psychic factors and also the symbolic meaning of archaic images.

Jung's finding that incest images, in the majority of cases, used analogies, such as sun, light, and sound for the father image, the cave and the city for the mother image, indicated to him a search for deeper meaning. Such tendencies then manifested an ill-defined religious struggle, a search for overcoming mere drives by spiritual yearning. How could a unipolar sexual common denominator—such as Freud proposed—do justice to the bipolarity of processes of psychic change? In Jung's view, the archaic image of God could never be equated with the mere fulfillment of an incestuous wish, nor could neurosis be exhaustively explained by the conflict between incestuous wish and incest taboo. Rather, the conflict was due to a disunion in life-energy itself: the wish created by the drive was opposed by an equally strong desire for liberation from the compulsion exerted by the drive—submersion in the bosom of the family was offset by the wish for psychic rebirth. The "will" clashed with an equally potent "won't,"[5] the concrete with the general, and finally, the natural with the spiritual. These opposites constitute a conflict inherent in the life process, in which neither one can be reduced to the other. As a result of this insight, Jung recognized the necessity of a unified concept of the libido which would do justice to the transformations of such basic

[3] Ibid.
[4] "The Future of an Illusion" (1927), p. 43.
[5] Jung, *Symbols of Transformation* (1952), p. 174. (Also in 1911–12 edn.)

expressions of life. He, therefore, proposed (like Schopenhauer) to conceive libido as will without any specification, a kind of continuous life urge which could find expression in affect, love, sexuality, as well as in intellectual ideas.

Another influence, equally strong, which impelled Jung to formulate a concept of psychic energy was Freud's theory of paranoia. Here, too, Freud tended to oversimplify matters. Jung had earlier mentioned, citing Janet (see G.I.2.c), that in dementia "all the functions of reality" are diminished or disappear;[6] in contrast, Freud emphatically advocated the view that the symptoms of dementia—megalomania and autoeroticism—owed their energy exclusively to detachment of the libido from sexual objects. As in hysteria and obsessional neurosis, symptom formation was explained as due to processes of repression and regression, which in paraphrenia reverts, not only to the libidinous objects of fantasy, but to the primary stage of infantile autoeroticism, with "a complete abandonment of object-love"[7] and simultaneous fixation to the ego.[8]

In opposition to this description of the principal characteristics of paranoia as "repression . . . detachment of the libido, together with its regression on to the ego,"[9] Jung stressed that in dementia praecox there was a considerable degree of loss of reality. Years earlier Janet had encountered in psychasthenia a deficiency in the *fonction du réel*, and Jung confirmed this finding in dementia praecox, based on dream analysis and association experiments.

> Earlier, in *The Psychology of Dementia Praecox*, I made use of the term "psychic energy" because what is lacking in this disease is evidently more than erotic interest as such. . . . But in schizophrenia far more is lacking to reality than could ever be laid at the door of sexuality in the strict sense of the word. The "fonction du réel" is absent to such a degree as to include the loss of certain instinctual forces which cannot possibly be supposed to have a sexual character.[10]

According to Jung, to derive the loss of reality from sexual drives would have been tantamount to artificial manipulation. Even though Freud was correct in tracing the introversion of libido back to auto-eroticism in cases of hysteria, this hypothesis was insufficient to elucidate the symptoms of autism (Bleuler) which are characteristic of the

---

6 "On Simulated Insanity" (1903), p. 171.

7 Freud, "Psycho-Analytic Notes on an Autobiographical Account of a Case of Paranoia (Dementia Paranoides)" (1911), p. 77.

8 "On Simulated Insanity," p. 72.   9 Ibid., p. 76.

10 *Symbols of Transformation*, p. 135. (Also in 1911–12 edn.)

schizophrenic patient. Jung understood this phenomenon primarily as an intrapsychic "substitute" for a disturbed reality function.[11]

Both of these considerations made it necessary for Jung to oppose Freud's concept of libido with the concept of a unified *"life-energy,"*[12] which explained the loss of libido as well as the loss of reality.

These facts have made it impossible for me to apply Freud's libido theory to dementia praecox.[13]

1. The Concept of Psychic Energy

Following Robert Mayer, who had introduced the concept of energy into the field of physics, Jung understood psychic energy as a general expression for effective action in the realm of the psyche. Just as electricity was not merely a transformation of water power, but was a manifestation of an abstract form of energy as well, psychic transformations also represented separate manifestations of one and the same energy. *It is not physical forces that change into one another but, strictly speaking, it is the energy that changes its outward form.*[14] Jung proposed that, like physical energy, psychic energy, too, could be conceived as *a dynamic unity,*[15] capable of the most varied manifestations.

The following definition sheds light upon Jung's energic point of view:

The energic point of view . . . is in essence final; the event is traced back from effect to cause on the assumption that some kind of energy underlies the changes in phenomena, that it maintains itself as a constant throughout these changes and finally leads to entropy, a condition of general equilibrium. The flow of energy has a definite direction (goal) in that it follows the gradient of potential in a way that cannot be reversed.[16]

The energic point of view, as defined here, seemed to Jung to be the only concept which could profitably explain the changes, shifts, and transformations of the libido.

Jung was well aware of the great difficulties caused by introducing the energic point of view into psychology. It raised the question of whether the approach of the natural sciences, that is, the method of

[11] "The Theory of Psychoanalysis" (1913), p. 120.
[12] "On Psychic Energy," p. 17.
[13] "The Theory of Psychoanalysis," p. 122.
[14] Ibid., p. 124.   [15] Ibid., p. 112.
[16] "On Psychic Energy," p. 4.

deducing pure laws of motion from observations, could be transferred to psychological factors. Didn't the nature of the psyche conflict with the basic principles of the energic view? Applying the concept of energy in the realm of psychology entailed much greater difficulties than in the natural sciences. It was possible for the natural sciences to ignore the substance and to consider only pure relations, because nothing other than objects that could be quantitatively determined were involved. Psychic phenomena, on the contrary, were largely inaccessible to such measurements and—as far as they were potentially admissible to consciousness—were greatly susceptible to subjectivity, arbitrariness, and inestimable conscious interference. Finally, the psyche was open to the collective unconscious and exposed to spontaneous manifestations of the unconscious, that is, indeterminate influences.

To transfer to the psychic realm concepts of the natural sciences, which were "exclusively those of moving bodies in space,"[17] was, therefore, highly problematic. Everything hinged on whether it was possible to establish relatively exact quantitative relations and relatively closed partial systems and on whether the principle of equivalence could be applied. Most of all, the efficacy of the concept of energy depended on whether the laws applicable to isolated systems could be transferred to actual phenomena, that is, to undisturbed, natural psychic processes. These were all very debatable assumptions, as pointed out so excellently by Toni Wolff.[18] And indeed, Jung's theory of energy might not be as convincing as his other concepts.

Jung attempted, first of all, to implement these assumptions by introducing an abstract and hypothetical concept of energy, to be used merely as a token or counter.

> . . . the libido with which we operate is not only not concrete or known, but is a complete X, a pure hypothesis, a model or counter, and is no more concretely conceivable than the energy known to the world of physics. . . . Forces are phenomenal manifestations; what underlies their relations with one another is the hypothetical idea of energy, which is, of course, entirely psychological and has nothing to do with so-called objective reality.[19]

The questions of exact quantitative determinations and whether these were possible in the approach to psychic energy were of basic

17 Ibid., p. 5.
18 "Einführung in die Grundlagen der Komplexen Psychologie," in *Die kulturelle Bedeutung der Komplexen Psychologie* (1935).
19 "The Theory of Psychoanalysis," p. 124.

importance. Jung answered these questions in the positive, with the qualification, however, that in contrast to physics only *"quantitative estimates of psychic energy"*[20] were feasible. He recognized that in a psychic content this was restricted to the degree of tension or, in other words, to the value intensity.[21] In this context, the findings in the association experiments were useful—for instance, the quantitative estimate of the indicators of complexes, which was connected to some degree with the feasibility of time measurements (see A.II.3).

Jung saw that the energic approach when applied to the realm of the psyche was considerably limited by the fact that energy—so far as it concerns pure relations—was not to be construed as an actual force. As experienced, energy always appeared to be connected with psychic forces, or a "something" tied to forces or psychic qualities. Instead of working with pure energic relationships, in the empirical world one is dealing only with dynamic relationships, that is, the play of forces, such as affects, drives, and so on. Jung traced the abstract concept of energy back to a potential of value intensities; consequently, the dynamic concept of energy was conceived as coping "with the behavior of forces, with substances in motion"[22] ("factor of *extensity*").[23] Freud's psychology was based mainly on the dynamic concept of energy, essentially on a definition of energy as a specific "drive."[24] Even though Jung by no means denied the existence of sexual dynamics, he found it impossible to build the theory of energy on a concept of dynamics which stressed the sexual aspect to such a degree. His approach called for a general psychological theory—an abstract concept of energy—which would account for the changes and transformations of psychic energy.[25]

This difference between the energic and dynamic points of view became a focus of controversy between Freud and Jung and contributed greatly to their final separation. As far as Freud was concerned, libido remained "a quantitatively variable force which could serve as a measure of processes and transformations occurring in the field of sexual excitation."[26] For Jung, the dynamic point of view regarded energy as always attached to substance; "from the energic standpoint, on the other hand, substance is nothing more than the expression or sign of an energic system."[27] The fact that energy became visible only in specific phenomena did not in any way prejudice his attempt to establish laws of pure movement.

20 "On Psychic Energy," p. 9.   21 Ibid., p. 13.
22 Ibid., p. 28.   23 Ibid., p. 20.
24 Ibid., p. 29.   25 Ibid.
26 Freud, "Three Essays," p. 217.   27 Jung, "On Psychic Energy," p. 22.

2. *Equivalent Transformations of the Libido*

Applying the energic approach to empirical phenomena, such as transforming conscious processes into unconscious processes (images, fantasies, and symbols) called for a further clarification, namely, the demonstration of equivalent relationships. For this, psychology had to find specific methods.

In the natural sciences, the application of the concept of energy primarily required attention to the principle of conservation of energy. Freud did this as early as 1892 when he mentioned the tendency to keep intracerebral excitation constant.[28] Jung stressed that the principle of conservation of the total energy in a closed system—an indispensable premise in physics—could not be directly applied to psychology. Since it is impossible to isolate totally closed systems in the realm of the psyche, Jung's choice between the two basic principles of energy—conservation and equivalence—was to give preference to the latter.

A. PRINCIPLE OF EQUIVALENCE AND TRANSFORMATION OF ENERGY

Jung believed that the principle of equivalence was in complete accord with the fact that in practical experience one never encountered total systems but only partial systems. He understood the principle of equivalence primarily as the energic relationship between quanta of energy: "The disappearance of a given quantum of libido is followed by the appearance of an equivalent value in another form."[29]

. . . for a given quantity of energy expended or consumed in bringing about a certain condition, an equal quantity of the same or another form of energy will appear elsewhere.[30]

Jung also established that considering equivalent relationships in empirical psychology was not a new idea. Charcot, in connection with his theory of trauma, had drawn attention to the transformation of conscious into unconscious states under the influence of shock. Janet, too, following Charcot's suggestions had investigated the parallelism between *abaissement du niveau mental* and dissociated memories. This point of view was elaborated in great detail by Freud who, from the very beginning of his interest in psychology, attempted to demonstrate that symptoms were equivalent substitute formations of quanta which had been withdrawn from consciousness. Consequently, no quantum of energy disappeared without reappearing in a correspond-

---

28 Breuer and Freud, *Studies on Hysteria* (1893–95), p. 197.
29 Jung, "On Psychic Energy," p. 19.   30 Ibid., p. 18.

ing substitute formation (parapraxis, fixation to the infantile level, and symptom). This extension of the causal connection between ego, trauma, and symptom (as established by Charcot) was to have great meaning in psychotherapy because cure became equated with detection of lost energies.

Freud—according to the model of the natural sciences which he followed—referred mainly to the principle of conservation. This approach, however, was not cogent as far as Jung was concerned. Freud missed the decisive issue in his "Project for a Scientific Psychology" (1895). In this work, conceived on physiological and neurological bases, Freud followed Fechner's suggestions, pointing out the tendency of the organism to keep the sum of excitation constant.[31] Consequently, he assigned to the pleasure drive the role of a regulating psychic principle, aimed at keeping the psychic apparatus as free from irritation as possible.[32] His ideal, first of all, was the reduction of drive tension to zero level, which seemed to be related to the law of entropy (Freud's economic model), as Rapaport,[33] too, assumed. Freud's hypothesis was confirmed in *Beyond the Pleasure Principle* (1920); here, he referred to Fechner's principle of the tendency towards stability,[34] which maintains that in every closed system there is a progression from unstable to stable states. Freud recognized in this principle the basis not only of the death instinct but of all drives in general. Accordingly, it was the essence of any drive to return constantly to the forms of earlier experiences—a fact which manifested itself, for example, in the always renewed repetition of drive stimuli, aimed at returning to the state of complete rest.

While Jung laid great emphasis upon the importance of the principle of equivalence, he felt obliged also to recognize the psychological effectiveness of the law of entropy. But, while Freud primarily envisaged attaining a state of absence of drives, Jung understood the principle of entropy as a tendency of energy transformations within *closed natural systems*, tending to balance the energy gradient by bringing the value differences of the entire system from a less probable to a more probable state.[35] The prerequisite for development of such a state was not only a relatively closed system (and therewith a constant level of energy) but also the goal-directedness and irreversibility

[31] Freud, "Project for a Scientific Psychology" (1895), p. 358.
[32] *The Interpretation of Dreams* (1908), p. 565.
[33] D. Rapaport, "The Structure of Psychoanalytic Theory: A Systematizing Attempt" (1959), p. 111.
[34] Freud, "Beyond the Pleasure Principle," pp. 8–9.
[35] Wolff, "Einführung," p. 133.

of natural processes—requirements which could not be directly transposed from the area of physical matter to the psyche. Jung always objected to the application of the law of entropy because, in the realm of the psyche, there were only partial systems; these subordinate systems were only relatively closed, and one had always to consider the possibility of a spontaneous interference of consciousness in the natural course of events.

The validity of the principle of entropy was, therefore, tied to the relative demarcation of subordinate systems from the whole as well as to the relative immobility of consciousness—phenomena which were encountered mainly in pathological cases. Jung saw such situations, for instance, in the overemphasized exclusion of conscious systems from the whole of the psyche (prejudices, obsessions), which would manifest a negative quality and might lead to congealing ideas to the point of numbness. In pathological cases there was "extreme detachment from the surroundings," particularly in catatonic schizophrenia. The law of entropy, however, could also have a positive effect—for example, in gradual compensatory processes such as might occur after periods of stormy affects or after acute inner tensions.

> Everyone speaks of the "storms of youth" which yield to the "tranquillity of age." We speak, too, of a "confirmed belief" after "battling with doubts," of "relief from inner tension," and so on. This is the involuntary energic standpoint shared by everyone.[36]

Freud referred several times to the law of entropy, without specifically naming it, but there are two instances in which he mentions it explicitly: in one case, in connection with the difficulty of undoing psychic developments which have been converted into neurotic symptoms;[37] in another, as a characteristic of very old people.[38] The principle of equivalence is, as far as I have seen, alluded to only once, in connection with a discussion of delusions:

> The delusions of patients appear to me to be the equivalents of the constructions which we build up in the course of an analytic treatment—attempts at explanation and cure, though it is true that these, under the conditions of a psychosis, can do no more than replace the fragment of reality that is being disavowed in the present by another fragment that has already been disavowed in the remote past.[39]

36 Jung, "On Psychic Energy," p. 27.
37 Freud, "From the History of an Infantile Neurosis" (1918), p. 116.
38 "Analysis Terminable and Interminable" (1937), p. 242.
39 "Constructions in Analysis" (1937), p. 268.

III. THE LIBIDO AS UNDIVIDED VITAL ENERGY (JUNG)

Jung stressed that the principle of equivalence was far from easy to apply in actual cases because they never presented clear-cut examples of the law; it was possible, however, to find certain analogies of equivalence in psychotherapy. In the first place, he emphasized the transference between physician and patient, which was frequently manifested in dream and fantasy symbols—equivalents substituting for conscious attitudes. In this context, he found examples of Freud's cases significant.

> Anyone who reads Freud's works with attention will see what an important role the equivalence principle plays in the structure of his theories. This can be seen particularly clearly in his investigations of case material, where he gives an account of repressions and their substitute formations. Anyone who has had practical experience of this field knows that the equivalence principle is of great heuristic value in the treatment of neuroses. Even if its application is not always conscious, you nevertheless apply it instinctively or by feeling. For instance, when a conscious value, say a transference, decreases or actually disappears, you immediately look for the substitute formation, expecting to see an equivalent value spring up somewhere else.[40]

B. SYMBOL FORMATION AND EQUIVALENCE PRINCIPLE

Jung pointed out, however, that the application of the equivalence principle was hardly sufficient in instances where *unconscious contents were transformed into symbols* or where an understanding of symbolic connections was required. In such cases, Freud's dynamic approach was bound to fail, because it was restricted to reducing symptoms to their equivalent substitute formations (for example, neurotic symptoms traced to repressed incestuous wishes); therefore, it could not do justice to the meaning and aim of the process nor to the significance of the symbol. The search for the teleological and symbolic meaning called for more than Freud's method. Viewed from the aspect of symbolic meaning, processes such as the transposition or translation of images into symbols involved an unconscious creation of psychic analogies which had a greater power of attraction than the original image. Such images manifested their power by producing a gradient for shifting energy from an instinctive to a spiritual level. From the energic point of view, they were equivalent to the original image, that is, they had at least the same value intensity as the original image.

[40] Jung, "On Psychic Energy." p. 19.

E. FROM LIBIDO TO PSYCHIC ENERGY

The application of the principle of equivalence to symbolic transformation was one of the specific and unique characteristics of Jung's
psychology. Here, the contrast between Jung and Freud stood out
particularly clearly. Jung emphasized that transformations of equivalent analogies always involved a transition from formations of lower
value to those of higher value or, from another angle, the discovery of
an unknown meaning hidden in the symbol. In contrast, Freud saw the
significance of equivalent contents as representing substitute formations of infantile and repressed drives, particularly incestuous wishes.

There were several more difficulties to be resolved before the problem
of the production of such analogies could be satisfactorily answered.
It became evident that in this process the aid of the unconscious was
indispensable, because transformations into symbols were never "consciously thought out," but always occurred spontaneously. Jung
ascribed such unconscious transformations to a *natural "tendency to
invent analogies,"*[41] which he conceived as one of the prerogatives of
the psyche. This tendency worked toward the constant equalizing of
unconscious and conscious ideas. The difficulties of analogy formation,
which Jung had already touched upon in *Transformations and Symbols of the Libido* (1912), were treated exhaustively in the revised
edition, *Symbols of Transformation* (1952).

> The libido has, as it were, a natural penchant: it is like water, which
> must have a gradient if it is to flow. The nature of these analogies is
> therefore a serious problem because, as we have said, they must be
> ideas which attract the libido.[42]

In the creation of psychic analogies, it was essential that the analogous image (for instance, the cave) should be subtly toned to the
underlying drive (such as the natural tie to the mother), or that it
should somehow subdue the original image. This process involved
harmonizing the "superior" and the "inferior," the "abstract" and
the "concrete." Such a symbolic analogy was, accordingly, an expression
combining natural and spiritual significance—for example: tower,
cave, rose, and church. Thus, a potential of opposites was created which
provoked further development. The analogy was important as an
attracting symbol, as a turning point which led from a natural expression of drives to a spiritual form.

Jung saw the primordial ideas, the archetypal images, as especially
suitable to produce an energic gradient. These universal, inherited
conformations, which were expressions of the structural relationships
of the unconscious, were predestined to function in energic transfor-

41 *Symbols of Transformation*, p. 141.   42 Ibid., p. 227.

mation or conversion.[43] Expressed in more general terms: Whenever the analogous ideas conformed to the structure of the psyche and were accordingly harmonized to what was destined to be changed, the archaic image had the function of energy transformer. In 1940–41, Jung greatly clarified the ideas he had expounded in *On Psychic Energy* (1928).

> A symbol cannot be made to order as the rationalist would like to believe. It is a legitimate symbol only if it gives expression to the immutable structure of the unconscious and can therefore command general acceptance.[44]

It was inevitable that concepts of the transformation of energy could be applied to psychotherapy only to a limited extent. One way to do this was to direct the patient's attention to suprapersonal processes in the collective psyche, that is, to spontaneous fantasy processes, such as active imagination.

In summary, I want to stress again that Jung designated very clearly the principle of equivalence as the basic law of energic transformations in general and, in particular, of symbolic transformations.

3. Tension of the Opposites and Energic Adjustment

The tension of the opposites represented an essential basis of the theory of energy, of the changes and transformations of the libido, and particularly of the origin of symbols. Freud had always considered the problem of the opposites only within the framework of the structure of the drives. In contrast, Jung saw in the opposites a phenomenon which comprised the two poles of drive and spirit. Whatever in human life manifested itself as opposition was the expression of an original principle inherent in the totality of the psyche.

Jung made the very important discovery that the tension of opposites was the basis of psychic intensity, illustrated by opposites such as willingness and unwillingness, nature and civilization, consciousness and the unconscious. The tension of the opposites, in fact, formed the whole basis of psychic energy. The combined action of opposite energic charges resulted in a difference in potential which determined vital flow. As early as 1928, Jung formulated these ideas as "the nature of the opposites that underlie psychic energy."[45] Even before this, he had clearly shown the direction of his thinking in *Psychological Types*:

43 "On Psychic Energy," p. 41.
44 "A Psychological Approach to the Dogma of the Trinity" (1940/1941), p. 188.
45 "On Psychic Energy," p. 55.

The concept of energy implies that of polarity, since a current of energy necessarily presupposes two different states, or poles, without which there can be no current. Every energic phenomenon . . . consists of pairs of opposites: beginning and end, above and below, hot and cold, earlier and later, cause and effect, etc.[46]

Jung described the interplay between the opposites as "the energetics of the life process, the polar tension that is necessary for self-regulation."[47] Starting from this point of view, he found the concept of psychic energy very productive because it pointed to something "like a living balance between opposites"[48] and at the same time adequately expressed the opposite movement in the psyche.

The tendency of the opposites to turn one into the other—*enantiodromia*—must be understood as an expression of the polarization of psychic contents. To his own great satisfaction Jung ascertained that in early antiquity Heraclitus demonstrated the law of counter-movement. This law meant that "sooner or later everything runs into its opposite."[49] Nietzsche, too, was for Jung a paramount authority, because he expressed something similar when he wrote that "with every growth of man his other side must grow as well."[50]

The polarization of opposites (or a constantly repeated falling apart of what was united) was a characteristic of living reality, and all human activity was determined by antagonistic tendencies; in the same way, Jung recognized the tendency toward a balance between the opposites as a basic principle of human existence. As early as 1917, he based this principle on the law of self-regulation. The psyche not only showed a tendency to polarization but also an inclination to strike a balance, even to establish continuous states of equilibrium. Both aspects were related to the law of self-regulation, which is of extraordinary importance for the psyche. The psyche regulates itself. Accordingly, Jung thought that a theory which would do justice to the living processes of the psyche would have to be built upon the principles of opposition and self-regulation.

A psychological theory, if it is to be more than a technical makeshift, must base itself on the principle of opposition; for without this it could only re-establish a neurotically unbalanced psyche. There is

46 *Psychological Types* (1921), p. 202.
47 "The Relations Between the Ego and the Unconscious" (1916), p. 196.
48 "On Psychic Energy," p. 55.
49 "On the Psychology of the Unconscious" (1917), p. 72.
50 Nietzsche, *The Will to Power* (tr. Ludovici), p. 316.

no balance, no system of self-regulation, without opposition. The psyche is just such a self-regulating system.[51]

Viewed from the external structure, a balance of opposites would depend on a gradient and could never be the result of merely voluntary effort. Transformations and changes of ideas, therefore, called for the natural happening of differences in potential, provided they tended in the correct direction. "It has become abundantly clear to me that life can flow forward only along the path of the gradient."[52] Only under such conditions were transformations into symbols feasible.

Whenever creative processes were in operation, a potential of the opposites as well as a tendency toward balance could be detected. Not only the products of civilization but also religious ideas and intellectual creations could be understood as the result of a profound tension between nature and intellect. While civilization revealed the opposition between natural demands and the nomothetic (that is, law-creating) processes, the antagonistic experiences of light and darkness reached an apex in various ideas of the godhead. Jung made the interesting statement that

God would thus be not only the essence of spiritual light, appearing as the latest flower on the tree of evolution, not only the spiritual goal of salvation in which all creation culminates, not only the end and aim, but also the darkest, nethermost cause of Nature's blackest deeps.[53]

Every symbol of a god was consequently the expression of a paradox which conformed with a deep psychological truth.

For it asserts the essential contradictoriness of one and the same being, a being whose innermost nature is a tension of opposites. Science calls this "being" energy, for energy is like a living balance between opposites.[54]

I mentioned earlier that Jung traced the origin of the tension of opposites back into earliest childhood. In following the bases of human existence back to the germinal disposition, Jung's idea coincided with Freud's, but one must not overlook the essential differences between the two investigators. As to Jung, the germinal disposition was never restricted to expressing tensions of drives (for example, ego-instinct

[51] "On the Psychology of the Unconscious," p. 61.
[52] Ibid., p. 53.   [53] "On Psychic Energy," p. 55.
[54] Ibid.

and sex-drive), but was the carrier of an immense incongruity, extending deep into the ancestral inheritance.

Thus every child is born with an immense split in his make-up: on one side he is more or less like an animal, on the other side he is the final embodiment of an age-old and endlessly complicated sum of hereditary factors. This split accounts for the tension of the germinal state and does much to explain the many puzzles of child psychology, which certainly has no lack of them.[55]

In the next chapter we will discuss how Jung's investigations led him to discover an increasingly deeper meaning of the tension of opposites. At this time it may suffice to point out that he never considered man's spiritual nature "only as an appendage, a by-product of the instincts,"[56] but always as a distinct element with the quality of a specific formative principle of psychic processes.

The phenomena of polarization and balance of the opposites became more meaningful in the second half of life, that is, after 35 years of age. As the individual developed, he was faced in his mature years with the necessity to integrate the "other within him" in order to fulfill the inherent principle of life. In the first half of life, the vital process involved him with the world around him, causing him to repress his infantile dependency on father, mother, and their substitute figures, in order to shape pressing drives and intellectual impulses to his needs. In the second half of life, however, such an attitude was bound to lead to phenomena of frustration. In this phase, an individual's confrontation with those areas of the personality which had remained unconscious, or were forgotten or repressed, could be avoided only by paying the price of severe disturbances. It was equally unavoidable for him to make contact with the contents of the collective unconscious, which exerted pressure but were still foreign to consciousness. This awareness determined Jung's basic attitude toward psychotherapy. For older subjects he did not see the goal of therapy as working-through infantile incestuous wishes (Freud) or inappropriate fantasies (Adler) or in liberating the ego from the burden of the past. He considered it essential to bring to consciousness and assimilate the function of the opposites hidden in the phenomena of blocking, frustration, and neurotic symptoms. Jung formulated this approach eloquently in 1926:

In a young man, the instinctual forces tied up in the neurosis give him, when released, buoyancy and hope and the chance to extend the scope of his life. To the man in the second half of life the development of the function of opposites lying dormant in the unconscious means a renewal; but this development no longer proceeds via the dissolution of infantile ties, the destruction of infantile illusions and the transference of old imagos to new figures: it proceeds via the problem of opposites.[57]

4. The Primary Connection of Archetypal Image and Instinct

Jung was always fascinated by the phenomenon of the tension of opposites in the human life process. Starting with *Studies in Word-Association* and continuing to his last works, he took up this problem again and again, always deepening his understanding of it. Initially, he encountered the tension of opposites as the confrontation of feeling-tone and idea; later (1912) he stressed the opposition of "will" and "won't" inherent in life; after another nine years (1921) he worked out the fourfold basic structure of the psyche. In 1919 he had conceived the problem of the opposites as antagonism of image and instinct. He recognized that both opposites were connected, even though causal reduction was impossible. Both belonged to the "characteristic quality of a living system."

Before looking at this problem more closely, we must know what Jung understood by the expressions "instinct" and "drive." From his statements it seems clear that he used both terms interchangeably. We find a definition only of the concept of instinct, but for the meaning of drive we are left with the characteristics of need, impulse, and desire. Jung described as instincts those unconscious processes which recur uniformly and regularly and present, above all, the characteristics of inner necessity[58] and inherited traits. Working on the latter problem he found the incredibly refined instinct of propagation in the yucca moth illuminating.[59] He concluded that the instinct functioned entirely independently from a person's individuality and that, in addition, it was of a collective nature—a finding which suggested its relationship to the archetypal image. The primordial images, too, which showed an autochthonous and uniform behavior, functioned autonomously and were anchored in the collective heritage.

Jung gained an understanding from these observations which was extraordinarily productive for his further investigations: The instincts (drives) and the basic forms of human orientation (archetypal images) were not only rooted in the collective unconscious but, owing

---

57 "On the Psychology of the Unconscious," p. 61.
58 "Instinct and the Unconscious" (1919), p. 130.
59 Ibid., p. 132.

to their common traits and regular qualities, they represented correlates, although with certain differences in detail.

And yet the way in which man inwardly pictures the world is still,
despite all differences of detail, as uniform and as regular as his
instinctive actions.[60]

Image and instinct characteristically regulated each event and presented typical forms—the instincts determining action, the archetypal
images influencing understanding.

Archetypes are typical modes of apprehension, and wherever we
meet with uniform and regularly recurring modes of apprehension
we are dealing with an archetype no matter whether its mythological
character is recognized or not.[61]

Jung described the instincts in an analogous manner:

Instincts are typical modes of action, and wherever we meet with
uniform and regularly recurring modes of action and reaction we are
dealing with instinct, no matter whether it is associated with a
conscious motive or not.[62]

However, he went even further. The connection between instinct and
archetypal image appeared to him so close that he drew the conclusion
that the two were coupled in the empirical world. He saw the primordial image as the *self-portrait of the instinct*—in other words, *the
instinct's perception of itself.*[63] Just as archetypal images always appeared together with a certain quantum of energy, the strivings of
the archaic drives were connected with mythological images. Jung
again expressed this, in much the same way, many years later:

. . . instincts are by no means blind, spontaneous, isolated impulses;
they are on the contrary associated with typical situational patterns
and cannot be released unless existing conditions correspond to the
a priori pattern. The collective contents expressed in mythologems
represent such situational patterns, which are so intimately connected with the release of instinct.[64]

After his first attempts to comprehend the relationship between
archetype (archetypal image) and instinct, Jung dropped the matter
for some twenty years and returned to the problem only in connection
with his investigation of synchronicity. For continuity's sake, it should

[60] Ibid., p. 136.   [61] Ibid., pp. 137–38.
[62] Ibid., p. 135.   [63] Ibid., p. 136.
[64] "Medicine and Psychotherapy" (1945), p. 92.

be mentioned that Jung, in 1946, had pursued the tension of opposites so far that a confrontation of drive and spirit became apparent. In the Appendix (I.2) I will try to show that this conclusion was based on the assumption of two transcendental principles.

5. Incest Image and Rebirth

In Jung's view of the incest complex we find a direct application of his concepts of the equivalence principle and of the transformation of unconscious contents into symbols. His idea culminated in the premise that not a concrete wish for an incestuous union but rather a symbolic occurrence was involved.

As early as 1912, Jung alluded to his basic difference from Freud's concretistic interpretation by referring to the dialogue between Nicodemus and Jesus.[65] Jung was impressed by Jesus' contrasting the natural birth from the mother's womb with the symbolic significance of a rebirth out of water and the Spirit. The latter clearly exhibited a higher potential as well as the fascinating power of the archaic image. Jung recognized a similar meaning in the image of the impregnation of the mother by the Spirit or by the fertilizing wind. In both instances, he made it an essential point that the intellect, imprisoned in concretive thinking, was given the opportunity of a new gradient which led from natural to spiritual reality.

"Nicodemus would remain stuck in banalities, if he did not succeed in raising himself above his concretism."[66] As Jung said in the revised edition:

> The symbolical truth, on the other hand, which puts water in place of the mother and spirit or fire in place of the father, frees the libido from the channel of the incest tendency, offers it a new gradient, and canalizes it into a spiritual form.[67]

While Jung accentuated one's rebirth which comes from the spiritual aspect of the psyche, the archaic image was to Freud a sign of the repressed impulse toward incest, of the wish for incestuous cohabitation. Jung was opposed to reducing the symbolic image to such concrete wishes and pointed out that

> It is not incestuous cohabitation that is desired, but rebirth. The incest prohibition acts as an obstacle and makes the creative fantasy

---

[65] *Psychology of the Unconscious (Transformations and Symbols of the Libido, 1912)*, p. 252.
[66] *Symbols of Transformation* (1952), p. 226.
[67] Ibid.

inventive; for instance there are attempts to make the mother pregnant by means of fertility magic. The effect of the incest-taboo and of the attempts at canalization is to stimulate the creative imagination, which gradually opens up possible avenues for the self-realization of libido. In this way the libido becomes imperceptibly spiritualized.[68]

Jung's premise that the unconscious aim of the incest image was not a desire to cohabit, but a longing for the rebirth of one's own nature through contact with the maternal soil, could be considered a re-valuation of all values. The finding that this wish was fundamentally a search for one's self and not just a decline into the infantile period—as Freud had assumed—was one of the most impressive aspects of Jung's psychology.

I have suggested that it is not just a relapse into infantilism, but a genuine attempt to get at something necessary. . . . We find that he [the patient] is seeking something entirely different, something that Freud only appreciates negatively: the universal feeling of childhood innocence, the sense of security, of protection, of reciprocated love, of trust, of faith—a thing that has many names.[69]

With such an approach Jung left unchanged the quality of the incest image as something unknown, just as the mother's womb sheltered an abundance of possibilities. Jung deserves great credit for attributing to the regressive process the potential of a renewal of the personality from the depth of the psyche—even though there was always the danger of coming to an impasse. He even saw that this regressive movement was often the only possible bridge toward establishing a living relationship to creative forces and also to the treasure of experiences accumulated in the psyche over centuries.

Wisdom dwells in the depths, the wisdom of the mother; being one with her means being granted a vision of deeper things, of the primordial images and primitive forces which underlie all life and are its nourishing, sustaining, creative matrix.[70]

The concept of regression, as formulated by Jung in his mature years, was not, however, the same as his view during his early work. Under the spell of Freud's psychology, Jung initially conceived of this phenomenon as a retrograde movement of the libido which "regresses

68 Ibid., p. 224.
69 "Some Aspects of Modern Psychotherapy" (1929), p. 32.
70 Symbols of Transformation, p. 413. (Also in 1911–12 edn.)

back to infantile reminiscences"[71] (from the individual's past history) and primarily revived the parental complex. Similarly, in the second part of *Transformations and Symbols of the Libido*, he described such regression (the "sacrilegious backward grasp," as Nietzsche called it) as "the specific inertia of the libido, which will relinquish no object of the past, but would like to hold it fast forever."[72] Although this idea agreed in part with Freud's views, one must not overlook the modifications Jung made in the second part of *Transformations and Symbols of the Libido*. They went hand-in-hand with his shift from a personalistic to an impersonal level. Transcending personal memory images or "activating collective images (archetypes)"[73] led Jung to the numinous and fateful quality of impersonal images. An example of activating such archetypes would be the awakening of the archaic mother image, the wisdom in the depth of the psyche.

During his years of struggle Jung possessed a dark feeling and a presentiment which he later succeeded in formulating with increasing clarity. His investigations enabled him to recognize unmistakably that regression to the incest image did not imply activating images of one's own parents nor concrete reminiscences of one's infantile period, but rather ideas of suprapersonal figures and of filial relationships more on the order of a religious nature. Only such a concept could bring the process of regression into correct focus, as stated in the revised edition (1952):

> If the regression goes still further back, beyond the phase of child-hood to the preconscious, prenatal phase, then archetypal images appear, no longer connected with the individual's memories, but belonging to the stock of inherited *possibilities of representation* that are born anew in every individual. It is from them that there arise those images of "divine" beings, part animal, part human.[74]

The perspective of mythological contents and religious allegories opened up new approaches for understanding symbols. It became apparent that regression—setting aside its reductive direction—suggested a tendency aiming at something greater.

Freud had seen the Oedipus complex, that is, the incest conflict, as a barely solvable split, which at best could be inactivated by sublimation or suppression or by adjusting to the demands of civilization. In contrast, Jung ascribed to the incest complex the potential of containing the germ for transforming the total personality. The prerequisite

71 Ibid., p. 30.
73 Ibid., p. 420.
72 Ibid., p. 174.
74 Ibid., p. 181.

for this was surpassing the intellectual and symbolic sides of the psychic conflict.

In the forties, Jung attempted to give a deeper significance to the difference between incestuous tendency and incest prohibition by distinguishing the underlying endogamous and exogamous aspects. Viewed alone, the endogamous (incestuous) tendency showed a spiritual inclination and, sociologically, an instinct "which serves to hold the family together."[75] The exogamous tendency, too, could be understood in a twofold manner. On the sociological level, it exhibited a tendency toward consolidating the personality and expanding one's own potentialities within society while, viewed from the inside, it imposed a restriction on the individual. Jung raised an interesting question: Which psychic tendencies were compensated by the two attitudes? It appeared to him that the exogamous attitude compensated for a too intense longing for the infantile milieu or for becoming submerged in one's self, while the endogamous attitude counteracted a too pronounced inclination toward losing one's self among the crowd. Jung recognized that both tendencies—the incestuous-endogamous as well as the restricting-exogamous—were combined in certain primitive tribes by a compromise solution, the so-called cross-cousin marriage.[76]

6. The Biological Hypothesis in Freud's Works

The question of the character of drive and instinct cannot be unequivocally differentiated in Freud's writing before 1920. Freud essentially limited himself to the question of the etiology of the drives, which he conceived as excitations determined by goal and object; he reserved the term "instinct" for an inherited faculty, which he ascribed almost exclusively to animals. Earlier, he had made statements on several occasions that pointed to a basic biological hypothesis. The first clear hint of a biological basis for psychic processes was given at about the time when he turned to ego psychology, primarily in narcissism (1914).

The preface to the third edition (1915) of *Three Essays on the Theory of Sexuality* characterized this work as "being deliberately independent of the findings of biology,"[77] but it also stated that "the concept of instinct is thus one of those lying on the frontier between the mental and the physical."[78] An almost identical formulation appeared

75 "The Psychology of the Transference" (1946), p. 224.
76 Ibid., p. 225.
77 Freud, "Three Essays on the Theory of Sexuality," p. 131.
78 Ibid., p. 168.

in the same year in "Instincts and Their Vicissitudes"[79] and again (although four years earlier) in "Notes on a Case of Paranoia."[80] Freud described instinct as "the psychical representative of the stimuli originating from within the organism and reaching the mind."[81] He was thinking of psychic characteristics like wishes, strivings, and ideas. He went on to say: "By the source of an instinct is meant the somatic process which occurs in an organ or part of the body."[82] The pressure of an instinct was seen as due to the tension of demands, and its psychic function as "removing the state of stimulation."[83] Such statements were to a large degree tantamount to basing drive psychology on biology. In 1938, Freud expressed this thought very clearly:

... instincts ... represent the somatic demands upon the mind.[84]

The basic biological hypothesis of Freud's psychology was definitely confirmed by this last remark as well as by his statement that the drive affected the psyche only by proceeding from its source (somatic excitation) to its aim.

Moreover, Freud stressed a series of specific points which demonstrated his inclination toward the biological approach. His emphasis on the erogenous zones and on the diphasic character of sexual development pointed in this direction as well as his remarks on the antagonism of the sexes and, particularly, his view of bisexuality. He continued to place more emphasis on the physical helplessness of the infant and the long period of dependency on his parents as an important biological substratum.

Some surprising statements of Freud from 1914 relate entirely to the area of biology. He declared man, from one point of view, to be an appendage to his germ-plasm.[85] He even proposed a chemical factor in psychic forces. He went so far as to say

... that all our provisional ideas in psychology will presumably some day be based on an organic substructure. This makes it probable that it is special substances and chemical processes which perform the operations of sexuality.[86]

While these remarks referred to the field of physiology, the distinction of the life- and death-instincts had to be understood as a concession to the inorganic world. Even while Freud wrote, "Eros, by

[79] (1915), pp. 121–22. [80] (1911), p. 74. (See above, n. 7.)
[81] "Instincts and Their Vicissitudes," p. 122.
[82] Ibid., p. 123. [83] Ibid., p. 122.
[84] "An Outline of Psycho-Analysis" (1938), p. 148.
[85] "On Narcissism: An Introduction" (1914), p. 78.
[86] Ibid.

bringing about a more and more far-reaching combination of the particles into which living substance is dispersed, aims at complicating life and at the same time, of course, at preserving it,"[87] he assigned to the death instinct (and to the coordinated repetition-compulsion) a strange "task . . . which is to lead organic life back into the inanimate state."[88]

> If we are to take it as a truth that knows no exception that every-thing living dies for *internal* reasons—becomes inorganic once again —then we shall be compelled to say that *"the aim of life is death"* and, looking backwards, that *"inanimate things existed before living ones."*[89]

Freud, following Fechner's principle of stability,[90] ventured to as-sume a gradual exhaustion of the instinct, aiming at a general state of rest. This statement, which revives a very pessimistic notion uttered in 1895,[91] seems to be significant because it reveals the destructive con-sequences of Freud's psychology of instincts.

7. Concluding Remarks

Considering the evidence presented in the foregoing, one can readily understand why Freud's theory of the libido was unacceptable to Jung. Yet, in his late writings Jung returned again to the theory of the libido in order to emphasize another fact which seemed to clarify the basis of his difference from Freud. What drew Jung's interest again and again to the sexual theory was the deep discrepancy underlying Freud's work which apparently had remained unconscious to him. On the one hand, Jung stated, sexuality had a numinous quality for Freud and assumed nothing less than "the role of a *deus absconditus*, a hidden or con-cealed god";[92] on the other hand, "his terminology and theory seemed to define it exclusively as a biological function."[93] Jung believed that this concealed dissension led Freud to regard sexuality as a highly threatening force, against which one had to protect oneself. His ex-treme preoccupation with the taboos revolving around sexuality pointed in this direction. The same was true of his constant emphasis on defense mechanisms as well as the importance he attributed in his later works to the renunciation of drives and the "education to real-

---

87 "The Ego and the Id" (1923), p. 40.   88 Ibid.
89 "Beyond the Pleasure Principle" (1920), p. 38.
90 Ibid., p. 8.
91 "Project for a Scientific Psychology," p. 357.
92 Jung, *Memories, Dreams, Reflections*, p. 151.
93 Ibid., p. 152.

ity."[94] All this not only showed that Freud thought of sexuality as an impenetrable, frightful secret but also pointed to an overpowering "other" in his psyche. From Jung's perspective, what Freud should have understood was the fact that sexuality meant to him an ultimate intellectual entity. If he could have visualized in his mind's eye the paradox of the coincidence of the "uppermost" and the "lowermost," of drive and intellect, it would hardly have been possible for him to reduce the sexual function to a biological formula. The two levels are simply incompatible.

It is of some historical interest that around 1950 Jung introduced a meaning into the framework of his own holistic concept which he presumed to be the basis of the sexual hypothesis (although Freud, to be sure, had never mentioned it). Faced with the threatening danger of instinct loss, Jung had no choice but to look searchingly into the significance of sexuality. But while Freud's observation of alienation from instinct became the motive of his theory of repression and superego, Jung used this experience as the foundation for his concept of the self and for the wholesome effect of establishing a relationship with this center of the individuality.

At all times, Jung took it as a matter of course that sexuality represented the natural expression of a drive which—like hunger, the power wish, and self-preservation—was a biological necessity. This natural aspect was never a serious problem either for Jung or Freud. Thus Jung never denied that sexuality, as one of the most potent drives, had to be counted among the vital bases of human existence. Its regulation—always presupposing natural impulses—was subject to the laws of biology as well as to the rules of society.

Just as the natural expression of the sex drive differed from repressed sexual function, the natural appraisal of sexuality was unlike its religious and symbolic evaluation. For Jung—as for Freud—sexuality became problematical only when it had lost its natural function and usurped the position of an unconscious psychic power which caught the individual unawares. Both investigators stressed the dangers involved when a person was unconscious of his sexual wishes or their repression. Jung, however, went farther than Freud, since he also investigated the dangers which could result from collective and impersonal factors. Whenever sexuality was underrated by the collective consciousness, it brought about dangerous compensatory processes in the unconscious of neurotic persons or those faced with current problems. In such cases, an overestimation of sexuality developed in the

[94] Freud, "The Future of an Illusion" (1927), p. 49.

collective unconscious corresponding to its conscious undervaluation, and sexual contents became amalgamated with archetypal images. The sexual function then assumed a numinous power which took possession of the person and enslaved him. Moreover, when sexual function became assimilated to the archetype of the self, the image of god, its power reached a culminating point. Because the archetype of the image of god always goes along with the claim of totality, it "can challenge the whole man and force him to react as a whole."[95] The phenomenology of such instances induced Jung again and again to consider seriously the sexual instinct and to fix his attention of the archetypal symbols connected with it and on the images of this situation. Since ultimate contents generally pointed to an opposite function, that is, to a function in opposition to the conscious attitude, their assimilation to the ego made an exacting demand on the individual. Nevertheless, bringing contents to consciousness is an absolute requirement for his self-realization.

From this orientation, sexuality assumed the value of a mystery which is indispensable for achieving totality. Sexuality could become the material for transformation, the starting point of a renewal of the personality, provided that the individual recognized its value in connection with the depth of the psyche. Jung could not help but acknowledge the extraordinary importance of the sex instinct in psychotherapy, especially when underestimated by the collective consciousness. However, in distinction from Freud, he attempted to understand the problem of sex in the framework of a holistic approach, looking at it from a symbolic point of view.

> The sexual hypothesis . . . carries considerable power of conviction because it coincides with one of the principal instincts. . . . The instincts are part of the living totality; they are articulated with and subordinated to the whole. Their release as separate entities leads to chaos and nihilism, because it breaks down the unity and totality of the individual and destroys him. It should be the task of psychotherapy, properly understood, to preserve or restore this unity. It cannot be the aim of education to turn out rationalists, materialists, specialists, technicians and others of the kind who, unconscious of their origins, are precipitated abruptly into the present and contribute to the disorientation and fragmentation of society. By the same token, no psychotherapy can lead to satisfactory results if it

95 Jung, "Flying Saucers: A Modern Myth of Things Seen in the Skies" (1958), p. 345.

confines itself to single aspects only. The temptation to do this is so great, and the danger of loss of instinct so threatening in the breath-less tempo of modern civilization, that every expression of instinct must be watched very carefully, since it is part of the total picture and is essential for man's psychic balance.[96]

[96] Ibid., pp. 349–50.

F. FROM THE CAUSAL TO THE HERMENEUTIC METHOD

I. FREE ASSOCIATION AND FREUD'S
CAUSAL METHOD

In the previous chapters, which discussed developments up to the 1930's, the question of the analytic method and its validity has been tacitly acknowledged. This leaves a gap which can be filled only by going back to the beginnings of the psychology of the unconscious.

The introduction of free association was one of Freud's principal contributions. It was so closely tied to psychoanalysis that Freud called it simply the psychoanalytic method. It was also one of the few discoveries to which he adhered throughout his life, although later somewhat modified or extended. For this reason and because the technique of free association played such a prominent role in later psychological systems, its importance can hardly be overestimated. Dalbiez was correct in regarding it as a truly genuine discovery which could claim objectivity. As he said, "The *original character of the method of spontaneous associations* is clearly seen."[1] Since the method of free association is at the core of the psychotherapeutic process, it can be considered only in the framework of Freud's overall concept.

Because of his training in the natural sciences, Freud made the basic assumption that the connection between cause and effect gave rise to rules governing natural events; he also accepted the postulate that a theory must be free of contradictions. His main interest in psychology was the investigation of neurosis; to detect the noxious event, the causes of disease, was the necessary prerequisite of cure. From the beginning, Freud saw the root of psychic illness in repressed childhood memories; accordingly, the goal of his therapeutic method was to bring to consciousness pathological memory traces and to work through the misdirected affects. Even in his first major psychological work, *Studies on Hysteria* (1893–95), he expanded Breuer's method of catharsis through the process of *remembering*,[2] which he recognized as a technique well suited to discover the causes of neurosis.

How did Freud arrive at the technique of free association? In the eighties of the last century, Freud was already using such methods as "abreaction," "hypnosis," "hypnotic suggestion" in the course of his practice—all of them leaving him dissatisfied.[3] Further steps were

[1] Dalbiez, *Psychoanalytic Method and the Doctrine of Freud* (tr. Lindsay, 1941), Vol. I, p. 47.

[2] Breuer and Freud, *Studies on Hysteria* (1893–95), p. 271.

[3] Ibid., pp. 256–57, 284–85. And see Frey-Rohn, "Die Anfänge der Tiefenpsychologie" (1955), pp. 33, 68.

based on Bernheim's experiences with posthypnotic suggestions and his demonstration that somnambulists upon awakening experienced only ostensible amnesia. These observations led Freud to expect a salubrious effect from asking the waking patient about the origin of his symptoms. However, frequent failures resulted, not only with hypnosis but also with the pressure technique as well as with assurance and insistence[4]—terms he used for encouraging the patient to remember. This made him suspect that disturbing, affect-toned factors occurred during therapy. From this predicament he conceived an ingenious idea: he tried to let the patient himself revive the pathogenic experiences. With this insight he laid the cornerstone of the indirect method, the so-called "psychoanalytic procedure."[5] In his little "Note on the Prehistory of the Technique of Analysis" (1920), he reported that he had been reminded of an essay by Ludwig Börne, entitled "The Art of Becoming an Original Writer in Three Days" (1823), especially this passage:

And here follows the practical application that was promised. Take a few sheets of paper and for three days on end write down, without fabrication or hypocrisy, everything that comes into your head. Write down what you think of yourself, of your wife, of the Turkish War, of Goethe, of Fonk's trial, of the Last Judgement, of your superiors—and when three days have passed you will be quite out of your senses with astonishment at the new and unheard-of thoughts you have had. This is the art of becoming an original writer in three days.[6]

Freud remembered that he had been given Börne's works when he was fourteen years old, and it was the only book that had survived from his boyhood, but he could not at first recall that particular essay. Jones commented that "we may be sure that Börne's startling proposal had sunk into Freud's mind and played its part twenty years later in stimulating him to give his patients' thoughts free play."[7] When Freud reread Börne's essay later, he was highly astonished to find not only a hint of free association but also of "censorship."[8] This possible cryptomnesia should not obscure the fact that Freud's scientific achievement was not alone in concentrating on free association but in applying the method to evoke the history of the disease and the foci of emotional disturbance.

4 *Studies on Hysteria*, p. 301.
5 "Sexuality in the Aetiology of the Neuroses" (1898), p. 282.
6 "A Note on the Prehistory of the Technique of Analysis" (1920), pp. 264–65.
7 Jones, *The Life and Work of Sigmund Freud*, Vol. I, p. 246.
8 "Sexuality in the Aetiology of the Neuroses," p. 265.

The great merit of Freud's contribution is little changed by the fact that the rules of association were theoretically established by Locke and Hume, centuries earlier, and were taken up again by Herbart. The decisive thing was that Freud applied the rules of association—such as similarity, contrast, and contiguity—to the empirical investigation of the unconscious and to psychotherapy. Thus, they received new appreciation and new significance.

The method of association was applied for the first time in 1895 in an attempt to stimulate the patient to recall lost memories. It was significantly extended when used in dream interpretation. From the very beginning, Freud based his method of free association on the patient's concentrated self-observation and in educating him "to give up the whole of his critical attitude"[9] and communicate everything that came to his mind. In this respect it was essential for the patient not to interfere with the production of "involuntary thoughts (most frequently regarded as disturbing elements and therefore ordinarily pushed aside)."[10] Freud regarded the so-called "Fundamental Technical Rule"[11] as indispensable:

> . . . the patient being required to put himself in the position of an attentive and dispassionate self-observer . . . to make a duty of the most complete honesty while on the other hand not to hold back any idea from communication, even if (1) he feels that it is too disagreeable or if (2) he judges that it is nonsensical or (3) too unimportant or (4) irrelevant to what is being looked for.[12]

The more involuntary the free association, the more certain it was to strike the repressed memory. In this way, "involuntary" ideas were transformed into "voluntary" ones.[13] The physician was supposed to remain as passive as possible and not to offer any explanation. His questions alone were supposed to uncover the particular causal connection between the subject and his symptoms, that is, the dreams which were interposed into the chain of psychic events. As J. H. Phillips pointed out, Freud's achievement was a turning point in empirical psychology comparable to the theory of Copernicus.[14] Freud recognized that the cooperation of the patient was absolutely necessary for successful therapy, less for his conscious evaluation than as a passive reflector for rising memories. He thought that this procedure

---

9 "Two Encyclopaedia Articles: (A) Psycho-Analysis" (1922–23), p. 238.
10 "Freud's Psycho-Analytic Procedure" (1903–4), p. 251.
11 "Sexuality in the Aetiology of the Neuroses," p. 265.
12 Ibid.
13 *The Interpretation of Dreams* (1900), p. 102.
14 Phillips, *Psychoanalyse und Symbolik* (1962), p. 125.

made it possible to accomplish his aim, to bring to consciousness repressed traumata or events of a personal nature in the life history of the patient. It is true that Janet, his predecessor, proceeded along a similar plan of assisting the ego to assimilate lost memories, but his method was built exclusively on hypnosis, that is, heterosuggestion.

Initially, Freud had expected that the technique of free association would enable him to make straight for the forgotten causes of the disease, but annoying obstacles showed him the error of this assumption. The veiling of childhood memories by fantastic stories (see C.I.1) and, more than that, the arousing of resistance thwarted the exposure of childhood experiences. Freud first became aware of it as "resistance to association,"[15] which manifested itself in "the fact that connections are broken,"[16] by ideas being blocked as well as by gaps in memory and distortions. As early as 1895, Freud established that patients' resistance corresponded in every respect to the original psychical force (defense) that prevented the painful trauma from becoming conscious.[17] Like repression, which pushes back painful stirrings of emotion, the patient's resistance tries to maintain his pathological state. Intellectualization, doubts, the compulsion to question, the wish for explanations, all were means to this end; Freud recognized transference resistance[18] as one of the most important forms of defense which work against psychoanalytic therapy. It always disclosed the presence of considerable affective disturbances in the relationship between patient and physician.

Later, the idea that resistance protected repression (or increased the degree of repression) was taken up again in Freud's concept of anti-cathexis (reaction-formation),[19] in which he recognized an extremely effective form of resistance.

Freud discovered another fact in connection with transference resistance: the tendency of the patient to repeat infantile behavior patterns. In such instances, acting out took the place of remembering.[20] Instead of reproducing certain memories, the patient unconsciously repeated a portion of his past. In spite of their dissimilarity, both remembering and acting out pursued the same unconscious goal of a fight to keep repressed drives from becoming conscious.

The appearance of various forms of resistance against uncovering the unconscious was by no means an insuperable obstacle to applying

15 *Studies on Hysteria*, p. 270.   16 Ibid., p. 281.
17 Ibid., p. 268.
18 "The Dynamics of Transference" (1912), p. 105.
19 *Introductory Lectures on Psycho-Analysis* (1915–17), p. 375.
20 "Remembering, Repeating and Working-Through" (1914), p. 150.

the method of free association. It was only necessary to keep in mind that the association had been distorted by the influence of resistance and could bring the traumatic occasion to consciousness only indirectly, by a roundabout route.

> The resistance accompanies the treatment step by step. Every single association, every act of the person under treatment must reckon with the resistance and represents a compromise between the forces that are striving towards recovery and the opposing ones which I have described.[21]

Just as neurotic symptoms have to be seen as compromise formations, the free-association technique must take account of the *yea and nay tendencies toward bringing the repressed to consciousness.* Therefore, a great many circuitous approaches, constructions, and intuitions were required to break through to the traumatic contents. The goal of therapy was thereby extended, since lifting the repression now also involved overcoming the resistance.

> First, the search for the repression and then the removal of the resistance which maintains the repression.[22]

This discovery was important not only for recalling the repressed but also for working through resistance and reliving the past.

In all such cases, Freud found the value of free association confirmed. With this method, he not only achieved great success in treatment but also gained his most decisive insights into the nature of the unconscious, that is, the laws governing the relationship between trauma and neurosis, resistance and neurosis, as well as those governing fantasy and dream. The method of free association also held an eminent position in dream interpretation, in spite of the complementary procedure of interpreting symbolic connotations, which, of course, was possible without the presence of the dreamer. For Freud, questioning the individual and uncovering his personal life history were always of fundamental importance.

Still, the validity and success of the technique of free association must be examined further. To what degree was free association due merely to chance and how much did it actually contribute in throwing light on the causes of neurosis? The answer is not complicated. As a matter of fact, associations were free only from the aspect of consciousness, that is, they were unintentional. Considered in relation to

21 "The Dynamics of Transference," p. 103.
22 *Introductory Lectures*, pp. 436–37.

the unconscious, they followed a *goal-directed inner urge*. Three remarkable conclusions seemed to establish the correctness and applicability of Freud's method: the recognition of the unbroken and meaningful chain of memory material,[23] the concentric layering of memories and resistances around an affect-toned nucleus of crystallization,[24] and finally the threefold stratification of the unconscious psyche, with its chronological, radial, and logical dimensions.[25] The surprising observation of meaning- and affect-toned causal connections between trauma, symptom, and association[26] convinced Freud of a psychic regularity which obviated the possibility of tracing associations to chance.

These findings, by confirming the aim of natural science in establishing a general connection between cause and effect, also guaranteed this basis for unconscious events. Freud was eminently satisfied to find that the effectiveness of unconscious purposes[27] was substantiated not only by the investigation of dream associations but also in jokes. (Later, he learned that Eduard von Hartmann had already mentioned in his *Philosophy of the Unconscious* [1890] that "in artistic creation . . . the association of ideas is governed by unconscious purposive ideas.")[28] The psychoanalytic method and the treatment of neurosis founded on it, as well as the interpretation of dreams, seemed to be justified by the fact that not only conscious but also unconscious processes followed an aim—even though the unconscious goal was not recognized.

> In the psycho-analysis of neuroses the fullest use is made of these two theorems—that, when conscious purposive ideas are abandoned, concealed purposive ideas assume control of the current of ideas, and that superficial associations are only substitutes by displacement for suppressed deeper ones. Indeed, these theorems have become basic pillars of psycho-analytic technique. When I instruct a patient to abandon reflection of any kind and to tell me whatever comes into his head, I am relying firmly on the presumption that he will not be able to abandon the purposive ideas inherent in the treatment and I feel justified in inferring that what seem to be the most innocent and arbitrary things which he tells me are in fact related to his illness. There is another purposive idea of which the patient has no suspicion—one relating to myself.[29]

23 "The Aetiology of Hysteria" (1896), p. 195.
24 *Studies on Hysteria*, p. 289. 25 Ibid., p. 288.
26 *The Psychopathology of Everyday Life* (1901), p. 278.
27 *The Interpretation of Dreams*, pp. 170, 246.
28 Ibid., p. 528, n. 1. 29 Ibid., pp. 531–32.

I. FREE ASSOCIATION AND FREUD'S CAUSAL METHOD

Freud used this observation by cautioning the patient or the dreamer to keep in mind a certain idea as a starting-point,[30] and in this way the associations were subjected to "enchaînement" and came under the spell of strongly emotional thought and unconscious complexes.[31]

In summary, the method of free association rested on the empirical demonstration that the unconscious exhibited a coherent totality of memories.

[30] *Introductory Lectures*, p. 106.   [31] Ibid., p. 109.

II. BOUND ASSOCIATION AND
JUNG'S FINALITY-ORIENTED POINT OF VIEW

The method of free association became one of the standardized techniques of Jung's psychology, although highly modified. Jung always
acknowledged that, historically, his method was derived from Freud's
psychoanalytic method. As late as 1929, he mentioned that he had
learned his own approach "from Freud's method of free association,"
and he regarded it "as a direct extension of that."[1] Certainly, he
expected to reach goals with the method of free association that were
essentially different from Freud's aims, that is, to disclose the center
of significance within the unconscious psyche and to understand the
lines of psychic development. But he nevertheless agreed with the
structural elements of Freud's approach. Jung, too, depended on
questioning the subject and on the spontaneity of ideas in his responses.

One of Jung's earliest differences from the Freudian method was
related to the psychological nature of association (or, to use Jung's
expression, the linguistic reaction in the association experiment).[2] Both
investigators agreed that the spontaneous idea was "a secret which he
[the patient] himself does not know . . . , which is hidden even from himself,"[3] that is, determined by an unconscious complex. However, Jung
stressed to a much greater degree that the reaction was basically not
"free." It corresponded much more to a symptomatic response and was
to a large extent the result of the autonomous action of a complex.

The reactions . . . are by no means random thoughts but simply
symptomatic acts, directed by a psychic factor that can behave like
an independent being.[4]

The *constellation* (Ziehen) of an association is mostly unconscious
(or not-conscious); the constellating complex here plays the part of a
quasi-independent entity—a "second consciousness."[5]

The recognition that associations are determined by the complex
was the basis of one of Jung's most essential objections to Freud's
assumption that the causes of the disease (the "lost memories") could

1 Jung, "The Aims of Psychotherapy" (1929), p. 47.
2 Jung and Riklin, "The Associations of Normal Subjects" (1904), p. 10.
3 Freud, "Psycho-Analysis and the Establishment of the Facts in Legal Proceedings" (1906), p. 108.
4 Jung, "The Reaction-Time Ratio in the Association Experiment" (1905), p. 245.
(Jung cited Freud, *The Psychopathology of Everyday Life*, for "symptomatic acts.")
5 Ibid., p. 262.

be uncovered in free associations, although by a circuitous route. According to Jung, whenever seemingly causative experiences are alluded to, one is faced with psychic impulses which previously had been constellated by complexes. It was never possible to draw a definite conclusion as to primary causes. As Jung saw it, the response connected with the initial idea "was already constellated by the complex. We are therefore justified in regarding the initial idea as a sign or symbol of the complex."[6] This observation was related to Jung's equally fundamental objection that combining the method of free association with Freud's causal approach missed the essential qualities of the psyche.

Because Freud traced all problems and difficulties to unsettled and unmastered experiences in the patient's past, it was only logical that he also connected the spontaneous ideas with causes in the past; thus, he remained trapped in the "enchaînement" of symptom, idea, and traumatic memory. Jung regretted that Freud's method was of no help in uncovering the meaning of the idea or the developmental tendencies of the unconscious psyche. He deemed it much more effective to investigate the associations from the viewpoint of intended aim and symbolic content. The discovery of the spontaneity, autonomy, and goal-directedness of the psyche resulted in a gradual change in applying free association.

1. The Prospective and Constructive Method

In Jung's early writings (1906 and 1907), the influence of Freud's causal method prevailed. In other words, the goal of uncovering past events predominated. In a lecture in French on "The Analysis of Dreams,"[7] Jung still based dream interpretation largely on free association. Nevertheless, he was already moving in the direction of uncovering the complex underlying the dream, with little attention given to past experiences. He came out publicly with his own point of view only in 1914, after his formal separation from Freud. His observation of the anticipatory significance of dreams (1912)[8] induced him to turn away from the causal-reductive method and to elaborate the prospective-constructive point of view.

The constructive standpoint asks how, out of this present psyche, a bridge can be built into its own future.[9]

6 "The Freudian Theory of Hysteria" (1908), p. 16.
7 "The Analysis of Dreams" (1909).
8 Psychology of the Unconscious (Transformations and Symbols of the Libido, 1912), p. 64.
9 "On Psychological Understanding" (1914), p. 183.

> In its immediate results the constructive method . . . traces, rather, the psychological path of development in a given individual.[10]

As Jung noted, the causal viewpoint, in contrast to his own, was largely reductive. It led back to instinctual causes, to primitive and elementary aspects, and, additionally, had a disintegrating and destructive effect. On the other hand, the constructive-prospective point of view was characterized by a tendency to synthesis and growth, with a forward-looking prospect. Freud's method was "retrospective understanding" in contrast to Jung's "prospective understanding."[11] From the reductive and causal point of view the question of "why" was of primary interest, and therefore emphasis was on attempts to ferret out the foci of disturbances in the past, that is, of faulty development and memory defects as well as misguided affective efforts to direct vital energy. In contrast, the constructive point of view was primarily oriented toward understanding the actual situation and finding a solution for current conflicts. Jung hoped that this approach would open an avenue to a more adequate understanding of new potentials for development and the possibility of new values for the individual.

> A man is only half understood when we know how everything in him came into being. If that were all, he could just as well have been dead years ago. As a living being he is not understood, for life does not have only a yesterday, nor is it explained by reducing today to yesterday. Life has also a tomorrow, and today is understood only when we can add to our knowledge of what was yesterday the beginnings of tomorrow.[12]

In emphasizing the constructive process, Jung did not by any means disavow the importance of exploring causes. He too recognized the need to go back to past events, for example, in cases of terrifying experiences, somatic symptoms, and particularly when repressed memories reappeared. It was, however, of far greater importance to him to supplement the exploration of causes by a search for meaning and purpose, or—to use a later formulation—"the question of the 'why' and the 'wherefore.' "[13] What is the purpose of a symptom or a complex, or what is the meaning of a dream? Jung also expected this approach to lead to new answers and to give access to understanding latent tendencies in the unconscious.

In the preface to the second edition of *Collected Papers on Analytical Psychology* (1917), Jung made an attempt to explain the difference

---

[10] Ibid., p. 192.   [11] Ibid., p. 181.
[12] "On the Psychology of the Unconscious" (1917), p. 46.
[13] "General Aspects of Dream Psychology" (1916/1928), p. 243.

between the causal and the finalistic points of view by the criterion of reversible vs. irreversible.

It cannot be disputed that, psychologically speaking, we are living and working day by day according to the principle of directed aim or purpose as well as that of causality. . . . What is plainly directed towards a goal cannot be given an exclusively causalistic explanation, otherwise we should be led to the conclusion expressed in Moleschott's famous dictum: "Man ist was man isst" (Man *is* what he eats). We must always bear in mind that *causality is a point of view.* It affirms the inevitable and immutable relation of a series of events: a-b-c-z. . . . *Finality* is also a point of view, and it is empirically justified by the existence of series of events in which the causal connection is indeed evident *but the meaning of which only becomes intelligible in terms of endproducts (final effects).* . . .

As a matter of fact, modern physics has necessarily been converted from the idea of pure mechanism to the finalistic concept of the conservation of energy, because the mechanistic explanation recognizes only reversible processes whereas the actual truth is that the processes of nature are irreversible. This fact led to the concept of an energy that tends toward relief of tension and hence towards a definite final state.[14]

Similarly, the recognition that the causalistic-reductive approach could not do justice to the images emerging from the collective sphere carried the issue beyond the Freudian method. Jung had first discovered from dream symbols that archaic images can become beneficial only through their meaning and scope; therefore, a method which traced such images exclusively to personal aspects and memories could not offer constructive possibilities. As early as 1917, Jung stressed the necessity of complementing the reductive-analytical procedure with the synthetic method.

. . . an exclusively causal and reductive procedure . . . breaks down at the point where the dream symbols can no longer be reduced to personal reminiscences or aspirations, that is, when the images of the collective unconscious begin to appear. It would be quite senseless to try to reduce these collective ideas to anything personal—not only senseless but positively harmful, as painful experience has taught me. . . . The images or symbols of the collective unconscious yield their distinctive values only when subjected to a synthetic mode of treatment. Just as analysis breaks down the symbolical fantasy-

[14] Prefaces to *Collected Papers on Analytical Psychology* (1916, 1917), pp. 295–96.

material into its components, so the synthetic procedure integrates it into a general and intelligible statement.[15]

The primordial images revealed their deeper substance, their prospective significance for the further development of the individual, only when the archaic material was not allowed to dissolve but an attempt was made to grasp its meaning and symbolic value.

Even though Jung recognized the reductive-causal nexus and applied the reductive method in certain cases of eccentricity, vanity, and loss of the sense of reality, a consideration of the finalistic method appeared to him to be indispensable. Not only was life a chain of causally connected events, consisting of a general chain of psychic facts with each new idea starting oscillations of the entire chain of reminiscences, but this continuity was also oriented toward final effects. In other words, the final causes ultimately depended on a kind of unconscious foreknowledge. Jung expressed this idea by describing the goal-directedness of the unconscious as "a system of directed aims which seek to fulfill themselves," even unto death.

> Life is an energy-process. Like every energy-process, it is in principle irreversible and is therefore directed towards a goal. That goal is a state of rest. . . . Life is teleology *par excellence*; it is the intrinsic striving towards a goal, and the living organism is a system of directed aims which seek to fulfil themselves. The end of every process is its goal.[16]

From this point of view, death too was to be considered a goal and a fulfillment. In spite of his increasing distance from Freud's causal approach, Jung attempted again and again to do justice to Freud's achievements. In retrospect, he wrote in the foreword to *Symbols of Transformation*:

> I have no wish to denigrate Freud, or to detract from the extraordinary merits of his investigation of the individual psyche. But the conceptual framework into which he fitted the psychic phenomenon seemed to me unendurably narrow. I am not thinking here of his theory of neurosis, which can be as narrow as it pleases if only it is adequate to the empirical facts, or of his theory of dreams, about which different views may be held in all good faith; I am thinking more of the reductive causalism of his whole outlook, and the almost

15 "On the Psychology of the Unconscious," pp. 80–81.
16 "The Soul and Death" (1934), pp. 405–6.

complete disregard of the teleological directedness which is so characteristic of everything psychic.[17]

2. The Method of Amplification

Jung's immediate task was to elaborate a method of association of
ideas which was fitted to help the individual in his tendencies toward
development and meaning. Even though the technique of free association was not necessarily related to basic psychological attitudes, still, a
certain affinity between the method of free association and the reductive-causal approach could be determined. Similarly, there appeared to
be an affinity between the prospective-finalistic approach and the
bound idea, tied to the center of significance of a symbol. This
technique, which Jung described as the amplification procedure, culminated in the finding that associations refer back to the nucleus of the
respective psychic unit—complex, dream, vision, or fantasy. Like the
linear technique of free association, the amplification method started
initially from the discrete parts of psychic conformations, that is, from
its elements. But while free association followed the chains of memories in order to advance from the manifest to the latent content (the
cause), the amplification method had an essentially radial character.
What Jung had in mind was "a careful and conscious illumination of
the interconnected associations objectively grouped round particular
images."[18] By a concentric method, which circled around the nucleus
of meaning, Jung hoped to limit ambiguity and at the same time
grasp the unique significance of the psychic formation as related to the
immediate state of affairs. (Jung thus came to findings similar to those
of Freud, who discovered the concentric arrangement of memory-
material about certain points of crystallization.) The expansion of the
meaning of the image until it became apparent was essential.[19]

> This amplification method means expansion, conscious enrichment.
> I thereby cause the dreamer to place the image in the center of inter-
> est and to produce all associations tied to the image.[20]

The aim of the amplification process was always oriented toward
elucidating the center of meaning of a psychic unit. From a formal
point of view the process was radial; from the standpoint of content,
however, it had a hermeneutic character. This elucidation could have

[17] *Symbols of Transformation*, Foreword to the 4th edn. (1952), p. xxiii.
[18] "The Practical Use of Dream-Analysis" (1931/1934), p. 148.
[19] "Seminar über Kinderträume," I (1938–39).
[20] Ibid., II (1939–40).

a personal as well as an impersonal quality. In personal amplification the individual contributed the essential associations from his personal life and his experiences, thereby establishing the so-called context of the particular elements of the psychic formation. The impersonal amplification, on the other hand, consisted of associations from the material of the collective unconscious, for instance, mythology, fairy-tales, and folklore. Just as the context served to increase the individual's understanding of his life story, and the conflicts connected with it as well as the unfulfilled possibilities of relationships, so the impersonal amplification enlarged his horizon and enabled him to view his personal difficulties in the perspective of experiences common to the entire human race. When viewed in contraposition to the store of objective experiences of civilization, his own troubles became relative; he participated in the general possibilities of conflict-solving and learned to recognize in himself the deeper, objective basis of human existence.

In general, Jung questioned the subject extensively, inducing him to look for associations relevant to the material he had so far uncovered—a principle which Freud had already established. However, Jung never regarded the subject as only a passive point of reference, which Freud did. In accordance with his concentric method which always circled around the nucleus of significance, Jung always involved the subject more actively in the process of interpretation.

Questioning the subject had the advantage of bringing out a relatively unambiguous selection among the possible associations; the numerous choices and the ambiguity of the meaning of words were restricted to connections which were essential to each individual. Jung, however, recognized that the presence of the patient or his assistance in the process of association was not an indispensable prerequisite, particularly when confronted with archetypal formations. In such cases, the psychotherapist was able to apply amplification by drawing on his own store of experience and familiarity with symbols and thus, as far as possible, objectively encircle the psychic formations.

Jung extended the method of free association to the process of bound association, changed the linear technique to that of shedding light on the image by amplification and supplemented the personal content by impersonal material gained from the wealth of symbols in the collective unconscious. Still, the prerequisites formulated by Freud retained their validity as far as their formal character was concerned. What Jung had stated in 1906 about the technique of the association procedure (referring to Freud) always remained an established principle.

He always maintained that "all human ideas are determined . . . by psychological laws";[21] this premise found expression in the unbroken chain of psychic events and in their affective regulation.

Anyone with practical experience of analysis can convince himself over and over again that under these conditions not just *anything* is reproduced, but always something that is related to the complex, though the relationship is, *a priori*, not always clear. . . .

This view is in agreement with already known psychological theories which maintain that the psychological situation at a given moment is nothing but the resultant of all the psychological events preceding it.[22]

Setting aside the inner links of unconscious contents, Jung also found that the psyche exhibited an original goal-directedness which was governed by the autonomous complexes as well as by the subjacent archetypal nuclei. This, however, did not change the fact of an unbroken regularity. The application of the amplification method and the conscious elucidation of associative connections could be smoothly reconciled with the "enchaînement." Last but not least, the impersonal interpretation of associations (the hermeneutic procedure), which Jung used to elucidate the archetypal contents of the unconscious, was anything but a result of chance. On the contrary, it fitted into the dominant order and, upon investigation, also revealed the value, meaning, and significance of the psychic process.

21 "Psychoanalysis and Association Experiments" (1906), p. 289.
22 "The Freudian Theory of Hysteria" (1908), p. 16.

G. NEUROSIS AND DREAM

I. NEUROSIS: A PROBLEM OF DRIVES
OR OF PERSONALITY?

1. Neurosis in the Light of Freud's Theory of Instincts

In his obituary for Freud, Jung made the following statement about Freud's work:

> As with his recognition that neurosis has the character of a medieval "possession," so, by treating dreams as a highly important source of information about the unconscious processes—"the dream is the *via regia* to the unconscious"—Freud rescued something of the utmost value from the past, where it had seemed irretrievably sunk in oblivion.[1]

The clarification of neurosis was not only Freud's starting point but remained the principal focus of his investigations. We will therefore briefly outline the basic ideas and main problems of his theory of neurosis. However, we will consider only the psychoneuroses, not the real neuroses, which, according to Freud, could not be traced to psychic conflicts nor to psychic mechanisms. The real neuroses (neurasthenia, anxiety neurosis, originally the phobias also) always pointed to actual disturbances, connected with the individual's sexuality and life style, with the vegetative nervous system, and also with his constitution.

Corresponding to the different levels that were characteristic of Freud's doctrine of the unconscious, one finds different phases of his theory of neurosis. His basic concept of psychoneurosis as a disturbed interplay of forces, an incompatible psychic conflict between the ego and an overpowering affective factor, never changed, but his definition of what this affect-toned factor comprised as well as what constituted the ego changed considerably. In succession, he placed his main emphasis on the etiological significance of an actual trauma, on a sexual trauma during childhood, on unfulfilled sexual desires, and—starting with his formulation of the sexual theory—on the misdirected development of the sex instinct. The problem of neurosis became more complex by making a distinction between Eros and the aggressive drive (1920), whereby the disharmonious development of ego and aggressive drive was recognized as a factor in causing neurosis. Up to that time, Freud had focused mainly on the problem of disturbed drives, but

[1] Jung, "In Memory of Sigmund Freud" (1939), p. 44.

during his work on ego psychology he took a radical turn. From then on, he placed the major emphasis on the weakness and immaturity of the ego—and on the problems of ego development in general; he recognized such disturbances as the basic cause of neurosis. The difference between the two approaches stands out clearly in a comparison of statements from the years 1913 and 1938. In 1913 Freud wrote:

> The primal conflict which leads to neuroses is one between the sexual instincts and those which maintain the ego. The neuroses represent a more or less partial overpowering of the ego by sexuality after the ego's attempts at suppressing sexuality have failed.[2]

In 1938, however, he made the following statement:

> The neuroses are, as we know, disorders of the ego; and it is not to be wondered at if the ego, so long as it is feeble, immature and incapable of resistance, fails to deal with tasks which it could cope with later on. . . .[3]

From the very beginning, a decisive factor in the theory of neurosis was Freud's recognition that situations of conflict between ego and instinctual wish unfailingly elicited the mechanism of defense (repression) on the part of the ego. Until the formulation of his ego psychology, Freud had maintained that neurosis primarily was caused by a miscarried attempt at repression, while later he traced it to the ego's inappropriate attempts to escape. In the latter case, not only secondary phenomena of repression ensued but also lasting restrictions in the development of the ego personality.

In explaining the origin of neurosis, Freud retained the basic concept that neurosis was caused by childhood experiences. He recognized that infantile sexuality and the organization of the libido were the bases of a normal person's later development in character, productive power, and the capacity to enjoy pleasure. He also saw the faulty development of infantile sexuality as one of the most important causes in the formation of neurosis. According to Freud, the crucial event of childhood was the diphasic beginning of sexual development —"something that is unknown except in man and evidently has an important bearing on hominization."[4] The consequences were not only such phenomena as amnesia regarding early experiences and fixation and attachment of the libido to objects of partial drives, but also

2 Freud, "The Claims of Psycho-Analysis to Scientific Interest" (1913), p. 181.
3 "An Outline of Psycho-Analysis" (1938), pp. 184–85.
4 Ibid., p. 153.

processes of repression under the influence of the awakening ego, and finally, object-choice occurring in two phases.

In the process of human maturation, infantile fixations constituted the truly sensitive points of development. On the one hand, the mobility of the libido and its capacity to sublimate were restricted; on the other hand, the points of fixation formed something comparable to magnetic centers, constantly attracting the conscious libido. Because of the tendency of everything unconscious to persevere, fixated and repressed contents continuously attempted to break through into consciousness—a phenomenon which Freud in later years characterized as the repetition compulsion of the repressed.

The repressive activity of the ego—which, according to Freud, originated during the latency period—was equally important in the development of neurosis and was essentially motivated by the castration complex. Repression as well as the formation of anticathexes against the assault of the repressed weakened the function of the ego. Just as fixation indicated a weakness of sexual development, repression created a weak point in ego development.

In addition to repression, frustration from outside sources and, particularly, regression played a part in the development of neurosis. The phenomenon of frustration had the well-known consequence of evading the demands of reality, that is, escaping into fantasy, thus revealing the subject's low degree of tolerance; at the same time, regression, with the libido returning to the fixation points, resulted in manifest neurosis. The choice of neurosis[5] depended on the level of fixation and could manifest itself at times as hysteria, phobia, obsessional neurosis, or narcissistic disease.

The discrete phases in the organization of the libido were also fundamental factors in the individual's love life. During the latency period, the two most essential mechanisms were formed: on the one hand, using the object for support and, on the other hand, concentrating on one's self. While identification was the overall model for overcoming the loss of love and operated during the oral phase as renunciation of the maternal breast, incestuous attachment, typical of the phallic phase, represented the high point in the mechanism of gaining support from the object.

According to Freud, the most significant stages in the development of neurosis were the phallic phase of sexual organization and the subsequent latency period. These stages were characterized by the

[5] "The Disposition to Obsessional Neurosis. A Contribution to the Problem of Choice of Neurosis" (1913).

Oedipus complex and the castration complex. The Oedipus complex represented the prototype of incestuous libido, but Freud regarded the castration complex as the exponent of both the subjective incest anxiety and the incest barrier imposed by civilization, which increasingly assumed greater significance in the individual's life. It was, if possible, even more fateful than the Oedipus complex. Consequently, the tenacity of the incestuous tie had a counterpart in the equally tenacious castration anxiety. The hold on the love object, at first the parent of the opposite sex, could not be maintained. The individual formed an ambivalent relationship with the paternal authority, which was fed by hate and guilt feelings. As an inevitable consequence, a conflict developed between incest-wish and incest-anxiety. Freud saw the incestuous tie to the parent as doomed—ontogenetically as well as phylogenetically. The mechanism of object-cathexis was superseded by introjection. Freud determined that as early as the oral phase "there quite often ensues an alteration . . . which can only be described as a setting up of the object inside the ego"[6] (lost object = mother's breast). This phenomenon was confirmed when the phallus was threatened by castration. At this time the incestuous object-cathexis was converted into narcissistic identification. In other words, the growing individual introjected the paternal authority; the superego developed, perpetuating the incest barrier and preventing the return of libidinous strivings.

Success or failure in overcoming the Oedipus complex depended on the course taken in the process of introjecting parental authorities. The first phase was characterized by the boy's relatively uncomplicated identification with his father and an equally uncomplicated, tender yearning for his mother. However, in the second phase, ambivalent attitudes in these relationships could already be recognized. A further entanglement of object-cathexes occurred when the castration complex appeared. Whether identification with the father—or, conversely, with the mother—increased, the result was always a consolidation of masculinity. In Freud's theory, all the implications in the Oedipus and castration complexes were considerably accentuated by assuming a constitutional tendency to bisexuality, a phenomenon to which Fliess had drawn Freud's attention. The concerted action of male and female qualities inherent in both sexes brought about positive as well as negative ties of the ego to these qualities in both parents. Freud thus came to the remarkable conclusion that not less than four components of incestuous relationships interacted.

[6] "The Ego and the Id" (1923), p. 29.

A boy has not merely an ambivalent attitude towards his father and an affectionate object-choice towards his mother, but at the same time he also behaves like a girl and displays an affectionate feminine attitude to his father and a corresponding jealousy and hostility towards his mother.[7]

The relationships of girls were similarly complex. With the fourfold conformation of the Oedipus and castration complexes, Freud expressed an extraordinarily important aspect of the unconscious. Disregarding the concretistic basis of Freud's arguments and, particularly, the assumptions of his psychology of instincts, one can detect certain analogies to Jung's observations of the fourfold structure of the psyche. This recalls the concept of the quaternio which, however, in contrast to Freud, was both purely psychic in nature and also indicated an archetypal principle which *a priori* set up a four-sided arrangement[8] (see H.II.3.a).

In the development of neurosis, the destiny of the individual was invariably decided by the manner in which the fight between incest-wish and incest-anxiety—that is, between the Oedipus and castration complexes—was resolved. In other words, everything depended on how the "conflict between the demand by the instinct and the prohibition by reality"[9] was worked through.

The findings based on the hypothesis of the sexual origin of neurosis were well stated in Rank's comment that "neurosis represented the inability of the ego to cope with a too powerful sexual drive."[10] With this in mind, Freud's assumption of a congenital aggressive and destructive drive made it even more difficult to deal with the aggressive tendencies in society in addition to those within one's self. Freud proposed the remarkable hypothesis that, whenever the aggressive tendency was obstructed in the outside world, the drive was turned inward with potentially dangerous effects. Just as anxiety about threatened castration by the father led to the formation of an authoritative superego within the psyche, thwarting the outward release of aggression resulted in a serious psychic reaction. In this context Freud was thinking of introjection of these impulses, which in very rare instances was harmless but most often constituted the cause of very grievous disturbances in the maturation of the individual. These could already be observed during the anal phase in tendencies toward self-destruction and anxiety.

---

[7] Ibid., p. 33. [8] Jung, *Aion* (1951), p. 159.
[9] Freud, "Splitting of the Ego in the Process of Defence" (1938), p. 275.
[10] Rank and Sachs, "Entwicklung und Ansprüche der Psychoanalyse" (1912).

The introduction of ego psychology brought several changes in the concept of the origin of neurosis. In the period of the sexual theory, Freud had attributed the primary role in the cause of neurosis to repression, but within the framework of ego psychology, this mechanism lost more and more importance compared to the part played by anxiety and the demands of the superego. The ego, threatened by inner and outer dangers, resorted to measures of protection and defense, while the superego, constantly faced with anxiety arising from conscience and fear of losing love, fended off the demands of the drives by various defense mechanisms. Just as the superego called for renunciation of instinct, the anxiety signal prompted the ego to start repression. Reversing an earlier assertion that anxiety was the consequence of repression, Freud arrived at the statement:

It was not the repression that created the anxiety; the anxiety was there earlier; it was the anxiety that made the repression.[11]

All these functions of ego and superego impaired the effectiveness of the ego. The individual was not only blocked but misled as well. Defense mechanisms used for a specific purpose were apt to become fixated in the ego and lead to regularly repeated character reaction formations. Lasting changes of the ego followed, culminating in a tendency to confine the ego[12] and favoring the outbreak of neurosis.

Freud always maintained that faulty development of instinctual life during childhood (that is, childhood neurosis, early attempts at repression, resistance, or anticathexes of the ego against the return of the repressed) always promoted the formation of neurosis; nevertheless, as time went on, he gave far less weight to the primary etiological significance of sexual factors. He supplemented the faulty evolution of the sexual instinct with the development of the aggressive drives; moreover, he recognized that faulty development of the ego, manifested by fixed defense reactions, anxiety-laden attempts at escape, and insufficient control of drives, was etiologically at least as important as disturbances in affectivity. The causes of neurosis were far from homogeneous: They included obstruction of drives (due primarily to the Oedipus and castration complexes) as well as damage from "inadequate reactions of the ego to instinct dangers,"[13] and, most of all, increased proneness to anxiety and escape attempts.

It is noteworthy that the biological factor became increasingly more obvious in Freud's concept of neurosis. In addition to the diphasic

[11] *New Introductory Lectures on Psycho-Analysis* (1933), p. 86.
[12] "Inhibitions, Symptoms and Anxiety" (1926), p. 99.
[13] Nunberg, *Principles of Psychoanalysis* (tr. Kahr, 1955), pp. 328–29.

origin of sexual development, he ascribed etiological importance to the long-time dependency of the child on his parents, the relatively late maturation of the ego, and to bisexuality, to say nothing of physical changes due to hormonal and chemical factors. Accordingly, the neuroses were "severe, constitutionally fixed illnesses, which rarely restrict themselves to only a few attacks but persist as a rule over long periods or throughout life."[14]

Freud drew certain conclusions about the nature of neurotic symptoms from his basic concept of neurosis. In an early letter to Fliess (February 19, 1899) he emphasized that reality and wish-fulfillment are a "contrasting pair," giving rise to all psychological phenomena, and that neurotic symptoms represent the wish-fulfillment of a repressing thought; they always originated where "the repressed and the repressing thoughts can come together in the fulfilment of a wish,"[15] that is, they achieved a compromise. This remained a guiding premise, and almost forty years later he made a very similar statement:

> The symptoms of neuroses are, it might be said, without exception either a substitutive satisfaction of some sexual urge or measures to prevent such a satisfaction; and as a rule they are compromises between the two.[16]

When the divided forces met in the symptom, the compromise was formed "in accordance with the laws operating between contraries in the unconscious"[17] (such as condensation, displacement, etc.). Symptoms represented thwarted attempts to reconcile threatening conflict situations; as such, they revealed all the signs of manifest neurosis: turning from the reality principle to the pleasure principle, regression to infantilisms and archaic attitudes, and tendencies to repeat repressed contents and increased susceptibility to anxiety. In all such cases, an intensified inclination to be obstinate and rigid could be observed, often leading to reduced productivity and capacity to enjoy, as well as impaired adaptation to reality.

Substitute gratifications and compromise formations assumed guises which conformed to the nature of the missing drive gratification and the type of neurosis. Freud had stressed as early as 1893 that conversion hysteria was accompanied by a total transformation of the repressed drives into somatic symptoms, with the patient completely unconscious of the disease process. In anxiety hysteria the repressed quantum of libido was channeled into anxiety—a concept later reversed (as men-

[14] Freud, *New Introductory Lectures*, p. 153.
[15] *The Origins of Psycho-Analysis* (1887–1902), p. 277.
[16] "An Outline," p. 186.   [17] Ibid.

tioned earlier) to anxiety-producing repression. Obsessive-compulsive neurosis was characterized by the mechanisms of displacement, reaction formation, and anticathexis, with constant oscillation between attempts to release repressed material on the one hand, and repression, on the other. We will not further discuss the changes in Freud's concepts of the various types of neurosis which occurred in connection with the discovery of the aggressive and destructive drive and with the introduction of ego psychology.

In conclusion, it should be stressed that neurosis was always a meaningful phenomenon for Freud. This remarkable idea brought him close to Jung's concepts. But we must not overlook that "meaning" had an entirely different connotation for Freud than for Jung. Because his approach was based on the method of the natural sciences, Freud found the meaning of the symptom primarily in the *enchaînement* of the patient's experiences, that is, in the causes hidden within the chain of experiences. Consequently, finding the meaning was tantamount to uncovering, in the sequence of symptom, trauma, and memories, the causes intertwined with the ego and the id. In the period before elaborating ego psychology, Freud put emphasis on remembering, working-through resistances, and repetition of forgotten past events,[18] but in later years he supplemented this goal with the idea of "strengthening the ego."[19] What he had in mind was "to tame an instinctual demand,"[20] to attain "intellectual mastery of our environment,"[21] and also to increase adaptation by the ability "to discover generalizations, rules and laws which bring order into chaos."[22] In brief, his object was "to replace repressions that are insecure by reliable, ego-syntonic controls."[23]

2. Neurosis as Personality Problem (Jung)

A. NEUROSIS AS DISUNION WITH ONESELF

Jung always acknowledged the value of Freud's contribution in creating a psychology of neurosis. As late as 1943 he wrote:

> To Freud belongs the undying merit of having laid the foundations of a psychology of the neuroses.[24]

Jung felt Freud's most significant achievement in this area lay in investigating the symptomatology and etiology of the disease and, particu-

18 "Remembering, Repeating and Working-Through" (1914), p. 151.
19 "Analysis Terminable and Interminable" (1937), p. 220.
20 Ibid., p. 225.   21 Ibid., p. 228.
22 Ibid.   23 Ibid., p. 229.
24 "On the Psychology of the Unconscious" (1917/1943), pp. 9-10.

larly, in analyzing the decisive mechanisms, chiefly repression and regression.

Jung was deeply impressed by Freud and was in many respects stimulated by him. But from the start he was less interested in the investigation of the causes of neurosis than in its meaning and significance within the framework of the personality. Since Jung's concept of neurosis was largely independent of Freud's, a detailed comparison of the two approaches does not seem to be necessary.

Symptomatology, although of central importance to Freud, was rarely referred to in Jung's work. The formulations he proposed during the 1940's could be applied to his earlier work. He was less interested in compiling symptoms than in understanding "the content of the neurosis."[25] For Jung, more important than the clinical diagnosis was the understanding of the diseased psyche, the fact that the patient who comes to psychotherapy "does not bring a part but the whole of his psyche and with it the fragment of world on which that psyche depends. . . ."[26] Ever since his college days, Jung had been interested in the sick person,[27] and he expressed the same idea forty years later even more profoundly: He emphasized "that sick people exist as well as sickness"[28] and "that the real point is the treatment of the whole psychic human being"[29]—not just his neurosis which, after all, was only a contrived diagnostic term. With this thought Jung tried to convey that there was something greater in man and that an orientation toward this greater dimension gives health-restoring meaning to the individual's life.

In contrast to Freud's tracing psychic disease back to a miscarried defense mechanism, Jung primarily had in mind the idea of a personality at variance with itself. He did indeed consider the psychic conflict to be fundamental in the development of neurosis—which was similar to Freud's concept—but for Jung the conflict was never restricted to the antagonism of drives. In addition to opposite instinctual strivings, intellectual tendencies and even facets of personality came into opposition. Neurosis was essentially a phenomenon of dissociation of the personality, an expression of unresolved opposites.

From a structural point of view, Jung (following Janet) had always considered neurosis as the dissociation of two personalities which were kept apart by strong emotional barriers.[30] Similarly, in 1912 Jung

25 "Medicine and Psychotherapy" (1945), p. 86.
26 "Psychotherapy Today" (1941), p. 95.
27 "On the Psychology and Pathology of So-Called Occult Phenomena" (1902).
28 "Medicine and Psychotherapy," p. 88.   29 Ibid., p. 89.
30 "Psychoanalysis and Association Experiments" (1906), p. 315.

stressed that neurosis was basically disunity with oneself,[31] a tension-laden discord with oneself, which was to be understood as the expression of an unconscious opposition between two contrasting psychic tendencies. The decisive point for Jung was always the discrepancy between a conscious and an unconscious attitude, which often was related to the antagonism between intellectual-moral and natural-amoral behavior. One of Jung's early descriptions of neurosis was:

> There are in a neurosis two [erotic] tendencies standing in strict opposition to one another, one of which at least is unconscious.[32]

Jung always maintained the premise that neurosis included two opposite complexes or personalities which were complete in themselves and together formed a whole. For instance, there might be a pathological one-sidedness in personality development, manifested as a conflict between a retained infantile attitude and a more mature outlook; or there might be discord between a relatively primitive motivation and another of an intellectual nature; or an antithesis between "knowing better" and acting instinctively; or, again, the antagonism between society's standards and personal inclination— Jung always saw in the neurotic conflict the expression of a more comprehensive tension between the opposites, which is inherent in human life.

Jung not only rejected the assumption that neurosis was due exclusively to an instinctual conflict, he also refused to place the main emphasis on past events as etiological factors. His approach did not focus on childhood memories but on the actual conflict. He saw neurosis, in the first place, as a maladapted "reaction to an actual conflict,"[33] which in the majority of cases culminated in escape into fantasy. Before the turn of the century Freud had already referred to flight from an unsatisfactory situation into fictional memories. Nevertheless, in his psychology the concept of the repressed fixation—of the repressed trauma—retained the significance of a primary starting point, endowed with a great power of attraction. In contrast, Jung saw in the desire to look backward, in the retreat of the ego from demands made by the outside world, a primary cause of the development of neurosis. It was imagination which produced both fictitious sexual experiences and childhood trauma and gave them the appearance of actual events.[34]

31 "New Paths in Psychology" (1912), p. 266.
32 Ibid., p. 257.
33 "The Theory of Psychoanalysis" (1913), p. 181.
34 Ibid., p. 131.

I. NEUROSIS: A PROBLEM OF DRIVES OR OF PERSONALITY?

As little inclined as Jung was to carry the origin of the neurotic conflict back to childhood, so was he, in general, reluctant to reduce it to personal problems. In 1912 he had already emphasized that problems common to all mankind could manifest themselves in neurosis. In such instances, neurotic disease seemed to represent "an unsuccessful attempt on the part of the individual to solve the general problem in his own person."[35] It is remarkable that at such an early date Jung complemented circumstances relevant to the patient's life with those pertinent to goals and issues common to all men. This approach was later much enhanced by Jung's investigations into the problems of the collective unconscious and the archetypes.

Like Freud, who envisaged a dynamic basis of neurosis, Jung expanded his early concept of neurosis as "disunity with oneself" by introducing the energic point of view. However, where Freud constructed an essentially sexual-toned dynamism based on the psychic mechanisms of repression, displacement, and regression, Jung started out from forms of relationships which grew out of the principle of the tension between the opposites as well as from the interplay between consciousness and the unconscious. Thus, the essential criterion was that differentiation in the process of becoming conscious must be unimpeded. Interference in the unfolding of opposite attitudes or in the development of consciousness could lead to neurosis.

Soon after Jung's separation from Freud, the beginnings of his totality-toned point of view could be clearly discerned. He discovered the opposite personality attitudes of extraversion and introversion,[36] which, when exaggerated unilaterally, seemed to throw a new light on the origin of hysteria or obsessive-compulsive neurosis. The new approach culminated in *Psychological Types* (1921), a work in which Jung investigated different types of attitude and the energic connection between the opposites of function: thinking-feeling, intuition-sensation.

In this context, Jung established the noteworthy tenet that, as long as the interplay of opposite attitudes and functions unfolded harmoniously in the individual, he was in harmony with the totality. In other words, energy unfolded progressively—progression, as understood by Jung, being "a continuous process of adaptation to environmental conditions."[37] The opposites were united and acted in coordination. From the energic point of view, disturbances resulted only when the progressive movement of the libido led to some degree of one-sided development in consciousness. When the conscious attitude became

[35] "New Paths in Psychology," p. 261.
[36] "A Contribution to the Study of Psychological Types" (1913), p. 505.
[37] "On Psychic Energy" (1928), p. 39.

215

absolute, the danger of neglect, devaluation, or even repression of the coordinated opposite contents might arise. The consequences could be such phenomena as blockage, disharmonious tensions, or formation of complexes and subsequent psychic conflicts—all of them paving the way for dissociation of the personality.

With segregation of the pairs of opposites, which up till then had been united, the unity between impulse and counterimpulse, between yea and nay,[38] collapsed. One part of the libido regressed and returned to the infantile, even to the archaic level. Complexes arose, consciousness was flooded by unconscious contents and experienced an "abaissement du niveau mental." This was patently a state which could barely maintain the bridges to the unconscious psyche. The dissociation of the pairs of opposites, which had hitherto acted in concert, produced manifest neurosis.

Jung gave regression a very important place among the causes of neurosis—as Freud had done earlier. However, Jung conceived regression not as a mechanical process but always in the context of the totality of the individual. Whenever the conscious attitude was unsatisfactory and consciousness shut itself off from unconscious contents and the personality as a whole, then the inferior functions and the complexes, which had formerly been excluded from the process of adaptation, were revived. Phenomena of blockage ensued, inducing the formation of neurotic symptoms. As Toni Wolff correctly stressed, the symptom was not a precise expression of the patient's psychic situation and could be understood as a blockage phenomenon only when considered from the energic point of view.[39]

Initially (1913), Jung described neurotic symptoms as "regressively reactivated reminiscences,"[40] but the causal explanation of neurosis became less and less interesting to him. He increasingly recognized the hidden meaning of the symptom—the underlying archetypal process— as the symptom's essential aspect. In line with his holistic approach, Jung considered regression not necessarily a pathological process—in contrast to Freud; that is, it was not "a retrograde step in the sense of a backward development or degeneration."[41] Rather, it seemed to him essential that regression should be understood as potentially positive, as stimulating new values, and as an incentive to a more productive attitude towards life. While Freud maintained that regression indicated a pathological "return [of the libido] to earlier phases of sexual

---

38 Ibid., pp. 32f.
39 Wolff, "Einführung in die Grundlagen der Komplexen Psychologie," p. 69.
40 "The Theory of Psychoanalysis," p. 162.
41 "On Psychic Energy," p. 37.

life,"[42] Jung conceived it as prospectively productive, provided the backward step had been taken toward a goal-directed introversion of the libido, that is, toward adaptation to the inner world of the psyche[43] and its tendencies to self-realization.

This last statement touches on an extraordinarily important difference between Jung's and Freud's psychology, namely, complementing the causal view by the finalistic-prospective outlook.[44] The search for the "wherefore" pushed into the background the question of "why." In other words, the disclosure of causes would have to be completed by questioning the meaning of the neurotic symptom within the framework of the total personality. This attempt at a new evaluation of neurosis was articulated as early as 1913 when Jung perceived that this disorder was not "an entirely pathological formation" but contained "a quite teleological significance,"[45] which very often heralded an attempt at a personal solution of hitherto insoluble problems. Viewed from this finalistic aspect, neurosis represented a miscarried attempt to incorporate the other, unrecognized side of the total personality into conscious life.[46] Neurosis revealed the abortive tendency in the process of integrating into the total personality those values and aspects which the ego lacked.

. . . the values which the individual lacks are to be found in the neurosis itself.[47]

In contrast to neurotic disintegration, Jung considered the integration of the absent and misunderstood values as tantamount (from the energic point of view) to a change from the regressive movement of energy to a progressive direction. He saw this in the individual's conscious attempt to withstand the approach of inferior contents and to grant them prospective possibilities—an attitude which stopped the pull of the unconscious. A new gradient between the opposites had been created and thereby the energic prerequisite for their transcendence in the symbol. This process of generating a third attitude from the opposites Jung called the birth of a symbol.

With the birth of the symbol, the regression of the libido into the unconscious ceases. Regression is converted into progression, the

---

[42] Freud, "Five Lectures on Psycho-Analysis" (1910), p. 49.
[43] Jung, "On Psychic Energy," p. 36.
[44] "General Aspects of Dream Psychology" (1916/1928), p. 241.
[45] "The Theory of Psychoanalysis," pp. 184f.
[46] "New Paths in Psychology," p. 266.
[47] "On the Psychology of the Unconscious," p. 61.

blockage starts to flow again, and the lure of the maternal abyss is broken.[48]

The application of the finalistic approach to the treatment of neurosis, the tolerant attitude toward regressive movements of the libido, and the vista of change with a new orientation toward hitherto unacceptable contents also included a re-evaluation of the phenomenon of anxiety. In *Transformations and Symbols of the Libido* (1912) Jung had already explained the connection between anxiety (as in the image of the dragon) and the development of consciousness, and he recognized that each step, each reviving of unconscious contents, and generally each sinking of energy to the level of drives was accompanied by anxiety and resistance. Just as the anxiety of being engulfed in the primitive and unconscious layer of drives was a recurrent subject in the myth of the hero and in mythical voyages into the nether world, so the conquest of anxiety and danger was hypothetically an ever-present theme. The feeling of anxiety was, therefore, never neglected in psychotherapy because it signified a persistent weakness, a lack of equilibrium, and unpreparedness for the tasks at hand. As a dark foreboding of danger, as doubt in the portent of experiences, and even as despair about the futility of the path ahead, anxiety was a steady companion along the course of development. Unlike Freud, who understood anxiety primarily as a signal pointing to possible danger and stimulating the ego to take protective measures, Jung gave anxiety a positive value as well: It could also be taken as an invitation to strengthen and extend the conscious attitude. Anxiety could become a motive for flight or for embarking on a heroic journey.

B. NEUROSIS AND CURE

The finalistic-prospective view led to a corresponding psychotherapeutic approach. The longer Jung searched for the meaning of unconscious psychic phenomena, the less importance he gave to bringing the causes of neurosis into consciousness, although this was the goal postulated by Freud. Jung was vitally interested in a therapeutic method which aimed not at shutting off repression, nor at clearing away amnesia, nor overcoming resistance. He never neglected repressed material with its inherent problems; but in his eyes it was much less the cause of neurosis than the carrier of hidden meaning and a so-far-unfulfilled purpose. This approach clarifies Jung's limited interest in dissolving repressed material and his endeavors to get at the meaning embodied in it. In his opinion, eradicating repressed material would

48 *Psychological Types* (1921), p. 263.

have been tantamount to "murdering" its essence. He also took the phenomenon of resistance so seriously that he would have considered surmounting it the same as crushing its potentials of hidden meaning. Not infrequently he saw resistance as the first sign of the patient's regaining autonomy, becoming himself, an attitude which was apt to find expression as antagonism to the analyst. Even in 1906 Jung had recognized in the resistance-toned attitude toward parents, teachers, or physician an unconscious wish for a new adaptation to reality—a concept which Freud adopted five years later in his distinction between the pleasure principle and the reality principle.

Getting to the meaning hidden in the neurotic symptom included, furthermore, the patient's change to a new, conscious attitude to his affliction. The attempt to reach an attitude conforming to the patient's total personality was Jung's singular psychotherapeutic endeavor.

. . . The task of psychotherapy is to correct the conscious attitude and not to go chasing after infantile memories.[49]

In general, the way this change came about in any particular case could not be detailed. Ultimately, it depended on the special need of the patient. Because the goal of transformation was always based in the individual himself, he could in each specific case change only to "what he essentially was." The attempts at solution aimed at bringing the patient to experience the immanent, unconscious bases of his symptoms; to bring this about Jung relied on questioning the patient, applying the technique of amplification. For discovering the meaning Jung also used spontaneous manifestations of the unconscious in dreams, fantasies, and visions. The primary factor was always what the patient himself unconsciously knew, not the knowledge of the physician, even though his information and understanding might be secondarily helpful.

This point of view naturally affected the much-debated problem of transference from patient to physician. Like Freud, Jung recognized in the transference situation a basic factor for cure, but there was an unbridgeable cleft between him and Freud. For Jung, the most important aim was not overcoming or dissolving the transference relationship but rather promoting the growth of tendencies hidden within this relationship. With such an approach, Jung hoped to have a chance to encounter the inner reality of the patient so that around this nucleus could cluster those values which were his immediate concern. Even when the patient brought out infantile wishes and archaic ideas,

49 "Some Aspects of Modern Psychotherapy" (1929), p. 31.

Jung did not consider them to be of less value, something to be over-come, but rather as still shapeless material which concealed the greater personality. Successful therapy depended a great deal on the per-sonality of the physician, his understanding, maturity, and degree of objectivity. According to Jung, "objectivity" did not mean standing outside the situation, but being in it, that is, to be conscious as far as possible of one's own personal stance and ready to serve suprapersonal aspects. Inasmuch as the physician implied disease as well as cure to the patient, building a satisfactory relationship was vitally important. The psychic rapport between physician and patient was anything but a bond which needed to be "overcome"; it was rather a relationship to be taken seriously and to be examined profitably, since this was often the patient's only possibility of attaining self-realization and a feeling of inner freedom. Jung never meant inner freedom as being entirely without ties but, on the contrary, as recognizing an inner connection with the other person.

C. DISSOCIATION IN NEUROSIS AND PSYCHOSIS

As mentioned earlier, Jung conceived neurosis to be, essentially, a disunion of the personality with itself, chiefly on the unconscious level. In the first decade of his investigations, he saw a certain contrast be-tween such dissociation of the personality and fragmentation of the personality which occurred in psychosis.

Now, to consider the psychological significance of the dissociation of the personality: Carrying on his and Freud's idea of the "in-congruity of idea and affect," Jung as early as 1907 observed an "atrophy of the complex," which might go so far as to cause complete disintegration of the personality. In this context, he followed Janet who had recognized "désagrégation mentale"[50] in cases of acute hysteria; he also applied Janet's finding of loss of reality[51] in the psychasthenic syndrome. With these tools Jung opposed Freud's con-cept that in paranoia the libido withdrew from objects, similarly to what happened in neurosis.[52] Freud's assumption that psychotic regres-sion of the libido went as far as the primary stage of infantile auto-eroticism did not conform with Jung's observations. Dementia praecox seemed to differ from mere introversion of libido, since the question was not loss of a quantum of libido, but rather loss of adaptation to reality.[53]

---

50 Janet, *Névroses et idées fixes*, Vol. 1, p. 145.   51 Ibid., p. 218.
52 Freud, "Psycho-Analytic Notes on an Autobiographical Account of a Case of Paranoia (Dementia Paranoides)" (1911), p. 72.
53 Jung, "The Psychology of Dementia Praecox" (1907), p. 97.

About twenty years later, after putting his psychology on an anthropological basis (1923), Freud gave loss of reality a foremost place in the development of both neurosis and psychosis. Although he retained the mechanism of the libido's withdrawal from objects, he increasingly connected the causation of psychic disturbances with failure of ego function. Not only did insufficiency of the reality function seem to be of etiological significance, but abortive attempts at controlling the drives as well. Failure could have a threefold effect on the relations of the ego: to the id, to the superego, and also to the external world.

Transference neuroses correspond to a conflict between the ego and the id; narcissistic neuroses, to a conflict between the ego and the super-ego; and psychoses, to one between the ego and the external world.[54]

In those years Freud saw a "loss of reality" as well as a "substitute for reality"[55] in all psychic symptoms. These phenomena had been differentiated by Jung as early as 1912,[56] when he wrote that "the whole adaptation to reality has ceased" for the patient with dementia praecox; in neurosis, on the other hand, "the former . . . psychologic adaptation to the environment remains preserved," although the patient substitutes fantasy images when reactivating parental images.

A position which both investigators held in common was that neither one laid the causes of psychic diseases exclusively to psychogenic factors but both gave attention to somatic sources. While Freud always stressed the importance of the chemical action of sexual secretions[57] and sex metabolism, Jung very early (1907) formulated the hypothesis that a toxin might be active in dementia praecox.[58] This assumption was one of his most predictive intuitions which, although it had little influence on the psychiatric research of that time, anticipated certain experimental findings of present-day psychiatry.

In the early years of his work with dementia praecox, Jung had "claimed that a great many cases of dementia praecox were psychogenic in origin, the toxic or destructive processes being secondary only."[59] Twelve years later, however, he was inclined to acknowledge "that

54 Freud, "Neurosis and Psychosis" (1924), p. 152.
55 "The Loss of Reality in Neurosis and Psychosis" (1924), p. 187.
56 *Psychology of the Unconscious* (*Transformations and Symbols of the Libido,* 1912), p. 142.
57 Freud, *The Origins of Psycho-Analysis,* p. 87.
58 Jung, "The Psychology of Dementia Praecox," p. 98.
59 "On the Problems of Psychogenesis in Mental Disease" (1919), p. 225 (referring to "The Psychology of Dementia Praecox").

there may be cases in which the organic processes are primary."[60] As time went on, he established that there were factors in dementia praecox (later, on the model of Bleuler, designated as schizophrenia)[61] which could not "be fitted into a purely personalistic frame of reference,"[62] in contrast to neurosis, but called for consideration of primary biological processes. At first, Jung concentrated on the investigation of psychological aspects, hoping to clarify and evaluate them sufficiently to permit an estimate of the feasibility of psychotherapeutic treatment. It was part of Jung's early discoveries that within certain limits schizophrenia could be psychotherapeutically treated.

It is now just about fifty years since I became convinced, through practical experience, that schizophrenic disturbances could be treated and cured by psychological means.[63]

Fairly narrow limits, however, are set to the psychotherapy of severe cases.[64]

In distinction from the psychological facts pertaining to neurotic dissociation of the personality, Jung always maintained that schizophrenia represented a split of the personality into "a plurality of *autonomous complexes*",[65] they were not only withdrawn from the control of the ego, but could even occupy the place of the ego personality.

Jung became more and more convinced of a primary destructive factor which disrupted the continuity of the psyche. This recognition led him from then on to completely new paths in the understanding of schizophrenia. Eleven years later (1939) Jung stressed that the "potential unity of the personality"[66] was characteristic of neurosis, that is, the presence of a unifying factor which held the opposites together in spite of their divergent tendencies. In contrast, schizophrenia presented the pathological picture of the personality's unity having been shattered into fragments,[67] with destruction of earlier relationships. It was easy to suspect the operation of a demonic power which caused the irreparable and irreversible dissociation. In the first place, an extreme "abaissement du niveau mental" became obvious, which represented the violent intrusion of archaic symbols from the collective uncon-

---

60 Ibid.
61 Bleuler, *Dementia Praecox or the Group of Schizophrenias* (1911; tr. Zinkin, 1950).
62 Jung, "Recent Thoughts on Schizophrenia" (1956), p. 251.
63 "Schizophrenia" (1957), p. 258.   64 Ibid., p. 265.
65 "Mental Disease and the Psyche" (1928), p. 227.
66 "On the Psychogenesis of Schizophrenia" (1939), p. 234.
67 Ibid., p. 235.

scious.[68] Although the symbols revealed a certain degree of meaning when considered separately and even presented a similarity with archaic dream symbols, they could hardly be compared with the dreams of neurotics because the psychic connection between the separate elements had gone to pieces.

> It is as if the very foundations of the psyche were giving way, as if an explosion or an earthquake were tearing asunder the structure of a normally built house.[69]

It became clear to Jung that the underlying factor had "no analogy with any kind of functional disturbance."[70] Not only were the associations mangled and the intrinsic logic of ideas subjected to the disarranging effect of certain factors, but the autonomous complexes also presented traits of deterioration.

About twenty years later, Jung arrived at a more precise distinction between neurosis and psychosis based on the criteria of systematic dissociation of the personality and unsystematic disintegration of psychic elements.[71] He conceived the systematic nature of neurosis as a group of single pathological traits around one or more nuclear complexes which always remained in contact. Schizophrenia, on the other hand, exhibited "unsystematic dissociation," that is, a multitude of unconnected fragments, an expression of the chaotic state of affectivity. While the emotional behavior in neurosis was still transparent and comprehensible, in schizophrenia the emotional values appeared to be paradoxically distributed. In Jung's words, the personality was like a "broken mirror." The systematic aspect of neurosis also showed the disunited personalities to be complete in themselves, related to a specific nucleus of personality. Hysterical dissociation was characterized by the opposites of emotionality and intellectuality, while the personality split of the compulsive neurotic showed the opposition of a moral and an immoral nucleus. In both instances, the emotional conflict was understandable, but in compulsive neurosis there was, in addition to a certain emotional inadequacy, an often-pronounced denial of the incompatible complex combined with the compensating compulsive ideas. Jung found in schizophrenia the acme of "unsystematic randomness"[72] of inadequate affects, the peak of nontransparent and incomprehensible emotional states. The phenomenon of "abaissement du niveau mental" appeared to assume exorbitant forms in this disease. While it occurred in normal subjects when fatigued or exhausted or in dreams, when consciousness was dimmed during sleep,

[68] Ibid., p. 239. [69] Ibid., p. 240. [70] Ibid.
[71] "Recent Thoughts on Schizophrenia," p. 251. [72] "Schizophrenia," p. 257.

abaissement in schizophrenics presented traits of an archaic, primitive world of ideas, which could not be assimilated by the ego; the "continuity of meaning was often maimed to the point of incomprehensibility," with grotesque, abstruse, and unintelligible thoughts coming to the fore.

Jung's observation that the complexes of ideas and their associative relationships were pulled apart in the disturbed expressions and communications of the patient was to become of incisive importance; on it he was able to base the conclusive understanding of personality decay. As early as 1907 he already had given a hint: "We have only the husks of the affect, the content is gone."[73] Jung extended this thought in 1957 to the notable hypothesis of "the self-destruction of the pathogenic complex."[74] In explaining this self-destruction, Jung was able to refer to the concept of the archetype-as-such (see App. I), which had meanwhile been developed and which served a regulating and directing function. He came to the completely novel discovery that the cause of affect decay in schizophrenia was connected with disturbed function of the central archetype.[75] Experience, however, demonstrated that at times of great mental disorientation some compensation was achieved by factors which pointed to a still-operating effectiveness of the regulating archetype.

The attempt to explain psychotic dissociation culminated in the hypothesis that the decay of the pathogenic complex of ideas was in all probability not only the effect of a specific toxin but also of "a kind of mistaken biological defence reaction"[76]—a theory which is an extremely interesting concession to the biological approach.

[73] "The Psychology of Dementia Praecox," p. 103.
[74] "Schizophrenia," p. 271.   [75] Ibid., p. 270.   [76] Ibid., p. 271.

Initially, Jung's understanding of the meaning and purpose of the unconscious had been derived from the fantasies of psychotics, but it was primarily the phenomenon of the dream which gave him basic insights into the nature of the unconscious psyche. Dreams confirmed his perception of the spontaneity of the psyche's background and led also to the idea of a compensating function of the unconscious. Moreover, from dream material Jung worked out the method of amplification as a means of interpretation, and thereby he gained some valuable approaches for investigating symbols.

Of all the followers of Freud, none was more searchingly occupied with the interpretation of dreams than Jung. He was deeply impressed by the fact that Freud had reopened the discussion of dreams and had assigned to them the status of a meaningful psychic occurrence. Jung gave Freud great credit for retrieving the dream from the domain of soothsayers and diviners, while taking it beyond the physiological description as mere bodily and sensory stimuli. Jung's high esteem of Freud's dream interpretation becomes clear in his obituary for Freud (1939):

> The Interpretation of Dreams is probably Freud's most important work, and at the same time the most open to attack. For us young psychiatrists it was a fount of illumination, but for our older colleagues it was an object of mockery. As with his recognition that neurosis had the character of a medieval "possession," so, by treating dreams as a highly important source of information about the unconscious processes. . . . Freud rescued something of the utmost value from the past, where it had seemed irretrievably sunk in oblivion. . . . It was an act of the greatest scientific courage to make anything as unpopular as dreams an object of serious discussion. . . . This line of investigation opened the way to an understanding of schizophrenic hallucinations and delusions from the inside, whereas hitherto psychiatrists had been able to describe them only from the outside. More than that, The Interpretation of Dreams provided a key to the many locked doors in the psychology of neurotics as well as of normal people.[1]

[1] Jung, "In Memory of Sigmund Freud" (1939), pp. 44–45.

G. NEUROSIS AND DREAM

1. Freud's Concept of the Dream

Freud was not only the first in medical psychology to attribute a scientifically demonstrable significance to the dream and to recognize in it *cogent determinants*, he was also the first to discern a structural unity[2] in the dream which was meaningfully connected with the psyche as a whole as well as with its individual parts. Freud saw the essence of this unity as based on an unconscious nucleus of the dream, more or less a point of crystallization which formed the common ground for consecutive dreams, not only during the same night but also in a succession of nights.[3] "The content of all dreams that occur during the same night forms part of the same whole,"[4] and "different dreams dreamt on the same night are, as a quite general rule, to be treated in their interpretation as a single whole."[5]

Freud also was the first to underline the significance of the dream as *"the royal road to a knowledge of the unconscious activities of the mind."*[6] His most important assumption in this respect was that the dream was embedded in the unbroken "enchaînement" of the memory material. Thus, the analytical access to the dream unconscious seemed to be assured. Because Freud understood the meaning and purpose of psychic events from the way their contents were determined, the discovery of the dream's meaning was nothing but a return to the unconscious causes of its elements. The purpose of dream interpretation was easily coordinated with that of psychotherapy: ". . . 'involuntary' ideas are transformed into 'voluntary' ones."[7] We have already mentioned that Freud considered the free associations of the dreamer to be of decisive importance. Later on, he supplemented the method of association with the interpretation of symbolic relationships (see H.I).

In contrast to Jung, Freud regarded the dream from the very beginning as the most valuable complement of the theory of neurosis. As early as 1897 he noted that ". . . dreams . . . contain the whole psychology of the neuroses in a nutshell."[8] In *The Interpretation of Dreams* he remarked that neurosis may serve as a model for the understanding of dreams.[9] In fact, from the processes involved in dreams he gained decisive insights into the working of psychic mechanisms—not only repression and regression, but also condensation, displacement, symbolization, and so on. Similarly, he arrived at a new psychological understanding of infantile experiences, fixation to childhood, and the

---

[2] Freud, *The Interpretation of Dreams* (1900), p. 179.   [3] Ibid., p. 525.
[4] Ibid., p. 333.   [5] Ibid., p. 525.   [6] Ibid., p. 608.
[7] Ibid., p. 102.   [8] *The Origins of Psycho-Analysis* (1887–1902), p. 212.
[9] *The Interpretation of Dreams*, p. 597.

sexual and archaic background of the psyche, since dreaming to him was "a piece of infantile mental life that has been superseded."[10]

Disregarding all similarities between dream and neurosis, which culminated in the interplay of opposing tendencies, the sleeping state was of critical importance for the dream. The dreamer was under the conditions of sleep, that is, a withdrawal of interest from the outside world and with limited mobility.

"Dreaming is evidently mental life during sleep."[11] From the biological point of view the dream had the essential function of protecting sleep—as Freud had established very early. This concept has again stirred up current interest because of the investigations of Dement and his pupils, who have been able to demonstrate empirically the life-preserving function of the dream.[12] Further investigations on dream and sleep have recently been made at the C. G. Jung Clinic and Research Institute, Zurich, under the direction of C. A. Meier.[13]

Now, we can further examine Freud's concept of the preservation of sleep, a function which was put in great jeopardy by the constant pressure of unconscious stirring. In his letters to Fliess, Freud had already acknowledged that unconscious wishes were the secret motives of the formation of dreams and symptoms. They seemed to accomplish their aim in wish-fulfillment[14]—an idea which to his great satisfaction came to him in 1895, like a revelation, as it were, unveiling the mystery of the dream. There seemed to be a connection between unconscious wishes and the pronounced visual character of the dream, which was produced by transforming the ideational content into sensory images,[15] as well as a connection with the dream's affinity for hallucinatory experiences, transposed into the present. As a rule, these tendencies or thoughts in dreams concerned infantile and archaic contents, mostly repressed, but which obviously were ready to break into consciousness and did not hesitate to exhibit both sexual drives and death wishes. Freud saw the dream thought as the essential active force of the dream, but it could be remembered only in a distorted guise, being unacceptable to the censor. In this context, Freud recognized a basic premise in psychoanalysis—that each remembered dream is the result of a mechanism of distortion[16] which, like the action of the ego in neurosis, brought about a compromise between unconscious wishes and the demands of the censor. On the strength of these insights,

[10] Ibid., p. 567.
[11] Introductory Lectures on Psycho-Analysis (1915–17), p. 88.
[12] Dement, "The Effect of Dream Deprivation" (1960).
[13] Meier, Die Bedeutung des Traumes (1972), pp. 14f., 62ff.
[14] Freud, Origins, p. 125.   [15] The Interpretation of Dreams, p. 547.
[16] Ibid., p. 144.

Freud described the dream as wish-fulfillment distorted by the censor—a definition which applied neither to dreams of children nor to dreams of adults which were of an "infantile type."

A dream is a (disguised) fulfilment of a (suppressed or repressed) wish.[17]

The two mentioned exceptions—dreams of children and adult dreams of the infantile type—Freud understood as an expression of pure wish-fulfillment, because the distorting agency of the censor either did not yet exist or functioned only to a reduced degree. Consequently, Freud saw in the manifest dream content—that part of the dream content which was remembered—a distorted substitute formation, while the latent dream content contained the hidden and essential aspects of the dream wish.[18] Three origins seemed to him to be decisive in the formation of the latent dream wish:

I can distinguish three possible origins for such a wish. (1) It may have been aroused during the day and for external reasons may not have been satisfied; in that case an acknowledged wish which has not been dealt with is left over for the night. (2) It may have arisen during the day but been repudiated; in that case what is left over is a wish which has not been dealt with but has been suppressed. (3) It may have no connection with daytime life and be one of those wishes which only emerge from the suppressed part of the mind and become active in us at night.[19]

The parallel which Freud drew between dream and neurosis was interesting, particularly because it was built on the mechanism of distortion. He conceived the neurotic symptom as a mnemonic symbol of a repressed traumatic excitation and treated "the dream itself as a symptom,"[20] that is, a sign of something else.

Freud recognized the censor as the actual agent of distortion and falsification, the supervisor *par excellence*, engaged in what he called dream-work. Its nature was revealed in always new aspects which Freud understood at times as the play of a cunning goblin with a fine scent, at times as the work of an intelligent and anticipating organizer. The most important aspect of dreams was dream-work, which Freud equated with the mechanisms of condensation and displacement as well as dramatization and symbolization. (We will return later to the problems of symbolization and symbol formation.) In describing dream-work, Freud used the whole gamut of artful combinations and gave free rein to his rich fantasies.

17 Ibid., p. 160.   18 Ibid., p. 144.   19 Ibid., p. 551.   20 Ibid., p. 101.

II. DREAM AS SYMPTOM (FREUD) AND AS SYMBOL (JUNG)

2. *The Dream in Jung's Psychology*

In the preface to *The Psychology of Dementia Praecox* (1907), Jung wrote: "I told myself, Freud could be refuted only by one who has made repeated use of the psychoanalytic method and who really investigates as Freud does."[21] This attitude applied particularly to the investigation of dreams. It is remarkable that Jung remained so long under the spell of Freud's ideas—especially since the subject of dreams from 1914 on occupied his central interest and was the source of new discoveries. Around 1910 the outlines of his concept of the collective unconscious had already begun to take shape, but his writing on dreams did not yet present a truly individual approach.

Jung's little paper on "The Analysis of Dreams"[22] (written in French, 1909) upheld without reservation Freud's concepts of the function of dream censorship, and two years later he still defended Freud's ideas in a critical review of an article by Morton Prince[23] on his findings in dream research. Unexpectedly perhaps, Jung later completely supported many of Prince's views which he had earlier criticized. In "New Paths in Psychology" (1912),[24] Jung frankly praised psychoanalysis and its method for the last time. However, a statement which he made in this essay might be surprising, although still following Freud's ideas: ". . . dreams are a symbolic substitute for a personally important wish which was not sufficiently appreciated during the day and was 'repressed.' "[25]

The separation from Freud (1913) marked a turning point in Jung's publications on the theory of dreams, but it is difficult to establish the precise point in time when his own ideas began to guide his thinking. The concepts of finality and compensation, which have illuminated to such a degree our understanding of Jung's dream psychology, were first explored in "The Psychology of Dreams" (1916)—revised and expanded under the title of "General Aspects of Dream Psychology" (1928, 1940)[26]—but were mentioned briefly in "On the Importance of the Unconscious in Psychopathology" (1914).[27]

In the field of dream research Jung had notable precursors. In 1910, Eugen Bleuler had established the importance of affectivity and conflicting affects in the dream, with particular emphasis on the reciprocal

---

[21] Jung, "The Psychology of Dementia Praecox" (1907), p. 3.
[22] "The Analysis of Dreams" (1909), pp. 25–34.
[23] "Morton Prince, 'The Mechanism and Interpretation of Dreams': A Critical Review" (1911), pp. 56–73.
[24] "New Paths in Psychology" (1912), p. 247.
[25] Ibid., p. 264.
[26] "General Aspects of Dream Psychology" (1916/1928), pp. 241ff.
[27] "On the Importance of the Unconscious in Psychopathology" (1914), p. 205.

inhibition of opposing affects.[28] To Bleuler's credit, he was among the first investigators to base the function of the dream on a strictly psychological concept, the reconciliation of complexes.[29] Also of great value were Silberer's studies on symbols, which Jung commended on several occasions, especially his "Phantasie und Mythos" (1910) and *Problems of Mysticism and Its Symbolism*.[30] The collaboration with A. Maeder, who had the distinction of discovering the prospective-finalistic function of the dream, was notably valuable for Jung.

Maeder has laid energetic stress on the prospective-final significance of dreams as a purposive unconscious function which paves the way for the solution of real conflicts and problems and seeks to portray it with the help of gropingly chosen symbols.[31]

Jung and Maeder seemed to have fertilized each other's thinking. In his early work Jung had begun to recognize the finalistic significance of fantasy, but Maeder took a further step by applying Jung's concepts to the dream, and he proposed his own theory in "Über die Funktion des Traumes" (1912). In contrast to Bleuler, he placed the principal emphasis of the function of the dream on the development of the individual. He stated that not only fantasies but also dreams "prepared egocentric solutions on the part of the dreamer"[32] and constellated his actions.[33] Two years later (1914) Maeder recognized that the dream was the most important source of information regarding prospective tendencies[34] in the life of the psyche. After these two advances made by Maeder, Jung published his paper on "The Psychology of Dreams" (1916), containing concepts which had developed two years earlier. He proposed the basic premise of a compensatory function of the dream,[35] applying Adler's general concept of compensatory function. At first glance it might be surprising that Jung—in spite of his earlier mention of the goal-directedness of psychic processes (1908) and the discovery of the anticipatory significance of dreams (1912)[36]—waited until 1914 to propose a specific theory of dreams, that is, the theory of compensation.

[28] Bleuler, "Die Psychoanalyse Freuds."   [29] Ibid., p. 725.
[30] *Problems of Mysticism and Its Symbolism* (1914; tr. Jelliffe, 1917).
[31] Jung, "General Aspects of Dream Psychology," p. 255.
[32] Maeder, "Über die Funktion des Traumes" (1912), p. 696.
[33] Ibid., p. 700.
[34] *The Dream Problem* (1914; tr. Hallock and Jelliffe, 1916).
[35] Jung, "General Aspects of Dream Psychology," p. 253.
[36] *Psychology of the Unconscious* (*Transformations and Symbols of the Libido*, 1912), p. 64.

II. DREAM AS SYMPTOM (FREUD) AND AS SYMBOL (JUNG)

A. THE DREAM AS MANIFESTATION OF THE UNCONSCIOUS

Jung's revolutionary discoveries in the realm of the unconscious during the first decade of his investigations were the primary basis for his concept of the dream. In 1931, he emphasized that the "problem of dream-analysis stands or falls with such an hypothesis" (that is, of the unconscious) and "without it, the dream is a mere freak of nature, a meaningless conglomeration of fragments left over from the day."[37] This thought could have been the motto for the years of transition (1912–14). Jung understood that "the dream is specifically the utterance of the unconscious,"[38] an "expression of an involuntary, unconscious psychic process . . . [which] shows the inner truth and reality of the patient as it really is."[39]

The interpretation of the dream, accordingly, depended completely on the way the unconscious was understood. Just as Jung's understanding of the unconscious began to deviate from Freud's concepts, his psychology of dreams parted from Freud's dream theory and developed in its own way. Jung's essential discovery of the creative and spontaneous character of the unconscious background had its immediate consequences in his concept of the dream: The dream was an autonomous utterance of the unconscious, presenting its own reality and forming a world of its own. Consequently, he was disinclined—at least after 1914—to reduce dreams to infantile, forgotten, or repressed wishes. Like any other unconscious phenomenon, the dream could be understood as a goal-directed event, with its own meaning and purpose.[40] Jung found it necessary to go back into the archaic levels of the psyche, and in this manner to establish contact with the image-creating aspect of the unconscious, that is, the original meanings and primal images. With this approach, Jung threw light on the *symbolic content* of the dream:

> By a symbol I do not mean an allegory or a sign, but an image that describes in the best possible way the dimly discerned nature of the spirit. A symbol does not define or explain; it points beyond itself to a meaning that is darkly divined yet still beyond our grasp, and cannot be adequately expressed in the familiar words of our language.[41]

The distinction between the personal and the collective unconscious proved particularly productive for understanding the dream. Based on

---

[37] "The Practical Use of Dream-Analysis" (1931/1934), p. 139.
[38] Ibid., p. 147.   [39] Ibid., p. 140.
[40] "General Aspects of Dream Psychology," pp. 239–40.
[41] "Spirit and Life" (1926), p. 336.

this distinction, the dream could be experienced not only as a source of information concerning personal problems, but also as a means of manifesting the content of archetypical meaning of the psychic background. This finding threw some light on the fact that "in ancient cultures . . . man always resorted to dreams and visions as a source of information"[42] regarding the concealed depths of the psyche. The dream was—like the vision, the enlightening idea, or the religious revelation—a kind of creative flash of thought which left a powerful impression on the psyche. Jung described this erupting thought thus:

> Light means illumination; it is an illuminating idea that "irrupts." Using a very cautious formulation, we could say that the underlying factor here is a considerable tension of psychic energy, evidently corresponding to some very important unconscious content.[43]

Such fascinating dream images and dream thoughts were the primary motives which induced Jung to see in the dream the expression of a superior wisdom, an "insight or knowledge which consciousness has not been able to produce."[44]

Establishing the affinity of the dream to the autonomous complex (1920)[45] became a rich source for Jung's further discoveries. Like the complex, the dream represented a psychic entity, its elements also being grouped around a nucleus. It had an affective and emotional tone, which manifested itself as a constellating power and as an influence determining the total character of the dream. In addition, the feeling-tone was coordinated with a center of significance,[46] which was meaningfully connected with each element of the dream as well as with the psyche as a whole. Like Jung, Freud conceived the dream to be a meaningful formation, but he understood this "meaning" in a basically different manner. For Freud, the meaning of the dream was tantamount to its causal determination—it was essentially a sign of something else. Jung, on the other hand, attributed to the dream a symbolic meaning. It was for him a unit of meaning, a symbolic expression of the unconscious,[47] the essence of which could be gained only through the interpretation of what was still unknown. In other words, the dream represented a *symbol* and could be understood only by a special technique of interpretation.[48]

---

42 "Basic Postulates of Analytical Psychology" (1931), p. 348.
43 "Brother Klaus" (1933), p. 320.
44 "Psychology and Religion" (1937/1940), p. 41.
45 "The Psychological Foundations of Belief in Spirits" (1920), p. 308.
46 "Seminar über Kinderträume," I (1938-39).
47 *Psychological Types* (1921), p. 422.
48 Wolff, "Einführung in die Grundlagen der Komplexen Psychologie," p. 73.

II. DREAM AS SYMPTOM (FREUD) AND AS SYMBOL (JUNG)

Jung made the remarkable observation that the dream has an exceptional "psychic structure";[49] there is a coherent structure of meaning in the dream as a whole. He recognized that in all cases in which the dream left a strong and lasting impression, it was possible to discern an intensified energy-tension with a corresponding organization of the meaning, comparable to the structure of a classical drama.

> With an increase of energy-tension, the dreams acquire a more ordered character; they become dramatically composed and reveal clear sense-connections, and the valency of the associations increases.[50]

Similar to the pattern of the classical drama, the dream could be divided into four meaningfully connected phases, dealing with the participating persons and place of action, exposition, climax, and resolution.

B. DISTORTION OR SYMBOLIC FORMATION?

From 1913 on, Jung's thinking on the concept of the dream became increasingly clear; since he and Freud started from such different basic concepts, it is no wonder that Freud's theoretical assumption of the dream as a product of distortion was so alien to Jung. In Jung's later theory of dreams, there was no longer a place for a distorting censor. However, it took some time until he freed himself completely from Freud's influence and abandoned the concept of a censor. In 1909 Jung, still following Freud, described the censor as "the resistance against the complex,"[51] which "will not allow the thought to pass until it is so disguised that the dreamer is unable to recognize it."[52] Even in 1916, Jung equated the inhibition exercised by consciousness with censorship, quoting Freud.[53] After that, a censoring agency is no longer mentioned in Jung's writings. His approach, which aimed at investigating the autonomy and structure of the psyche, no longer permitted the assumption of a "hobgoblin" which concealed unconscious wishes by "crafty cunning" and falsified the truth.

With the rejection of the censoring agency, Freud's hypotheses of dream distortion effected thereby and of dream work naturally became untenable. It is true, Jung retained the psychic mechanisms of condensation, displacement, symbolization, and so on as the formal prerequisites for dream formation, and he even recognized condensation as the

[49] "General Aspects of Dream Psychology," p. 237.
[50] "The Transcendent Function" (1916), p. 77.
[51] "The Analysis of Dreams," p. 31.   [52] Ibid., p. 29.
[53] "The Transcendent Function," p. 69.

formal basis of symbol formation; however, after 1920 he viewed this mechanism neither as connected with a censor nor as the product of distortion. The background of the psyche was responsible for the obscurity of the dream content, not a censoring agency. This obscurity was due to the general and mutual contamination of all unconscious contents.

Similarly, the distinction between the manifest and latent content of dreams, built on the censoring agency, had to be abandoned. It could, however, be misleading to note that Jung still referred in *Psychological Types* (1921) to the opposition of manifest and latent meaning in dreams.[54] At about that time he also declared that manifest dream formations were fragmentary and unsatisfactory. The explanation of this surprising statement is that Jung awkwardly tried to indicate the obscurity inherent in the memory of a dream. In spite of the meaningful structure which Jung attributed to the dream, it was very often felt as a fantastic, illogical, or even absurd experience—a situation implying that the meaning of the dream could not immediately be grasped. This lack of clarity and, occasionally, even incomprehensibility came about because the dream represented a *communication in images*—which both Jung and Freud took for granted. The dream hardly ever expressed itself in logical-abstract terms, but always "in the language of parable or simile."[55] While Freud understood this lack of clarity to be a disguise of the true meaning, Jung on the contrary saw in the still opaque manifest content the expression of the true essence: It was a spontaneous expression of background processes, the rational transparency largely missing due to the often pronounced state of being independent of consciousness and untouched by it. The often high degree of incomprehensibility of the remembered dream, therefore, called for interpretation. A dream always needed to be read and explained. For this reason, the problem of interpretation played a great role with both investigators. Until well into the 1920's, Freud declared that interpretation, in the first place, involved going back to unconscious and unknown causes, but later he also considered an explanation based on symbolic relationships which, after all, were typical and constant. In contrast, Jung understood interpretation as an art, the deeper meaning being revealed through understanding the symbol (see Part H). In order to understand the dream, Jung thought it was indispensable to grasp its language and to elucidate its meaning by amplification. Even though the remembered dream at first presented

54 *Psychological Types*, p. 429.
55 "General Aspects of Dream Psychology," p. 248.

an incomprehensible jumble of words, Jung understood it neither as a façade nor as a distortion, as Freud had done.

> . . . the so-called façade of most houses is by no means a fake or a deceptive distortion; on the contrary, it follows the plan of the building and often betrays the interior arrangement. The "manifest" dream-picture is the dream itself and contains the whole meaning of the dream. . . . What Freud calls the "dream-façade" is the dream's obscurity, and this is really only a projection of our own lack of understanding. We say the dream has a false front only because we fail to see into it. We would do better to say that we are dealing with something like a text that is unintelligible not because it has a façade—a text has no façade—but simply because we cannot read it. We do not have to get behind such a text, but must first learn to read it.[56]

Jung, thus, agreed with the Talmud, in which the dream was understood as "its own interpretation."[57] In the Terry Lectures (1937/ 1940), Jung made the remark:

> The dream is such a difficult and complicated thing that I do not dare to make any assumptions about its possible cunning or its tendency to deceive. The dream is a natural occurrence, and there is no earthly reason why we should assume that it is a crafty device to lead us astray.[58]

After Jung developed his own concept of the dream (1914–16), he maintained that basically what is remembered of the dream is an involuntary, spontaneous phenomenon which faithfully portrayed the inner truth of the dreamer.

> . . . the dream comes in as the expression of an involuntary, unconscious psychic process beyond the control of the conscious mind. It shows the inner truth and reality of the patient as it really is: not as I conjecture it to be, and not as he would like it to be, but *as it is*.[59]

C. WISH-FULFILLMENT OR SELF-PORTRAYAL

Freud's hypothesis of the dream as a distorted wish-fulfillment was foreign to Jung's deepest convictions. He had as little interest in the dream as the result of wishes and wish-fulfilling tendencies as he had (after 1913) in tracing back the unconscious to repressed wishes. What-

[56] "The Practical Use of Dream-Analysis," p. 149.
[57] "Psychology and Religion," p. 26.   [58] Ibid., pp. 26–27.
[59] "The Practical Use of Dream-Analysis," p. 142.

ever applied to the unconscious psyche as a whole was evidently valid for the dream as well. He could not see sexual wishes as the exclusive motivating force of dream events nor could he accept the principle of pleasure and displeasure, connected to wish-fulfillment[60] as the regulating tendency of the psyche. As far as he was concerned, wish-fulfillment was useful only as an expression. Even though he agreed with Freud in assuming a teleological basis for unconscious events, it was never as a merely drive-determined goal-directedness, and certainly not hedonistic. From his experience, the psyche presented a tendency to self-fulfillment but never restricted to the satisfaction of sexual drives and always including the realization of spiritual goals. Besides sexual desires, Jung also acknowledged a number of drive tendencies—toward nourishment, power, value, and self-preservation, to mention only a few. Furthermore, the drive was always coupled with patterns of archetypal situations[61] and with archetypal motives.[62] Just as archaic images were frequently connected with a numinous affect-tone, conversely, intense affectivity in dreams suggested the presence of still-unknown images. In each instance, it was left to dream interpretation to bring to life the connection between affect and image, which may have been conscious or unconscious, and to assimilate the content of the dream with the ego.

All these observations motivated Jung to denounce ever more sharply the concept that "the unconscious . . . knows no other aim than the fulfillment of wishes"[63] and is entirely directed toward wish-fulfillment and the wish-satisfaction of repressed contents.

The view that dreams are merely the imaginary fulfilments of repressed wishes is hopelessly out of date. There are, it is true, dreams which manifestly represent wishes or fears, but what about all the other things? Dreams may contain ineluctable truths, philosophical pronouncements, illusions, wild fantasies, memories, plans, anticipations, irrational experiences, even telepathic visions, and heaven knows what besides. One thing we ought never to forget: almost half our life is passed in a more or less unconscious state.[64]

As discussed earlier, because he had demonstrated the ability to create new formations and had observed tendencies toward a positive

60 "General Aspects of Psychoanalysis" (1913), p. 237.
61 "On the Nature of the Psyche" (1946/1954), p. 201.
62 "Instinct and the Unconscious" (1919), p. 137.
63 Freud, The Interpretation of Dreams, p. 568.
64 Jung, "The Practical Use of Dream-Analysis," p. 147.

development within the unconscious psyche, it was impossible for Jung to share Freud's assumption that during the night all the slime of objectionable and inferior contents, all repressed incestuous wishes, and even all evil thoughts[65] (such as hatred, egotism, and death wishes) attempted to find their way into consciousness or into motoric discharge. On the contrary, in Jung's experience, moral tendencies[66] as well as new spiritual possibilities could be detected in the dream.

Opposed to Freud's theory of wish-fulfillment, which in the last analysis was based on biological assumptions, Jung advocated as early as 1913 a concept of the dream founded exclusively on psychological premises, that is, on self-portrayal.[67] Instead of seeing the function of the dream as wish-fulfillment of repressed drive tendencies, he conceived its function as self-portrayal, while the theory of dream wishes was replaced by the idea of an image-creating psychic activity, which was feeling- and value-toned. Accordingly, the dream was seen as a picture mirroring the inner situation of the dreamer.

> For Freud, the dream is essentially a symbolic disguise for repressed wishes which would come into conflict with the aims of the personality. I am obliged to regard the structure of a dream from a different point of view. For me the dream is, in the first instance, a subliminal picture of the actual psychological situation of the individual in his waking state.[68]

Several years later Jung reformulated this thought, with the dream representing not only a symbolic self-portrayal but also a reproduction of the actual situation of the unconscious.

> As against Freud's view that the dream is essentially a wishfulfilment, I hold with my friend and collaborator Alphonse Maeder that the dream is a *spontaneous self-portrayal, in symbolic form, of the actual situation in the unconscious.*[69]

This first attempt at an understanding of the function of the dream was complemented in the following year (1914) by Jung's discovery of the compensatory function of the dream, which eclipsed all earlier theories.

[65] Freud, *Introductory Lectures*, p. 143.
[66] Jung, "General Aspects of Dream Psychology," p. 245.
[67] "General Aspects of Psychoanalysis," p. 240.
[68] Ibid.
[69] "General Aspects of Dream Psychology," p. 263.

G. NEUROSIS AND DREAM

3. Sleep-Preservation vs. the Function of Compensation

A. DREAM AND SLEEP

Like Freud, Jung too granted an exceptional position to the dream because of the conditions of sleep and based on the highly varying degree of "abaissement du niveau mental."

> Since the dream originates in sleep, it bears all the characteristics of an "abaissement du niveau mental" (Janet), or of low energy-tension: logical discontinuity, fragmentary character, analogy formations, superficial associations of the verbal, clang, or visual type, condensations, irrational expressions, confusion, etc.[70]

This exceptional position of the dream by no means signified that the lowering of ego-consciousness connected with the state of sleep was by itself tantamount to a reduction of psychic activity, as Freud had assumed. On the contrary, Jung recognized that the inner activity remained fully alive in spite of being severed from the outside world. As he determined in early investigations, this applied particularly to the dream complexes and their affective nuclei, which he had consistently noted as lively expressions of the unconscious psyche. Because of this unceasing activity of the complexes, Jung assumed—contrary to Freud —an intensification of inner life during sleep which could go so far as to put an end to sleep.

> . . . we should not overlook the fact that the very dreams which disturb sleep most—and these are not uncommon—have a dramatic structure which aims logically at creating a highly affective situation, and builds it up so efficiently that the affect unquestionably wakes the dreamer.[71]

Even though painful affects were occasionally held back in dreams (as suggested by Freud), in many other cases the dream was accompanied by intensive affects, which could increase to such a degree that they penetrated consciousness or even triggered awakening. However, it would have been contrary to Jung's entire thinking, with its finalistic orientation, to approach such phenomena exclusively from the point of view of sleep disturbance or even vital damage. Freud's concept of the function of the dream as veiling the affect and protecting sleep, which was the outcome of his biological approach, seemed too narrow to Jung. He considered the biological approach to be suitable only when the energy-tension in the dreamer was low. In such cases, the function

---

[70] "The Transcendent Function," p. 77.
[71] "General Aspects of Dream Psychology," p. 252.

of the dream could be ascribed entirely to biological factors. However, Jung considered the psychological evaluation as far more important. He determined, for instance, that suppression of the affects in the dream not only failed to accomplish the biological purpose of preservation of sleep—as Freud also recognized—but could result beyond that in negative effects on the psyche, impeding its development. However, the opposite might also occur: In contrast to Freud, Jung observed that intensified dream affects might also constitute a source of life-promoting values. He became more and more convinced that one of the principal values of the dream was that it stimulated conscious orientation, which could be understood as inviting reflection and coming to terms with still-unconscious contents.

> They [the dreams] preserve sleep whenever possible: that is to say, they function necessarily and automatically under the influence of the sleeping state; but they break through when their function demands it, that is, when the compensatory contents are so intense that they are able to counteract sleep. A compensatory content is especially intense when it has a vital significance for conscious orientation.[72]

The consequences of the dream process had to be distinguished from the psychic effects of the dream content. As Maeder had already emphasized, dreaming in itself had a beneficial influence on sleep—a concept which Jung expanded by demonstrating that *objectifying affects as dream symbols* (that is, investing the symbols with meaning and content) benefited the subject's psyche. The value of dreaming has been experimentally investigated by C. T. Frey in collaboration with C. A. Meier.[73]

B. THE COMPENSATING FUNCTION OF THE DREAM

One of Jung's extraordinary merits is that he utilized the above-mentioned experiences to formulate a completely new concept of the dream. Like Maeder, he recognized the necessity of a purely psychological basis for the dream. To be sure, Jung was not satisfied with an explanation which was founded on working through psychological problems in the dream (Maeder, Bleuler). It seemed to him of primary importance to base the function of the dream on its relationship to the conscious psyche. Indeed, Jung was the first in the field of empirical psychology to propose the hypothesis that the dream had a compensa-

[72] Ibid.
[73] Frey-Wehrlin, "Probleme der Traumdeutung" (1963), p. 75.

tory relationship to the content of the dreamer's consciousness[74]—a principle which subsequently proved very productive in psychotherapy.

In medicine, the idea of compensating certain excessive processes by other balancing functions had been familiar for a long time, but only Alfred Adler made it the basic concept of his individual psychology. He proceeded from the idea of a life-plan which developed in childhood out of the individual's clash with the powerful environment and the attempt to compensate inferiority feelings by power configurations. Earlier, Freud had referred to compensating activity (without, however, using this term) by mentioning that wish-fulfillment in dreams appeases the psyche.[75] He did use the term in 1908 in referring to a hypothetical man who had "become over-kind as a result of a violent suppression of a constitutional inclination to harshness and cruelty."[76] Even *before* the appearance of Adler's first work dealing with compensation (1907),[77] Jung's *Psychology of Dementia Praecox* (1907) contained the statement that the fantasies of psychotics "substitute . . . for a life of toil and privation."[78] Still, it took a considerable time until Jung discovered compensation to be a general tendency of the unconscious psyche. He was then able to confirm earlier conjectures, primarily in psychopathological phenomena, such as hallucinations and sensory delusions, which showed signs of compensation. One of the earliest of these passages was written in 1914:

> To sum up, one could say that the function of the unconscious in mental disturbances is essentially a compensation of the conscious content.[79]

Jung soon recognized that compensation was not limited to psychopathological phenomena but constituted a *basic law of the unconscious.*

> In normal people the principal function of the unconscious is to effect a compensation and to produce a balance. All extreme conscious tendencies are softened and toned down through a counterimpulse in the unconscious.[80]

This concept was made complete two years later by recognizing that dreams had the function of balancing the state of the conscious psyche.

74 Jung, "General Aspects of Dream Psychology," p. 250.

75 *The Interpretation of Dreams,* p. 570.

76 " 'Civilized' Sexual Morality and Modern Nervous Illness" (1908), p. 203.

77 Adler, *Study of Organ Inferiority and Its Psychical Compensation* (1907; tr. Jelliffe, 1917).

78 "The Psychology of Dementia Praecox," p. 145.

79 "On the Importance of the Unconscious in Psychopathology," p. 210.

80 Ibid., pp. 205–6.

II. DREAM AS SYMPTOM (FREUD) AND AS SYMBOL (JUNG)

Dreams, I maintain, are compensatory to the conscious situation of the moment.[81]

The discovery of dream compensation cannot be overrated. Jung earned extraordinary merit for demonstrating not only a psychological function in the dream but also a meaningful interplay between the conscious and the unconscious systems. Particularly important was his grasp of these actions in the context of psychic energy, and even of life processes as a whole. The regulating activity in the world of organic life was paralleled by self-regulation in the realm of the psyche.[82]

The psyche is a self-regulating system that maintains its equilibrium just as the body does. Every process that goes too far immediately and inevitably calls forth compensations, and without these there would be neither a normal metabolism nor a normal psyche. . . . Too little on one side results in too much on the other.[83]

In general, Jung conceived compensation as an attempt by the psyche to bridge psychic opposites. As an expression of the differentiated relationship between consciousness and the unconscious, compensation also shed light on the "Janus-face" of the dream. By this means the dream satisfied both sides: On the one hand, it was a spontaneous expression of unconscious processes, on the other it constituted a meaningfully compensating response to conscious convictions and tendencies. The elements of the dream were constituent factors of the unconscious as well as compensations of the momentary status of consciousness with which they were "linked together associatively and . . . selected by the conscious situation of the moment."[84]

Jung saw compensation as a basic rule of general significance, valid for all psychic formations—fantasy, vision, and dream. The only exception was the pure reaction-dream[85] which always identically repeated the traumatic starting-point.

In general, the dream established a balance of disturbed equilibrium, constellating not only forgotten material and habitually unconscious and repressed ideas, but also matters which up to then had been intrinsically unknown. In subjects who were relatively well adjusted to the environment, the dream was limited to the role of complementing the conscious attitude. In those with a one-sided conscious attitude, on the other hand, the response of the dream was equally one-sided: It

---

[81] "General Aspects of Dream Psychology," p. 252.
[82] "On the Psychology of the Unconscious" (1917/1926/1943), p. 61.
[83] "The Practical Use of Dream-Analysis," p. 153.
[84] "General Aspects of Dream Psychology," p. 153.
[85] Ibid., p. 260.

took the "opposite position," thereby making manifest the latent conflict situation. The regulating action of the dream was thus by no means
always parallel to conscious intentions, "particularly when the conscious attitude [tended] too exclusively in a direction that would
threaten the vital needs of the individual"—in such cases, "vivid
dreams with a strongly contrasting but purposive content"[86] appeared.
In other instances, in which the dream approached the center of the
personality more or less closely, the dream was satisfied with variants.[87]
If, finally, the conscious attitude was adequate to the psyche as a whole,
the dream was found to "coincide with conscious contents and tendencies"[88] without, however, losing its characteristic autonomy.

Jung emphasized particularly the mythological or *archetypal compensation*, with its tendency to balance conscious convictions with the
deeper layers of the psyche. This included religious compensations
which became of decisive importance in shaping the further life of the
dreamer, in spite of their distance from the conscious mind.

> In these cases one must always remember that every man, in a sense,
> represents the whole of humanity and its history. What was possible
> in the history of mankind at large is also possible on a small scale in
> every individual. . . . It is therefore not surprising that religious
> compensations play a great role in dreams. That this is increasingly
> so in our time is a natural consequence of the prevailing materialism
> of our outlook.[89]

Such "big dreams" were characteristic not only for the biologically
significant phases of life—childhood, puberty, menopause—but also
for periods in which an individual was no longer in harmony with his
total personality and, finally, for times of contemporary crisis. In all
such instances compensations occurred, attempting a better adaptation
of the dreamer to physical changes, tendencies toward self-realization,
or even to the spirit of the time.

As pointed out in the preceding chapter, Jung opposed the causalistic
approach with the prospective-constructive point of view, which allowed finding new potentialities of meaning. With this method a
"bridge into the future"[90] could be built from the elements of the
dream. In agreement with Maeder, Jung saw in the finalistic orientation of the dream-unconscious a function which anticipated "future

86 Ibid., p. 253.
87 "Seminar über Kinderträume," I (1938–39).
88 "On the Nature of Dreams" (1945/1948), p. 287.
89 "General Aspects of Dream Psychology," p. 250.
90 "On Psychological Understanding" (1914), p. 183.

conscious achievements, something like a preliminary exercise or sketch, or a plan roughed out in advance."[91] However, he cautioned against an incorrect understanding of the prospective function of the dream as prophetic, that is, "to suppose that the dream is a kind of psychopomp (guide of the psyche) which, because of its superior knowledge, infallibly guides life in the right direction."

> However much people underestimate the psychological significance of dreams, there is an equally great danger that anyone who is constantly preoccupied with dream-analysis will overestimate the significance of the unconscious for real life.[92]

However, Jung observed, some conscious attitudes were so poorly adapted to the total personality that the unconscious attitude appearing in the dream corresponded much better to the whole and, therefore, brought out unsuspected potentialities of meaning. As an example, in 1914 Jung adduced the dream of Nebuchadnezzar, who at the zenith of his power had a dream which anticipated his downfall.[93]

4. The Meaning and Interpretation of the Dream

Jung's interpretation of the meaning of the dream—largely differing from Freud's method—opened up new avenues of understanding. As far as the formal principles were concerned (for instance, questioning the dreamer or utilizing his associations), Jung continued along the course which Freud had outlined. His own unique achievement became apparent only when seeking the meaning contained in the dream.

Although both investigators saw the dream as a segment of the comprehensive structure of the psyche and both recognized the dream's coherent design, they conceived its meaning and significance in essentially dissimilar ways. Freud was led by the idea of "enchaînement" and understood the dream as a fragment of a causally determined continuity of memories; Jung conceived the dream as part of a goal-oriented process through which images, values, and archetypal symbols became manifest. In this respect the dream was not unusual, but adhered to the same rules governing fantasies, visions, and neurotic symptoms. In contrast to Freud, Jung could neither accept fantasy formation as a symbolic disguise of basic drives, nor neurotic symptoms as compensatory gratification; similarly, for Jung the dream was in no way merely a symbolic substitute,[94] but rather a spontaneous creative

[91] "General Aspects of Dream Psychology," p. 255.
[92] Ibid., p. 256.   [93] Ibid., p. 257.
[94] Freud, *Introductory Lectures*, p. 154.

manifestation of the depth of the psyche, which had an irreducible value.

Meaning and the search for meaning, therefore, implied entirely divergent paths for the two investigators. While Freud took the meaning of the dream to be the equivalent of detecting its causes, Jung recognized a significant value in the meaning of the dream, derived from its relationship to the psyche as a whole.

Freud's quest for the meaning of the dream was initially limited to uncovering repressed experiences (later, he also took into consideration fixed symbol relationships); Jung was occupied with deepening self-knowledge and self-understanding. This included grasping the current attitude of consciousness as well as throwing light on the developmental tendencies concealed in the content of the dream, that is, bringing out that which wanted to come forth and rouse the dreamer to creative production. Archetypal images were of primary importance in finding the meaning of the dream, since from time immemorial they expressed "the harmony of the experiencing subject with the object experienced."[95] Inasmuch as the dream consisted of symbolic relationships circling around the nucleus of significance, its meaning was determined by the relationship of this nucleus to impersonal structures of higher significance. Just as the immanent meaning of the dream was detected by elucidating the kernel of significance which formed its basis, the transcendent meaning of the dream was unraveled by clarifying the relationship of the conscious ego to the nucleus of significance. This meant nothing less than expanding the momentary picture of the world into an *image of wholeness concealed in experiences of higher significance*. In attempting to bridge the gap between conscious and unconscious attitudes, the ego transcended the conscious point of view and reinstated the connection with the primordial experiences of mankind that gradually appeared in dreams.

All of this makes it clear that the interpretation of a dream could never be exhausted by an explanation. Just as the causal approach was supplemented by the finalistic approach oriented toward the future, Jung opposed explanation with understanding, and interpretation of signs with the hermeneutic method.[96] Even though he by no means completely rejected the reductive method, which goes back to infantile drive fixations, still, it seemed to him more productive for the individual's self-understanding to apply the finalistic procedure (related to meaning and the subject's goal of realization) as well as the her-

95 Jung, "Analytical Psychology and *Weltanschauung*" (1927/1931), p. 380.
96 "The Structure of the Unconscious" (1916), p. 293.

meneutic method, based on the understanding of the archetypal symbols of the dream.

As pointed out earlier (see F.II.2), this procedure depended on elucidating the symbolic expressions of the dream and expanding their meaning by establishing a relationship to analogous formations. The more the separate symbols of the dream were brought into relation with each other and with analogous connections of meaning, the more understandable became the particular content of the dream. In 1916 Jung described the outstanding feature of hermeneutics in this way:

> The essence of hermeneutics . . . consists in adding further analogies to the one already supplied by the symbol: in the first place subjective analogies produced at random by the patient, then objective analogies provided by the analyst out of his general knowledge. This procedure widens and enriches the initial symbol, and the final outcome is an infinitely complex and variegated picture. . . . Certain lines of psychological development then stand out that are at once individual and collective. There is no science on earth by which these lines could be proved "right." . . . Their validity is proved by their intense value for life.[97]

Thus, Jung supplemented the method of free association with amplification and proceeded from the interpretation of personal data important in the patient's life history to an understanding of the elements of the dreams from their relationships to the collective treasure of civilization.

Application of hermeneutics presupposed a consideration of certain, symbolically delineated paths. Jung conceived them as individually designed "life-lines,"[98] that is, currents of libido,[99] indicated by emotional reactions as well as by symbolic transformations. His early conjecture was confirmed during the fourth decade of the century by demonstrating a continuity of unconscious images in a dream series, that is, successive and continued dreams. In the course of dream development, the emerging *leitmotivs* and concepts of goals manifested a degree of continuity which suggested the hypothesis of an underlying archetype. In 1937 Jung made this statement:

> I never, if I can help it, interpret one dream by itself. As a rule a dream belongs in a series. Since there is a continuity of consciousness despite the fact that it is regularly interrupted by sleep, there is

[97] Ibid., p. 291.   [98] Ibid., p. 294.   [99] Ibid., p. 295.

G. NEUROSIS AND DREAM

probably also a continuity of unconscious processes—perhaps even more than with the events of consciousness.[100]

On the basis of the dream series Jung was able to verify his hypotheses regarding interpretation, eliminate certain mistakes,[101] and trace the gradual crystallization of archetypal motifs. Beyond that, he discovered in the unconscious psyche the outline of "a kind of developmental process in the personality itself."[102] In connection with his studies on "Individual Dream Symbolism in Relation to Alchemy,"[103] which followed the process of individuation as revealed in several hundred dreams extending over many months,[104] Jung determined that particular dreams compensated for the conscious situation in an independent manner; however, single efforts at compensation developed in accordance with a firmly established inner regularity, an inner organization.

At first it seems that each compensation is a momentary adjustment of one-sidedness or an equalization of disturbed balance. But with deeper insight and experience, these apparently separate acts of compensation arrange themselves into a kind of plan. They seem to hang together and in the deepest sense to be subordinated to a common goal, so that a long dream-series no longer appears as a senseless string of incoherent and isolated happenings, but resembles the successive steps in a planned and orderly process of development. I have called this unconscious process spontaneously expressing itself in the symbolism of a long dream-series the individuation process.[105]

Jung was confirmed in this assumption by the further, highly important finding that the background of the dream was capable of exhibiting autonomy and activity which even manifested itself as a *guiding and directing function* of particular events.

Active orientation towards goals and purposes would not be the privilege of consciousness alone but would also be true of the unconscious, so that it too would be just as capable of taking a finally oriented lead. The dream, accordingly, would then have the value of a positive, guiding idea or of an aim whose vital meaning would be greatly superior to that of the momentarily constellated conscious content.[106]

100 "Psychology and Religion," pp. 32–33.
101 "The Practical Use of Dream-Analysis," p. 157.
102 "On the Nature of Dreams," p. 289.
103 (1936/1943), in *Psychology and Alchemy*.   104 Ibid., pp. 41–42.
105 "On the Nature of Dreams," pp. 289–90.
106 "General Aspects of Dream Psychology," pp. 254–55.

II. DREAM AS SYMPTOM (FREUD) AND AS SYMBOL (JUNG)

The foregoing should make evident how productive a tool the hermeneutic method was in elucidating motives, tendencies, and concepts in the life of the dreamer of which he hitherto had been insufficiently aware, as well as his potentialities for spontaneous development; the method was particularly useful in clarifying the relationship of dream symbols to the psyche as a whole.

In so far as psychic entities, the centers of meaning, were always connected with feeling tones, the affective tension of the dream was an invaluable guide through the thicket of dream symbols. In this respect Jung concurred with Freud, who as early as 1900 had stressed that "affects are always appropriate."[107] To be sure, Jung saw affect less as evidence for uncovering repressed strivings than as a tool for fathoming what was still unknown at the bottom of the psyche, still not expressed nor articulated. For him, the emotional charge primarily had the value of a presentiment and a dim feeling of the nucleus of significance. Therefore, he made it a golden rule to ask the dreamer about his feeling- and affect-reactions to the dream and to observe his own emotion and evaluation of the dream.

A. DREAM INTERPRETATION AND STATE OF CONSCIOUSNESS

Jung considered the second step in dream interpretation—immediately after clarifying the immanent meaning of the dream—to be the important effort to connect the meaning of the dream to the dreamer's state of consciousness. This he felt was the habitual attitude of the dreamer, his convictions, value judgments, and interests as well as his educational level, his store of knowledge, and his human qualities. Jung, therefore, always stressed that interpretation should never neglect the life values of conscious personality nor the cultural level. Accordingly, an adequately reliable interpretation of the dream called for not inconsiderable qualifications on the dreamer's part as well as the psychotherapist's.

It needs psychological empathy, ability to co-ordinate, intuition, knowledge of the world and of men, and above all a special "canniness" which depends on wide understanding as well as on a certain *intelligence du coeur.*[108]

The guiding principle in confronting the meaning of the dream with the conscious state of the dreamer was always the question: *"What conscious attitude does it [the dream] compensate?"*[109] Without attention

---

107 *The Interpretation of Dreams*, p. 461.
108 Jung, "On the Nature of Dreams," p. 286.
109 "The Practical Use of Dream-Analysis," p. 153.

to the conscious attitude no dream could be interpreted with any degree of certainty. Because, indeed, one could never exactly specify the state of consciousness, questioning the dreamer as to his actual psychic condition was of extraordinary heuristic value. Particularly, when dreams pointed to personal events in the dreamer's life, the interpretation was contingent on his associations.

Depending on the substance of the dream, its interpretation might be limited to correcting the dreamer's conscious attitude by complementing it or adding to it. In other cases, the dream might draw attention to tendencies opposing conscious ideas and thereby evoke conflict situations. Furthermore, the dream could gravitate toward the meaning of archetypal symbols, with general compensation of consciousness from the primordial levels.

Jung limited the reductive method, commonly used by Freud, to selected cases where it was indicated to bring the dreamer down to primitive and fundamental aspects, to cut him down to proper dimensions. In such instances, it was pertinent for the psychotherapist to draw the dreamer's attention to his "illusions, fantasies, and exaggerations" and forcibly to confront him with his persistent infantilism. Applying the prospective-finalistic technique, on the other hand, made it essential to accentuate the tendencies in the dreamer which indicated a potential for development and thus to supplement his conscious attitude. The hermeneutic method, in turn, aimed at expanding the conscious attitude by demonstrating the relationship of the ego to the values hidden in the archaic and archetypal images and so reconcile the archaic with the conscious picture of the world.

B. THE ASSIMILATION OF THE MEANING OF THE DREAM

For Freud, the aim of his theory of neurosis as well as his interpretation of dreams, was to uncover hidden wishes and motives and bring to consciousness disguised thoughts. In contrast, Jung saw the goal of dream interpretation as helping the individual to assimilate the immanent meaning of the dream into the conscious attitude.[110] Assimilation, then, was the third step in dream interpretation. While, according to Freud, disclosing and working through the causes of dreams were sufficient prerequisites for connecting unconscious contents with the train of conscious ideas, Jung felt that establishing the meaning of dreams by no means guaranteed that it would be adequately incorporated into consciousness. On the contrary, the dreamer was still faced with the crowning achievement of "mutual penetration of conscious and unconscious" contents. As Jung emphatically stressed, he did not

110 Ibid., p. 152.

have in mind "a one-sided evaluation, interpretation, and deformation of unconscious contents by the conscious mind."[111] Assimilation was rather a mutual approximation and adjustment of the opposite values of consciousness and the unconscious, aimed at outgrowing any still-existing dissociation of the personality. Thereby, the possibility of partial participation of the unconscious was re-established and, ultimately, a better self-understanding attained. In this process it was "of overriding importance that no real values of the conscious personality should be damaged, much less destroyed,"[112] because compensation by the unconscious could be effective only in the presence of an integral consciousness. Jung considered it equally important that the dreamer should neither again repress the newly detected unconscious values (which would have sacrificed the possibility of expanding consciousness) nor relinquish his former values, which would have been tantamount to the personality shattering into a chaos of values.

> Assimilation is never a question of "this *or* that" but always of "this *and* that."[113]

As Jung pointed out, with an attitude of "this *and* that," the dreamer would be enabled to attain a point of view which would bridge the opposites and again permit him to approach the natural law of his own being.

> Through the assimilation of unconscious contents, the momentary life of consciousness can once more be brought into harmony with the law of nature from which it all too easily departs, and the patient can be led back to the natural law of his own being.[114]

C. INTERPRETATION ON THE SUBJECTIVE AND OBJECTIVE LEVELS

By considering both philosophical and psychological facets, Jung was able to make a distinction between interpretation at the subjective and objective levels. This resulted from contrasting the naïve and the critical view of the world. As he often emphasized, Jung regarded Silberer as a precursor of this approach. The significant contrast of material and functional categories[115] in the psychic area is connected with Silberer's name. He placed the content of symbol-toned formations in the material category, while the functional category applied to psychic mechanisms, "the events in the psychic apparatus proper."[116] With this approach he expected a deeper understanding of fairy-tale and myth as well as fantasies and dreams. Consequently, Silberer conceived the

---

111 Ibid.   112 Ibid., pp. 155–56.   113 Ibid., p. 156.
114 Ibid., p. 160.   115 Silberer, "Phantasie und Mythos" (1910).
116 Ibid., p. 547.

elements of dreams and the symbols of fantasy as representations of systems and tendencies in the psyche. According to Silberer, furthermore, mythical formations might represent images of split-off affects and ideas, or rather, repressed and suppressed drives.

The first beginnings of a subjective interpretation of dream elements can probably be detected in Freud's work rather than in Silberer's paper. In *The Interpretation of Dreams* Freud recognized that certain character traits of the dreamer himself may appear as personifications in the dream. These would not only be collective and composite figures[117] but also those representing certain inner qualities and the "confluence of many sources" in the figures of hero, helper, enemy, and so on[118]—phenomena which Freud had observed in daydreams as well as in psychological novels. Rank—probably following in Freud's footsteps—had also pointed out that "all persons coming on the stage in a dream represent a part of the dreamer's individuality, the personal psychic life of the dreamer himself."[119]

The method of subjective interpretation reached its peak in opposing the subjective and objective levels of interpretation, as proposed by Jung. On the objective level he conceived the separate parts of the dream as contents belonging to the environment, while he saw subjective interpretation as an attempt to understand the images of the dream as "personified features of the dreamer's own personality."[120] This distinction was obviously based on a critical evaluation of whether the parts of the dream belonged more to the objective than to the subjective sphere.

I call every interpretation which equates the dream images with real objects an *interpretation on the objective level*. In contrast to this is the interpretation which refers every part of the dream and all the actors in it back to the dreamer himself. This I call *interpretation on the subjective level*.[121]

The distinction between interpretation on the subjective and the objective levels was to become extraordinarily important for Jung. Interpretation on the objective level was called for whenever conflicts connected with vital interests or paramount relationships to the environment[122] were touched upon, while interpretation on the subjective

117 *The Interpretation of Dreams*, p. 293.
118 Freud, "Creative Writers and Day-Dreaming" (1908), p. 153.
119 Rank, "Ein Traum, der sich selbst deutet" (1910).
120 "General Aspects of Dream Psychology," p. 266.
121 "On the Psychology of the Unconscious," p. 84.
122 "General Aspects of Dream Psychology," p. 269.

level was indicated primarily in cases of overvaluation of the object.[123] For, when the tie to the outside world was too close, the danger of impairing comprehension and self-reflection developed. Psychotherapeutically, it was therefore often vitally important for the individual's further development to notice instances when the inner images began to stand out from exterior objects. Such cases were quite frequently observed in transference situations where it might be advisable or even necessary to withdraw dream contents from the projection and direct them to the real object, the therapist. By withdrawing the projection, the individual's concretistic fixation to the exterior object was loosened, and at the same time the inner psychic reality, analogous to the dream events, was revealed. To be sure, situations could be encountered in which less value was given to the object, and it might be important to retain the projection to the physician in order to concentrate on the "greater" aspect in the individual and on self-realization. In such cases, it appeared to be particularly helpful to understand the dream images also as parts of the subject, in other words, as function complexes of the unconscious. The resulting gain for the dreamer was equivalent to strengthening the subject against the objective environment, that is, strengthening his self-consciousness and his feeling of responsibility.

5. Historical Survey of the Concept of Projection

The importance of the concept of projection in the psychology of the unconscious justifies a short reference to the history of its development. Jung took over the concept of projection from Freud, who in turn owed it to the neurologist and psychiatrist Meynert. As M. Dorer[124] showed, Meynert's merit was to demonstrate in his brain physiology that the fiber systems consisted of association systems (the connections between the individual portions of the cerebral cortex) as well as projection systems.[125] These projection systems served to transmit exterior stimuli to the cortex and, contrariwise, established a connection between the subcortical centers and the spinal cord, thereby with the peripheral nerves as well.

Freud first mentioned Meynert's theory of projection in *On Aphasia* (1891).[126] The question which he himself raised had to do with the manner in which the body was represented in the cortex and he an-

---

[123] Ibid., p. 275.
[124] *Historische Grundlagen der Psychoanalyse* (1932).
[125] Meynert, *Klinische Vorlesungen über Psychiatrie* (1890), p. 11.
[126] Tr. Stengel, 1953.

swered his own question by referring to the projection mechanism as follows:

> Meynert calls this representation a "projection," and some of his comments indicate that he actually envisages a projection, i.e., a point by point representation, of the body in the cerebral cortex.[127]

Five years later, Freud used the concept of projection in the psychological sense to elucidate delusions of persecution in paranoia.[128] In 1911, he described this form of repression as projecting "the causes of certain sensations to the external world, instead of looking for them . . . inside ourselves."[129] In 1917, finally, Freud expanded the range of the concept of projection to mean transposing outwards certain inner (repressed) processes.[130] He even went so far as to conceive *the dream as a projection*, "an externalization of an internal process."[131]

Jung, too, initially saw "projection [as] the repressing of the conflict and the setting forth of the repressed contents into seeming objectivity,"[132] but relinquished this assumption to the extent that he was able to detect impersonal contents in the unconscious. With the discovery of primordial images, autonomous complexes and, foremost, of archetypal ideas, a fundamental change took place in Jung's concept of projection; he recognized that projection referred to everything that had been constellated but had remained unconscious.[133] Consequently, as Jung stressed again and again, the individual was in a constant state of projecting because all those unconscious contents of which he was not aware could be found in the outside world.

> Nature, the object par excellence, reflects all those contents of the unconscious which as such are not conscious to us. Many nuances of pleasure and pain perceived by the senses are unthinkingly attributed to the object, without our pausing to consider how far the object can be made responsible for them.[134]

Forty years earlier, Jung had expressed the same thought in a similar manner:

> The projection into the "cosmic" is the primitive privilege of the libido, for it enters into our perception naturally through all the

127 Ibid., p. 47.

128 "Further Remarks on the Neuro-Psychoses of Defence" (1896), p. 184.

129 "Psycho-Analytic Notes on an Autobiographical Account of a Case of Paranoia (Dementia Paranoides)" (1911), p. 66.

130 "A Metapsychological Supplement to the Theory of Dreams" (1917), p. 233.

131 Ibid., p. 223.   132 *Psychology of the Unconscious* (1912), p. 73.

133 *Symbols of Transformation* (1952), p. 59.   134 Ibid., p. 112, n. 84.

avenues of the senses, apparently from without, and in the form of pain and pleasure connected with the objects. This we attribute to the object without further thought, and we are inclined, in spite of our philosophic considerations, to seek the causes in the object, which often has very little concern with it.[135]

Moreover, seen from the point of view of development, projection was an intricate problem. Just as projections in the present could anticipate future knowledge, one had to assume that much of the contents ascribed nowadays to the personal psyche had been projections in remote antiquity. A large part of the thoughts and ideas which today stir the psyche could most probably in early times be experienced only as projections, a point which Jung raised in his later years (1956).

Everything that we today would call "mind" and "insight" was, in earlier centuries, projected into things, and even today individual idiosyncrasies are presupposed by many people to be generally valid.[136]

Freud had considered it possible, on principle, to disentangle projections by releasing repressions, but Jung was far less optimistic. To be sure, he also was of the opinion that it was possible to terminate projections, as far as they were of an unconscious-personal nature. However, in the presence of projections of impersonal contents, he seemed to have doubts as to whether what had been projected could be reclaimed. More generally, only projections within the reach of consciousness could be retrieved. In order to maintain continuity, we cite another statement by Jung from 1956:

Projections can be withdrawn only when they come within the possible scope of consciousness. Outside that, nothing can be corrected.[137]

Accordingly, Jung thought that contents which the individual experienced as being outside of himself, that is, belonging to the extrapsychic sphere, could be neither perceived nor dissolved.

[135] *Psychology of the Unconscious*, p. 505, n. 69.
[136] *Mysterium Coniunctionis*, p. 488.   [137] Ibid., p. 489.

H. FROM SIGN TO SYMBOL

In the foregoing, some aspects of the symbol have been examined in connection with discussing energics and methods of interpretation. Among others, we saw that Jung conceived the symbol from the energic point of view as a vital balance of opposites (see E.III.2.b), while Freud saw it expressed as a fixed, constant relationship in so far as it was universal. For Jung, the symbol was "the psychological mechanism that transforms energy";[1] as such, it canalizes the physical event into a psychic experience, whereas Freud interpreted the symbol as repeating the identity between sexuality and verbal expression which has existed since time immemorial. The meaning of the symbol, according to Freud, rested in identifying the symbol with already known data; Jung, on the other hand, discovered the hermeneutic technique and the method of amplification, making it possible to understand symbols as psychic analogies, and he thereby opened new paths and perspectives for the creative development of the personality. (See E.III.2.b.)

[1] Jung, "On Psychic Energy" (1928), p. 45.

I. SYMBOLIZATION AND SYMBOL
IN FREUD'S WORK

The differences between Freud's and Jung's attitudes regarding the nature of the symbol can be understood only by a rather detailed review of the development of these concepts. Freud's career was already well advanced before he took up "symbolic interpretation" (around 1917). In so far as his scientific approach permitted, he regarded symbols exclusively from the causal point of view, without giving attention to the general content of symbols. Like all other contents of the unconscious psyche, the symbol had value only as a symptom and could be understood by the technique of free association. This concept, which prevailed up to 1917, has been aptly expressed by Dalbiez: "The meaning of the dream are its causes."[2] As time went on, Freud felt compelled to give more attention to the meaning of symbols, as several of his disciples (Abraham,[3] Rank,[4] Riklin,[5] and Silberer[6]) had done earlier.

Freud's discovery of symbolizations[7] was a step toward establishing a general meaning of symbols. He recognized that dreams replace ideas with images. In 1900, he wrote that "the key to the symbolization is . . . laid down by firmly established linguistic usage."[8] He also observed the connection between symbols and sexual objects.[9] As J. H. Phillips[10] rightly emphasized, as early as 1895 Breuer and Freud had repeatedly found symbolization in hysterical symptoms—for instance, the relationship between vomiting and suppressed affects. To be sure, it was not until the development of the libido theory that Freud was in a position to formulate a comprehensive theory of symbols which also encompassed the universal symbols.

The incentive for Freud's pursuit of symbolism in general came from the work of Stekel,[11] and from that of Rank and Sachs,[12] who

[2] Dalbiez, *Psychoanalytic Method and the Doctrine of Freud* (1941, tr. Lindsay), Vol. I, p. 40.

[3] *Dreams and Myths: A Study in Folk-Psychology* (1909; tr. H. C. Abraham and Ellison, 1955, pp. 151–209.

[4] *The Myth of the Birth of the Hero: A Psychological Interpretation of Mythology* (1909; tr. Robbins and Jelliffe, 1914); and "Ein Traum, der sich selbst deutet" (1910).

[5] *Wish-Fulfillment and Symbolism in Fairy Tales* (1908; tr. White, 1915).

[6] "Phantasie und Mythos" (1910); "Über die Symbolbildung" (1912).

[7] *The Interpretation of Dreams* (1900), p. 349.   [8] Ibid., pp. 341–42.

[9] Ibid., pp. 256ff.   [10] *Psychoanalyse und Symbolik* (1962).

[11] *Die Sprache des Traumes* (1911).

[12] *The Significance of Psychoanalysis for the Mental Sciences* (1913; tr. Payne, 1916).

helped him in mythological research.[13] Freud's discovery of symbolization was later enlarged into a general system of interpretation (1914).
It was necessary to pursue the subject more deeply because it became
apparent that the components of many dreams were symbols which
could not be interpreted by free associations; that is, they were not
the result of distortion by the censor nor were they important as
references to earlier events in the individual's life. Above all he could
not avoid recognizing that symbolism was not restricted to dreams, but
was a matter of general importance. In each instance, the symbol involved an indirect visualization which, in addition, had to be understood in the dream in connection with the disguise of latent thoughts.

Thus, he was faced with the problem that the symbolic relations of
such dreams were fixed or, in other words, appeared as constant trans-
positions of unconscious ideas into images. This presented a considerable dilemma for him. Could he ignore the "mute" components of
dreams which were beyond the reach of personal associations, making
it impossible to find a satisfactory meaning of the dream—or was it
necessary to enlarge the method of free associations? In that case,
however, he faced the danger of falling prey to the arbitrary approach
of ancient dream interpreters, that is, deciphering dreams by using
some sort of code and assigning to dream symbols a meaning arrived
at by purely mechanical methods. This procedure hardly did justice to
the ambiguity of dream symbols. Therefore, Freud demanded a cau-
tious and critical approach to dream interpretation, including chiefly a
comprehensive knowledge of the meanings of symbols. He took the
position that only when the dream interpreter was familiar with
common symbols, with the personality of the dreamer, with his particular situation and the events of the day preceding the dream, was
there any guarantee that using generally accepted symbolism could
lead to productive results. However, it remained a basic rule of Freud's
dream interpretation that the symbolic point of view could never take
the place of the technique of free association but could be used merely
to complement the conventional method.

We are thus obliged, in dealing with those elements of the dream-
content which must be recognized as symbolic, to adapt a combined
technique, which on the one hand rests on the dreamer's associations
and on the other hand fills the gaps from the interpreter's knowledge
of symbols.[14]

13 Jones, *The Life and Work of Sigmund Freud*, Vol. II, p. 361.
14 *The Interpretation of Dreams*, p. 353.

An interesting point here is that the recognition of symbol interpretation necessarily led to a curtailment of the long-standing psychoanalytic principle of questioning the dreamer in order to elicit his associations.[15]

According to Freud, the validity of general symbols was based on three considerations:

First, symbols appeared to be "an ancient but extinct mode of expression," a kind of " 'basic language' of which all . . . symbolic relations would be residues."[16]

Second, Freud suspected "that there is a specially intimate relation between true symbols and sexuality,"[17] between verbal expressions and sexual phenomena, and he assumed that "the symbolic relation seems to be a relic and a mark of former identity."[18]

Things that are symbolically connected to-day were probably united in prehistoric times by conceptual and linguistic identity.[19]

Accordingly, present-day symbols could easily be understood as repetitions of equivalent relationships in ancient times.

Third, all such identities were based on the immutable coordination of verbal expression and sexual object. All "things which were once called by the same name as the genitals could now serve as symbols for them in dreams."[20] Because such verbal expressions were rooted in sexuality, all elongated objects denoted the male penis and every hollow shape the female genital; similarly all weapons and tools represented the male, all hand-fashioned objects, the female. The interpretation of symbols revealed a general pattern, in some way relating to the human figure.[21]

The application of this concept to the dream created certain difficulties. The symbolic relations, though general and consistent, remained completely unconscious to the dreamer. Freud was, therefore, forced to assume an unconscious knowledge[22] or unconsciously connected ideas, but was unable to describe how they could be woven into the dream. For this purpose he would have needed an acceptable hypothesis explaining how unconscious thought patterns became conscious.

As advanced as Freud's theory of symbols might appear, in the end he reduced it to his earlier concepts. Not only did he trace symbols to

[15] Ibid.
[16] *Introductory Lectures on Psycho-Analysis* (1915–17), p. 166.
[17] Ibid.
[18] *The Interpretation of Dreams*, p. 352.
[19] Ibid.
[20] *Introductory Lectures*, p. 167.
[21] Ibid., p. 153.
[22] Ibid., p. 165.

regressive processes reaching back into the prenatal state, but he also detected them in repressed contents. Only that which had been repressed could be expressed as a symbol. Since repressed material was also always distorted, the theory of symbolism could without any difficulty be subordinated to the principle of dream distortion. Freud, therefore, arrived at the conclusion that dream symbols were nothing other than still operative distortions from earlier times. As remnants of the early identity of verbal expression and sexual object, symbols still retained the original character of signs representing the meaning of words. In effect, Freud conceived dream symbols, as well as symbols in general, as standing for the one essential, the sexual organs.

II. THE SYMBOL AS A RELATIVELY UNKNOWN
ENTITY (JUNG)

Freud's causal explanation of a symbol had no value for Jung as a true description of the symbol because it merely reduced a known thing to something other, but also known. Freud's statement that the symbol should be understood as a mnemonic symbol, that is, a substitute for repressed childhood memories, and his attempt to supply the symbol with a consistent sexual meaning were completely contrary to Jung's concept. The mnemonic symbol only shifted the problem, while reduction to sexual objects made the so-called symbol appear to be a sign rather than a "true" symbol. When Freud described universal symbols as "a relic and a mark of former [conceptual and linguistic] identity,"[1] Jung viewed this as being as much a spurious symbolization as tracing the symbol back to distorted sexual events. In both instances, the symbol was "an abbreviated designation for a *known* thing"[2]—a symptom. He could never see the meaning of a symbol "as an intentional paraphrase or transmogrification of a known thing,"[3] but considered it essentially a reference to something yet unknown. What Freud had in mind—as he himself stated—was a symptomatic action and not symbolization; this was clearly expressed, for example, by tracing back the unconscious humming of melodies to a symptomatic action.

> ... for him [Freud] these phenomena are not symbolic in the sense here defined, but are symptomatic signs of a definite and generally known underlying process.[4]

According to Jung, there are two categories of events: ". . . processes obviously exist which express no particular meaning, being in fact mere consequences, or symptoms; and . . . there are other processes which bear within them a hidden meaning."[5] By assuming a consistent coordination, Freud divested the symbol of its finalistic significance and of its psychic content altogether. For Jung, on the other hand, the symbol always meant a spontaneous attempt of the unconscious psyche to express in known images something relatively unknown, at the time only dimly divined.

An expression that stands for a known thing remains a mere sign and is never a symbol. It is, therefore, quite impossible to create a

---

[1] *The Interpretation of Dreams* (1900/1914), p. 352.
[2] Jung, *Psychological Types* (1921), p. 474.
[3] Ibid.   [4] Ibid., p. 477.   [5] Ibid., p. 478.

living symbol, i.e., one that is pregnant with meaning, from known associations. . . . Every psychic product, if it is the best possible expression at the moment for a fact as yet unknown or only relatively known, may be regarded as a symbol, provided that we accept the expression as standing for something that is only divined and not yet clearly conscious.[6]

In spite of all his reservations, Jung never overlooked Freud's great merit in having worked out the formal foundations of the symbol, particularly condensation and identification of ideas. Jung himself conceived condensation as the process of compressing different qualities into a single one, for example, the personification of personality aspects or the formation of archetypal ideas. To be sure, Jung drew a line when it came to content: he never assumed that the process of identification was no more than an unconscious analogy of sexual generalities—as Freud did, for instance, with regard to verbal expression and sexual object; nor was he able to accept the symbol as nothing more than the transformation of sexual characteristics. For Jung, identification always consisted of an equalization of data which were essentially unknown. In his view, Freud's theory missed the special nature of the symbol. Moreover, he was convinced that a monopolar approach, in which the opposites were based solely on drive activity, was unable to elucidate the basic transformations of the libido. For example, it could never account for the transition from lower to higher levels (cf. E.III.5) and was certainly not able to explain the specific nature of the symbol, anchored as it was in the depth of the human personality. For accomplishing that, the gradient was missing from Freud's concept, and therefore the prerequisite of the symbol.

1. The Incest Symbol

Jung's concept of the symbol became apparent in his early comments on the symbolism of incest. He saw the essential features of the incest image (those aspects that made it seem so important, so fascinating, and so stubbornly resistant to resolution) in the symbolic content of incest rather than in the incestuous wish. This symbolic content gave the fantasy of an incestuous relation with a parent its overpowering quality and accounted for the air of mystery floating around it. The hints Jung discovered in *Transformations and Symbols of the Libido* (1912) were subsequently confirmed in his psychotherapeutic practice. The most remarkable expression of the problems connected with in-

---

[6] Ibid., p. 475.

cest—and the one most basic for psychotherapy—Jung found in the relationship of transference between physician and patient, just as Freud had before him. It became evident that the incest symbol was the psychological model for any erotic relationship. But unlike Freud, who interpreted the incest image as a wish for cohabitation harking back to childhood, Jung saw it primarily as a recurring archetypal expression of man's longing for shelter in the primeval past, in the blissful state of complete unconsciousness, in which man was still united with himself and the primordial maternal soil.

The incest-toned parental images were most frequently projected in the transference situation, the physician attracting either the father or the mother image. In this context, it was highly irrelevant whether the subject was aware of his projection or not. Even when he was fully conscious of these contents, they persisted in their activity, revealing that the deep psychic background still contained another hidden and completely inaccessible content.

We must therefore assume that, over and above the incest-fantasy, highly emotional contents are still bound up with the parental imagos and need to be made conscious. They are obviously more difficult to make conscious than the incest-fantasies.[7]

From such emotionally toned fantasies Jung also concluded that unconscious religious ideas of highly suggestive power were active. Characteristically, they usually followed a line far from the traditionally transmitted dogma, but rather presented a pronounced heretical character. It was also striking that images of the parent, as a rule, suggested a motif of a divine couple of rare perfection, radiating a superhuman glow. The symbol may sometimes have suggested Plato's androgynous creature, or might be analogous to the primordial images of heavenly King and Queen, or else might present some other male/female duality (Niklaus von der Flüe). Yet, Jung felt that such incest fantasies never represented a mere incestuous relationship but rather the activity of an archetype of general significance. The genesis of such images, in Jung's opinion, could never be explained by the incest theory.[8] What was active in the depth of the incest fantasy was the archetype (primordial image) of the divine couple, the syzygy,[9] the ubiquitous image of a male/female totality, encountered in mythology and ethnology.

[7] "Concerning the Archetypes, with Special Reference to the Anima Concept" (1936/1954), p. 61.
[8] Ibid., p. 69.   [9] Ibid., p. 59.

For instance, everything that we would like, in infantile fashion, to attribute to our parents or blame them for is blown up to fantastic proportions from this secret source, and for this reason it remains an open question how much of the ill-reputed incest-fantasy is to be taken seriously. Behind the parental pair, or pair of lovers, lie contents of extreme tension which are not apperceived in consciousness and can therefore become perceptible only through projection.[10]

These images were distinct from traditional concepts, exhibiting a high intensity. On closer examination, they represented the subject's attempts to grow beyond personal fetters or to use such images of totality (cf. H.III.3.a) to compensate for the personality's tendency to fall apart into opposites. Most of all, these images showed a propensity to heighten the tie to father or mother by presenting them as supra-human images.

The image of the syzygy, revealing man's female part as the mother image, suggested the anima, and correspondingly the woman's male part, or father image, could be seen as the animus.

Jung did not by any means conceive the anima as an idea which could be grasped intellectually, but rather as a naturally grown symbol which represented the life-giving aspect of the psyche in general. The anima

. . . is always the *a priori* element in his moods, reactions, impulses, and whatever else is spontaneous in psychic life. It is something that lives of itself, that makes us live; it is a life behind consciousness that cannot be completely integrated with it, but from which, on the contrary, consciousness arises.[11]

The anima was almost always projected, appearing in various shapes. Water-sprites, witches, and goddesses were among the forms in which she manifested herself.

In the animus, Jung saw the counterpart of the anima. It was the image of the male spirit, acting within the woman's psyche, and representing a precipitation of the most essential experiences which she had had with men. Depending on the extent of such experiences, the symbol of the animus took concrete shape in opinions absorbed from others, in unswerving convictions and incontestable arguments, as well as in productive insight and creativity. When projected, the animus might appear as a ski instructor, a singer, a religious teacher, or as a spiritual leader.

10 Ibid., p. 63.
11 "Archetypes of the Collective Unconscious" (1934/1954), p. 27.

It was fundamentally important for the individual to try to cope with the projections, the psychic images of animus and anima, and bring them to consciousness. Inasmuch as they constituted life and psychic activity "behind consciousness," they became bridges to the unconscious when brought into relationship to the ego. In other words, they had the essential role of mediating between the conscious and the unconscious, or of communicating with the figures of the collective unconscious hidden within them. Just as the anima represented the archetypal symbol of life in whom, regardless of meaning, the image of the old wise man was concealed, the image of the Magna Mater was latent in the animus.

2. *The Symbol as Mediator*

One of Jung's most remarkable insights was the concept of the symbol as a mediator, unifying the opposites of conscious and unconscious. The symbol was an image which, on the one hand, was a manifestation of the primordial psychic background not yet rationally shaped and, on the other hand, participated in conscious reality. Jung saw the symbol as a paradoxical expression, aiming at the unification of the Yea and the Nay and encompassing both.

Only that can be symbolic which embraces both.[12]

Not infrequently, some things could be bridged in the symbol which, when viewed in a logical perspective, would seem to preclude each other and present an insoluble conflict on the practical level. It was, so to speak, a "tertium quid," an unforeseen third position, which was likely to appear at the time of apparently deadlocked clashes between obligations. Being irrational and taking place in the depth of the psyche, the symbol released the individual from a presently insoluble conflict between his conscious and unconscious attitudes. In a similar vein, about twenty years later, Jung wrote:

What takes place between light and darkness, what unites the opposites, has a share in both sides and can be judged just as well from the left as from the right, without our becoming any the wiser: indeed, we can only open up the opposition again. Here only the symbol helps, for, in accordance with its paradoxical nature, it represents the "tertium" that in logic does not exist, but which in reality is the living truth.[13]

[12] *Psychological Types*, p. 111.
[13] "Paracelsus as a Spiritual Phenomenon" (1942), p. 162.

Jung expressed the irrational double nature of the symbol in the following pithy comment:

> The symbol is neither abstract nor concrete, neither rational nor irrational, neither real nor unreal. It is always both.[14]

This double nature produced a paradox which increased the opposites and, at the same time, revealed something more than the tension brought on by the opposition of rational and irrational. The function of the symbol in establishing a synthesis was the true secret of transforming the personality, "synonymous with progressive development towards a new attitude."[15] This was referred to earlier as the transcendent function.

> The process of coming to terms with the unconscious is a true labour, a work which involves both action and suffering. It has been named the "transcendent function" because it represents a function based on real and "imaginary," or rational and irrational, data, thus bridging the yawning gulf between conscious and unconscious. It is a natural process, a manifestation of the energy that springs from the tension of the opposites, and it consists in a series of fantasy-occurrences which appear spontaneously in dreams and visions.[16]

The function of forming symbols was therefore vitally important in the process of self-realization or individuation, as Jung stated in 1928. He understood it as "a process or course of development arising out of the conflict between the two fundamental psychic facts"[17] of ego and the unconscious. Individuation was largely irrational and aimed at establishing and unfolding the original wholeness.[18] In line with his orientation toward wholeness, Jung saw the realization of the individual not only in distinguishing the ego from its opposites but also in elaborating a point beyond these opposites.

> Whatever man's wholeness, or the self, may mean *per se*, empirically it is an image of the goal of life spontaneously produced by the unconscious, irrespective of the wishes and fears of the conscious mind. It stands for the goal of the total man, for the realization of his wholeness and individuality with or without the consent of his will.[19]

14 *Psychology and Alchemy* (1944), p. 283.
15 "On the Psychology of the Unconscious" (1917/1926/1943), p. 99.
16 Ibid., p. 80.
17 "Conscious, Unconscious, and Individuation" (1939), p. 288.
18 Ibid., p. 289.   19 "Answer to Job" (1952/1956), p. 459.

According to Jung, the essential aspect in the process of symbol-formation was that the symbol leads from a more natural level to a more spiritual one, that is, increases the opposition of nature and spirit. The symbol was, so to speak, the "middle way along which the opposites flow together in a new movement."[20] Inasmuch as *the conscious experience of life* demanded an always new balance of opposites, a constantly renewed bridging of the powers of drive and spirit, the unifying symbol really had a creative function in guiding the individual to a deeper psychological truth.

> Considered from the standpoint of realism, the symbol is not of course an external truth, but it is psychologically true, for it was and is the bridge to all that is best in humanity.[21]

Because the unifying symbol was essentially an indefinable third position between the opposites of rational and irrational, conscious and unconscious, it was impossible to coin a completely lucid expression of its meaning. In Jung's view, that which was real and essential in human experience could only be expressed symbolically, and its meaning could be formulated only by approximation. The symbol would lose part of its fullness and power, its compactness and vitality, if expressed in rational terms. Even so, in view of self-realization, the image would have to approximate consciousness. Yet this always bore the risk that the individual would become split from the primordial soil and the source of creativity. The danger could be avoided only by preserving the relationship between the symbol and the whole. As Jung said, a symbolic expression was alive only when it was pregnant with meaning. It stayed alive only as long as it "expressed the inexpressible in unsurpassable form." In such cases, it represented "the best possible expression at the moment for a fact as yet unknown or only relatively known"[22] and was accompanied by a life-giving and life-promoting effect.

The characteristics of the symbol (its transforming and modulating qualities, unifying the opposites) should make it sufficiently clear that the symbolic truth was anything but a compromise formation, the result of distortion and falsification—as was Freud's contention. In Jung's psychology, the symbol has the function of a creative "transition from one attitude to another."[23] This comment points out the extraordinary significance which Jung attributed to the psychic attitude. Granted that the conception of analogies, the ability of the psyche to

20 *Psychological Types*, p. 262.
21 *Symbols of Transformation* (1912/1952), p. 231.
22 *Psychological Types*, p. 475.   23 Ibid., p. 480.

form symbols, and the quality of unifying opposites were indispensable prerequisites, still the perception of a symbol depended just as much on the conscious attitude of the individual.

> Whether a thing is a symbol or not depends chiefly on the attitude of the observing consciousness; for instance, on whether it regards a given fact not merely as such but also as an expression for something unknown. Hence it is quite possible for a man to establish a fact which does not appear in the least symbolic to himself, but is profoundly so to another consciousness.[24]

People fell into different classes according to their type of attitude. Depending on psychic characteristics, temperament, or type of individual, one's attitude toward the nature of the symbolic truth varied.

Without going too far afield, we may say that it was this kind of difference in psychic attitude that was responsible for the basic dissension between Freud and Jung, in spite of their largely similar observations. Behind Freud's psychology one could feel the power of the castrating father's image, while Jung was affected by the mother's image, by the vital and nourishing aspects in the depth of the psyche. Accordingly, Jung evaluated psychic contents not only in their relationship to the individual's life history, but also, on principle, in their relationship to the psyche as a whole and to the prospective potentialities of each specific subject. For instance, Jung recognized in regression both the danger of attachment to past experiences and the germ of new, vital potentials; consequently, he attributed to the archaic image the capacity of preparing the way for a rebirth from maternal primordial soil. Hence, for Jung, the symbol never implied a mark of prehistoric identity between sexuality and language, but rather the psyche's spontaneous attempt to express something relatively unknown in known images. While Freud exhaustively described the symbol as compromise-toned wish-fulfillment, Jung recognized in it a creative ability to form analogies between drive and spirit and, further, an irrational tendency to unify the psychological opposites.

Jung's concept of the symbol was, of course, soon attacked by the psychoanalytic school. Ferenczi's review (1913) of *Transformations and Symbols of the Libido* is a good example:

> Jung, too, found the motive for symbol formation in the tendency to take unconscious complexes "which have not received recognition and have been treated as if they did not exist" and to cast them into a distorted form which is unintelligible to consciousness. . . .

24 Ibid., p. 475.

At this point, Jung still regarded the unconscious tendency as the *essential feature*, the *symbol* being nothing but the fantastic product of substitution. . . . In the second part of the book on libido, however, symbols are no longer the images which have been displaced into consciousness, but the unconscious psychic tendencies themselves are declared to be "symbols"—in spite of the fact that the role Jung attributed to repression in the development of symbols precludes such an inversion. This would be a good opportunity to point out the need for coming at last to an agreement on the unequivocal use of the term "symbol." Not everything that stands for something else is a symbol. . . . In the context of psychoanalysis, a simile becomes a symbol as soon as the censor has repressed the original meaning of the simile into the unconscious. Therefore, for example, the church steeple, after repression has occurred, may symbolize a phallus, but never the phallus a church steeple.[25]

3. The Symbol of the Self

One of Jung's most important achievements was the discovery (1928) of a center of the personality, the self, which is prominent in the symbolic formations of the unconscious. Since he understood the self as something which formed the beginning of psychic life and was also the goal toward which all things were oriented, he conceived self-realization as a developmental process "by which a man becomes the definite, unique being he in fact is."[26]

From the psychological point of view, the symbol of the self was experienced as a central point, not coinciding with the ego, but felt as rising virtually to an apex. It indicated an unrecognizable midpoint and at the same time was felt as a preeminent whole. As such, it represented the image of a total personality which formed the "middle between conscious and unconscious" as well as the unifying point of reference for the numerous personality fragments, complexes, and autonomous figures in the collective unconscious. The idea of the self could never be completely demonstrated and could only be inferred and divined from the manifestations of the psyche; still, it brought into the reach of personal experience a primordial idea of man, of his potential wholeness. From the philosophical point of view, the idea of the self was an unknowable entity which completely surpassed the individual's comprehension.

[25] Ferenczi, "Kritik der Jungschen 'Wandlungen und Symbole der Libido'" (1913). (Tr. F.E.E. and E.K.E.)

[26] Jung, "The Relations Between the Ego and the Unconscious" (1916/1928/1935/1948), p. 174.

I have called this centre the *self*. Intellectually the self is no more than a psychological concept, a construct that serves to express an unknowable essence which we cannot grasp as such, since by definition it transcends our powers of comprehension.[27]

Similarly, thirty years later Jung stressed that the symbol of the self had only potentially an empirical meaning. As an image of totality, only its smallest part could be experienced, its major portion remaining unrecognizable. Because of this indeterminable character the self pointed, on the one hand, to the concrete reality, on the other to transcendence. In other words, its nature was subjective as well as objective. In 1958 Jung added the following definition to *Psychological Types*:

> As an empirical concept, the self designates the whole range of psychic phenomena in man. It expresses the unity of the personality as a whole. But in so far as the total personality, on account of its unconscious component, can be only in part conscious, the concept of the self is, in part, only *potentially* empirical and is to that extent a *postulate*. In other words, it encompasses both the experienceable and the inexperienceable (or the not yet experienced). It has these qualities in common with very many scientific concepts that are more names than ideas. In so far as psychic totality, consisting of both conscious and unconscious contents, is a postulate, it is a *transcendental* concept, for it presupposes the existence of unconscious factors on empirical grounds and thus characterizes an entity that can be described only in part but, for the other part, remains at present unknowable and illimitable.[28]

The peculiarity of the self, expressing the rational as well as the irrational, the empirical as well as the transcendental, made it difficult to coin a rational formula expressing its essence. Only the symbol could satisfactorily convey the totality of the psyche.

A. THE SELF AS A UNITING SYMBOL

Jung found the deepest and most complete expression of totality in the so-called unifying symbol which represented the elusive essence of the self. Symbolizing the totality of experience, that is, the "bipolarity of the archetype,"[29] it combined the conscious and the unconscious areas, the superior and inferior functions, and also the male and the

27 Ibid., p. 238.   28 *Psychological Types*, p. 460.
29 *Psychology and Alchemy*, p. 471.

female aspects. In particular, it meant that the symbol of the self was always both—rational and irrational, good and bad, light and dark—embodying the opposites (*complexio oppositorum*).

> Anything that a man postulates as being a greater totality than himself can become a symbol of the self.[30]

While investigating the psychology of religion Jung stated time and again that, as a rule, the quaternary and circular symbols most adequately expressed wholeness. As a very ancient idea of humanity, the quaternio of symbolic elements pointed to totality: the four temperaments, the four seasons, the four chief points of the compass, as well as the four psychic functions. Among the oldest religious symbols in the history of civilization belonged the mandala (ritual or magic circle). Its definitely numinous nature was presumably connected with the symmetry of the components of the image, which impressed the beholder with a mirror-like relationship of the conscious to the unconscious and at the same time manifested a principle of transcendental order in the unconscious. The relationship between the circle and its center, too, pointed to a transcendent core which in the various religions assumed the image of the God within. Wherever a concentric and radial pattern of images and motifs was arranged around a central hub, a focal point appeared which differed from the ego. The experience of an impersonal center in the psyche was significant because something that had existed at all times, and which the viewer had always searched for, had finally become apparent. What was conceived psychologically as the symbol of the self appeared in Christianity as the dogmatically delineated figure of Christ and in the East as Purusha, Atman, Hiranyagarbha, Buddha, etc. The concept of the center stood out, for instance, in the image of Christ surrounded by his disciples as well as in the ritual circumambulation of the center (as in the medieval ballgame).

> At all events, the aim and effect of the solemn round dance is to impress upon the mind the image of the circle and the centre and the relation of each point along the periphery to that centre. Psychologically this arrangement is equivalent to a mandala and is thus a symbol of the self, the point of reference not only of the individual ego but of all those who are of like mind or who are bound together by fate.[31]

[30] "Transformation Symbolism in the Mass" (1940/1941), p. 156.
[31] Ibid., p. 276.

Jung found that the holistic character of the unifying symbol expressed the conjunction of the opposites—either in the simpler combinations, for example, in syzygies, or in constellations of double character, as could be seen in the quaternio, which knitted together four elements.

In the archetypal image of the syzygy, for instance, the aspect of totality always became apparent in the shape of a duality of male/female. It expressed the idea that the male principle was always linked with the female in the superhuman and divine spheres. The motif of syzygy could refer to a luminous vision of the deity (which always was presented as an epicene figure) as well as to the pairing of the father and mother (exalted to the realm of the gods). As noted earlier, syzygy at first glance brought to mind the incest motive, but in Jung's view an incestuous character was precisely what it did not have; it had to be understood as an image of totality. Therefore, he rejected the bisexuality basis of Freud's explanation and preferred to interpret the motif of the divine couple as a purely intra-psychic relationship. This concept was confirmed again and again in his investigations of the psychology of religion, particularly in gnostic speculation and in Chinese philosophy (Yang-Yin). The motif of syzygy was of universal significance and was as deeply rooted in primitive mythology as the motif of the anima, which was always present as the female aspect of the archetypal image of the couple. In psychotherapy, Jung very frequently encountered such motifs in the attitudes of sons attached to their mothers, who compensated for their fear of stern reality with images of unearthly beauty. Once they were able to recognize the holistic meaning of the motif of syzygy, they could accept it as the decisive experience in the process of individuation. When the transference situation reached a certain intensity, the archetypal motif of the divine couple generally appeared as the central issue in the relationship between physician and patient. These images were always characterized by a definite archetypal arrangement of symbols, a definite order, which took the form of opposite structures and indicated the establishment of a holistic relationship.

Jung considered the gnostic and alchemical writings on the quaternio, particularly the marriage quaternio,[32] to be prototypes for the symbols just described. The quaternio was generally understood as a symmetrical arrangement of opposites in a quadrangular shape which, in the marriage quaternio, presented the structure of an antagonistic position of figures. Whether the opposites were those of endogamous and exogamous libido, of brother and sister, of bright and dark, light

---

32 *Aion* (1951), p. 209.

and shadow, the arrangement of the figures always conformed to the following quaternary model:[33]

Adept _____ Soror mystica

Rex (animus) _____ Regina (anima)

In this context, one might mention the analogy of the marriage quaternio to the quaternity of relationships demonstrated by Freud (cf. E.II.2). But while Freud based the quaternity of persons on the assumption of bisexuality and the psychosexual nature of man, Jung recognized in the quaternio the fourfold basis of wholeness *per se*.[34]

> Only the production of these four aspects makes a total description possible.[35]

In contrast to Freud, Jung saw in the quaternity of relationships an exclusively psychic expression. Basically, the marriage quaternio postulated wholeness; it was an assertion of the holistic structure of the psyche.

The holistic aspect of the marriage quaternio contained a hint of the incest image and implied a tendency to expand the psychic structure of the "ordinary" man in both directions—the superhuman as well as the subhuman. Depending on the conscious orientation of the individual, he would reveal his affinity toward the spiritual, "higher" man (Anthropos Quaternio) or to the "lower" man (Shadow Quaternio).

> Since the schema is a primary one characterizing the psychology of love relationships and also of the transference, it will, like all characterological schemata, obviously manifest itself in a "favourable" and an "unfavourable" form . . . everything a man does has a positive and a negative aspect.[36]

B. THE RELIGIOUS FUNCTION OF THE SELF

Jung became increasingly more occupied with the relationship between the idea of the self and the God-image. Only toward the middle of the 1920's did he make the idea of the self the focus of his psychology, but the phenomenology of the God-image had already interested him in earlier years. It was one of Jung's most remarkable achievements that as early as 1912 he liberated the God-image from the shackles of

---

[33] "The Psychology of the Transference" (1946), p. 227.
[34] *Aion*, p. 159.   [35] Ibid., p. 259.   [36] Ibid., p. 229.

personalistic interpretation. He saw more and more clearly that the outline of something deeper than the ego appeared in the God-image, just as in dreams, fantasies, and in visions. They expressed a natural function of the psyche, referring to immediate inner experiences and living processes in the unconscious. In this context, the symbol of the god's renewal was particularly revealing, because it usually indicated the highest psychic value, which prepared a new conscious attitude and, at the same time, "a new manifestation of life."[37] Psychotherapy and the regression it fostered to the archaic image of the world also drew Jung's attention to how important the renewal or reactivation of the God-image was for the process of self-realization.[38]

Jung's discussion of the existence of a primordial or archetypal God-image in the psyche can be found mainly in *Psychology and Religion* (1939). He had in mind a "psychological function of an irrational nature,"[39] which indicated the presence of a numinous quality, but "which has nothing whatever to do with the question of God's existence."[40] Just as religion was related to the *numinosum*, the *homo religiosus* meant an individual whose psychic attitude had "been changed by experience of the *numinosum*."[41] Jung's attempt to explain the relationship of man with the divine came from his deep insight that the God-image was essentially derived from a correspondence between the soul and the essence of God.

> It would be going perhaps too far to speak of an affinity [between God and psyche]; but at all events the soul must contain in itself the faculty of relation to God, i.e., a correspondence, otherwise a connection could never come about. *This correspondence is, in psychological terms, the archetype of the God-image.*[42]

Jung's occupation with the religious function of the self and the question of the relationship of the God-image to the self became always more his central interest during the 1940's. He recognized increasingly that the symbols of the self could in no way be distinguished from those of the godhead.

> But as one can never distinguish empirically between a symbol of the self and a God-image, the two ideas, however much we try to differentiate them, always appear blended together, so that the self appears synonymous with the inner Christ of the Johannine and

[37] *Psychological Types*, p. 193.
[38] "The Relations between the Ego and the Unconscious," pp. 137–38.
[39] "On the Psychology of the Unconscious," p. 71.   [40] Ibid.
[41] "Psychology and Religion" (1937/1940), p. 8.
[42] *Psychology and Alchemy*, p. 11.

Pauline writings, and Christ with God ("of one substance with the Father"), just as the Atman appears as the individualized self and at the same time as the animating principle of the cosmos, and Tao as a condition of mind and at the same time as the correct behaviour of cosmic events.[43]

Both forms of awareness, psychological experience of the self as well as religious experience, arose on the same basis, that is, something which was experienced as comprehensive unity and wholeness. Like the God-image, the archetype of the self, too, could take hold of the individual with such force that he could hardly doubt the "truth" of his experience. In both cases, the individual was seized by the *numinosum* which furnished him with an ominous experience of wholeness. There seemed to be no criterion distinguishing between the experience of the self and that of God.

At any rate, I personally have found it impossible to discover a criterion of distinction. Here faith or philosophy alone can decide, neither of which has anything to do with the empiricism of the scientist.[44]

Because of this concept he also considered the value of statements about the self and about the God-image to be merely subjective knowledge. For both, the individual had only the evidence of personal experience, which could not be based on any objective criteria, neither as to the similarity nor as to the disparity of the underlying transcendence. Even though all such statements referred to an objective essence endowed with extraordinary numinosity, they were only based on subjective truth. Therefore, Jung could never have assumed an equation between the archetype-as-such and God nor between the unconscious and God. What applied to the experience of self and God was true in general of all religious testimonies: as Jung had emphasized so strongly, their experiential value was limited in that they always referred only to the image or simile, never to the transcendent background itself.

That is why whenever we speak of religious contents we move in a world of images that point to something ineffable. We do not know how clear or unclear these images, metaphors, and concepts are in respect of their transcendental object. If, for instance, we say "God," we give expression to an image or verbal concept which has undergone many changes in the course of time. We are, however, unable

[43] "A Psychological Approach to the Dogma of the Trinity" (1940–41/1948), p. 156.
[44] Ibid., p. 190.

to say with any degree of certainty—unless it be by faith—whether these changes affect only the images and concepts or the Unspeakable itself.[45]

Concerning the ambiguity of religious tenets, Jung expressed himself as follows: From the intellectual point of view such observations merely had the value of a hypothesis regarding something inexpressible. In the historical perspective, they manifested a certain degree of objectivity inasmuch as they represented recurrent primal ideas native to the human race. Finally, because of their numinosity these tenets put an almost absolute obligation on the individual.

C. ARCHETYPE OF THE SELF AND INNER EXPERIENCE

Although the truth of religious beliefs was relative and knowledge gained through metaphysical generalizations had only a relative value for Jung, he never questioned the subjective validity of inner experiences. His own experiences, historical evidence, and the reports of his pupils convinced him again and again of the extraordinary value of inner experiences for each individual. Even though he strictly rejected hypostatizing in any way, he still felt a deep conviction that the individual can be overwhelmed by the archetype-as-such. Just as he had never doubted the existence of a transcendental reality, he saw the process of becoming aware of God and of the self as an inner secret of the highest numinosity. In whatever image the meaning of this inexpressible presence revealed itself, it existed as an experience; it was real and it was effective.

In the same way that Kant had opposed pure reason to the practical, Jung distinguished between the claim of a metaphysical truth and the individually valid experience. He expressly stressed that even though religious statements were incommensurable with reason, it could in no way reduce the reality and vitality of the inner experience.[46] On the contrary, Jung put a far higher value on the personal experience of transcendental reality than on intellectual judgment about this unknown quality.

The experience itself is the important thing, not its intellectual representation or clarification, which proves meaningful and helpful only when the road to original experience is blocked.[47]

And again he wrote with equal profundity:

45 "Answer to Job," pp. 360–61.
46 Mysterium Coniunctionis (1955/1956), p. 551.
47 Ibid., p. 545.

II. THE SYMBOL AS A RELATIVELY UNKNOWN ENTITY (JUNG)

> What counts in religious experience is not how explicitly an arche-
> type can be formulated but how much I am gripped by it. The least
> important thing is what I think about it.[48]

In the practice of psychotherapy, therefore, the inner awareness of
the archetype of the self and of the God-image were guideposts for
Jung. Such awareness was gained through dreams and fantasies and by
observation of the phenomena of the process of individuation. Above
all, Jung envisioned the archetypal image of something greater, "a
virtual centre,"[49] which organized ideas and experiences. Consequently,
in his view the foremost goal of psychotherapy was to establish a
relationship between the ego and the reality of the inner center.
Orientation towards this goal appeared to him to be the only way
for man to become that which he really was. The experience of the pure
essence of self and the God-image, in Jung's view, could not be assailed
on psychic grounds, since it was founded on transcendental premises.
Although such experiences always took the form of subjective images
and symbols, they nevertheless rested on an emotional basis of the
most pronounced numinosity, supremely binding for shaping the
individual's life.

> But, although our whole world of religious ideas consists of anthro-
> pomorphic images that could never stand up to rational criticism, we
> should never forget that they are based on numinous archetypes,
> i.e., on an emotional foundation which is unassailable by reason.[50]

For Jung, therefore, this background of the psyche, beyond any doubt,
was an inexhaustible source of strength for those who searched for it
and were concerned with it.

It cannot be said too often that Jung refrained from any opinion
regarding the essence of this transcendental background—even though
he equated the experience of the self with the God-image, that is,
acknowledged the inability to differentiate between psychological and
religious images. The unknowable nature of the unconscious made it
impossible to gain any objectively valid information about the archetype of the self or about God. But this did not preclude archetypal as
well as religious experiences from presenting the earmarks of wholeness
which gave them the character of numinous experiences replete with
meaning of the highest order.

48 Ibid., p. 524.
49 "The Relations between the Ego and the Unconscious," p. 237.
50 "Answer to Job," p. 361.

APPENDIX:
JUNG'S CONCEPTS FROM
1936 TO 1961

I. THE ARCHETYPE-AS-SUCH

In his works during his last years Jung's view of the world deepened to such an extent that it not only transcended its earlier framework but put it into a wholly new perspective. He ventured into areas so little known to medical psychology that it is hardly possible to see Jung's mature concepts in the same context as those Freud had voiced earlier. This survey of Jung's psychology of the unconscious would not be complete without discussing his later ideas as they developed after Freud's death.

Jung had coined the expression "archetypal image" to designate typical basic forms, prefigurative determinants, and the tendency to repeat the same psychic experiences. In 1943, he formulated his thought in this way:

> Not only are the archetypes, apparently, impressions of ever-repeated typical experiences, but, at the same time, they behave empirically like agents that tend towards the repetition of these same experiences. For when an archetype appears in a dream, in a fantasy, or in life, it always brings with it a certain influence or power by virtue of which it either exerts a numinous or a fascinating effect, or impels to action.[1]

Jung discovered in archetypal images not only the focus on which earlier paths converged, but also a center from which fascinating effects proceeded. They were the creative forces which shaped and transformed the life and actions of each individual and were largely responsible for his ideas and artistic products. Earlier, Jung had discovered a reciprocal relationship between the archetype and the conscious psyche; the image needed to be formed by the conscious ego just as much as, conversely, consciousness required an evocative idea.

The more Jung focused his attention on the phenomena of the collective background—whether on the phenomenon of synchronicity or on spiritual manifestations—the more it became evident that the archetype was unfathomable and that the human mind could merely paraphrase or approximate an ultimately unconscious nucleus of meaning.

The ultimate meaning of this nucleus was never conscious and never will be. It was, and still is, only interpreted, and every interpretation

[1] Jung, "On the Psychology of the Unconscious" (1917/1926/1943), pp. 69–70.

that comes anywhere near the hidden sense . . . has always, right from the beginning, laid claim not only to absolute truth and validity but to instant reverence and religious devotion.[2]

As early as 1921, Jung stated that the creative power of the archetype, in the final analysis, coincided with the secret of the creative activity of the spirit:

> The organism confronts light with a new structure, the eye, and the psyche confronts the natural process with a symbolic image, which apprehends it in the same way as the eye catches the light. And just as the eye bears witness to the peculiar and spontaneous creative activity of living matter, the primordial image expresses the unique and unconditioned creative power of the psyche.[3]

1. The Archetype as a Regulator

One of Jung's most significant discoveries during the 1940's was the hypothesis of a regulating activity of the archetypes. Again, fantasy formations of the unconscious psyche led his investigations in this direction, more precisely those fantasies produced by active imagination and extending over long periods. In them he recognized that unconscious regulators existed in the depth of the psyche which, independent of personal choice, arranged the elements of the images. Jung saw nothing new in certain motifs repeating themselves and conforming to mythological symbols. The surprising thing was that the fantasy material was organized in a rather orderly way around a focal point. It seemed as if spontaneous factors, even an unconscious nucleus of significance, operated in the depth of the psyche and served to stimulate all happenings.

The numinosity of the archetype, particularly, was a case in point, which Jung was able to demonstrate principally with the archetype-as-such. Wherever it appeared, it had a compelling force, "and whenever its effect becomes conscious it has a distinctly numinous quality."[4] Whether the archetype was encountered in a dream or as an image, as an idea or in human shape, the common quality of all such manifestations was the feeling of the presence of the numen. In other words, the individual gripped by the experience felt its source to be an extra-conscious psychic reality, presenting the special quality of something

2 "The Psychology of the Child Archetype" (1940), p. 156.
3 *Psychological Types* (1921), pp. 444–45.
4 "A Psychological Approach to the Dogma of the Trinity" (1940–41/1948), p. 149.

"illuminating" and helpful but, at the same time, strange. Jung gave a very impressive description of this process:

A dark impulse is the ultimate arbiter of the pattern, an unconscious *a priori* precipitates itself into plastic form, and one has no inkling that another person's consciousness is being guided by these same principles at the very point where one feels utterly exposed to the boundless subjective vagaries of chance. Over the whole procedure there seems to reign a dim foreknowledge not only of the pattern but of its meaning.[5]

This assumption of the archetype's apparent foreknowledge, which also originated during the 1940's, was an entirely new concept. Just as new was the hypothesis of an *a priori* possession of the envisioned goal.

As a numinous factor, the archetype determines the nature of the configurational process and the course it will follow, with seeming foreknowledge, or as though it were already in possession of the goal to be circumscribed by the centring process.[6]

Since the unconscious regulators of psychic formations could be recognized only by their effects, and never in their exact nature, they seemed to indicate an abstract pattern of organization, that is, a basic form of conception coming to light again and again in various images.

These experiences and reflections lead me to believe that there are certain collective unconscious conditions which act as regulators and stimulators of creative fantasy-activity and call forth corresponding formations by availing themselves of the existing conscious material.[7]

In so far as such organizing forms implied an agent totally different from the specific representations, Jung selected the term archetype-as-such to cover this basic pattern.

The archetypal representations (images and ideas) mediated to us by the unconscious should not be confused with the archetype as such. They are very varied structures which all point back to one essentially "irrepresentable" basic form. The latter is characterized by certain formal elements and by certain fundamental meanings, although these can be grasped only approximately.[8]

[5] "On the Nature of the Psyche" (1946/1954), p. 204.
[6] Ibid., p. 209.   [7] Ibid., p. 204.   [8] Ibid., p. 213.

The archetypal images provided a means of giving a somewhat definite shape to these numinous organizing factors, and at the same time their presence concealed the core of meaning in the background of the psyche; however, the organizing nucleus itself revealed numinous effects, often surprising in their "fulness of meaning."[9]

Such effects led Jung to compare the psyche's luminous experiences with the light impressions described by the alchemists. In this connection, he thought of the "seeds of light broadcast in the chaos" (Khunrath),[10] of the "scintillae" (Dorn),[11] of fish-eyes at the bottom of the sea,[12] or images of luminous serpent's eyes. From such numinous impressions, experienced so to speak as sparks of light emerging sporadically from the darkness of the unconscious, Jung arrived at the highly important assumption of a spirit factor in the depth of the psyche which was incapable of becoming conscious.

The concept of the archetype-as-such accordingly achieved the prominence of a psychic model: Even though structured itself from the recognizable effects of symbolic representations, it had a function in bringing about a clearer understanding of certain structural connections in psychic material, such as orderedness, goal-directedness, or centering process. In this way, further enlightenment about the relationship of archetype and consciousness could be gained.

It is not a question of his [the psychologist's] *asserting* anything, but of constructing a *model* which opens up a promising and useful field of inquiry. A model does not assert that something *is* so, it simply illustrates a particular mode of observation.[13]

The origin of the archetype, whether it is acquired or not, and the question of the nature of this metaphysical entity composed one of the problems for which there were no ready answers.

I have often been asked where the archetype comes from and whether it is acquired or not. This question cannot be answered directly. Archetypes are . . . factors and motifs that arrange the psychic elements into certain images, characterized as archetypal, but in such a way that they can be recognized only from the effects they produce. They exist preconsciously, and presumably they form the structural dominants of the psyche in general. They may be compared to the invisible presence of the crystal lattice in a saturated solution. . . . Empirically considered, however, the archetype

9 Ibid., p. 206.   10 Ibid., p. 190.   11 Ibid., p. 192.
12 Ibid., p. 196.   13 Ibid., p. 184.

did not ever come into existence as a phenomenon of organic life, but entered into the picture with life itself.[14]

Since the metaphysical nature of the archetype-as-such did not allow for any answerable question, one could only state with any degree of certainty that it represented a kind of psychic entity which was inherited and existed *a priori*; or, to put it differently, it was an accumulation of modal elements which time and again produced similar ideas.

2. *Archetype and Instinct (Drive)*

Throughout his investigations Jung was occupied with the relationship between the biological and the psychological aspects of the background of the psyche. The problem arose again after he had established a clearly unconscious nucleus of meaning in the archetype-as-such.

As early as 1919 Jung had stated that instinct and archetypal image together formed the foundation of the collective unconscious. One could not be separated from the other. The principles of action and apprehension were linked in such a manner that the primordial image could be designated as the "self-portrait of the instinct" (cf. E.III.4).

> ... the way in which man inwardly pictures the world is still, despite all differences of detail, as uniform and as regular as his instinctive actions ...
>
> The collective unconscious consists of the sum of the instincts and their correlates, the archetypes. Just as everybody possesses instincts, so he also possesses a stock of archetypal images.[15]

Findings in animal psychology resulted in an important further step in understanding the relationship between instinct and archetype. The investigations of renowned biologists (Portmann, Hediger, Lorenz) demonstrated preformed tendencies in animal behavior, for instance, when nesting or in ritualistic dances.[16] Chickens, too, know exactly when to crack the shell and creep out of the egg, while spiders exhibit typical behavior when building their artful webs—all indications of preformed primordial images. Proposing inherited structures of behavior in human beings followed naturally, and connecting such tendencies with archetypal patterns seemed just as natural. However, the empirical demonstration of typical instinctual patterns in man was

14 "A Psychological Approach to the Dogma of the Trinity," p. 149.

15 "Instinct and the Unconscious" (1919), pp. 136–38.

16 Jacobi, *Complex, Archetype, Symbol in the Psychology of C. G. Jung* (tr. Manheim), p. 41.

rather difficult because consciousness could alter or even obstruct the regulating process of instinctual images. Such instinctual patterns could be quite clearly demonstrated in young children, but in adults they were mainly limited to creative processes, for example, active imagination or certain dream series. The similarity between the organizing activity of the archetypes and the regulatory processes in drives and instincts was nevertheless so striking that Jung felt bound to equate the regulating function of the archetype with that of instincts. Both coincided in their pattern of behavior.

Instinct and the archaic mode meet in the biological conception of the "pattern of behaviour."[17]

This concept could also be expressed as one aspect of the archetype pointing upward, another downward. While the biological facet could become overtly apparent in instinctual action, the archetypal principle of organization manifested itself only within, as in the experience of images.

Jung's hypothesis of a primary connection between drive and image, archetype and instinct, must never be mistaken for a biological assumption. On the contrary, he never mentioned in his writings that psychic contents were in any way derived from the area of biology. The dynamism of the drive as well as its image always followed their own special rules. For instance, "the meaning or purpose of the instinct . . . may easily mask a sense of direction other than biological, which only becomes apparent in the course of development."[18]

Under certain circumstances this special character of spirit and instinct manifested itself in the greatest imaginable opposites.[19] The archetypal image could function so completely independent of instinctual feeling that a frank opposition ensued. The contrast between one individual ruled by drives and another overwhelmed by the spirit demonstrate this point.

The link between archetype and instinct led Jung to another, even bolder hypothesis: the outward appearance of a connection between biological and psychological factors seemed to him to indicate the presence of two transcendental principles which were, in the final analysis, incompatible. Although spirit and drive were coordinated in human experience, these two principles were quite separate in a transcendental sense. And just as the empirical connection between the two principles was essential for understanding their dynamism, Jung believed that the hypothesis of transcendental factors was productive

17 "On the Nature of the Psyche," pp. 200–201.
18 Ibid., p. 182.   19 Ibid., p. 207.

in discussing metaphysical and religious subjects. In the practical world, as noted earlier, Jung saw that the tension between the opposites, particularly the antithesis of drive and spirit, sparked a deeper source of energy. They cooperated in so far as the archetype embodied the "meaning of the instinct,"[20] and the instinct, the dynamic aspect of the spirit.

In his late works, Jung understood the term "spirit" in the sense of spirit-as-such, giving, as it were, meaning and purpose to life, as "spiritus rector." Up to that time he had limited himself to a scientific investigation of the spiritual factor as an image-creating principle, as the uplifting and inspiring breath of the psyche, in short, as a primordial image of the psyche.

With this turn from the primordial image to the concept of the spirit, Jung significantly deepened the basic concepts of his psychology. He was well aware that he transgressed the limits of empirical science by assuming a factor incapable of becoming conscious, that is, a psychoid factor; yet, he did not hesitate to describe the archetypes as metaphysical principles, which "determine the orientation of consciousness."[21]

In my previous writings I have always treated archetypal phenomena as psychic, because the material to be expounded or investigated was concerned solely with ideas and images. The psychoid nature of the archetype, as put forward here, does not contradict these earlier formulations; it only means a further degree of conceptual differentiation, which became inevitable as soon as I saw myself obliged to undertake a more general analysis of the nature of the psyche and to clarify the empirical concepts concerning it and their relation to one another.[22]

To illustrate the psychic tension between drive and archetype, Jung employed the analogy of the spectrum, the image of the drive operating at the ultraviolet end of the color band, its dynamism at the infrared end.[23]

Just as the "psychic infra-red," the biological instinctual psyche, gradually passes over into the physiology of the organism and thus merges with its chemical and physical conditions, so the "psychic ultra-violet," the archetype, describes a field which exhibits none of the peculiarities of the physiological and yet, in the last analysis,

---

20 Ibid., p. 201.
21 "Flying Saucers: A Modern Myth of Things Seen in the Skies" (1958), p. 366.
22 "On the Nature of the Psyche," p. 215.   23 Ibid., p. 211.

can no longer be regarded as psychic, although it manifests itself psychically. But physiological processes behave in the same way, without on that account being declared psychic.[24]

From these and similar observations, Jung saw that the transcendental nature of the drive, essentially irrepresentable, was as irrefutable as that of the archetype, because the drive not only was rooted in the organism but also, in effect, formed "the bridge to matter."

In archetypal conceptions and instinctual perceptions, spirit and matter confront one another on the psychic plane. Matter and spirit both appear in the psychic realm as distinctive qualities of conscious contents. The ultimate nature of both is transcendental, that is, irrepresentable, since the psyche and its contents are the only reality which is given to us *without a medium*.[25]

From these hypotheses, Jung developed the further, equally bold premise that analogous to the archetype (the spirit-as-such) a drive-as-such also existed. Just as the archetypal image exposed the psychoid nature of the archetype-as-such, drive perception, too, flowed into something ineffable—the essence of matter. The next chapter takes up the questions of whether these opposites of matter and spirit could be surmounted by a third quality and how far this would extend, as well as whether they could be fused into a unified world view (see App. II.2.d, end).

[24] Ibid., p. 215.   [25] Ibid., p. 216.

II. THE PSYCHE VIEWED FROM TRANSCENDENTAL FACTORS

1. The Archetype-As-Such: A Form of a priori Orderedness

By demonstrating the psychoid nature of the archetype, Jung took a step of consummate importance, advancing from the subjective to the objective approach, that is, from the idea of the archetypal image to a transpsychic concept of the archetype-as-such. This orientation permitted him to fix his attention on borderline phenomena which, for the most part, transcended the realm of what could be experienced by the psyche. Such phenomena could be experienced in part, but beyond that could not be recognized. Being open to new observations, his investigation of synchronistic phenomena became the starting point for new discoveries. He considered the most remarkable property of such coincidences to be a meaningful, but completely acausal, concurrence of certain psychic states (such as presentiments of death, anxieties, or expectations) with one or more events in the outside world[1] (for example, extraordinary natural phenomena, accidents, etc.). All these synchronistic events occurred completely by chance and exhibited an "existing quality, an irreducible contingency which is 'Just-So.'"[2] Jung found such contingencies operating in Rhine's experiments on ESP phenomena, in astrological correlations, and in the I Ching, as well as in contemporary physics.

From such pregnant coincidences Jung arrived at a completely new hypothesis, which opened up entirely unsuspected perspectives for the science of psychology. He recognized that synchronistic phenomena can be understood by the human mind only when the idea of causal determinism has been supplemented by the equally universal concept of a connection through equivalence or "meaning."[3] This appeared to be another dimension, one transcending the causal connection and suggesting an "acausal orderedness"[4] of data, that is, the operation of an a priori ordering principle, which Jung equated with the archetype-as-such. In a further analogy, the archetype-as-such seemed to have the quality of a metaphysical act of creation in time.[5] What he had in mind was "continuous creation,"[6] either "a series of successive acts of creation . . . (or) the eternal presence of the *one* creative act."[7]

[1] Jung, "Synchronicity: An Acausal Connecting Principle" (1952), p. 441.
[2] Ibid., p. 516.   [3] Ibid., p. 514.   [4] Ibid., p. 516.
[5] Ibid., p. 517.   [6] Ibid., p. 518.   [7] Ibid., p. 516.

All this made it clear that Jung assigned to the archetype-as-such the function of a transpsychic ordering agency, that is, not only an *a priori* principle but one which also entailed an *a priori* distribution and organization of factors. Jung summarized the progressive steps of the work devoted to the archetype as follows: "The archetype *is* the introspectively recognizable form of *a priori* psychic orderedness."[8]

2. *The Relativity of Consciousness and the Unconscious*

The remarkable change in the concept of the archetype, having the quality of an imperceptible structural element, could not fail to have repercussions on the ideas of the unconscious and on consciousness. Both ideas manifestly became less distinct, less determinable, and less unequivocal.

A. THE INDETERMINACY OF THE UNCONSCIOUS

Initially, Jung conceived the unconscious as a body of contents which, on principle, could become conscious and could be clarified by the conscious psyche. With the assumption of psychoid factors in the background of the psyche, this approach underwent a fundamental change. In 1934, Jung conjectured that the collective unconscious could be a guide to a "form of existence *without* space and time,"[9] and it became increasingly more evident that this assumption was highly justified. The hypothesis of a transpsychic function of the archetype induced Jung to embrace the further premise of an irrepresentable background in the psyche, incapable of becoming conscious and ultimately independent of any man's judgment. Jung's revolutionary discoveries culminated in the proposition that the collective unconscious represented a psychoid sphere, comprising the "darkness beyond the categories of the mind" and including "things which are not capable of consciousness and are only 'quasi-psychic.' "[10] The *a priori* ordering principle of the archetype had a counterpart in the psychoid nature of the collective unconscious.

The discovery of a form of existence, incommensurable for the mind to take in, was responsible for a considerable enlargement of the hitherto prevailing concept of the unconscious. From then on, Jung saw the unconscious as embodying a realm which extended from personal to psychoid categories.

The unconscious is not simply the unknown, it is rather the *unknown psychic*; and this we define on the one hand as all those things

8 Ibid.   9 "The Soul and Death" (1934), p. 414.
10 "On the Nature of the Psyche" (1946/1954), p. 188, n. 51.

in us which, if they came to consciousness, would presumably differ in no respect from the known psychic contents, with the addition, on the other hand, of the psychoid system, of which nothing is known directly.[11]

The extension of the concept of the unconscious went hand in hand with the assumption that this sphere darkened and became less definite. Up to that time the concepts of consciousness and the unconscious had been clear and unequivocal, but now they became increasingly more indistinct. Jung established that, when psychic energy sank into the deeper layers of the unconscious, personal experiences also became progressively assimilated with the nature of the instinct, that is, with primitive and automatic qualities which were beyond influence. In other words, the unconscious was less and less accessible to conscious correction or reasoning.

Although at first sight the process continues in the unconscious as though it were conscious, it seems, with increasing dissociation, to sink back to a more primitive (archaic-mythological) level, to approximate in character to the underlying instinctual pattern, and to assume the qualities which are the hallmarks of instinct: automatism, non-susceptibility to influence, all-or-none reaction, and so forth. Using the analogy of the spectrum, we could compare the lowering of unconscious contents to a displacement toward the red end of the colour band.[12]

The unconscious became increasingly darker until it finally lost itself in the indiscernible and nonrepresentable.

B. THE APPROXIMATE ASPECT OF CONSCIOUSNESS

In connection with Jung's investigations of synchronicity, the quality of consciousness, too, became considerably less well-defined. Until the middle of the twentieth century an unequivocal concept of consciousness had prevailed, the limits between conscious and unconscious being more or less clearly delineated, and consciousness was associated with a certain degree of brightness. Now, none of these premises could be maintained any longer. It became more and more evident that the quality of luminosity was not limited to the sphere of so-called consciousness. Likewise, investigations on individual states of consciousness and research on the unconscious—particularly on the luminous state of unconscious contents—necessitated a modified approach to the ideas of consciousness and self-consciousness. On the one hand, no

11 Ibid., p. 185.   12 Ibid., p. 187.

conscious states existed which, under certain circumstances, were not at the same time unconscious; on the other hand, there were no unconscious states which did not exhibit a minimal degree of brightness. Consequently, under certain conditions consciousness dominated, while in others the unconscious came to the fore.

> Between "I do this" and "I am conscious of doing this" there is a world of difference, amounting sometimes to outright contradiction.[13]

Seen from another angle, Jung recognized that consciousness displayed degrees of lucidity, which represented a kind of intermediate state between absolute "blackout" and the most intense brightness. States of pathological dissociation fell into this intermediate range, those split-off complexes which (as Janet had demonstrated earlier) exhibited certain personality characteristics; infantile and primitive attitudes were also included and, finally, archetypal formations. All these psychic contents showed some "luminosity" in spite of the absence of an ego nucleus and a reflexive capacity. In such processes of "approximative consciousness,"[14] as Jung designated them, a second ego-consciousness was out of the question, but they nevertheless were so pregnant with meaning as to resemble the quality of consciousness.

> And when we observe the psychic processes in the higher vertebrates and particularly in domestic animals, we find phenomena resembling consciousness which nevertheless do not allow us to conjecture the existence of an ego. As we know from direct experience, the light of consciousness has many degrees of brightness, and the ego-complex many gradations of emphasis. On the animal and primitive level there is a mere "luminosity," differing hardly at all from the glancing fragments of a dissociated ego. Here, as on the infantile level, consciousness is not a unity, being as yet uncentred by a firmly-knit ego-complex, and just flickering into life here and there wherever outer or inner events, instincts, and affects happen to call it awake. At this stage it is still like a chain of islands or an archipelago. Nor is it a fully integrated whole even at the higher and highest stages; rather, it is capable of indefinite expansion. . . . Therefore, we would do well to think of ego-consciousness as being surrounded by a multitude of little luminosities.[15]

These new observations constituted an unexpected scientific achievement which further advanced the modification of the earlier psychology of consciousness, which had equated consciousness with psyche. The

[13] Ibid.   [14] Ibid., p. 189.   [15] Ibid., pp. 189–90.

absolute dominance of consciousness had already become questionable with Freud's discovery of unconscious processes, but it was far more severely challenged by Jung in demonstrating the relative quality of consciousness.

C. THE PSYCHE AS A CONSCIOUS/UNCONSCIOUS WHOLE

The concept of the relativity of psychic phenomena culminated in the observation that the contents of consciousness were, as a rule, conscious only from a certain aspect, but unconscious from another. Jung drew attention to some paradoxical cases in which the individual, although clearly conscious of certain contents, was not aware that they were in fact unconscious in an essential respect and might even lead to disturbances in the unconscious psyche.[16] Jung formulated this observation in a way which, in the 1940's, had an extremely novel and exceedingly bewildering effect:

> So we come to the paradoxical conclusion that there is no conscious content which is not in some other respect unconscious.[17]

The contents of consciousness were, on principle, "at the same time conscious and unconscious." In other words, "the psyche is a conscious-unconscious whole."[18] William James had observed something similar with respect to phenomena close to consciousness, which he described as "fringe of consciousness."[19] Jung took a step beyond that by proceeding from the quality of relative consciousness to the assumption of mere luminosities, that is, degrees of minimally intense brightness which occasionally flared up. In summary, Jung observed that, parallel with the increasing dissociation of unconscious processes from the ego, a scale of intensity of consciousness extended from states of the most intense lucidity to those completely incapable of becoming conscious.

D. THE PSYCHOID-UNCONSCIOUS AS AN ACAUSAL ARRANGEMENT
IN PSYCHOLOGY AND PHYSICS

As noted earlier, the discovery of synchronistic phenomena sharpened Jung's understanding of new aspects in the background of the psyche. These observations unexpectedly showed that coincidences in time, in spite of their apparently incidental connection, presented far-reaching similarities in their meanings. These phenomena, however, could not be explained without expanding the psychological point of view. A relative concept of causality as well as of space and time[20] was required,

16 Ibid., p. 188.   17 Ibid.   18 Ibid., p. 200.
19 Ibid., p. 185.   20 Ibid., p. 231.

shifting the emphasis of these observations to a transcendental reality, that is, the reality of nonpsychic phenomena.[21] Jung assumed that only acausal arrangements of these indefinable contents could be established, since they were beyond conscious approach. He considered the archetype-as-such to be the principle which justified such organization because of its homogeneity and meaning. He saw in it a "living idea that constantly produces new interpretations."[22] In his opinion, the archetype-as-such was not only the imperceptible, *a priori* principle giving order to all ideas, but was completely integrated with the reality of that which was nonrepresentable and nonpsychic.

Jung gave great importance to the analogous ideas and thought patterns found in physics. Just as psychologists had advanced to the borderline phenomenon of the archetype-as-such, that is, to the principle of an *a priori* orderedness and distribution of data, physicists had established certain laws of probability related to acausal arrangements of physical factors. In order to explain various disturbances on the atomic level, caused by the presence of an observer, the physicist was forced to sacrifice the idea of causality. In the first place, problems arising from observations and from complementary circumstances (for example, the mutual exclusion of wave and particle in the theory of light) necessitated supplementing the idea of causality with statistical laws of nature. Both led to including the nonrepresentable in theoretical considerations.

In 1954, Pauli stressed the remarkable analogies between physical and psychological data, for instance, between the concepts of the "field" and the "unconscious." He also proposed extending the idea of causality in both branches of knowledge by presupposing universal connections in nature.

The "unconscious" has a certain analogy to the "field" in physics, and both psychology and physics, because of the observer situation, have essentially been forced into the areas of the non-representable and the paradoxical. In physics, no mention is made of self-reproducing "archetypes," but rather "statistical laws of nature with primary probabilities" are assumed; however, both formulations coincide in their tendency to extend the old narrow idea of "causality" (determinism) to a more general form of "organization" in nature—a premise which is also indicated by the psychophysical problem.[23]

21 Ibid., p. 384.
22 *Mysterium Coniunctionis* (1955/1956), p. 523.
23 Pauli, "Naturwissenschaftliche und erkenntnistheoretische Aspekte der Ideen vom Unbewussten" (1954). (Tr. F.E.E. and E.K.E.)

II. THE PSYCHE VIEWED FROM TRANSCENDENTAL FACTORS

The relationships between discoveries in physics and in depth psychology were brought up for discussion for the first time by C. A. Meier (1935). His essay also contained the bibliographical references necessary for an understanding of developments in physics.

Contemporary physics has, through the *creation of new ways of thinking*, discovered a kinship and connection with complex psychology, but it is hard to say which of the two disciplines should take greater pride in the other. Over many years of work in their separate fields, both branches of science have accumulated observations and have set up applicable systems of thought. Both have arrived at certain boundary lines . . . which in principle are similar. The *subject being investigated is indivisibly connected with man*—with all his sensory organs, his possibilities of understanding, and the extensions of these faculties that he has devised, such as measuring instruments and procedures. *These complementary factors are the same in physics and in psychology. The reaction of the one on the other* forms a reciprocal "symmetrical" relationship.[24]

In this same work Meier also commented:

When we examine any conscious content closely enough, we will soon encounter underlying unconscious motives. These premises are indispensable if we want to make cogent statements (or exact measurements). When these "unconscious" contents, however, are brought into consciousness, they will react upon the primary content of consciousness and *modify* it. Bringing unconscious material into consciousness also changes the unconscious contents while it modifies the conscious attitude; this interaction has its analogy in physics.[25]

Empirically, Jung's investigations of synchronicity largely confirmed Meier's earlier conjectures. They demonstrated the principle of reciprocity (complementarity) between conscious processes and phenomena of synchronicity. As Bavink pointed out, the term "complementarity" in general implies a relationship between scientific determinations, one factor limiting the validity of another. According to this finding, Jung could, for example, observe that synchronistic phenomena always occurred when psychic energy was drawn into the unconscious, as in a trance. However, the reverse could also be observed, synchronistic phenomena coming to an end at the moment when conscious

24 Meier, "Moderne Physik—Moderne Psychologie" (1935), p. 362. (Tr. F.E.E. and E.K.E.)
25 Ibid., pp. 359–60.

processes started. As a parallel to the complementary relationship between synchronicity and consciousness, Jung discovered an analogous relationship between the presence of neurotic symptoms and awareness of these symptoms. In other words, the symptoms disappeared when the contents reached the threshold of consciousness. Freud had recognized this fact early in his investigations but never connected it with the principle of complementary relationships. As far as could be determined from his writing, this idea (not the term, which only later was introduced into physics) appeared as early as *The Interpretation of Dreams*. In this work he drew attention to the relationship of memory and consciousness, in which one excluded the other.[26]

Jung was able to demonstrate another feature common to psychology and physics. Just as, in atomic physics, the observer caused uncontrollable effects on the observed system, the investigation of phenomena in the background of the psyche made it necessary to take the observer into consideration. Likewise, in psychology, the observing subject not only modified the phenomena in the background but, in addition, the psychoid-unconscious changed conscious results by its organizing effects. The presence of an observer limited the objectivity of the transcendental reality, that is, deflected it toward subjectivity; in the same way, the psychological approach gained an objective element under similar circumstances. In support of his concepts Jung cited a letter from the physicist Pauli, who had looked over his manuscript:

> As a matter of fact the physicist would expect a psychological correspondence at this point, because the epistemological situation with regard to the concepts "conscious" and "unconscious" seems to offer a pretty close analogy to the undermentioned "complementarity" situation in physics. On the one hand the unconscious can only be inferred indirectly from its (organizing) effects on conscious contents. . . . Thus the physicist will conclude *per analogiam* that this uncontrollable reactive effect of the observing subject on the unconscious limits the objective character of the latter's reality and lends it at the same time a certain subjectivity.[27]

Jung saw a paradoxical situation in psychology, similar to that in physics. All intellectual models drawn from the nonpsychic background contained an indeterminant factor; in one respect they appeared to be objective, yet more subjective in another. Jung maintained this point of view in all references to matters which transcended the perceptible.

26 Freud, *The Interpretation of Dreams* (1900), p. 538.
27 "On the Nature of the Psyche," p. 229, n. 130.

The reality underlying the unconscious effects includes the observing subject and is therefore constituted in a way that we cannot conceive. It is, at one and the same time, absolute subjectivity and universal truth, for in principle it can be shown to be present everywhere. . . . The elusiveness, capriciousness, haziness, and uniqueness that the lay mind always associates with the idea of the psyche applies only to consciousness, and not to the absolute unconscious.[28]

From such data Jung drew the remarkable conclusion that the so-called "archetypes . . . have a nature that cannot with certainty be designated as psychic."[29]

The indeterminant factor inherent in transcendental reality made any claim to perceptibility untenable. While scientific instrumentation expanded the area of physical phenomena considerably, the ideas expressed above referred only to the individual's fantasies, images, and thoughts. Jung himself never doubted the existence of transcendental reality, but he considered it to be self-evident that all models of it were incommensurable with intellectual constructs or judgment.

The existence of a transcendental reality is indeed evident in itself, but it is uncommonly difficult for our consciousness to construct intellectual models which would give a graphic description of the reality we have perceived. Our hypotheses are uncertain and groping, and nothing offers us the assurance that they may ultimately prove correct.[30]

The limited possibility of perceiving the transcendental background applied equally to the inner and the outer worlds.

That the world inside and outside ourselves rests on a transcendental background is as certain as our own existence, but it is equally certain that the direct perception of the archetypal world inside us is just as doubtfully correct as that of the physical world outside us.[31]

The scientific approach could only follow the path which physics had taken before: to eliminate indeterminate factors by formulating laws of probability, or correlations between subjective and certain acausal factors. However, a metaphysical approach, aiming at a possible meaning of wholeness, would not prevent the construction of models related to the nature of the transcendental, as long as no claim of scientific validity crept in.

28 Ibid., p. 230.   29 Ibid.
30 *Mysterium*, p. 551.   31 Ibid., p. 481.

Jung doubted that an objective intellectual judgment on the transcendental background of the psyche could ever be reached, but he always upheld the subjective value of an image or simile in so far as it conveyed the meaning and importance of the background's numinous quality. He, therefore, did not hesitate to construct models clarifying the complementary relationship between physics and psychology, on the one hand, and matter and spirit on the other. Such models, however, could never be regarded as truths; they were important only in their function of raising "useful questions."

Starting from the surprising phenomenon of coincidences with a like meaning, Jung found it helpful to use a model in which the transcendental reality was conceived as a kind of imperceptible space-time continuum, that is, "a space-time continuum in which space is no longer space, nor time time."[32] On the other hand, the space-time continuum was split into a duality of physical and psychic events. Yet, because of the indeterminate factor in the effects of the background reality which blurred the boundary line between objective and subjective, it was equally possible, and perhaps even more probable, that matter and psyche could constitute two aspects of one and the same reality.

> Since psyche and matter are contained in one and the same world, and moreover are in continuous contact with one another and ultimately rest on irrepresentable, transcendental factors, it is not only possible but fairly probable, even, that psyche and matter are two different aspects of one and the same thing. The synchronicity phenomena point, it seems to me, in this direction, for they show that the nonpsychic can behave like the psychic, and vice versa, without there being any causal connection between them. Our present knowledge does not allow us to do much more than compare the relation of the psychic to the material world with two cones, whose apices, meeting in a point without extension—a real zero-point—touch and do not touch.[33]

About ten years later Jung, in complete agreement with the alchemists, developed a conceptual model: "The background of our empirical world . . . appears to be in fact a *unus mundus*"[34] which consisted of the "identity of the psychic and the physical."[35] This conjecture—that matter and psyche form the two aspects of the transcendental background of our empirical reality—may be regarded as the end of Jung's metaphysical deliberations. They represent not

32 "Synchronicity," p. 481. 33 "On the Nature of the Psyche," p. 215.
34 *Mysterium*, p. 538. 35 Ibid., p. 537.

so much well-founded results as prospective solutions of the problems of analytical psychology.

3. Freud and Transcendental Reality

The term "transcendental" is meant to cover a nonpsychic factor to which is ascribed an objective meaning, even though it cannot be rationally explained[36] nor psychologically interpreted. It should not, then, be too difficult to appraise Freud's position as to the reality of the transcendental and the spiritual-as-such. It would be completely wrong to say that he entertained no assumptions of transcending qualities.

Still, Freud's writings show that the transcending quality he recognized was exclusively drive-as-such, even lifeless matter-as-such. A truly spiritual, transcendental meaning was foreign to him. Ultimately, beyond the psychic reality, was the body with its demands. Freud saw it as the true carrier of psychic processes. He even did not hesitate, as he said in 1920, to recognize the beginning and the end of everything alive in inorganic-lifeless matter. He never used the term "transcendental" but rather "metapsychic" in order to establish a boundary line between that and metaphysics.

> I believe that a large part of the mythological view of the world, which extends a long way into the most modern religions, *is nothing but psychology projected into the external world.* The obscure recognition . . . of psychical factors and relations in the unconscious is mirrored . . . in the construction of a *supernatural reality*, which is destined to be changed back once more by science into the *psychology of the unconscious.* One could venture to explain in this way the myths of paradise and the fall of man, of God, of good and evil, of immortality, and so on, and to transform *metaphysics* into *metapsychology.*[37]

Freud was very outspoken in declining to accept the description of the unconscious as psychoid,[38] because this term would presuppose too great a discrepancy between consciousness and the unconscious. For him, not only the life- and death-drives had a metapsychical nature, but also the so-called principle of constancy, which he understood—

---

[36] "A Psychological Approach to the Dogma of the Trinity" (1940–41/1948), p. 140.
[37] Freud, *The Psychopathology of Everyday Life* (1901), pp. 258–59.
[38] "The Ego and the Id" (1923), p. 15.

according to Fechner's principle of stability[39]—as a tendency to inertia, the return of the psychic apparatus to "zero" (1895).[40]

Freud's reference to the metapsychic was in no way intended to draw a boundary line between the recognizable and the unrecognizable. In spite of imputing to unconscious (repressed) processes a relative incapability of becoming conscious, he maintained that they were, in principle, discernible, even though this depended on certain conditions (return of the repressed and working through resistance). He thought he had found the prerequisite for recognizing unconscious processes in the typical features of neurosis and dream—that is, regression of the libido to earlier stages of development and their consequences.[41] Bringing such consequences of early childhood fixations to consciousness was largely equated with recognizing the unconscious. However, we should not overlook the single exception which Freud allowed: primal repression, which could not be cathected and consequently remained unrecognizable.

There is no doubt that Freud saw organic and somatic matter (products of metabolism, sexual hormones, "chemical forces of sexuality") as substances existing as such. It is just as certain that he never recognized the archetype or spirit-as-such. When he used the term "Geist," it might mean psyche, intellectual interest, or "ruach" (breath of wind). In every instance, "Geist" was in direct opposition to the physical world, that is, to what could be perceived by the eye. Therefore, neither his assumption of primary repressed contents nor his hypothesis of archaic inheritance could be interpreted to indicate anything nonpsychic. Even though Freud conceived the primary repressed as a level which, by its very nature, was incapable of being brought to consciousness, he still believed that it could be reduced to constantly renewed emotional states and to repetition compulsion, showing that it was exclusively drive-conditioned and, in the final analysis, not spiritual in character.

The concept of archaic inheritance, too, was in no way related to a transcendental reality, much less to anything spiritual-as-such. On the contrary, it had an historical quality, recalling the precipitate of experiences of early man, "memory-traces of the experience of earlier generations."[42] Freud even traced it ultimately to memories of the "historic" event of the killing of the primal father.

39 "Beyond the Pleasure Principle" (1920), p. 9.
40 "Project for a Scientific Psychology" (1895), in *The Origins of Psycho-Analysis*, p. 358.
41 "The Unconscious" (1915), pp. 175–76.
42 "Moses and Monotheism: Three Essays" (1937/1939), p. 99.

But could not the superego be said to have a spiritual quality, could it not be viewed as representing a spiritual category? Freud's description of the superego as supporting the categorical imperative and man's striving for perfection and higher aims,[43] certainly makes a positive interpretation possible. Yet, some doubts are bound to arise when one learns that this superior agency in man represented an introjection of the castration threat by the father and was the nucleus around which fear of conscience focused.[44] The defenses imposed by parental authority or by society against all feelings of lust, life, and drive were embodied in the castration threat—not only that, but this threat resulted in the negation of drives, regarded as an absolute principle. Once moral demands became absolute, the superego, that principle of morality, turned suddenly into an agency inimical to life, which sometimes, as Freud pointed out, might give rise to highly immoral acts.[45] The destructive aspect of the superego became especially apparent in relation to the aggressive- and death-drives. Its origin from introjecting paternal authority was not only connected to the threat of castration but also to the aggressive tendency originally associated with the father; this tormented the individual with anxiety and the threat of punishment and finally entangled him in guilt feelings. In Freud's view, the aggressiveness of conscience continues the aggressiveness of authority,[46] forcing the individual into an incessant attitude of defense. He even went so far as to see in melancholia— which he considered the high point of the life-destroying activity of the superego—an increasing aggressive tendency, culminating in a pure culture of the death instinct.[47] Instead of being a principle of morality, the superego turned into an immoral agency. Instead of expressing an objective-spiritual background, it became a subjectively toned evil spirit. The harshness of the superego, growing evermore aggressive the more control the individual exerted on his overt aggressiveness,[48] placed him in a position of constraint which doomed an ethical solution of his conflicts.

The Logos,[49] which Freud extolled in 1927, was only a meager substitute for transcendental reality. In so far as Freud recognized in it a tool of the ego which essentially served in renouncing and controlling drives, the Logos presented not only a rational force but also a power based deep in the human personality. The further function of the ego,

---

[43] *New Introductory Lectures on Psycho-Analysis* (1933), p. 65.
[44] "The Ego and the Id," p. 57.   [45] Ibid., p. 52.
[46] "Civilization and Its Discontents" (1930), p. 123.
[47] "The Ego and the Id," p. 53.   [48] Ibid., p. 54.
[49] "The Future of an Illusion" (1927), p. 54.

"education to reality,"[50] pointed more to a limitation of the personality than to openness toward something greater. Freud assumed that the aim of securing a relationship to reality could be effected only through sacrifice of restriction, that is, by the ego restricting its own organization.[51] I believe that we can unhesitatingly interpret this attitude as a refutation of the principle of the greater and more constructive aspect of the human psyche. In the final analysis, Freud offered the individual subjection under the ascetic principle of self-restriction and drive negation. In any case, recognition of the reality of a suprapersonal meaning was lacking. This statement applied, as mentioned earlier, also to the religious ideas which Freud traced back to the father complex.

> Psycho-analysis has made us familiar with the intimate connection between the father-complex and belief in God; it has shown us that a personal God is, psychologically, nothing other than an exalted father, and it brings us evidence every day of how young people lose their religious beliefs as soon as their father's authority breaks down. Thus we recognize that the roots of the need for religion are in the parental complex; the almighty and just God, and kindly Nature, appear to us as grand sublimations of father and mother, or rather as revivals and restorations of the young child's ideas of them. Biologically speaking, religiousness is to be traced to the small human child's long-drawn-out helplessness and need of help; and when at a later date he perceives how truly forlorn and weak he is when confronted with the great forces of life, he feels his condition as he did in childhood, and attempts to deny his own despondency by a regressive revival of the forces which protected his infancy. The protection against neurotic illness, which religion vouchsafes to those who believe in it, is easily explained; it removes their parental complex, on which the sense of guilt in individuals as well as in the human race depends, and disposes of it, while the unbeliever has to grapple with the problem on his own.[52]

One cannot help but be impressed with Freud's intention to exclude from psychoanalysis everything that bordered on an impersonal aspect of the spirit—an attempt, however, which did not completely succeed. Freud, notwithstanding his defense of the scientific basis of psychoanalysis, was always secretly attracted by the phenomena of occultism.[53] He was excited by Charcot's pronouncement that possession by the

---

50 Ibid., p. 49.
51 "Inhibitions, Symptoms and Anxiety" (1926), p. 91.
52 "Leonardo da Vinci and a Memory of His Childhood" (1910), p. 123.
53 Jones, *The Life and Work of Sigmund Freud.* Vol. III, pp. 375–407.

devil in the Middle Ages was caused by hysterical phenomena.[54] He also connected anal eroticism with hysterical possession and demoniac epidemics;[55] he described the "uncanny," which he had observed in the repetition compulsion and in reactions to the persistent recurrence of certain situations[56]—for example, repeatedly encountering the same number, possibly 62.[57] Finally, he acknowledged the phenomena of thought transmission and telepathy. What he initially had rejected as occult, he later accepted as an objective possibility,[58] with probably "a real core of yet unrecognized facts."[59]

> Psycho-analysis cannot give a direct answer to the question that no doubt interests you the most—whether we are to believe in the objective reality of these findings. But the material revealed by its help makes an impression which is at all events favourable to an affirmative reply.[60]

A little later Freud made the following statement:

> If one regards oneself as a sceptic, it is a good plan to have occasional doubts about one's scepticism too. It may be that I too have a secret inclination towards the miraculous which thus goes half way to meet the creation of occult facts.[61]

In spite of recognizing a core of reality in the amazing phenomenon of occultism, Freud placed it outside of scientific research. His concession that "the theory of instincts is so to say our mythology,"[62] made just as little change in his basic scientific assumptions. The phenomena of the drives and their causes at all times referred to concrete data, either biological or historical. This approach obscured his view of the impersonal and suprapersonal aspects of the nucleus of significance, which alone would have conferred the dignity of deeper human qualities to the drive processes. Anyone who considers the question of a transcendental spirit-as-such finds Freud's work lacking the recognition of an objective meaning within the metapsychical background of the drives. Reducing the higher and more inspiring aspects of the psyche to wish, urge, and drive led to a great danger of life becoming demoniac. This was the unavoidable end result of an attitude which ruled out the presence of a numinous quality. Such a process, that is, the life of

54 Freud, "Charcot" (1893), p. 20.
55 "Character and Anal Eroticism" (1908), p. 174.
56 "The 'Uncanny'" (1919), p. 236.   57 Ibid., pp. 237–38.
58 New Introductory Lectures on Psycho-Analysis, p. 54.
59 Ibid., p. 36.   60 Ibid., p. 47.
61 Ibid., p. 53.   62 Ibid., p. 95.

an individual becoming demoniac, stood out clearly in Freud's essay "A Seventeenth-Century Demonological Neurosis" (1923). In this work, Freud interpreted the highly interesting phenomenon of a pact with the devil as a substitute-formation for the subject's ambivalent relationship either to the father or to the deity. Tracing this neurosis to a misguided relationship with the *numinosum* shows that, willy-nilly, the inescapable danger of life becoming demoniac is present if one disregards the archetype of the self.

III. CONCLUDING REMARKS

In contrast to the pessimistic turn shown in Freud's later work, Jung's psychology is incomparably more optimistic and constructive. In trying to achieve an adequate understanding of the suffering individual, he again and again raised the question of the meaning of human existence. In his discussions of the spirit-as-such and the archetype of the self, he pursued this central problem to the very boundaries set by the human condition. In formulating the transcendent essence which cannot be expressed in words, he resorted to image and simile. Aniela Jaffé gave beautiful expression to Jung's idea when she described the myth as a form of thought which attempts to answer that for which there is no answer.[1]

The psychology of C. G. Jung can remove neither the individual's insecurity nor his anxiety and uncertainty of his destiny; but, by directing him to his own experience, it can provide him with an idea of "what basically holds the world together." This may be a great deal or very little. It is very much, compared to the dark spirit which holds man captive in blind desperation; but it contributes little toward that certainty which only the charisma of faith can provide. Psychology is just as little a substitute for religion as personal experience is a replacement for knowledge through faith. However, the great significance of psychology is to enable the individual to understand the opposites within himself and to help him bear his destined limitations.

[1] Jaffé, *The Myth of Meaning in the Work of C. G. Jung* (1968).

BIBLIOGRAPHY

Abbreviations

Freud, SE = The Standard Edition. See below.
Jahrb. = *Jahrbuch für psychoanalytische und psychopathologische Forschungen.*
Jung, CW = The Collected Works. See below.

The Collected Editions in English

The Standard Edition of the Complete Psychological Works of Sigmund Freud. Translated from the German under the general editorship of James Strachey, in collaboration with Anna Freud, assisted by Alix Strachey, Alan Tyson, and Angela Richards. London: The Hogarth Press and the Institute of Psycho-Analysis. / New York: distributed by Macmillan. 1953–.

I. Pre-Psycho-Analytic Publications and Unpublished Drafts (1886–1899)
II. Studies on Hysteria (1893–1895)
III. Early Psycho-Analytic Publications (1893–1899)
IV. The Interpretation of Dreams (I) (1900)
V. The Interpretation of Dreams (II) and On Dreams (1900–1901)
VI. The Psychopathology of Everyday Life (1901)
VII. A Case of Hysteria, Three Essays on Sexuality and Other Works (1901–1905)
VIII. Jokes and their Relation to the Unconscious (1905)
IX. Jensen's "Gradiva" and Other Works (1906–1908)
X. The Cases of "Little Hans" and the "Rat Man" (1909)
XI. Five Lectures on Psycho-Analysis, Leonardo and Other Works (1910)
XII. Case History of Schreber, Papers on Technique and Other Works (1911–1913)
XIII. Totem and Taboo and Other Works (1913–1914)
XIV. A History of the Psycho-Analytic Movement, Papers on Metapsychology and Other Works (1914–1916)
XV. Introductory Lectures on Psycho-Analysis (Parts I and II) (1915–1916)
XVI. Introductory Lectures on Psycho-Analysis (Part III) (1916–1917)
XVII. An Infantile Neurosis and Other Works (1917–1919)
XVIII. Beyond the Pleasure Principle, Group Psychology and Other Works (1920–1922)

XIX. The Ego and the Id and Other Works (1923–1925)

XX. An Autobiographical Study, Inhibitions, Symptoms and Anxiety, Lay Analysis and Other Works (1925–1926)

XXI. The Future of an Illusion, Civilization and Its Discontents and Other Works (1927–1931)

XXII. New Introductory Lectures on Psycho-Analysis and Other Works (1932–1936)

XXIII. Moses and Monotheism, An Outline of Psycho-Analysis and Other Works (1937–1939)

XXIV. Indexes, Bibliography, etc.

The Collected Works of C. G. Jung. Editors: Sir Herbert Read, Michael Fordham, Gerhard Adler; William McGuire, executive editor. Translated from the German by R.F.C. Hull (except Vol. 2). Princeton, N.J.: Princeton University Press (Bollingen Series). / London: Routledge & Kegan Paul. 1953– .

1. Psychiatric Studies (1902–1906)

2. Experimental Researches (1904–1910) (tr. Leopold Stein in collaboration with Diana Riviere)

3. The Psychogenesis of Mental Disease (1907–1914; 1919–1958)

4. Freud and Psychoanalysis (1906–1914; 1916–1930)

5. Symbols of Transformation (1911–1912; 1952)

6. Psychological Types (1921)

7. Two Essays on Analytical Psychology (1912–1928)

8. The Structure and Dynamics of the Psyche (1916–1952)

9.i. The Archetypes and the Collective Unconscious (1934–1955)

9.ii. Aion: Researches into the Phenomenology of the Self (1951)

10. Civilization in Transition (1918–1959)

11. Psychology and Religion: West and East (1932–1952)

12. Psychology and Alchemy (1936–1944)

13. Alchemical Studies (1929–1945)

14. Mysterium Coniunctionis (1955–1956)

15. The Spirit in Man, Art, and Literature (1929–1941)

16. The Practice of Psychotherapy (1921–1951)

17. The Development of Personality (1910; 1925–1943)

18. The Symbolic Life (miscellany)

19. Bibliography and General Index

Abraham, K. (1909): *Dreams and Myths: A Study in Folk-Psychology.* Tr. H. C. Abraham and D. R. Ellison. London: The Hogarth Press, 1955.

—— (1914): A review of C. G. Jung's "Versuch einer Darstellung der psychoanalytischen Theorie" (Attempt at a Representation of Psychoanalytical Theory). In H. C. Abraham, ed.: *Clinical Papers and Essays on Psycho-Analysis.* Tr. H. C. Abraham and D. R. Ellison. London: The Hogarth Press and the Institute of Psycho-Analysis, 1955.

Adler, A. (1907): *Study of Organ Inferiority and Its Psychical Compensation.* Tr. S. E. Jelliffe. New York: Nervous & Mental Disease Publishing Co., 1917.

—— (1912): *The Neurotic Constitution.* Tr. B. Glueck and J. E. Lind. New York: Moffat, Yard & Co., 1917.

Aschaffenburg, G. (1896): "Experimentelle Studien über Assoziationen," in E. Kraepelin, ed.: *Psychologische Arbeiten*, I, Leipzig.

Bleuler, E. (1904): "Upon the Significance of Association Experiments," in Jung, ed.: *Studies in Word-Association.* Tr. M. D. Eder. London: Heinemann, 1918. (Reprinted: Routledge & Kegan Paul, 1969.)

—— (1911): *Dementia Praecox or the Group of Schizophrenias.* Tr. J. Zinkin. New York: International Universities Press, 1950.

—— (1910): "Die Psychoanalyse Freuds," *Jahrb. u. psychopathol. Forsch.*, 2:623–731.

Breuer, J., and Freud, S. (1893–95): *Studies on Hysteria.* SE 2.

Dalbiez, R. (1941): *Psychoanalytical Method and the Doctrine of Freud.* Vol. I. Tr. T. F. Lindsay. London: Longmans, Green & Co.

Dement, W. (1960): "The Effect of Dream Deprivation," *Science*, 131:1705–1707.

Dorer, M. (1932): *Historische Grundlagen der Psychoanalyse.* Leipzig: Meiner.

Evans, R., ed. (1964): *Conversations with Carl Jung and Reactions from Ernest Jones.* Princeton, N.J.: D. Van Nostrand Co., Inc.

Fechner, G. T. (1860): *Elements of Psychophysics.* Tr. H. E. Adler. New York: Holt, Rinehart & Winston, 1966.

Ferenczi, S. (1913): "Kritik der Jungschen Wandlungen und Symbole der Libido," *Internat. Z. f. ärztl. Psychoanal.*, 1:391–403.

Freud, S. (1887–1902): *The Origins of Psycho-Analysis.* Tr. E. Mosbacher and J. Strachey. New York: Basic Books, 1954.

Freud, S. (1891): *On Aphasia*. Tr. E. Stengel. New York: International Universities Press, 1953.

―――― (1893): "Charcot," SE 3.

―――― (1893): "Some Points for a Comparative Study of Organic and Hysterical Motor Paralyses," SE 1.

―――― (1893): "On the Psychical Mechanism of Hysterical Phenomena," SE 3.

―――― (1894): "The Neuro-Psychoses of Defence," SE 3.

―――― (1895): "On the Grounds for Detaching a Particular Syndrome from Neurasthenia under the Description 'Anxiety Neurosis,' " SE 3.

―――― (1895): "Project for a Scientific Psychology," in *Origins*, supra.

―――― (1896): "Heredity and the Aetiology of the Neuroses," SE 3.

―――― (1896): "Further Remarks on the Neuro-Psychoses of Defence," SE 3.

―――― (1896): "The Aetiology of Hysteria," SE 3.

―――― (1898): "Sexuality in the Aetiology of the Neuroses," SE 3.

―――― (1899): "Screen Memories," SE 3.

―――― (1900): *The Interpretation of Dreams*, SE 4 and 5.

―――― (1901): *The Psychopathology of Everyday Life*, SE 6.

―――― (1903–4): "Freud's Psycho-Analytic Procedure," SE 7.

―――― (1905): "Three Essays on the Theory of Sexuality," SE 7.

―――― (1906): "My Views on the Part Played by Sexuality in the Aetiology of the Neuroses," SE 7.

―――― (1906): "Psycho-Analysis and the Establishment of the Facts in Legal Proceedings," SE 9.

―――― (1906): *Collection of Shorter Writings on the Theory of the Neuroses from the Years 1893–1906*. Mostly in SE 3.

―――― (1907): "Delusions and Dreams in Jensen's *Gradiva*," SE 9.

―――― (1908): "Character and Anal Eroticism," SE 9.

―――― (1908): "Creative Writers and Day-Dreaming," SE 9.

―――― (1908): " 'Civilized' Sexual Morality and Modern Nervous Illness," SE 9.

―――― (1908): "On the Sexual Theories of Children," SE 9.

―――― (1909): "Analysis of a Phobia in a Five-Year-Old Boy," SE 10.

―――― (1910): "Five Lectures on Psycho-Analysis," SE 11.

―――― (1910): "Leonardo da Vinci and a Memory of His Childhood," SE 11.

―――― (1911): "Formulations on the Two Principles of Mental Functioning," SE 12.

―――― (1911): "Psycho-Analytic Notes on an Autobiographical Account of a Case of Paranoia (Dementia Paranoides)," SE 12.

―――― (1912): "The Dynamics of Transference," SE 12.

———— (1913): "The Claims of Psycho-Analysis to Scientific Interest," SE 13.

———— (1913): "A Note on the Unconscious in Psycho-Analysis," SE 12.

———— (1913): "The Disposition to Obsessional Neurosis. A Contribution to the Problem of Choice of Neurosis," SE 12.

———— (1913): "Totem and Taboo," SE 13.

———— (1914): "Remembering, Repeating and Working-Through," SE 12.

———— (1914): "On Narcissism: An Introduction," SE 14.

———— (1915): "The Unconscious," SE 14.

———— (1915): "Instincts and Their Vicissitudes," SE 14.

———— (1915): "Repression," SE 14.

———— (1915): "A Case of Paranoia Running Counter to the Psycho-Analytic Theory of the Disease," SE 14.

———— (1915–17): *Introductory Lectures on Psycho-Analysis*, SE 15 and 16.

———— (1917): "A Metapsychological Supplement to the Theory of Dreams," SE 14.

———— (1918): "From the History of an Infantile Neurosis," SE 17.

———— (1919): "The 'Uncanny,' " SE 17.

———— (1919): Introduction to "Psycho-Analysis and the War Neuroses," SE 17.

———— (1920): "A Note on the Prehistory of the Technique of Analysis," SE 18.

———— (1920): "Beyond the Pleasure Principle," SE 18.

———— (1922–23): Two Encyclopaedia Articles. (A) Psycho-Analysis, SE 18.

———— (1923): "The Ego and the Id," SE 19.

———— (1923): "The Infantile Genital Organization," SE 19.

———— (1923): "A Seventeenth-Century Demonological Neurosis," SE 19.

———— (1924): "The Loss of Reality in Neurosis and Psychosis," SE 19.

———— (1924): "Neurosis and Psychosis," SE 19.

———— (1925): "An Autobiographical Study," SE 20.

———— (1926): "Psycho-Analysis," SE 20.

———— (1926): "Inhibitions, Symptoms and Anxiety," SE 20.

———— (1927): "The Future of an Illusion," SE 21.

———— (1930): "Civilization and Its Discontents," SE 21.

———— (1933): *New Introductory Lectures on Psycho-Analysis*, SE 22.

———— (1937): "Analysis Terminable and Interminable," SE 23.

———— (1937): "Constructions in Analysis," SE 23.

Freud, S. (1938): "An Outline of Psycho-Analysis," SE 23.

────── (1938): "Some Elementary Lessons in Psycho-Analysis," SE 23.

────── (1938): "Splitting of the Ego in the Process of Defence," SE 23.

────── (1939): "Moses and Monotheism: Three Essays," SE 23.

────── (1950): *The Origins of Psycho-Analysis, 1887–1902.* Tr. E. Mosbacher and J. Strachey. New York: Basic Books, 1954.

────── and C. G. Jung (1974): *The Freud / Jung Letters,* ed. W. McGuire, tr. R. Manheim and R.F.C. Hull. Princeton University Press (Bollingen Series).

Frey-Rohn, L. (1955): "Die Anfänge der Tiefenpsychologie," in *Studien zur analytischen Psychologie C. G. Jungs,* I. Zurich: Rascher.

────── (1961): "Evil from the Psychological Point of View," in *Evil: Essays by Carl Kerényi and Others,* tr. R. Manheim and H. Nagel. Evanston, Ill.: Northwestern University Press, 1967.

──────: *Jenseits der Werte seiner Zeit: Friedrich Nietzsche im Spiegel seiner Werke.* Zurich: Daimon Verlag, 1984. Tr., *Friedrich Nietzsche: A Psychological Approach to His Life and Work.* Einsiedeln: Daimon Verlag, 1988, 1989.

────── (1971): "The Shadow Revealed in the Works of Friedrich Nietzsche," in H. Kirsch, ed., *The Well-Tended Tree.* New York: C. G. Jung Foundation (G. P. Putnam's Sons).

Frey-Wehrlin, C. T. (1963): "Probleme der Traumdeutung," in C. A. Meier, ed., *Traum und Symbol.* Zurich / Stuttgart: Rascher.

Glover, E. (1950): *Freud or Jung.* London: George Allen & Unwin.

Jacobi, J. (1957): *Complex, Archetype, Symbol in the Psychology of C. G. Jung.* Tr. R. Manheim. New York: Pantheon Books (Bollingen Series) 1959.

Jaffé, A. (1968): *The Myth of Meaning in the Work of C. G. Jung.* Tr. R.F.C. Hull. Zurich: Daimon Verlag, 1984, 1986.

Herbart, J. F. (1816): *A Text-book in Psychology.* Tr. M. K. Smith. New York: D. Appleton & Co., 1895.

Janet, P. (1898): *Névroses et idées fixes,* Vol. I. Paris: Félix Alcan.

Jones, E. (1953, 1955, 1957): *The Life and Work of Sigmund Freud.* 3 vols. New York: Basic Books.

Jung, C. G. (1902): "On the Psychology and Pathology of So-Called Occult Phenomena," CW 1.

────── (1903): "On Simulated Insanity," CW 1.

────── (1905): "Cryptomnesia," CW 1.

────── (1905): "On the Psychological Diagnosis of Facts," CW 1.

────── and Riklin, F. (1906): "The Associations of Normal Subjects," CW 2.

────── (1906): "The Reaction-time Ratio in the Association Experiment," CW 2.

—— (1906): "Freud's Theory of Hysteria," CW 4.

—— (1907): "The Psychology of Dementia Praecox," CW 3.

—— (1908): "The Content of the Psychoses," CW 3.

—— (1908): "The Freudian Theory of Hysteria," CW 4.

—— (1909/1949): "The Significance of the Father in the Destiny of the Individual," CW 4.

—— (1909): "The Analysis of Dreams," CW 4.

—— (1909/1946): "Psychic Conflicts in a Child," CW 17.

—— (1911): "Morton Prince, 'The Mechanism and Interpretation of Dreams': A Critical Review," CW 4.

—— (1912): *Psychology of the Unconscious* (= *Wandlungen und Symbole der Libido* [*Transformations and Symbols of the Libido*], 1911–12). Tr. B. M. Hinkle. New York: Moffat Yard, 1916.

—— (1912): "New Paths in Psychology," CW 7 (2nd edn.).

—— (1913): "The Theory of Psychoanalysis," CW 4.

—— (1913): "General Aspects of Psychoanalysis," CW 4.

—— (1913): "A Contribution to the Study of Psychological Types," CW 6.

—— (1914): "Some Crucial Points in Psychoanalysis: A Correspondence Between Dr. Jung and Dr. Loÿ," CW 4.

—— (1914): "On the Importance of the Unconscious in Psychopathology," CW 3.

—— (1914): "On Psychological Understanding," CW 3.

—— (1916/1958): "The Transcendent Function," CW 8.

—— (1916): "The Structure of the Unconscious," CW 7 (2nd edn.).

—— (1916/1928/1948): "General Aspects of Dream Psychology," CW 8.

—— (1916/1935/1938): "The Relations Between the Ego and the Unconscious," CW 7 (2nd edn.).

—— (1916/1917): Prefaces to "Collected Papers on Analytical Psychology," CW 4.

—— (1917): "The Psychology of Unconscious Processes," in *Collected Papers on Analytical Psychology*. New York and London, 2nd edn., 1917. Revised as the following.

—— (1917/1926/1943): "On the Psychology of the Unconscious," CW 7 (2nd edn.).

—— (1919): "Instinct and the Unconscious," CW 8.

—— (1919): "On the Problem of Psychogenesis in Mental Disease," CW 3.

—— (1920): "The Psychology Foundations of Belief in Spirits," CW 8.

—— (1906): "Psychoanalysis and Association Experiments," CW 2.

—— (1906): "Association, Dream, and Hysterical Symptom," CW 2.

Jung, C. G. (1921): "The Therapeutic Value of Abrecation," CW 16 (2nd edn.).

—— (1921): *Psychological Types*, CW 6.

—— (1924/1926): "Analytical Psychology and Education," CW 17.

—— (1926): "Spirit and Life," CW 8.

—— (1927/1931): "Analytical Psychology and *Weltanschauung*," CW 8.

—— (1928): "On Psychic Energy," CW 8.

—— (1928): "The Structure of the Psyche," CW 8.

—— (1928): "Mental Disease and the Psyche," CW 3.

—— (1928): "A Psychological Theory of Types," CW 6.

—— (1929): "Freud and Jung: Contrasts," CW 4.

—— (1929): "The Aims of Psychotherapy," CW 16 (2nd edn.).

—— (1929): "Problems of Modern Psychotherapy," CW 16 (2nd edn.).

—— (1929): "Some Aspects of Modern Psychotherapy," CW 16 (2nd edn.).

—— (1930): "The Stages of Life," CW 8.

—— (1931): "Basic Postulates of Analytical Psychology," CW 8.

—— (1931/1934): "The Practical Use of Dream-Analysis," CW 16 (2nd edn.).

—— (1932): "Sigmund Freud in His Historical Setting," CW 15.

—— (1932): "The Development of Personality," CW 17.

—— (1933): "Brother Klaus," CW 11.

—— (1933): "The Meaning of Psychology for Modern Man," CW 10.

—— (1934/1954): "Archetypes of the Collective Unconscious," CW 9, i.

—— (1934): "The Soul and Death," CW 8.

—— (1934): "A Review of the Complex Theory," CW 8.

—— (1935/1953): Psychological Commentary on *The Tibetan Book of the Dead*, CW 11.

—— (1936): "Psychological Typology," CW 6.

—— (1935/1944): "Individual Dream Symbolism in Relation to Alchemy," CW 12 (2nd edn.).

—— (1936/1954): "Concerning the Archetypes, with Special Reference to the Anima Concept," CW 9, i.

—— (1936): "Yoga and the West," CW 11.

—— (1936): "Psychological Factors Determining Human Behaviour," CW 8.

—— (1937/1940): "Psychology and Religion," CW 11.

—— (1938–39): "Seminar über Kinderträume," I. (Unpublished.)

—— (1939): "On the Psychogenesis of Schizophrenia," CW 3.

—— (1939): "Conscious, Unconscious and Individuation," CW 9, i.

—— (1939): "In Memory of Sigmund Freud," CW 15.

—————— (1939): "Psychological Commentary on the *Tibetan Book of the Great Liberation*," CW 11.

—————— (1939–40): "Seminar über Kinderträume," II. (Unpublished.)

—————— (1940–41/1948): "A Psychological Approach to the Dogma of the Trinity," CW 11.

—————— (1940–41/1954): "Transformation Symbolism in the Mass," CW 11.

—————— (1941): "The Psychology of the Child Archetype," CW 9, i.

—————— (1941): "The Psychological Aspects of the Kore," CW 9, i.

—————— (1942): "Paracelsus as a Spiritual Phenomenon," CW 13.

—————— (1944): *Psychology and Alchemy*, CW 12 (2nd edn.).

—————— (1945): "Psychotherapy Today," CW 16 (2nd edn.).

—————— (1945/1948): "On the Nature of Dreams," CW 8.

—————— (1945): "Medicine and Psychotherapy," CW 16 (2nd edn.).

—————— (1946): "The Psychology of the Transference," CW 16 (2nd edn.).

—————— (1946): "On the Nature of the Psyche," CW 8.

—————— (1951): *Aion*, CW 9, ii.

—————— (1952): *Symbols of Transformation*, CW 5. Revision of *Transformations and Symbols of the Libido* (1911–12).

—————— (1952): "Synchronicity: An Acausal Connecting Principle," CW 8.

—————— (1952/1956): "Answer to Job," CW 11.

—————— (1955–56): *Mysterium Coniunctionis*, CW 14.

—————— (1957/1959): "Recent Thoughts on Schizophrenia," CW 3.

—————— (1958): "Schizophrenia," CW 3.

—————— (1958): "Flying Saucers: A Modern Myth of Things Seen in the Skies," CW 10.

—————— (1958): "A Psychological View of Conscience," CW 10.

—————— (1963): *Memories, Dreams, Reflections*: Recorded and edited by A. Jaffé. Tr. R. and G. Winston. New York: Pantheon Books.

—————— (1974). See Freud (1974).

Kraepelin, E. (1896): "Der psychologische Versuch in der Psychiatrie," *Psychologische Arbeiten*, I. Leipzig.

Lindner, G. A. (1858): *Manual of Empirical Psychology*. (Tr.) Boston: D. C. Heath & Co., 1889.

Lipps, T.: *Psychological Studies*. 2nd edn., tr. H. C. Sanborn. Baltimore: The Williams & Wilkins Co., 1926.

Maeder, A. (1912): "Über die Funktion des Traumes," *Jahrb.*, 4:692–707.

Maeder, A. (1913): "Zur Frage der teleologischen Traumfunktion," *Jahrb.*, 5:453–454.

—————— (1914): *The Dream Problem*. Tr. F. M. Hallock and S. E. Jelliffe. New York: Nervous & Mental Disease Pub. Co., 1916.

———— (1957): *Der Psychotherapist als Partner*. Zurich / Stuttgart: Rascher.

Meier, C. A. (1935): "Moderne Physik—Moderne Psychologie," in T. Wolff, ed.: *Die kulturelle Bedeutung der Komplexen Psychologie*. Berlin: Springer.

———— (1957): *Jung and Analytical Psychology*. Newton Center, Mass.: Andover Newton Theological School, 1959.

———— (1968): *Die Empirie des Unbewussten*. Zurich: Rascher. Tr., *The Unconscious in Its Empirical Manifestation*., Boston: Sigo Press, 1984.

———— (1972): *Die Bedeutung des Traumes*. Olten: Walter.

Meynert, T. (1890): *Klinische Vorlesungen über Psychiatrie*. Vienna: Wilhelm Braumüller.

Miller, Miss Frank (1906): "Quelque faits de l'imagination créative subconsciente" (tr. T. Flournoy), *Archives de psychologie* (Geneva), 8:36–51.

Nietzsche, F.: *Human, All-Too-Human*. Tr. H. Zimmern and P. V. Cohn. London and New York, 1909, 1911.

————: *The Will to Power*. Tr. A. M. Ludovici. New York: Macmillan, 1924.

Nunberg, H. (1955): *Principles of Psychoanalysis*. Tr. M. and S. Kahr. New York: International Universities Press, Inc.

Pauli, W. (1954): "Naturwissenschaftliche und erkenntnistheoretische Aspekte der Ideen vom Unbewussten," *Dialectica*, 8:283–301.

Phillips, J. H. (1962): *Psychoanalyse und Symbolik*. Bern / Stuttgart: Hans Huber.

Rank, O. (1909): *The Myth of the Birth of the Hero*. Tr. F. Robbins and S. E. Jelliffe. New York: Nervous & Mental Disease Pub. Co., 1914.

———— (1910): "Ein Traum der sich selbst deutet," *Jahrb.*, 2:465–540.

———— and Sachs, H. (1912): "Entwicklung und Ansprüche der Psychoanalyse," *Imago*, 1:1–16.

———— (1913): *The Significance of Psychoanalysis for the Mental Sciences*. Tr. C. R. Payne. New York: Nervous & Mental Disease Pub. Co., 1916.

Rapaport, D. (1959): "The Structure of Psychoanalytic Theory: a Systematizing Attempt," in S. Koch, ed.: *Psychology: A Study of a Science*. New York: McGraw-Hill Book Co., Vol. 3, pp. 55–183.

Riklin, F. (1908): *Wishfulfilment and Symbolism in Fairy Tales*. Tr. W. A. White. New York: Nervous & Mental Disease Pub. Co., 1915.

Silberer, H. (1910): "Phantasie und Mythos," *Jahrb.*, 2:541–622.

———— (1912): "Über die Symbolbildung," *Jahrb.*, 3:661–723.

———— (1914): *Problems of Mysticism and Its Symbolism*. Tr. S. E. Jelliffe. New York: Moffat, Yard, 1917.

Stekel, W. (1911): *Die Sprache des Traumes*. Munich and Wiesbaden: Bergmann.

Wolff, T. (1935): "Einführung in die Grundlagen der Komplexen Psychologie," in *Die kulturelle Bedeutung der Komplexen Psychologie*. Berlin:
Springer. Reprinted in *Studien zu C. G. Jungs Psychologie*, Zurich: Daimon Verlag, 1981.

INDICES

NAME INDEX

Not including Freud and Jung.

SUBJECT INDEX

abaissement du niveau mental, 164, 216, 222ff, 238

abreaction, 187

action, 233, 284; modes (typical) of, 146, 149, 174; symbolic, 46f; symptomatic, 44, 46, 61, 194, 261

adjustment (adaptation), 212, 242; to civilization, environment, life, inner and outer world, reality, society, 28, 31, 49, 89, 108, 114, 141, 148, 177, 211, 215, 217, 219f; to inner man, world, 89

adult, 38, 141f, 150, 152; neurotic, 141, 148f, 155

affect, -toned (*see also* emotion), 5, 7, 13, 17, 19f, 22f, 64, 118, 120, 139, 166, 187f, 224, 257; content of, 224; displacement of, 49f, 101; dissociation (incongruity, splitting) of idea and, 22, 32f, 49f, 55, 120, 220, 250; image and, 236; opposite (conflicting), 36, 229f; *see also* complex; defense; meaning

affectivity, 15, 20, 55, 229; as basis of personality, 67, 137; chaotic, 223; complex as measurement of, 16; disturbance in, 210; resistance to, 56; *see also* content; development; dream; ego; regulation; stability

aggression (destructive), 53, 106, 136, 146, 222, 301; eros and, 205; frustration and, 146; release of, 209; *see also* drive

aim: *see* goal

alchemy, alchemist, 272, 284, 298

allegory, 231

all-or-none reaction, 291

ambivalence, 144f; *see also* object; parents

amnesia, 17, 153, 188, 206

amplification (*see also* hermeneutics), 200, 234, 245; method, 199f, 256, 219; —, as expansion, hermeneutic, radial, 199; personal and impersonal, 200

analogy, -formation, 81, 167f, 238, 294, 296; attraction of, 167; drive and, 168; equivalent, 167f; objective and subjective, 245; search for, 83; *see also* meaning (expansion); symbol

analysis, analyst, 101; self-analysis, 75, 102, 104, 135

ancestor: *see* experience; life

anima, animus, 264f, 272; as bridge to the unconscious, 265; and divine couple, 272; projection of, 264f

animal, 96, 128, 178, 285, 292

anthropology, 105, 111

anthropos: *see* quaternio

anticathexis, 190, 207, 212

anticipation, 85, 87, 89, 253; *see also* dream

anxiety, 53, 107, 120, 145, 148, 209ff, 218, 289; castration and, 208, 301; incest-, 145, 208; moral, neurotic, realistic, 107; repression (primal) and, 120, 210; as signal, 107, 210; superego and, 209, 301; *see also* ego (seat); hysteria

anxiety-neurosis, 205

apprehension, 285; (typical) modes of, 174

archetype (*see also* image), 95, 127, 245, 263, 284; bipolarity of the, 270; and brain, 95; (disturbance of) central, 223; and instinct, 118, 152, 285f; and Karma, 92; as such (*per se*), xii, 117, 224, 275f, 288, 300; —, as centring process, goal-directedness, 283; (*a priori*) existence, 285; —, as irrepresentable, psychoid, transcendental, 96, 117, 286ff, 289f, 294; —, as metaphysical, 285, 287, 289; —, as (primary) model, 96, 284; —, as nucleus of meaning, 281, 285; —, numinosity of, 277, 282f; —, as (*a priori*) ordering, arranging, directing, organizing, regulating, 224, 282, 284, 286, 289f, 294; —, as (universal) pattern of perception, 92; as structural dominants, elements, 117, 284; *see also* consciousness; drive; God-image; image (archetypal); representation; self

arrangement (*see also* organization), acausal, 294; archetypal, 272, 282, 284; concentric, 8, 199; four-sided, 209; quaternary, 272; symmetrical, 272

assimilation, 291; *see also* complex; dream; ego; memory; opposites

association, -process, 13ff, 44, 71, 192, 195, 199f, 243, 248, 259; and affect, 15; and attention, 14; bound, 199f; chance and, 191f; disturbance of, 14f, 17; enchainement of, 14, 193; law (rule) of, 8, 189; method (technique) of (free), 8, 16, 187ff, 190f, 193ff, 199f, 226, 245, 257f; —, as linear, 199f; personal, 258; resistance to, 8, 190f; superficial, 192, 238; *see also* (causal) nexus

association experiment, 6, 13f, 16f, 19, 44, 54, 194; as dialogue, 17; (as) objective (evidence of), 16, 18; psychoanalysis and, 17; psychotherapy and, 17, 20

consciousness *(cont.)*
109, 115, 291, 292f, 300; collective, 114,
181f; compensation and, 240ff, 246,
249; degrees of, 4; development of, 34,
58, 116, 153, 218; differentiation of, 58,
116; as discrimination, 58, 116; double,
4f, 32; fragmented, 32; fringe of, 119,
293; inadmissible to, 49, 54, 56, 61, 64,
101f, 120, 131; indeterminacy, indis-
tinctness of, 290, 291; integration into
(assimilation to), 38, 90, 97, 248; interference of, 162, 166, 215; and memory,
108, 116, 296; as observation, 109; one-
sidedness of, 58, 215; perception and,
108, 116, 119; preconscious and, 108,
116; psychology of, xi, 31, 107, 109, 112,
292; relativity of, 293; split-off (banished) from, 27, 34; threshold of, 88,
101; *see also* attitude; complementarity; dissociation; dream; ego-; excitation; incompatibility; projection; psyche; repressed (the); unconscious
conservation, -principle, 137, 165, 197
constancy, -principle, 91, 115, 161, 164,
299
constellation, 91, 139; infantile, 86; *see
also* complex
constitution, 51, 126, 131, 141, 205; *see
also* neurosis
contamination, 61, 83, 139, 234
content, 20, 81, 118ff, 224, 261f; affective,
19, 27, 263; and emotion, 22; (two)
groups of, 119; personal, 34f; impersonal, 34f, 54, 90, 252; not yet perceived, repressed, subliminal, 64, 101,
118f, 131, 150, 227, 252; unconscious,
34, 83, 90, 140, 167, 175, 252; —, and
conscious, 27f, 64, 293, 295; *see also*
dream; symbol
context, 200
contingency, 289
continuity, 113; *see also* ego
control, 27f, 50, 210, 301; repression and,
212; *see also* ego
conversion, 8, 50, 168; *see also* hysteria
cooperation, 56; *see also* ego; patient
correction, 27, 120, 291
cortex, 251
cosmos, 252
couple: divine, 263, 272
creation, creativity, 30, 35, 44f, 64, 78, 81,
96f, 111, 118, 123, 171, 176, 231, 264,
267f, 281f, 286; continuous, 289; *see
also* fantasy; product
crisis, 242
cryptomnesia, 63, 188

crystallization (point of), 8, 101, 192, 199,
226, 246
culture, 51, 146, 232, 247; instinct and, 38
cure, 39, 330, 333; detection of causes
and, 187; *see also* energy; physician;
transference
curiosity (inquisitiveness), 86, 151; intellectual, 150; *see also* mind

dance; ritualistic, 285; round, 271
danger, 181, 210, 218, 303f
death, -drive, -instinct, 104, 136, 165, 180,
198, 289, 301; aggressive and, 301; as
spiritual, 138; *see also* eros; life; wish
decay, 224
defense, 7, 49ff, 52, 57, 101, 111, 190, 210,
301; affect and, 48; miscarried (attempt
at), 8, 49, 213; trauma and, 50; *see also*
ego; neurosis; (causal) nexus
deficiency (defect, gap), 160; *see* memory
deity, 272, 304
delinquent, 16
delusion, 31, 166, 225, 240, 252
dementia praecox *(see also* psychasthénie,
schizophrenia), 19, 55, 77, 136, 221;
atrophy of complex in, 55; loss of
reality in, 77, 160; as organic, toxic
process, 221
demon, 33, 303f
demonstration: empirical (of the Ucs), 8,
18, 69, 100, 103, 227, 285
denial, 52, 145, 223
depression, 44f
derivative: *see* fantasy, repressed (the)
désagrégation mentale, 220
destiny, 85, 135
destruction *(see also* aggression), 222;
self-, 209, 224
detachment, 160
determination, determinism, 10, 16, 67,
136, 141, 158; causal, 8, 13, 43, 232, 289,
294; historical, 88; quantitative, 158,
161f; sexual, 139
deus absconditus, 180
devaluation, 56f, 216
development (expansion, extension), 53,
60, 127, 141f, 145, 148f, 154, 178, 195f,
198, 207, 218, 247, 251; affective, 148;
diphasic, sexual, 141, 149, 179, 206,
210f; disturbance of (ego, sexual), 136,
141f, 151f, 205f, 209f; historical, 181;
intellectual, 87, 140, 151; lines of, 245;
process of, 5, 111, 115, 246; *see also*
child; consciousness; ego; individual;
individuation; personality; sexuality
(infantile)
devil, 81, 303; pact with, 304

dialogue, 17

differentiation; *see* consciousness, function, individuation

directedness, 58, 85f; *see also* goal

discharge, 50

discrimination: *see* consciousness

disease (*see also* illness, sickness), 213; causes of, 187, 190, 194; —, as psychogenic and somatic, 221; history of, 188; mental, 61; uncovering, 8; *see also* personality (neurosis)

disguise, 44, 76, 228, 233, 258

disintegration, 217; unsystematic, 223; *see also* personality

displacement, 9, 22, 27, 46, 56, 158, 212, 215, 228; *see also* affect

disposition, 24, 94, 127, 131, 155; collective, constitutional, inherited, innate, instinctual, 25, 122, 126ff; in the ego, 127; germinal, 171; —, incongruity of, 171; —, polyvalent, 150ff; polymorphous (perverse), 141, 149f, 153

dissociability, dissociation (incongruity), 4, 7, 22, 37, 55, 58, 64, 164, 222, 224, 291f; centralization and, 69; from consciousness, 65, 118; from ego, 56, 293; irreversible, 222; psychotic, 38, 55, 224; and repression, 33, 65; and subliminal process, 65; systematic, unsystematic, 223; *see also* affect; complex; connection; neurosis; opposites; personality; psyche; union

distortion (falsification), 9, 44, 49, 80, 128, 147, 227f, 260, 267; *see also* censor; fantasy; memory

disturbance (disorder), 10, 20, 30, 137, 172, 196, 215, 221, 223, 294; actual, 205; in the ego, 52, 206; emotional, 14, 16, 18, 188, 190; mental, 13, 63, 240; neurotic, 17; *see also* affectivity; association; development; drive; indicator; memory

dogma, 263

dominants, 92, 117, 284

doubt, 198

drama, classical, 233

dramatization, 228

dream, -formation, 10, 19, 118, 230f, 236, 238, 258, 259; affect, affectivity in the, 232, 236, 238f, 247; —, and symbol, 239; amplification of, 234, 245; anticipating, 87, 195, 220, 242f; (as) archaic, 102; assimilation of, 236, 248f; big, 242; cause, causal determination of, 226, 232, 243, 257; censor and, 227f, 234; —, as distorting, 227f, 233, 258; child and, 102, 228; (as) compensating,

complementing, 230, 237, 241; —, consciousness and, 239ff, 242, 248; complex and, 232, 238; as compromise, 227; as constellating, 230, 232, 241; content of, 226, 239, 244, 258; —, archaic, infantile, repressed, sexual, 227; —, latent, manifest, 228, 234f, 242; day-dream, -dreamer, 75f; as disguised, distorted, 228, 233f, 238; element of, 232, 241, 250; as façade, 235; as finalistic, prophetic, prospective, 89, 230, 243; four phases in, 233; as goal-oriented, guiding, 231, 243, 246f; as hallucination, 227; as image (sensory, simile), 227, 234, 236f, 251; as infantile (type of), 102, 228; interpretation of, 10, 191f, 196, 225f, 231f, 234f, 243, 244, 247ff, 250, 258; as knowledge, wisdom, 232; as life-preserving, 227, 239; meaning (-fulness) of, 87, 225f, 231f, 234f, 243f, 246, 248, 257f; —, structure of, 233; —, transcendent, 244; as natural, 235; neurosis and, 226ff; nucleus of, 226, 232, 244; —, feeling of, 247; obscurity (incomprehensibility) of, 234f; as projection, 252; psychology of, 231, 237, 239, 243; purpose of, 231; reaction-, 241; regression in, 146; as regulating, 242; remembered, 227, 234; as royal road, 26, 205, 226; as self-portrayal, 237; series of, 245f, 286; —, and individuation, 246; as sign, symptom, 228, 232; significance (center) of, 10, 232, 344; sleep (-preservation) and, 88, 227, 238f; as source of information, 5, 205, 225, 230, 232; spontaneity of, 234f, 241, 243; structure of, 10, 226, 234, 237; as substitute, 229, 243; (as) symbol, symbolic, symbolism (of), 10, 197, 231, 237, 245ff, 258ff; and the unconscious, 231, 237; uncover, 189; and whole, 226, 233, 243, 247; working through, 239, 248; (as) (and) wish (distorted, repressed, sexual), 10, 76, 228, 235ff, 240; *see also* analogy

dream-analysis, 231, 243

dream-ego, 114; as archetype of ego, 114

dreamer, 191, 227, 235, 247f, 250, 258f; questioning the, 243, 248, 259

dreaming (the), 227, 239

dream-thought, 227, 292

dream-wish, 228, 237

dream-work, 228, 233

drive (striving) (*see also* instinct), 23, 104f, 122f, 135f, 152, 156, 165, 169, 173f, 181, 236, 286, 288, 301, 303; aggressive (self-) destructive, 106, 136, 209f; —, eros and, 205; aim, goal of, 22, 138;

SUBJECT INDEX

reaction-time, -word, 14f
reality, 5, 57, 85, 166, 207, 209, 211, 276, 299, 302; adjustment to, 31, 108, 114, 211, 219ff; detachment from, 57; devaluation of, 57; education to, 180f, 302; fear of, 272; function of (fonction du réel), 56, 77, 160, 221; inner, 97, 219, 231, 235, 251; —, and outer, 24, 91; loss of, 77, 85, 143, 160f, 209, 220f; psychic, (intra-), 24, 159, 251, 282; substitute for, 161, 221; as symbolical, 267; transcendental, 294, 300; —, existence of, 276, 290, 297; —, experience of, 276f; —, as indeterminant, 297f; —, matter and psyche as aspects of, 298; —, model of, 297f; —, as objective and subjective, 296, 298; —, and perception, 296f; —, as space-time-continuum, 298; see also event; fantasy; instinct; motive; (unconscious) wish
reality-principle, 88, 135; ego as, 107f; see also instinct; pleasure-principle
reason, 129, 277, 291; see also ego
rebirth, 116f, 130, 159, 175; see also incest-fantasy
recognization: see unconscious
reconciliation, 211, 230, 248
recurrence: see repetition
reduction: see conflict (neurotic); drive; incest-fantasy; method; person; point of view (causal); wish
regression, 36, 51f, 76, 136, 143, 145f, 160, 176f, 207, 215ff, 220, 260, 300; as pathological, 216; —, and as new value, renewal, 87, 176, 260, 268; and progression, 217; psychotic, 220; religious, 155; as search for oneself, 155f; see also anxiety; childhood; dream; fantasy; fixation; incest-fantasy; infantilism; layer; memory (personal); neurosis; phase (libidinal)
regulation, regulator, 88, 131, 155, 201, 236, 241f, 283, 286; affective, 201; archetypal image, archetype and, 95, 174, 282, 286; instinct as, 174, 286; self-regulation, 112, 118, 241; value and meaning as, 88; see also function; opposites (self-); pleasure; psyche (self-); system (self-)
relatedness: see eros
relation, -ship; complementary, 108, 296, 298; dynamic, 163; equivalent, 164, 259; filial, 177; fixed, constant, 256, 258; holistic, 272; incestuous, 208; love-, 273; model of, 263; quaternity of, 273; religious, 177; (with) self, 181; symbolic, 46f, 226, 234, 244, 258f; sym-

metrical, 295; see also center, energy
relativity: see consciousness; psyche; space; truth
release, 265; see also aggression; drive; instinct; repressed
relief: see tension
religion, 53, 71, 177, 181, 242, 302; experience, 275; —, evidence of, 275f; as obsessional neurosis, 53, 159; parental complex and, 302; psychology of, 271f; and reason, 276; as (sexual) sublimation, 86, 159; substitute for, 305; see also belief; experience; father; idea; projection; relationship; symbol; thought
remembrance, 153, 187f, 212; acting out and, 190; see also dream, method
removal (dissolution), 179; see also complex; repression (lifting)
renewal, 76, 117, 173, 274; see also personality
renunciation, 207, 210; see also drive (negation); wish fulfillment
repetition (recurrence), 15, 128, 136, 140, 212, 281, 303; see also conflict; drive; image (primordial); memory; motive; past; repression symbol; trauma
repetition-compulsion, 30, 106, 120, 136, 180, 207, 300, 303
representation, 177, 179, 250, 252; archetypal, 283; in the cortex, 252; drive and object-, 22; instinct as psychic, 104; see also word-representation
repression, (the) repressed, (see also defense), 7, 27, 30, 33, 43f, 48, 50ff, 53ff, 56ff, 62, 64f, 103, 120, 129, 131, 142, 144f, 151, 156, 160, 167, 172, 181, 190, 207, 215f, 269; as appendix, 120; censor as, 10, 142; as (previously) conscious, 55, 65, 119, 121; derivatives of the, 104; dissolving, 218; ego (ideal) and, 52, 120, 207, 210; lifting, removal of the, 103, 191; (carrier of) meaning (of), 65, 218; miscarried attempt of, 10, 62, 206; as moral liberation, 65; motives of, 56, 63; natural and, 181; original, primary, 64, 100, 120f, 300; —, attraction of, 120; —, non-psychic, 300; projection of the, 252; release of, 27, 103, 253; repetition of, 136, 211; repressing and repressed, 10, 52, 211; return of the, 9f, 50, 131, 210, 300; sexual, 51, 137, 153; shadow as, 59, 61; uncover, 244, 247; see also civilization; complex; control; dissociation; drive; memory; neurosis; religion; superego; symbol; symptom; unconscious; wish
reproduction, 14f, 20, 120, 148, 201

340

image; id; idea; knowledge; memory; motive; performance; psyche; purpose; structure; thought

unconsciousness, 27, 32, 57, 180f, 263

uncovering (detection): resistance against, 190; *see also* cause; complex; disease; event (past); experience; life (history); motive; repression; unconscious; wish

understanding (the), 4, 6, 77, 97, 111, 196, 235, 237, 305; explanation and, 244; method of, 149; prospective and retrospective, 196

undoing, 52, 166

unfolding: *see* development

union (conjunction, reunion) unification, 69, 118; dissociation and, 69, 88; with source, 124; *see also* life; opposites; self; symbol

uniqueness, 68f

unit, 28, 117, 199; *see also* complex

unity, 8, 33f, 40, 69, 111, 136, 182; dynamic, 161; structural, 10, 226; *see also* complex; multiplicity; person; personality

universality, 122f; *see also* motif, symbol, unconscious (coll.)

unus mundus, 298

usurpation, 143

validity, 282, 295, 297; subjective, 276

value, 20, 24, 44, 88, 201, 249, 276, 374; assimilation of opposites, 249; chaos of, 249; equivalent, 167; integration of lacking, 217; life, 239, 247; moral, 60, 107; new, 196, 216; revaluation of, 39, 176; subjective, 297; transition from lower to higher, 168; *see also* energy; feeling; judgment

vision, 62, 232

vitality, 268; interest, 250

voice, 31

vomiting (hysterical), 257

water, 175

weakness, 207, 218; perceptive, 48; *see also* attention, ego

Weltanschauung, 124

whole, wholeness (*see also* totality) 43, 67, 111, 182, 244, 266, 273, 297; conscious and unconscious, 298; experience of, 275, 277; individual, individuation and, 61, 69, 266; instinct as part of the, 182; quaternio and the, 271, 273; *see also* image (primordial); personality; psyche; symbol; syzygy

will, 160; and won't, 36ff, 58, 159, 173

wind, 175

wisdom, 232; *see also* man, mother

wish, -fulfillment, 77, 88, 107, 206, 211, 227, 236f, 268; death-, 37, 227; distorted, 83f; incest-, 144f, 156, 159, 172, 175, 208f, 237, 262f; —, and incest-barrier, 36, 79, 178; infantile, 122, 172, 219, 231; reality and, 76, 175, 219; for rebirth, 159; reduction to, 121, 156, 231, 235; renunciation of, 53, 106; repressed, suppressed, 46, 102, 122, 181, 228f, 231, 235ff; sexual, 76, 122, 154, 181, 205; unconscious (and), 10, 46, 122, 127, 236; —, censor and, 227; uncover, 248; *see also* dream; fantasy; idea (religious); myth; symptom

withdrawal (retrieval), 55, 214, 227; *see also* complex; ego; object; projection

womb: *see* mother

word (verbal): meaning of, 200, 260; *see also* sexuality (identity)

word-representation, 103, 108f; as residues of perception, speech, 109

working-through, 36, 38, 49, 172, 187, 212, 248; *see also* resistance

world, 137, 298; devaluation of, 57; empirical, 163; (archaic) image (picture) of the, 79, 122, 248, 274, 285; —, inner (interior), 123; —, mirror-, 94, 125; —, as objective, subjective, 79; inner (inside), 125, 209, 217, 297; outer (outside), 28, 107, 125, 148, 209, 214, 251f, 289, 297; —, ego and, 107, 214, 221; —, projection into, 252, 299; —, withdrawal from, 214; two aspects of the, 227, 298

writer, 76

writing: automatic, 31

zero, 298, 300; reduction to, 165

zone: erogenous, 135, 179

OTHER C.G. JUNG FOUNDATION BOOKS
FROM SHAMBHALA PUBLICATIONS

*The Child, by Erich Neumann. Foreword by Louis H. Stewart.

*Depth Psychology and a New Ethic, by Erich Neumann. Forewords by C.G. Jung, Gerhard Adler, and James Yandell.

The Golden Ass of Apuleius: The Liberation of the Feminine in Man, Revised and Expanded Edition, by Marie-Louise von Franz.

A Guided Tour of the Collected Works of C.G. Jung, by Robert H. Hopcke. Foreword by Aryeh Maidenbaum.

Knowing Woman: A Feminine Psychology, by Irene Claremont de Castillejo.

In Her Image: The Unhealed Daughter's Search for Her Mother, by Kathie Carlson.

Power and Politics: The Psychology of the Soviet-American Partnership, by Jerome S. Bernstein. Forewords by Senator Claiborne Pell and Edward C. Whitmont, M.D.

The Wisdom of the Dream: The World of C.G. Jung, by Stephen Segaller and Merrill Berger.

Woman's Mysteries: Ancient and Modern, by M. Esther Harding. Introduction by C.G. Jung.

*Published in association with Daimon Verlag, Einsiedeln, Switzerland.